TALK TO SYBEX ONLINE.

Second Edition

Stan Kelly-Bootle

SYBEX®

SAN FRANCISCO • PARIS • DÜSSELDORF • SOEST

Acquisitions Editor: Dianne King
Developmental Editor: Gary Masters
Editors: Odile Sullivan-Tarazi, Armin Brott
Project Editors: Kathleen Lattinville, Valerie Potter
Technical Editors: Dan Tauber, Aaron Kushner
Book Designer: Suzanne Albertson
Production Artist: Claudia Smelser
Technical Artist: Cuong Le
Desktop Specialists: Thomas Goudie, Len Gilbert, Stephanie Hollier
Production Coordinator: Sarah Lemas
Production Assistant: Lisa Haden
Indexer: Ted Laux
Cover Designer: Design Site
Cover Photographer: Mark Johann
Cover Photo Art Director: Ingalls + Associates

Library of Congress Card Number: 94-68434
ISBN: 0-7821-1499-7

Manufactured in the United States of America

10 9 8 7 6 5 4 3 2 1

For my born-again Anna

ACKNOWLEDGMENTS

I want to thank the many people who knowingly or unwittingly helped me to write this book. First, the wonderful folk at SYBEX who have, at various times, held my hand, wiped my brow, slapped my back, or nudged my ribs according to the prevailing circumstances. I value especially the friendly encouragement I have received from Dr. Rudolph Langer, who first suggested Unix as the topic of my fourth SYBEX title.

My warmest thanks also go to Barbara Gordon, Managing Editor, and Dianne King, Acquisitions Editor, for patiently goading me past the regular, monthly deadline crises.

Between any Unix manuscript and its published product, there lurk a thousand stylistic and typographical quirks and traps where a wrong case-shift, a misplaced dot, or an obtusely-angled quotation mark can noticeably increase the entropy of the cosmos. I therefore salute the SYBEX team of editors, production assistants, desktop publishers, and artists who spared no effort to ensure a smooth and accurate transition from my error-prone keystrokes to these unblotted pages.

In particular, and not in any order of merit, I want to express my gratitude to Gary Masters, Developmental Editor; Odile Sullivan-Tarazi and Armin Brott, Editors; Kathleen Lattinville and Valerie Potter, Project Edtiors; Dan Tauber and Aaron Kushner, Technical Editors; Lisa Haden, Production Assistant; Sarah Lemas, Production Coordinator; Thomas Goudie, Len Gilbert, and Stephanie Hollier, Desktop Publishers; Claudia Smelser, Artist; and Cuong Le, Technical Artist.

I would also like to thank all those in the Unix community who have at different times and levels freely downloaded their wisdom. In particular, I remember early VI sessions with Jim Joyce and Bob Toxen: their enthusiasm for Unix was (and remains) infectious. My colleagues and fellow columnists at *UNIX Review* and *Computer Language* have also helped me over the years, more by informal osmosis than

by structured discourse: Steve Bourne, Ken Arnold, Joe Celco, Michael Godfrey, Eric Allman, Nicole Freeman, Tim Parker, Greg Chesson, Bill Plauger, Warren Keuffel, Dave Burnette, Mark Compton, Ken Broadhurst, Dave Chandler, John Dlougosz, Chip Rabinowitch, Lea Anne Bantsari, J. D. Hildebrand, and the mysterious, collective Ellipsis.

I am most grateful to Steve Bourne for his foreword.

And finally, can a parsable sentence express my gratitude to my bien aimée wife, Iwonka? Jamais!

CONTENTS AT A GLANCE

TABLE OF CONTENTS

FOREWORD

Twelve years ago the Unix system was mainly of interest to technical users and research scientists. Today it is a major operating system in use by millions of people on every widely available computer.

For those familiar with the "Devil's Advocate" column in *UNIX Review*, Stan needs little introduction as a writer. Stan has also written a number of other successful books on computing topics. Stan's introduction to computing, like my own, began in Cambridge, England, in the pioneering days of the EDSAC I and II. It was at the Computer Laboratory in Cambridge that Maurice Wilkes pioneered microprogramming and that David Wheeler invented subroutines, so it is fitting that Stan is now writing about Unix, considered by many to be the programming development environment of choice.

The first Unix books appeared in the early 80s and were aimed at the technically sophisticated. Many books on Unix have appeared since then, targeted at different audiences. This book is aimed at the literate, nonexpert user and provides a valuable addition to your Unix bookshelf.

The Unix system has increased significantly in functionality since its original implementation at Bell Laboratories in the early 70s. However, the basic system functions and structure remain unchanged. *Understanding UNIX* provides an easy-to-read description of these basic system functions. It also contains many helpful hints on how to use Unix via the standard system shells.

Dr. Stephen R. Bourne
Cupertino, California

INTRODUCTION

Yaub?

I suppose that *YAUB* (Yet Another Unix Book) calls for some explanation. There are, without doubt, many wonderful texts already circulating that cover almost every facet of Unix from almost every perspective and level of expertise. Nevertheless, I do feel that a new new-to-Unix audience has emerged recently that may find the existing treatments either too elementary or too abstruse. My aim, therefore, is straight down the middle, like the golfer's *juste milieu*: a practical approach to Unix, gentle but not juvenile. The authors of many computer books seem to confuse ignorance with stupidity and the resulting tone is too often one of condescension. The readers I have in mind are intelligent and curious (you know who you are); but through a happy twist of fate have not been exposed to the rigors of a computer science education. Nonetheless, you may find yourselves faced with a Unix computer, a mile-high stack of manuals, and a burning desire to squeeze some useful work out of this beast. The number of people finding themselves in this situation has grown significantly over the last few years with the dramatic growth of Unix applications in both the academic and commercial sectors.

On campuses and in research centers throughout the world, Unix has long been the standard operating system for computer scientists, physicists, engineers, biologists, and even for scholars in the so-called softer sciences of economics and sociology. More recently, computing has started to play a major role in the humanities, too, so that more and more students of history, archeology, music, linguistics, and literature are now faced with a Unix terminal that says login:. And apart from the direct application of computers in these disciplines, there is the universal use of word processors, replacing the typewriter for document preparation. The typical "Unix Made Easy" books are not quite the answer here either, and neither are the Unix-guru-in-a-cave books.

The progress of Unix in the commercial arena has been even more startling. After years of unfulfilled prophecies, Unix systems have now reached the office in large numbers. All the major mainframe computer vendors now offer some version of

Unix, and many corporations have adopted Unix for both their R&D and their general office computing. With the advent of faster Intel and Motorola microprocessors, cheaper memory and hard disk storage, the PC now has the power to support serious Unix applications—both networked and stand-alone. The RISC (reduced instruction set computer) chips have helped create a new market; the Unix workstation. Workstations from Hewlett-Packard, Sun Microsystems, IBM, Silicon Graphics, and others are moving from the lab to the front office, especially as network servers and for sophisticated financial modeling and other computer-intensive work.

The microprocessor revolution has profoundly changed the look and feel of the Unix world. Many thousands of small-to-medium companies now use Unix-based PCs for their daily accounting, electronic mail, and word-processing chores. The success of the Microsoft/SCO XENIX implementation on the 80286 has been followed by even more successful System V versions for later and more powerful Intel microprocessors such as the Pentium. All the staple applications found on DOS or Microsoft Windows PCs are available under Unix; spreadsheets, database management, accounting, word processing, desktop publishing, and so on. The X Window System developed at MIT provides a machine-independent, network-independent, and hardware-independent graphical user interface (GUI), with far more capability and elegance than Microsoft Windows.

Unlike the traditional mainframe Unix sites, these smaller installations seldom enjoy the luxury of a full-time system administrator or Unix guru. This, along with the X Window System developments just mentioned, has encouraged many Unix vendors to develop GUIs that simplify some of the trickier aspects of Unix maintenance and operation. You can discount the canard that Unix is wildly arcane and hairy, but it is equally misleading to claim that Unix is as simple as DOS. The fact that there are no limitations in Unix (as there always will be in DOS) does not hide the fact that Unix is, by necessity, a more complex system to master. I hope that *Understanding Unix* helps you in this endeavor.

What Is Unix?

Like most interesting subjects, Unix is not that easy to define. At the lowest level it is simply the *kernel* of an operating system, a set of supervisory routines devised by Ken Thompson *et al* in 1969 at Bell Labs to control and coordinate the activities of a

multiuser computer system. Above the kernel, you must add the unique and elegant Unix *filesystem* that organizes your data files, directories, and devices. Then, at the next level, Unix includes a *shell*, a special intercessory program that intercepts your commands and shields you from the kernel. Next, you need to consider the ever-growing collection of Unix tools and utilities that has accrued over the last 25 years. Even when you have added all these elements together—the kernel, the filesystem, the shell, and the tools—you still don't have the full picture. Understanding Unix means much more than learning the command options and the shell syntax. As I hope to reveal in this book, Unix is also a remarkable success-against-all-odds story, and a cultural phenomenon with considerable historical and socio-economic, nay, even mystical implications.

The famed portability of Unix helped to break the dominance of proprietary software that tied you to a specific vendor's hardware, yea unto death. As Unix spread to the universities in the 1970s and beyond in the 1980s, a whole generation of students and programmers enjoyed this "wind of change" and became addicted to this new, open style of computing. Incidentally, many of these students and programmers are now in high places, influencing the current directions in computing research and development.

Versions, Versions, Versions...

As you will soon see, the Unix philosophy does have a darker side; many slightly different dialects have been developed over the years, and some of these differences between versions are undoubtedly irritating. In computing, more than any other field, even the tiniest of differences can have diabolical implications. In *Understanding Unix*, I have tried to cover the basic features found on all Unix systems, but please be patient when you read "some versions do this, but yours may not." If you are new to Unix, you are coming in at just the right time. The release of System V successfully pulled most of the divergent strands together into one strong standard.

After 25 years of maturation, Unix is seen by some pessimists as declining into a dull, standardized commodity. However, the "Unix or die" battle cry is far from silent, and the Unix community can take much of the credit for the emergence of the open system philosophy that is permeating every aspect of computing today.

Read on.

Syntax Conventions

But first a short diversion on the typographical conventions used throughout this book. Certain typefaces and fonts are used to indicate different classes of tokens:

- `This font` indicates programming elements, Unix command and file names, and screen output. For example, `termcap, ftp`.

- *`This font in italic`* indicates place-holders and variables in syntax definitions. For example, *`file_name`*, *`count`*, where *`file_name`* would be replaced by a real file name, and *`count`* would be replaced by a number.

- **`This font in boldface`** indicates something that you type at a shell prompt, such as $ **`cat poem.1`**.

The solid vertical line | used in this book to represent pipes and logical OR is equivalent to the broken vertical line found on most PC keyboards.

CHAPTER

ONE

Are You Online Yet?

- Getting started—accessing a Unix system

- Logging in

- Commands

- Logging out

- Choosing passwords

The first stage of your journey is a mental one. You must accept that Unix is a large, complex system to tackle. Unless you take one careful, diligent step at a time, it is easy to become somewhat overawed. If you flip aimlessly through the mountains of official documentation, you can be forgiven for feeling daunted by the number of commands and options, and by the sheer weight of quirky detail. The good news is that you need learn only a few Unix basics in order to become productive. As you build on this solid foundation, layer by layer, the climb becomes more gentle. This book stresses constant practice with useful examples so that you see cause and effect rather than ponder textbook abstractions. It also emphasizes motivation: knowing *why* the Unix designers provided certain features often clarifies *how* they are implemented. It proves much easier to assimilate facts when they are interrelated in some way, rather than picked up in isolation.

We can certainly discount any rumors that Unix is impossibly arcane unless you have an advanced degree in computer science. The proof can be found in thousands of ordinary office installations worldwide. Although Unix dominates the academic and research arenas, its presence in the business world has been growing rapidly on every platform from mainframe to PC.

Gaining Access—What You Need to Get Started

As with any computer system, there are several prerequisites before you can gain access and start using Unix. You obviously need a suitable terminal correctly connected to a computer that is running Unix. (The latter caution is not as dumb as it seems—many computers nowadays are capable of running several operating systems, so you need to be sure that you are talking to the right one.) Each Unix vendor supplies precise documentation for installing a particular combination of hardware and version of Unix.

When you are connected and ready to go, you are said to be *online* to the computer. When you lose connection for any reason, you go *offline*, and life becomes simple again. Your terminal may be local, directly cabled (or *hard-wired*) to the computer, or it may be remotely connected via modems and telephone lines. The difference affects only the way you establish a connection; once you are online, the type of connection, local or remote, does not normally affect the way you work.

Remote connection is made by dialing the number of the Unix system just as you would make a normal telephone call. In most cases, the dialing is automated with suitable telecommunications software. The actual procedures are very much site-dependent, so you will need to consult your local guru or Unix vendor. Operating remotely, of course, exposes you to the random gremlins of the telecommunications underworld—glitches on the lines, electrical interference, broken connections, and so on—as well as the psychological stresses of isolation if things go wrong.

Terminals

Unix supports almost every type of terminal ever invented, and indeed is designed so that terminals not yet invented can be handled by simple software changes. As far as the beginner is concerned, a terminal can be looked on as a device with a *keyboard* for typing in instructions and data to the computer (*input*), and a CRT or monitor screen to *echo* your input and display messages or responses from the computer (*output*). The computer itself usually has a hard-wired terminal referred to as the *console* or *systems console*.

Terminals can be *dumb* or *intelligent*, although it is not always easy to tell the difference. A dumb terminal has a keyboard and CRT but no local processing power—it relies on the central computer for all its processing needs. An intelligent (or *smart*) terminal, in addition to a keyboard and CRT, has some built-in processing power and local memory. With the low costs of microprocessors and integrated circuits, the completely dumb terminal is now quite rare. The same cost factor has also led to the widespread use of PCs (personal computers) as very intelligent devices capable of working both online as Unix terminals and offline as stand-alone PCs. Indeed, with the advent of superfast microprocessors such as the Intel 80486 and Pentium and Motorola 68030/40, which can handle high-capacity disks and lots of RAM, your Unix may well be running on a PC or workstation while supporting other terminals and PCs.

Keyboards

Whether you have a dumb or intelligent terminal, an online PC, or a PC running Unix, you will have a keyboard for input and a screen for output. With all the varieties of keyboard layout and key labeling currently on the market, you will appreciate that the instructions in this book may need some adjustment for your particular keyboard. To further complicate matters, most smart terminals allow you

to personalize the keyboard in various ways. In other words, you may be able to *remap* the keyboard, thereby changing the action of certain keys or sequences of keys.

An extreme form of remapping is the use of *emulation* software that makes a brand X terminal behave like a brand Y model. Whatever tricks you perform, Unix needs to know the type and mode of the terminal being used so it can correctly interpret the stream of characters you are sending. The normal alphanumeric printable characters are fairly standard (usually the so-called ASCII set), but the invisible control characters are subject to the more diverse interpretations of the hardware jungle of keyboards, screens, and (especially) printers. The parts of Unix that cope with these vagaries are, perforce, correspondingly messy. Until you know more, therefore, it is best to have your vendor or system administrator set up Unix for your particular terminal.

To avoid too many diversions, I will assume the standard PC keyboard conventions. When we encounter the need for special keystrokes other than the universal alphanumeric keys, I will point out some of the most common variants. For example, the key called Enter on the PC plays an essential role in Unix input. Your Enter key may be marked as Return, CR, Car Ret, or ↵.

Screens

Variations in your monitor screen and video adapter are less problematic at this stage. I will be assuming monochrome text displays on a standard 25-lines-x-80-columns character screen, unless specifically stated otherwise. Unix, of course, supports color and graphics applications and other screen layouts, but you will use text mode for the basic commands in this book.

Who Does What?

In larger installations, there are staff specially assigned to manage the system, so you would not normally be concerned with such mundane tasks as installing terminals and ensuring that Unix is set to handle them. In particular, you'll find a system administrator (SA for short) who will be the chief liaison between you as user and the Unix system. Whether system administration is a single full-time job or spread among staff members according to shifts or particular responsibilities will depend on the size and complexity of your Unix site. At smaller installations, the system administrator may simply be a designated user selected (or sentenced) to

play this role in addition to other duties. The system administrator may even be you! Fear not, this book explains the chief responsibilities of the SA. For the moment, I will assume that you have someone who can get you online.

The first sign that your terminal awaits you is that your screen displays the *prompt*

```
login:
```

with the cursor blinking impatiently after the colon. A prompt is any message or symbol that indicates that input is expected—in other words, you are being *prompted* to type something! The cursor is a distinctive symbol on the screen indicating where your next typed character will appear.

Although you are online to Unix and Unix is talking to you, you are not yet an active user. You must first log in (some say log on) and satisfy Unix that you are a legitimate user. Let's see how.

Logging In

In a single-user environment, such as DOS, anyone booting up the system can usually start operating it without permission. DOS itself just doesn't care. If you want to control access, you must install some additional security system (either mechanical locks or software barriers). With a multiuser system such as Unix, the need for security has to be taken more seriously since access may be possible from terminals beyond your immediate control. Unix offers a host of built-in security features that allow the system administrator to control who can get online as well as what the users can and cannot do when they get online. The system administrator is free to decide how much security is appropriate for a given installation, but there is a minimum level found at most sites.

The basic idea is that the system administrator assigns each user a unique *user name*, also called a *logon*, and an initial *password*. The SA sets up your logon and password on the system and tells you what they are. Once you have logged on (you'll see how soon), you are free to change your password but not your logon name. The latter is usually your first name in lowercase letters, such as stan or mary. In larger installations, it may be necessary to use fuller names and/or initials to ensure uniqueness. Whatever scheme is adopted, your logon *must* be in lowercase, and it serves to identify you to Unix at all times.

5

The choice of passwords needs careful consideration and we'll be discussing this in detail later on. For now, make sure you know your password and keep it to yourself. And try not to forget your password—it means more work for the system administrator, who may be annoyed enough to issue you a temporary, deflating password such as dummy.

At the login: prompt, type your logon. As you type, you'll see your keystrokes echoed on the screen. The stream of characters you type is actually going to a temporary storage area inside Unix known as a *buffer*. Each character in turn is sent back to the screen as you type—hence the terms *echo* and *echoing*. Most of your keyboard entries will be echoed in this way, but there are important exceptions as you'll see shortly.

Typing Errors

Your keyboard entry builds up in the buffer until you press Enter, at which point Unix starts examining what you have typed. You therefore have a chance to correct your input *before* you press the Enter key.

If you make a conscious typing error, there are two ways to recover: erase and retype characters or scrub the entire entry and start over again.

To erase characters to the left of your cursor, you can press the Backspace key. If your keyboard lacks a Backspace key, use Ctrl-H. Ctrl-H means holding down the Ctrl key and pressing the H key. You may see this written ^H in Unix documentation.

To delete a whole line, type Ctrl-U, then retype from the beginning. (Your system may allow the use of # to delete the previous character, or @ to delete the whole line. Check with your system administrator or experiment!)

The Enter Key

When you think you have correctly typed your user name, press the Enter key. Until you press Enter, Unix will simply wait for more keystrokes. This is a general rule: pressing Enter signals the end of your typing and asks Unix to process what you have typed. Unix responds with the prompt

```
Password:
```

The password is case-sensitive. Carefully type your password exactly as the system administrator set it up (using the proper upper- and lowercase letters); then press Enter. (This is the last time I'll remind you that Enter is needed after every completed line of input.) I stress the word *carefully* for two reasons:

- What you type in the password field is *not* echoed on the screen, lest Peeping Toms are lurking behind you.

- Passwords are (or should be) strange, un-English, hard-to-type combinations.

Unix now checks both your logon name and your password. If the logon is valid and matches the password previously assigned, you will be logged into Unix.

Login Errors

If you make a login error, you get the message

```
Login incorrect
```

followed by another login prompt:

```
login:
```

Note that Unix plays its cards pretty close here. If you type `stam` in place of `stan`, followed by Stan's password, Unix will not say `logon name invalid`. If you type `stan` followed by Mary's password, Unix will not say `password invalid`. All you know is that either the logon name, the password, or both do not match. This withholding of clues is all part of the cloak and dagger game—no help for the potential intruder. If you keep getting `Login incorrect` messages, check the Caps Lock key; you may be using the wrong case. If this doesn't help, you'll have to double-check with your system administrator.

Logged In at Last!

Once you've passed the login hurdle, Unix can respond in many ways depending on the way your system is set up. Both you and the system administrator can tailor your environment to suit your lifestyle. This is the two-edged sword of Unix: infinite

flexibility! In the simplest case, your successful login is greeted by a single character, known as the *shell prompt*. A $ symbol indicates that you have the Bourne shell; a % means you have the C shell. (There are other shells and other prompts, but these two are the most common.)

The differences between the Bourne shell and C shell will not affect you until we reach more advanced Unix operations. The examples here display the Bourne shell, so when you see the $ prompt in the following examples, make the mental adjustment to % if you are using the C shell.

I'll have more to say about shells later. For now, look on them as special Unix programs that will interpret your typed commands and pass them on for further action. A Unix shell is something like the command-line interpreter, COMMAND.COM, in DOS. Most Unix systems now offer you a choice of shells so that you or your system administrator can select the default shell to suit your tastes. The word *default* crops up frequently in data processing, so let's take a brief time-out to discuss what it means.

Defaults

If you have a simple situation where the computer expects a yes or no response, it may be that 90 percent of the time yes is the more appropriate response, as in `Are you sure you want to Exit? y/n?`. If the program has been arranged so that the Enter key works as though y had been entered, we say that y is the *default*. More generally, if one option among many is the one programmed to be selected in the absence of user input to the contrary, that option can be the default. In many Unix situations, you can change a default permanently or for a particular session. In the latter case, you would revert to the default default, as it were, in subsequent sessions.

Login Greetings

In addition to the shell prompt, Unix may reward you with a message or two. If Unix is uncertain as to your type of terminal, it may prompt you for information before proceeding:

```
TERM=(unknown)
```

or

```
TERM=(vt100)
```

In the latter case, the vt100 (or some similar set of characters in parentheses) represents the default terminal type for your system. To pass this hurdle, you need to confirm this default name by pressing Enter or supply the actual terminal type. Your system administrator can help you here. Each terminal type supported by Unix has a mnemonic name such as vt100 (the DEC VT-100), wyse60 (for the Wyse 60), and so on. In most cases, the system administrator can set up the system so that the TERM message does not appear or simply requires you to press Enter.

The system administrator can also set up a message of the day (known as *motd* in Unix jargon) that will be displayed to all users when they log in. The message may be an important newscast (The system will be down next Friday) or a cheery Welcome aboard! My SCO UNIX also tells me useful facts about disk usage. You may see the message

```
You have mail.
```

This alerts you to the fact that the Unix electronic mail service has received one or more messages since the last time you cleared your incoming mailbox. Mail can originate from users on your system (you can even send yourself a letter) or from users on any other remote system that has your Unix mailing address and the right connections.

Commands

What is the shell prompt prompting you for? The answer is Unix *commands*. These commands come in all shapes and sizes, from simple and common to rare and hellish. The command itself is a rather brief set of letters (usually, but not always, with a hint of mnemonicity), possibly followed by *options* and/or *arguments*. I'll explain these terms in the next chapter, but for now, let's try a few simple commands. I'll use boldface to show what you type and lighter type to indicate the response. First, enter the command date. The dialogue will look something like this:

```
$ date
Thu Feb 16 09:35:12 PST 1995
$ _
```

Note that after the date, time, and time zone are displayed, the shell prompt reappears ready for your next command. Next enter who to see who is on the system.

The response is a list of all active users, the terminals they are logged on, and the date and time they last logged on.

```
$ who
iwonka tty1a Feb16 10:05
stan   tty2a Feb16 15:23
$ _
```

Unix lets you enter two or more commands on the same line. Simply enter a semi-colon between each command; then press Enter after the final command:

```
$ date; who
Thu Feb 16 09:35:12 PST 1995
iwonka tty1a Feb16 10:05
stan   tty2a Feb16 15:23
$ _
```

The next example shows what happens if you enter a nonexistent command.

```
$ amelia
amelia: not found
$ jimmy_hoffa
jimmy_hoffa: not found
$ _
```

No, Unix is not an expert in aviation and trade union history. If you enter a command that is unknown to Unix, you get the not found message, followed by the shell prompt.

It is important at this early stage to realize that it is almost impossible to damage a computer system by mistyping a command. There are, to be sure, a few dangerous commands, such as rm and rmdir, that if used rashly, can erase files you may not want to erase. I'll show you how to avoid such calamities, so there is no need to develop computophobia.

Logging Out Already?

WARNING   Be sure to log out after each Unix session.

After logging in and typing a few commands, it may seem premature to show you how to log out (some say log off). In fact, it is an essential operation to master as soon as possible. The whole point of security and passwords is lost if you leave your terminal in an active logged-in state, whether remotely or locally. Anyone can take advantage of your hard-gained access, and who knows what evil lurks in the hearts of men and women? In addition, some sites charge you real money or set quotas for connect time. The logging out procedure varies according to the shell you are using. The Bourne shell logout works as follows:

```
$ exit
```

The C shell requires this command to log out:

```
% logout
```

At most sites, you can also log out with Ctrl-D. (Remember to hold down the Ctrl key and press D.) A successful logout is signaled by the appearance of the login prompt, so if you or anyone else wishes to become an active user, the full logging in sequence is required. If you are connected by modem, you must follow the vendor's instructions for hanging up. Many online Unix systems will hang up for you when you log out, but check this before you run up unnecessary phone bills.

Choice of Passwords

Passwords must strike a balance between memorability and lack of obviousness. These aims conflict somewhat. Passwords should be reasonably memorable; otherwise you'll have to write them down in too many accessible places. They should also be fairly long, say, six characters minimum. You have probably heard all the stories of hacker break-ins. Often the passwords were broken because the user used obvious words such as names of husbands, wives, dogs, or children. The SCO UNIX and other Unix systems offer the automatic generation of "pronounceable" but otherwise highly obscure passwords such as `klibrugak`, which you would remember in syllables as "kli-bru-gak." Another useful trick is to mix alphanumeric characters with punctuation or even invisible control characters.

Summary

You have seen how to log in and log out, and how to enter a few simple commands in between. You now know how to enter your user name and password, and how to correct typing errors noticed before you have used the Enter key to terminate an input line.

You have also been exposed to some of the Unix jargon. There is more to come.

CHAPTER

TWO

Simple Commands

- About the shell

- Finding the kernel

- Files—a quick introduction

- Command arguments

In Chapter 1 you logged in to Unix and entered the two commands date and who. In this chapter I'll introduce a few more simple commands and give you a better idea of what is going on when Unix receives and obeys your instructions. This discussion will introduce or expand on several important topics including shells, kernels, programs, files, and permissions, although fuller treatments await you in later chapters. As in all pursuits of knowledge, a general framework is needed upon which you can slot in the nitty details.

More on the Shell

The shell prompt, $ or %, indicates that a shell program designated by you or your system administrator is running on your piece of the system. When we talk about a program *running* or *executing*, we mean that the CPU is carrying out the program's instructions step by step. Some of these instructions may temporarily halt the run for various reasons. For example, the shell program regularly requests input from you and waits for your response. After you enter your command, the shell program "revives" to examine your input.

Less obviously, Unix itself may temporarily halt a program to allocate processing time to other active programs. In fact, Unix can service many users by switching from one user's program to another's. It does this so quickly that each user seems to have sole control of the system. Operating systems, such as Unix, that can handle several programs concurrently are said to be *multitasking*. The related term *multiuser* refers to any system that can support more than one user terminal. All multiuser systems must provide multitasking, but you can also have multitasking on a single-user system. OS/2 on a PC, for instance, is not a multiuser system, but it lets the single user run several programs concurrently. Unix is both a multitasking and multiuser system.

While we are on the terminological treadmill, a *multiprocessor* system is one with several CPUs (central processing units). Since modern systems, large and small, now tend to have auxiliary microprocessors lurking in disk controllers, graphics boards, and laser printers (sometimes more powerful than your main processor), the true meaning of multiprocessor is somewhat clouded. This is a common problem to all escalating technologies: the dictionaries cannot be updated quickly enough. But back to the shell.

The shell, although a miracle of coding that will play a vital role in your Unix life, is just a program residing in a file like any other Unix program. The Bourne shell, for instance, was largely written by Dr. Stephen R. Bourne in the Fall of 1976 while he was with the Unix development team at AT&T Bell Laboratories.

The Bourne shell serves not only as a command interpreter but as a programming language, complete with named variables, conditional branching, and all the other trappings of a high-level programming language. You can write your own programs, known as *shell scripts*, by listing a sequence of commands. The shell then interprets and runs your script. (If you've been exposed to DOS, you can think of the shell as a highly sophisticated COMMAND.COM command-line interpreter, and of the shell script as an advanced form of batch file.)

If You Want to Find the Kernel...

Sitting at the heart of Unix is a mastermind program called the *kernel*. The Unix kernel interacts with your computer and peripherals (disks, printers, terminals, and so on), allocating resources and scheduling jobs behind the scenes. You don't have to know much about the kernel's machinations; just be glad it's there protecting you from the endless hardware jungle. When Unix is *ported* from one system to another—that is, rewritten to run on a different computer—it is the kernel that gets modified to cope with the new CPU. Unlike DOS, which is tied to one family of Intel microprocessors, Unix can run on any computer that has the appropriate kernel. The kernel program itself is written largely in a high-level programming language called C (also developed at AT&T Bell Labs). This reduces the effort needed to port Unix to other systems and explains the famed Unix ubiquity.

In simplified terms, the kernel protects you from the computer hardware, and the shell protects you from the kernel. Yes, you can also seek protection from the shell! There exist many Unix applications and user interfaces that hide the shell and its prompt, offering you menus, windows, and other mollycoddling devices with which to select commands and run your jobs.

Files—A Quick Introduction

Computer files are so called because they bear a nodding relation to the old-fashioned manila files people once used to store bits of paper. Such files had tab markers with headings such as "Gas Receipts, 1908–1909," allowing a primitive form of *random access*. For the moment, you can think of a computer file simply as a place for storing data and programs on your disk. Disk files also have tab markers known as *file names*. Groups of files are stored in *directories*, which also have names. Both you and Unix use these directory and file names when locating a file and accessing its contents. You'll see how in Chapter 3.

A major service offered by Unix (and most other operating systems) is handling files by name. You usually do not need to be concerned with the physical location or structure of a file—Unix keeps track of these boring details. Your accounts payable data may reside on cylinder 87 starting at sector 102, and it may even move about during processing. All you need to know is the directory name, `/usr/payables` or whatever, and the file name, say, `ac.payable`.

You (or your application program) may want to access a data file to examine or update its contents. Data or *text* files normally contain visible, printable characters encoded in ASCII format. You'll meet commands that will display or print the contents of a text file by reading a sequence of characters from the disk. There are yet more commands that allow you to write to the disk in order to create and modify text files. You can also copy and rename files, or append one file to another. You can, dare I mention it, all too easily erase (or *kill*) files.

Multiuser systems need to offer safeguards to prevent other users from reading and/or erasing your files without due authority. Unix has an elaborate scheme of file ownerships and permissions whereby users and groups of users can protect their files. Each file in the system carries read, write, and execute permissions that dictate who can do what with a file.

Binary files contain program code in a form understood only by your CPU. Some bytes in this code may coincide with ASCII characters, but printing or displaying an executable file will give you gibberish or lock up your printer or terminal.

If you want to run a program, Unix needs to locate it by name. When you enter the command `date`, for example, Unix looks for a program file called `date`. It looks in various places, as you'll see in Chapter 5. If it fails to find the target file, you get a *filename: not found* message, as you saw with `amelia` in Chapter 1.

Command Arguments

Unix is not just the kernel and shell. Even the most basic versions of Unix come with a set of utility programs for editing and manipulating files: searching, sorting, and so on. Each of these can be invoked by entering the appropriate command, usually followed by additional, optional information known as *command arguments* and *options* (or *switches*). To reduce verbosity, the term *argument* is often applied to any extra information you type after a command, whether it is a file name or the symbol for a switch. Even when you enter a command such as date with no arguments, Unix usually supplies a default argument behind your back. You'll find that some arguments are needed simply to override or modify such defaults.

The precise nature and format for these arguments and options varies from command to command, and getting to know their quirks is a major part of mastering Unix. Each command has a *syntax*, or set of rules, governing its legal arguments. In addition, of course, you need to learn the semantics behind each syntactical variation: what does the command do, and how is the action modified by the presence of arguments? And, as I mentioned earlier, most commands have default arguments that you need to know about.

The bulk of the Unix documentation, in fact, is devoted to listing the syntax and semantics of the commands and their permissible arguments. Some commands you will use daily so they become familiar friends. Others are quite esoteric, requiring even the experts to take a sly peek at the manual to refresh their memory. Most systems have some or all of the Unix command reference manual online for instant access via the man command.

Who Do People Say That I Am?

Try adding the arguments am i to the command who:

```
$ who am i
stan     tty01     Mar 23 13:07
$ _
```

> **NOTE** Unix distinguishes arguments from commands and, in most cases, other arguments by the spaces that separate them.

Your response, I imagine, will be different. Note the space between the command and its first argument. This is a general rule, otherwise Unix would be unable to distinguish the command name from what follows. We also have a space between the two arguments am and i, but other commands may accept arguments with or without spaces or other separating symbols.

In the interests of gooder English, Unix also accepts who am I with a capital *I*. The extra arguments alter the normal action of who. Rather than list all active users, it tells you about yourself: your login name, the name of the terminal or *line* you are wired to, and the date and time you logged in. The question is not as dumb as it may seem, by the way. You may be working away from home on a strange terminal and need to know its name; you may be registered under several user names; you may want to check when you logged in; or you may encounter a terminal that has been rashly left by someone in a logged-in state. (In the latter case, the who am i really asks "Who *was* that fool?")

Here is a useful shorthand to show the syntax of the who command so far presented:

```
who [am i]
who [am I]
```

We use the square brackets to enclose any argument or arguments that can be legally omitted. Note carefully that it would be wrong to write who [am] [i], since this would imply that who am and who i are legal (which is not true).

Now enter the command

```
$ who
```

immediately followed by the command

```
$ who -s
```

NOTE	A hyphen usually indicates that the following symbol is an option.

Can you spot any difference in the responses displayed by Unix? Unless someone logged in or out between your two entries, the two commands will give you the same result. They are equivalent because the switch −s (s here means short) is the default option for who. This option tells Unix to display just the name, line, and time fields of all active users. Unless you use another option that overrides the −s, who will assume you want the short option. The - sign (minus or hyphen) is commonly used in Unix to indicate that the following symbol is an option. When more than one option is allowed, you often find that a single - can be followed by a string of option symbols.

Instant Calendars

Next we'll try the calendar display command cal to illustrate another use of arguments and defaults. Enter cal as follows:

```
$ cal
Thu Mar 23 13:08:14 1995
       Feb                     Mar                     Apr
 S  M Tu  W Th  F  S     S  M Tu  W Th  F  S     S  M Tu  W Th  F  S
          1  2  3  4              1  2  3  4                       1
 5  6  7  8  9 10 11     5  6  7  8  9 10 11     2  3  4  5  6  7  8
12 13 14 15 16 17 18    12 13 14 15 16 17 18     9 10 11 12 13 14 15
19 20 21 22 23 24 25    19 20 21 22 23 24 25    16 17 18 19 20 21 22
26 27 28               26 27 28 29 30 31        23 24 25 26 27 28 29
                                                30
$ _
```

With no arguments, cal shows you the present date and time (as seen with the date command), then lists a three-month calendar for the previous, present, and following months of the current year. The full syntax for cal is

```
cal [[month] year]
```

Notice the positions of the square brackets used to indicate optional groups of arguments. They indicate that you can enter cal, cal *year,* or cal *month year,* but you are not allowed to enter cal *month.* Try some of the following combinations:

```
$ cal 1995
```

Whoops, the calendar for a whole year quickly scrolls off the screen. Time for a ReadSpeed enrollment? Not really. Unix offers a trick whereby you can display one screenful of text at a time:

```
$ cal 1995 | more
```

After the first part of the calendar fills the screen, you'll see the legend -- More --, and scrolling halts until you press the spacebar. Scrolling then resumes until another screen is full, and so on until the output is over and the prompt reappears. You can scroll one line at a time by pressing the Enter key.

Pipelines

The | (vertical bar) symbol represents a *pipeline* that takes the output of one program and sends it as input to another program. The second program is known as a *filter.* The output from a filter can either be displayed, or it can be passed on to another filter by using the pipeline symbol again. In $ x | y | z, the output from program x feeds into filter y, the output of y feeds into filter z. The output of z, if any, would normally be displayed on the screen.

In the above example, | redirects the output of cal from the screen to the filter called more. We won't delve deeply into this important mechanism just now—suffice it to say that more soaks up the data coming from cal and passes it on one screen or line at a time with a convenient pause and prompt. Other filters, provided by Unix or user-created, allow a wide range of data manipulation to and from files and screens.

More Calendars

The optional month argument can be entered numerically:

```
$ cal 9 1990
```

or alphabetically:

```
$ cal sep 1990
```

Both will display the calendar for September 1990. This is less than a screenful, so the more trick is not required. Unix is quite tolerant over the format for the month. Try

```
$ cal s 1990
```

Since s (or S) uniquely determines September (no other month can claim this initial letter), September is what you get. With June, you need at least jun to avoid clashing with July. May needs three letters because of March, and so on. The rule for the month entry is this: either a number between 1 and 12, or enough letters (lower- or uppercase) to uniquely identify the name of a month.

A common error is to type the year as 90 when you mean 1990. The Unix calendar goes back to 1 C.E. (Common Era, also known as A.D.), so 90 is taken as, well, 90! The legal range for year is 1 to 9999, so you can play around with calendars past and future. I confirmed, for example, what my mother told me: I was born on a Sunday. Run your birth month and year past cal and check your day of birth.

To explore more useful Unix commands, you need to know more about the Unix file system. This forms the subject of our next chapter.

Summary

Chapter 2 covered the following topics:

- Unix is a multitasking, mulituser operating system.

- The shell is a program that interprets your commands and passes them to the kernel for processing.

- The Unix kernel is the central mastermind program that schedules jobs and allocates resources (time, memory, disks, and other peripherals), thereby shielding the user from most of the foibles and intricacies of the hardware.

- Unix is not tied to any particular computer model. The kernel is written in a high-level language (C), which makes it relatively easy to port from one machine to another.

- Files are grouped into directories. Both files and directories are accessed by their names. Files are either text or binary. Some files are executable, that is, they represent scripts or programs that can be run.

- Commands are executable programs supplied with Unix. Commands usually have arguments and options that you enter in order to vary the default action of the command.

- You met the command who with the argument am i and the cal command with various date arguments.

CHAPTER

THREE

Meet the Unix
File System

- Directories

- The name of the file

- Trees and hierarchies

- The root of the matter

- Absolute path names

Files play an important and pervasive role in Unix. In Chapter 2, you learned that the file is a place where data and programs are stored. In this and the following chapter, you'll see how Unix extends this simple idea so that files can also represent devices, such as printers, terminals, and disk drives, and even less tangible objects such as *processes*.

To recap the four most important facts about files that were introduced in Chapter 2:

- Files are grouped into directories.
- Files and directories have names.
- Within a directory, each file has a unique name.
- The command names you type correspond to the names of program files that are interpreted by the shell.

Let's delve more deeply into files and directories by exploring a familiar analogy: your home filing system.

Directories

A typical home filing system might start life with separate manila folders filed alphabetically:

Cajun Recipes

Dad's Recipes

Gas Receipts 1993

Gas Receipts 1994

Gas Receipts 1995

IRS 1993

IRS 1994

IRS 1995

John's Recipes

John's School

Mary's College

Mom's Recipes

For a small collection of files, this organization might be adequate, but as the number of files increases, your access time and frustration would grow—with most of the time spent in trying to recall the exact name of the folder holding your target data. Suppose now that you buy some larger folders and label them

Education

Gas Receipts

IRS

Recipes

Within each large folder you store the appropriate files. Your new file might be restructured and relabeled to look like this:

Education

    John

    Mary

Gas Receipts

    1993

    1994

    1995

IRS

    1993

    1994

    1995

Recipes

    Cajun

    Dad

John

Mom

In Unix terms the larger folders represent directories, while the individual folders represent the files. Notice that the "search time" is reduced, mainly because you are better organized! You can go quickly to, say, *Education* by thumbing through the major categories, then quickly locate *John* or *Mary*.

You will immediately note that there are now two files named *John*. However, the two *John* files are distinct: one is under *Education* and the other is under *Recipes*. Similarly, the file names *1993*, *1994*, and *1995* each appear twice but represent different sets of data. In Unix, you can indicate these distinctions as follows:

`Education/John`	The `John` file in the `Education` directory
`Education/Mary`	The `Mary` file in the `Education` directory
`Recipes/John`	The `John` file in the `Recipes` directory
`Gas.Receipts/1995`	The `1995` file in the `Gas.Receipts` directory
`IRS/1995`	The `1995` file in the `IRS` directory

and so on. Each directory/file combination, you'll notice, is unique, although the file names may be duplicated.

The Name of the File

The period in `Gas.Receipts`, by the way, is not a typo. Unix file and directory names cannot have intervening spaces, so you tend to use a symbol such as . or _ or - to increase legibility: `GasReceipts`, `Gas.Receipts`, `Gas-Receipts`, and `Gas_Receipts` are all permitted, but `Gas Receipts` would look like two separate names to Unix. Most of the naming rules we'll be looking at apply equally to file and directory names, so to reduce verbiage, I'll often just refer to file names. In fact, you'll see that Unix, being file-centered, treats directories rather like files in many situations.

In DOS, the period is reserved to show a file *extension*. In CONFIG.SYS or WS.COM, for example, SYS and COM are extensions, limited to three characters at most, used to tell you something about the nature of the file. Unix is more flexible: periods are optional, but if used, they can be placed anywhere in a file or directory name. A

period at the *beginning* of a name does have a special significance, so we'll avoid using names such as .thingy until I've explained this usage.

Unix names are usually limited to fourteen alphanumerical characters, and there are a few symbols that are illegal or inadvisable. For instance, using the / character within a name would confuse Unix and everyone else, as it is used to distinguish directory names from file names; something like Gas/Receipts would be interpreted as a file called Receipts in a directory called Gas.

WARNING Avoid * / ? " ' ` [ ] and any control characters in your Unix file names.

Similarly, the invisible control characters should not be used, again for obvious reasons. The other forbidden characters are * ? " ' ` [and], for reasons that will emerge later.

You should strike a balance between a short, ambiguous file name, such as things or stuff, that barely indicates its contents, and a long-winded essay that may prove difficult to recall and type consistently. Of course, if your directories are succinctly named, the file names can be short and simple, as in the examples above.

HISTORY The prepackaged command names of Unix are often notoriously short and cryptic. There are sound historical reasons for this. In the late 1960s, when Ken Thompson and Dennis Ritchie were developing the first Unix, the available terminals were slow, 10-character-per-second teletypewriters, so it made sense to keep both command lines and error messages as short as possible.

Remember too that Unix, unlike DOS, distinguishes upper- and lowercase letters in file and directory names. The files irs, Irs, and IRS are different, so watch your Shift and Caps Lock keys. Traditionally, though, programmers have never been slick touch typists, so command names have tended to be short and in lowercase.

Trees and Hierarchies

As you've seen, Unix uses the symbol / (forward slash) between the directory name and the file name. (DOS users will recognize this trick—see the next section.) It provides a file structure known, I'm afraid, as *hierarchical*. So far you've only seen a two-level hierarchy, `directory_name/filename`, but both DOS and Unix build on this in a natural way: a directory can itself hold several directories, known as *subdirectories*, and subdirectories can hold *subsubdirectories*, and so on, until you reach "real" files.

UNIX AND DOS   DOS borrowed the Unix hierarchical file structure when DOS matured from Version 1.0 to Version 2.0. For some obscure reason, though, DOS uses a \ (backslash) rather than the / (forward slash) used in Unix. DOS would use `IRS\1995.DAT`, for example, for a file in the IRS directory. This difference can be a nuisance if you are constantly switching between DOS and Unix. Either system will quickly tell you if you use the wrong slash, and usually no real damage results: you'll just get an annoying `file not found` or similar message.

Paths

The Unix notation for these hierarchies is quite simple. If you see a file named `usr/stan/memo`, you know at once that `usr` is a directory with a subdirectory called `stan` that holds a file called `memo`. The *path* to `memo` is the sequence of directories you need to traverse to reach `memo`, namely `usr/stan/`. You can also say that the path to `stan` is `usr/`. The path concept turns out to be of great practical importance when working with Unix files. If this concept is a little fuzzy to you, have patience. There will be plenty of examples before long.

Figure 3.1 shows a *tree* diagram, a common and convenient way of looking at paths and file hierarchies. Unlike Mother Nature's trees, file trees traditionally grow upside down, with the branches spreading downwards away from the light.

Quick test: what is the path to `mail`? Yes, you climb down the tree via the directories `usr` and `mary` to `mail`, so the path is `usr/mary/`. What is the path to `temp`? Ah, gotcha! Both `stan` and `mary` have a file called `temp`, so the question needs reframing.

You Call That a File?

The labels in Figure 3.1 identify which names are directory names and which are file names. Without these labels, you could certainly deduce that `usr`, `stan`, and `mary` are directories. How? Well, they are each shown holding (or providing a path to) a named object on the lower level: `usr` holds `stan` and `mary`, `stan` holds `memo` and `temp`, and so on. Only directories can hold other directories and files. Files can hold data (not shown in the tree), but they cannot hold directories or other files.

FIGURE 3.1:

The file tree

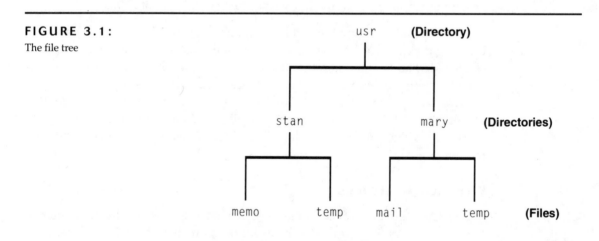

If I removed the label showing `memo` as a file, however, you could not tell from the tree whether `memo` was a file or an *empty* directory. As you can guess, an empty directory is a perfectly valid directory that by some quirk of fate happens not to

hold any subdirectories or files. If you erased the files `stan/memo` and `stan/temp`, for instance, `stan` would still exist, but it would now be an empty directory.

You'll be pleased to learn that Unix offers commands that tell you whether a given name is a file or a directory. There are also commands to create and remove both directories and files, as well as commands that let you "move" around the tree in all directions and explore the contents of directories and files (limited only by any security restrictions imposed by other users and the system administrator). Before rushing into these commands, you need a little more background on Unix file organization.

File Name Duplicates

Although you can have more than one Unix file called `John`, each must reside in a different directory. In the manila-folder world we looked at earlier, there's nothing to stop you from misfiling *John's Education* stuff in the *Recipe* section. The two files marked *John* would just sit there. This would be a nuisance and would hinder prompt retrieval, but it would not violate the known Laws of Physics.

In this area Unix files are less tolerant, and here the manila-folder analogy starts breaking down. Two `John` files cannot coexist in the `Recipes` directory. Putting a second file named `John` into the `Recipe` directory would overwrite the existing `John` file with the second `John` file, regardless of the relative sizes of the two files. By overwriting, I mean *completely* replacing the contents of one file with another. The original data is lost: the `Recipe/John` file would now contain his grades and curriculum vitae! The name of a Unix file or directory has no magical influence over its contents.

Files and i-Nodes

In fact, Unix files and directories are stored and retrieved using internal numbers known as *i-nodes*. All you need to know for the moment is that Unix keeps track of how file and directory names correspond, or *map*, to their i-nodes. Unix also knows how the i-nodes relate to specific blocks and tracks on your disk. The sequence of steps taken by Unix when you key in a file name is (briefly) as follows:

1. Use the path to get to the relevant table.

2. Find the name in that table.

3. Note the corresponding i-node.

4. Use the i-node to locate the file on the disk.

5. Manipulate the data in the file (read, write, and so on) according to your command.

Flat Files

Unix files are what we call *flat files*. You can think of them as simple streams of characters or bytes without any intrinsic format or structure. They can grow and shrink freely as they are manipulated and massaged in various ways. The upper limit in file size is huge and well beyond a mortal's total disk capacity. Unix maintains in its tables a number giving the current length in bytes of each file, and this is updated whenever the file size changes. When a program tries to read beyond the end of a file, Unix generates an EOF (end-of-file) message—end of reading!

Other operating systems have elaborate sets of formats defining specific headers and fields for different files, strict rules that must be adhered to by all user programs. With Unix, it is up to individual application programmers to impose some structure on the string of bytes sitting in a Unix flat file. When we come to editing text files, you'll see that the usual layout codes, such as tab and carriage return, are written into files by the editor program just like normal characters. It is the editor, not Unix itself, that interprets them to give you nicely formatted documents.

Two Names for the Same File?

The chunk of flat data sitting in a file "knows" only its unique i-node. You could not determine its Unix name by reading this data; you would have to trace back to the tables where Unix keeps its lists of i-nodes and names. Each name has a unique i-node, but several different names can have the same i-node value. Consequently, if two different file names, stan and joe, share the same i-node value, they represent the same file. Changes to stan would immediately show up if you examined joe, and vice versa. How did stan and joe achieve this strange status? Well, Unix provides a command called ln (link) that lets you link an existing file to another name. Assuming you set up stan first, you could enter

```
$ ln stan joe
```

Thereafter, the name joe has the same i-node as stan, giving you two names for the same physical file. I-nodes and links are important in the theory of the Unix file system. But ln also has a practical application: given a long path name, you can save keystrokes by linking that file to a shorter "alias."

The root of the Matter

The tree in Figure 3.1 is just a part of the total Unix file tree. At the base of the whole tree is a special directory appropriately called the root. Remember that file trees are inverted with respect to natural timber, so the root will be shown at the top!

Changing the symbolism to family trees, you can see that other directories have one (unique) parent and may possibly have children, but the root has only children. The root is the only directory with no parent. The whole tree grows (down!) from the root, the Adam of the family.

The symbol for the root is /, which beginners find rather strange at first. Yes, the selfsame slash that is used to separate directory and file names when listing paths and path names. You may think it confusing and ambiguous to use the one symbol in two apparently conflicting ways, but once you start using the root symbol, it soon emerges as a natural and indeed elegant approach.

First, let's add the root to our earlier tree. The result is shown below in Figure 3.2.

FIGURE 3.2:
File tree with root

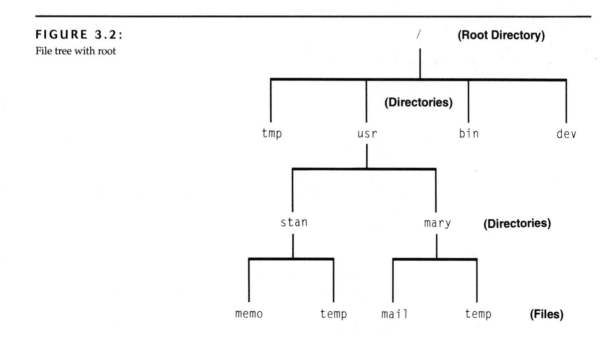

Notice that usr is now a subdirectory of root, and that I have added a few more subdirectories to root, namely tmp, bin, and dev. These three standard directories have many branches, but I've omitted them to avoid clutter.

Absolute Path Names

We can now give the full path names for our four files as follows:

```
/usr/stan/memo
/usr/stan/temp
/usr/mary/mail
/usr/mary/temp
```

The first / is the root. This is a fixed point of reference. The subsequent / symbols are our familiar directory/file separators.

Path names starting with /, the root, are called *absolute* path names: they specify the file completely.

Home Is Best

The beauty of the Unix file hierarchy is that you do not always have to specify these lengthy, absolute path names. If you are already partway down the path to your target file, all you need to specify is the *rest* of the path. Unix knows where you are, and will construct the full, absolute path name for you. If you are already "sitting at" mary, say, you can access the file /usr/mary/mail by simply asking for mail. Unix supplies the /usr/mary/ part for you.

To see how this works, you need to understand two new concepts: the *home* directory and the *working* directory.

Every user is assigned a home directory by the system administrator. When you first log in, you are placed in this home directory. Home is your starting point in the file tree. From there you can roam around the tree, up, down, and sideways, landing in different directories, and returning home for love and dinner. The directory you happen to be in at any point in your Odyssey is called your *current* or *working* directory, and has the special nickname (or alias) . (pronounced *dot*). Most times, this will be your own, home, dedicated, private directory. Here you are king or queen, free to establish your own subdirectories and files, set visiting rights (permissions) for other users, and so on. Only the system administrator can override your protective shield. Otherwise, your home directory is safe and cozy. It is almost

always named in your honor. Home directories for users are usually subdirectories of /usr. My home directory is called stan just like my login name, so I start at /usr/stan. Mary will start in the directory /usr/mary.

How do you know where you are in the file tree as you move around? Read on.

You Are Here

The pwd command means "print working directory." In Unix, the word "print" often means "display," another hangover from the early teleprinter terminal days.

The response to pwd gives you the absolute path name of your current place in the file tree, namely your working directory. For example:

```
$ pwd
/usr/stan
$ _
```

Next, try creating your own subdirectory and moving to it, as in

```
$ mkdir test
$ cd test
$ pwd
/usr/stan/test
$ _
```

Since I was already in /usr/stan, the mkdir test (make new directory called test) command created a new, empty subdirectory with the absolute path name of /usr/stan/test. Its name *relative* to /usr/stan, my home directory, is simply test. So while I'm in my home directory, I can refer to the new directory "just below me" simply as test—there is no need to use the longer absolute path name. Knowing where you are in the tree is therefore vital: your current, working directory quietly "adds" its path to any relative directory or file-name arguments you type.

The cd test (change working directory to test) command therefore moves me from /usr/stan to /usr/stan/test. I could have used

```
$ cd /usr/stan/test
```

with exactly the same results but with more keyboard effort.

You can use cd without an argument to get to your home directory at any time. For example:

```
$ pwd
/usr/stan/test
$ cd
$ pwd
/usr/stan
```

After cd, I used pwd to confirm my present whereabouts. While you are getting used to navigating the directories, it's an excellent idea to use pwd frequently. Remember that if you have several files called John, the one you are accessing is the one in your current directory, unless you explicitly supply an overriding path name. If you are working in /usr/joe/Education, the name John refers to /usr/joe/Education/John. If you want to access the other John without changing directories, you could type its full, absolute path name: /usr/joe/Recipes/John. Or, you could change your working directory with this command:

```
$ cd /usr/joe/Recipes
```

Now, of course, you can access /usr/joe/Recipes/John by using good old plain John. Confused? Well, it does take some practice. Like riding a bike, some things are easier to do than to write about. The key point to watch is that absolute path names start with the root symbol /. They take you all the way back to the root, then lead you down to your target. Relative path names do not have an initial /, so they lead you from where you are to your target.

Back Home

Suppose I'm in /usr/stan/test/temp. To get back to the parent directory, /usr/stan/test, I could use this command:

```
$ cd /usr/stan/test
```

but Unix offers a simpler method. The special argument .. (two periods, pronounced *dot-dot*) always means "the parent of the current directory." So

```
$ cd ..
```

gets me to /usr/stan/test a little sooner!

Wherever you are, cd .. moves you one level back towards the root. If you are already at root, then cd .. has no effect.

Removing a Directory

Let's get rid of the `test` directory. It's empty and has served its purpose. The command to use is `rmdir` (remove directory):

```
$ rmdir test
```

If `test` had contained any files or directories, Unix would warn you and would refuse to delete the directory. Now that `test` has been deleted, try `cd test` for a giggle. Yes, you get a `directory: does not exist` error message. You may get this error message on occasions when you are convinced that the target directory *does* exist. The usual reason is that you are not in the correct working directory. If you are in `/usr` and type `cd memo`, Unix looks in vain for `/usr/memo`. Now memo does exist, but it's a subdirectory of `/usr/stan`. So, either supply the full path name, or make `/usr/stan` your working directory.

With the commands `pwd`, `mkdir`, `cd`, and `rmdir`, you can gain some useful insights into the Unix file tree. To progress further, you'll need to know how to create files. This is the subject of our next chapter.

Summary

Chapter 3 covered the following topics:

- As far as Unix itself is concerned, files are "flat" (structureless) sequences of bytes. It is up to the programs that write and read files to impose a structure (such as fixed- or variable-length fields).

- Files are given names that usually relate in some helpful way to their contents: `gas_bills.jan95`, `quicksort.c`, `passwd`, and so on. File names should not exceed 14 alphanumeric characters. Avoid the following characters when naming files: `*` `/` `?` `"` `` ` `` `'` `[` `]` and Ctrl-x.

- A special kind of file called a directory holds file names, together with data used by Unix to locate these files on the disk. Directories are used to group related files. Within each directory, file names must be unique, although the same name can be used for different files in different directories.

- Using the ln (link) command, a given disk file can be assigned more than one file name. Each disk file has a unique i-node, but you can link (map) several names to this i-node.

- Directories can hold both files and subdirectories, forming the famous Unix file hierarchy. This hierarchy (or inverted tree) starts at the root, called /. The full path name of a file tells you its position in the tree:

  /usr/stan/poem

  is a file called poem in the stan subdirectory of usr, which in turn is a subdirectory of the root, /. If you are logged into the directory /usr/stan, you can refer to this file simply as poem (the full path name is not needed).

- The symbol / is used both as the name for root and as a separator between directories and file names.

- Each user is assigned a (usually eponymous) home directory. For example, Mary's home directory would normally be /usr/mary. You can build up your private file hierarchy from this point without disturbing other users' file hierarchies.

- You create new directories with mkdir.

- You can remove empty directories with rmdir.

- Your current (or working) directory has the special nickname (or alias) . (pronounced *dot*). As you move around the tree, the "value" of dot changes. The parent directory of your current directory has the special nickname .. (pronounced *dot-dot*).

- You move about the file tree with cd (change directory). cd alone moves you to your home directory. If you are in /usr/stan, cd dir moves you to directory /usr/stan/dir. If you are anywhere, cd /etc/mail moves you to the directory /etc/mail. cd .. moves you to the parent of the current directory.

- You find out where you are in the tree by using pwd (print working directory).

CHAPTER

FOUR

Creating Your Own Files

- Standard input and output

- Redirecting output

- The `ls` and `cat` commands

- Using `cat` to create files

- The `lc` command

- Redirecting input

- Comparing redirection and pipelines

Now that you know how to navigate the Unix file hierarchy, it's time to create some files of your own. In this chapter, you'll learn how to store the output of commands in disk files and how to key text into files. (In Chapter 8 you'll be able to edit these files with ed, a simple text editor found on all Unix systems.)

You'll also meet the ls and lc commands that list the names and attributes of your files in various formats, and the curiously named cat command that lets you read the contents of files. As the number of commands you learn continues to grow, you'll see how they can be combined to create useful tools.

Standard Input and Output

Recall my earlier comment that files are omnipresent in Unix. In fact, you have already been using two special files without being aware that they *were* files. Since a Unix file can represent any stream of characters, it is not surprising to find that the characters you enter on the keyboard and the characters displayed on your screen can be associated with two files called *standard input* and *standard output*. For brevity, I'll call them stdin and stdout, the internal names used by C programs and their programmers. (Note that you do not use these names as file-name arguments in commands—more on this anon.)

- The stdin file, the command's standard input, is initially attached (or linked) to your terminal *keyboard.*

- The stdout file, the command's standard output, is initially attached (or linked) to your terminal *monitor screen.*

You do not have to create or name these two standard files as you do with normal user disk files. Unix *opens* them for you whenever a command starts to operate. Opening a file simply means priming it for action, an internal Unix operation the mechanics of which are of no immediate concern to us.

The stdin and stdout files are clearly different in many ways to the disk files you met in Chapter 3. Unless you save your keystroked input somewhere, your default stdin file is simply a source of volatile characters, discarded as soon as they have served their purpose. Likewise, the characters sent to the default stdout file appear fleetingly on the screen, then move on to oblivion ("The Bourne shell from which no traveller returns," as Shakespeare once explained).

On the other hand, it turns out to be extremely fruitful to treat the streams from stdin and to stdout in exactly the same way as data from or to conventional files. Here's a simple example.

In the dialogue below, the first line uses the pwd command introduced in Chapter 3. It confirms that I am "at home" in my usual working directory, /usr/stan. Your own home directory will usually be /usr/*xxx*, where *xxx* is your login name. If you are not in your home directory, you should use cd on its own to get there. Recall that cd without an argument defaults to cd /usr/*xxx*, or whatever your home directory happens to be. In this chapter, you'll be creating and messing about with junky test files, so it's safer to be in your own personal directory where you cannot bother other (anxious) users.

```
$ pwd
/usr/stan
$ date
Mon Apr 3 17:33:28 PDT 1995
$ date >today.test
$ _
```

WARNING Using $ command > *filename* without care may overwrite valuable data in *filename*!

The first date command displays the current date on the screen in the time-honored fashion, similar to the example shown above. But where is your date display from the fifth line? The answer is that you have asked Unix to *redirect* the output from date into a file called today.test, and in response Unix quietly and temporarily reassigns stdout from your screen to this file. If this file already exists, it will be overwritten; otherwise Unix creates a new file called today.test. This is why I picked a rather unusual file name, and why you should become familiar with those commands that can quietly overwrite existing files.

Redirecting Output

The greater-than sign (>) is a redirection operator (on PC keyboards, you'll find that > is shift-period). Note that a space before and/or after > is optional. Common practice is to add a space before > but not after. Some find that another space after > improves legibility—it's your own call.

As its name and shape suggest, > effectively takes the stream of characters produced by date and redirects them *from* the screen file *to* today.test, a "real" disk file.

We'll concentrate on output redirection for a while, but it should come as no surprise to hear that Unix can also redirect stdin using the symbol < (note the direction), so that many commands can take their input data either from the keyboard or from a disk file.

Before I go any further, let's verify that your redirection has worked as planned. Enter the following commands:

```
$ ls
...
lp0
mbox
today.test
...
$ cat today.test
Mon Apr 3 17:33:50 PDT 1995
$ _
```

There are two new important commands here: ls and cat.

The ls Command

ls stands for "list" because it lists the names of the files and subdirectories in your current directory. ls has many options that I'll discuss later. For now, I am using the plain ls without options to prove that a new file called today.test has indeed been created. When you type the ls command, you may well get a different list from mine. The ellipses in the last example indicate that there may be other file names showing, since I've no way of knowing what files exist in your current directory. What I do know is that if you entered date >today.test correctly, then ls will reveal the new file, test.today. Furthermore, you'll find it listed in the correct alphabetical sequence, since ls kindly sorts the names alphabetically for you by default. Later you'll see how to vary this ordering by supplying options.

Note also that ls without options lists both your files and subdirectories by name only, without telling you which is a file and which is a directory.

Another way of using ls to check the existence of files (or directories) is as follows:

```
$ ls today.test
today.test
$ ls teddy.bear
teddy.bear not found
$ _
```

Here you've supplied a file-name argument, and ls will list just that file if it exists; otherwise you get a *name* not found message, where *name* is the file name you specified. In our simplified notation, the syntax for ls, so far, is

```
ls [name]
```

Omitting the optional *name*, the names of all files and subdirectories in your current directory are listed. It's easy to extend this syntax by adding an optional path:

```
ls [path][name]
```

For example, ls/usr or ls/usr/ will list all the files and subdirectories of /usr even if your current directory is /usr/stan.

Similarly, ls/usr/memo will tell you if memo exists in /usr, whatever your current directory may be. A good way to picture this is that when you omit the optional path name, Unix assumes your current directory by default. You simply override this default by adding a specific path name.

Wildcards

ls, like many Unix commands, also supports *wildcard searches*. Try the following:

```
$ ls *
...
lp0
mbox
today.test
...
$ ls *test
today.test
$ ls ??day.test
today.test
$ ls *.*
today.test
$ _
```

The wildcard * provides a match with any number of characters (including none). For instance, with

```
ls *test
```

any names *ending* with the characters test, such as today.test, mytest, your-test, and even the file test, would all match and be listed.

The wildcard ? matches any single character in that position. If you had a file called myday.test, then ls ??day.test would find and list it as well as finding and listing today.test. Wildcards can also be used in directory-path arguments with ls. ls /usr/*/temp, for example, would search all subdirectories of usr for files called temp. Any such found would be listed. Excessive use of * in path arguments, of course, can easily generate an overwhelming response. ls /*/*/* will generate a depressing number of file names and waste your time in the process!

I'll show you further wildcard examples when we have some more files to play with.

Advanced Topic

Unix also provides a more sophisticated pattern-matching argument format for ls and similar commands. ls [abc]*, for example, will list all files starting with "a", "b", or "c", and ls *[vqz] will match all files ending with "v", "q", or "z". ls [a]??[s] will match all four-letter names starting with "a" and ending with "s". I'll have more to say on matching in Chapters 8 and 9.

Within the [and] you can place any sequence of characters for *individual* matching. More interestingly, you can ask for a *range* of characters as follows: ls [a-m]* will match any file starting with a letter in the range a to m inclusive. You could use ls [s-u]???[1-9] to list any five-letter files starting with "s", "t", or "u" and ending with a digit between "1" and "9".

The shell turns arguments featuring wildcards into sets of matching names for ls to process. ls itself, contrary to appearances, does not receive wildcard arguments. You'll see the implications of this when I discuss echo and other commands.

An interesting quirk of Unix wildcards concerns the matching of names beginning with a period. You may recall that I warned you in Chapter 3 against using an initial period when naming files and directories. The reason is twofold.

First, any file such as .profile that starts with a period is *not* normally reported by ls and similar commands. So I lied when I said that * matched all character strings! Such files are *hidden* for various reasons. To "see" them, you must use

ls .*

Second, as you saw in Chapter 3, Unix uses the period in its shorthand for two important directories: one period for your current directory, and two periods for the parent of your current directory. So, ls . and ls .. list the contents of your current and parent directories respectively. If ls * also matched initial periods, it would generate a host of unwanted names. Try

ls .*

It will find list files such as .profile, then all the files and subdirectories of your current directory (also known as .), then finally it will list all the files and subdirectories of .., the parent of your current directory. Better use ls .* | more to give you a pause after each screenful.

I mentioned the many options available with ls. Although this is not the place to enumerate them, I will now take a brief detour to show you how to learn more about ls without having to comb the documentation.

Exploring ls with the man Command

Although Unix has the reputation of being user-indifferent, it has one eminently friendly facility that has been widely imitated, without acknowledgment, by other putatively amiable systems. From the earliest days, the man command has provided easy access to an online manual. Its size and quality, however, may vary from site to site, depending on factors such as available disk space and the system administrator's devotion to updates. Try entering the command

```
$ man ls
```

The online manual pages for ls will scroll by one screenful at a time, with a pause for digestion. At the end of each screen, a colon appears. Press the Enter key to see the next page. Eventually, you'll get back to the $ prompt.

Any command name will serve as the man argument. Commands are uniformly explained under the following sequence:

Name (Section)	LS(C)
Command	ls
Syntax	ls [-ACFRabcdfgilmnopqrstux] [*names*]
Description	Describes the effect of each option and lists the default options.
Files	Lists any associated files, e.g., files where defaults may be stored.
See Also	Lists related commands.
Notes	Gives additional information or samples of usage.
Standards Conformance	Lists the Unix standards with which the command conforms, e.g. AT&T SVID, X/Open.

The online manual uses a standard Unix section coding scheme to facilitate reference to the Unix cornucopia. The header LS(C) means that the ls command is in the C (command) section; CRASH(ADM) references the crash command in ADM, the system administration section; TERMINFO(M) is all about terminfo in the Miscellaneous section, and so on. A LOCAL section documents all commands that are specific to your installation. You'll gradually become familiar with which section holds which command. You can ask man to search all or selected sections. From now on, when I introduce a new command, I will provide the section code to guide you.

Digesting the Syntax

The syntax line usually looks daunting. The twenty-two letters shown inside [and] after ls mean that you can use either some, all, or none of them with ls. Note that case is important: a and A are different options. A single option would be written as ls -l [names], for example, with a hyphen before the chosen letter and a space after the command and before the file or directory names (if any). The - has no negative connotations: some options are subtractive while others are additive.

Multiple options can either be written out in full

    ls -l-a name

or combined with a single hyphen:

    ls -la name

The option letters are sometimes mnemonics: -l means list in the *long*, comprehensive format. Sometimes they are less so: -a means list the hidden files and directories (those beginning with a period), so you can think of a as standing for *all*. Sometimes no obvious mnemonic appears: -u means sort the list by time of last access.

Occasionally, two options exist that are mutually contradictory or conflict in some way, or one option may already include the properties of the other, in which case you have wasted a keystroke. Some combinations of options are so commonly used that Unix provides a single, time-saving command offering those options as the default. For example, ls -l is so frequently used that the command l (single letter ell) can be used as an exact equivalent. You can still add other compatible options with l.

In the syntax line, [names] means that one, several, or no names are all admissible. So both ls and ls -la name1 name2 name3 are legal.

Table 4.1 lists some of the more popular ls variants.

TABLE 4.1: Common options for ls, l, and lc

Option	Description
Default	Lists in alphabetic sequence, excluding .*names* (that is, names starting with a period)
-a	Lists all matching entries, including .*names*
-l	Provides a long listing showing type of entry (file or directory), permissions, owner, size, and date last modified
-r	Reverse listing order
-s	Gives size of each file
-t	Lists in order of time-date last modified (latest first)
-u	Lists in order of time-date last accessed (latest first)

The man command itself has many options for customizing and printing the manual in different formats. Naturally, you can read all about these by typing

```
$ man man
```

Be warned that man can become quite addictive. For now, just note that the manual text files are stored in /usr/man; your system administrator can add to these for any local commands or instructions.

The cat Command

Returning to the date >today.test experiment outlined in the section "Redirecting Output," you'll recall that we used cat today.test to prove that redirection worked as promised.

The cat command (in man section C), used with a single file-name argument, simply displays the *contents* of the given file. So cat today.test displays the sequence of characters stored in today.test. As you saw earlier, cat gave a display on your screen similar to

```
Mon Apr 3 17:33:50 PDT 1995
```

which was exactly like the original date command with no redirection. Ah, not exactly! The time of the second date entry was a few seconds later! However, you must agree that the output from date was successfully redirected into today.test. It's quite neat to realize that you have created a file and filled it with meaningful data without resorting to word processors or text editors!

The name cat is short for *catenate*, which in turn is short for *concatenate*, a fancy, $500 term for joining things together. You have seen cat display only a single file, so you may wonder what this has to do with concatenation. The reason is that cat can be used with several file-name arguments: cat x y will display the contents of file x, followed by the contents of file y. Using our newfound friend >, cat x y > z will concatenate the two files x and y into one new, big file called z.

Using Output Redirection with Other Commands

Redirection works with any command that generates output to stdout. We often talk about a command *writing* to its standard output. Try the following:

```
$ who >who.dat
$ cat who.dat
iwonka tty1a Apr5 10:04
stan   tty2a Apr5 10:32
$ ls >list.dat
$ cat list.dat
list.dat
lp0
mbox
today.test
who.dat
$ cat who.dat list.dat >combo
$ cat combo
iwonka tty1a Apr5 10:04
stan   tty2a Apr5 10:32
list.dat
lp0
mbox
today.test
who.dat
$ _
```

Your displays will differ somewhat, but they should convince you that with redirection, commands such as who and ls can create useful files. Note how cat with two file-name arguments concatenates the files to the third argument, combo. The second argument, list.dat, although nearer to combo in the command line, appears at the end of combo, which may seem counterintuitive. cat reads and transfers its arguments, though, from left to right.

You should experiment on your own by creating a calendar file using cal > cal.dat or cal 1990 > cal.year. Note that the optional arguments for cal are entered before the redirection arguments. Use ls and cat to check your new files.

The syntax for output redirection is simple:

```
commandname [options] [>filename]
```

Omitting the optional > filename arguments gives the default: command output goes to the screen. (Note that you should never actually use >stdout as an argument. Unix would take date >stdout literally, creating a disk file called stdout!)

Before I move on from output to input redirection, let's see a simple way of creating a file from keyboard input. You'll be using cat in a new way. So far, we have been creating files with data determined by other commands, such as date, cal, and who; it would be nice to have some files with our own written texts in them. You'll meet some new commands: lc and wc (both in man section C).

Using cat to Create Files

Enter the following sequence:

```
$ cat >poem.1
Mary had a little lamb,
Its feet were white as snow;
^d
$ _
```

Press Enter after typing poem.1, lamb, and snow; to get line spaces as shown. During text entry Unix stores the Enter key action as the ASCII *newline* code (value 10). When text files are read back to screens or printers, the newline code gives you the familiar carriage-return/linefeed action.

After the final Enter, you should hold down the Ctrl key and type a d or D. Ctrl-D, traditionally written as ^d or ^D, is the Unix EOF (end-of-file) character, telling the command that input is finished. (You may recall the use of ^D to log out—you were actually telling the shell program to quit.)

Let's see the result of our efforts:

```
$ cat poem.1
Mary had a little lamb,
Its feet were white as snow;
$ _
```

The miracle is readily explained: cat was reading data from your default standard input, the keyboard, and passing it to its redirected standard output, the file poem.1. Let's try another:

```
$ cat >poem.2
And everywhere that Mary went,
The lamb was sure to go.
^d
$ cat poem.2
And everywhere that Mary went,
The lamb was sure to go.
$ _
```

Now it's concatenation time:

```
$ cat poem.1 poem.2 >poem
$ cat poem
Mary had a little lamb,
Its feet were white as snow;
And everywhere that Mary went,
The lamb was sure to go.
$ _
```

cat will not replace WordPerfect, but at least we have a file with a poem in it.

To test your ls and wildcard skills, try the following:

```
$ ls poem.?
poem.1
poem.2
$ ls poem*
poem
```

```
poem.1
poem.2
$ _
```

The lc Command

Now for a new command from the ls family:

```
$ lc poem*
poem     poem.1    poem.2
$ _
```

 NOTE   lc is standard for SCO UNIX, but may not be available on your system.

Yes, lc (in man section C) means "list in columns," but otherwise works very much like ls. Without any name arguments, lc lists the files and subdirectories of your current directory.

Normally, lists are sorted lexicographically (in dictionary order). You can vary this with the −t option, giving time-of-last-data-modification order, with the latest modified file listed first:

```
$ lc −t poem*
poem     poem.2    poem.1
$ _
```

The −u option sorts by time of last access, with the most recently accessed file first. Here is a case where two options conflict, so avoid the combination −ut. The −r option reverses the order given by the other options, so −rt (sort by time modified, with earliest first) and −ru (search by time accessed, with earliest first) are legal and useful.

```
$ lc −rt poem*
poem.1    poem.2    poem
$ _
```

Counting Words with wc

You can also determine some statistics about your file contents using the wc (word count) command (in man section C):

```
$ wc poem
        4   22  108  poem
$ wc poem.1
        2   11   53  poem.1
$ wc poem.2
        2   11   55  poem.2
$ _
```

wc gives you the number of lines, words, and characters in the target file. Note that the number of characters is more than you might expect because the newline codes count as characters.

It's interesting, and in the true spirit of Unix, to combine commands. Try ls | wc. The output of ls (a list of your files) will be counted by wc and the result displayed. The first number from wc is the number of files in your current directory.

Redirecting Input

If you feel comfortable about output redirection using >, the next topic, input redirection, should present no real obstacles. Since the directions are reversed, the input redirection symbol is naturally reversed also: you use

```
command <filename
```

to indicate that the command will take its input from the file *filename* rather than from the default standard input, namely your keyboard.

To illustrate this concept, I'll introduce a useful command called pr (in man section C) that performs relatively simple text formatting for screen display or hardcopy printers. As I mentioned earlier, many Unix names reflect the days of yore when most terminals were printing devices, so the pr (print) command should not be taken literally. You still find Unix folk talking about "printing on the screen" when they really mean "displaying." Anyroad, pr accepts text from stdin and writes the formatted output to stdout, which as you now know can be the screen, a disk file,

or a special file representing a hardcopy printer. You can see that pr meets all the criteria for being a filter (see Chapter 2), and such it is.

> **NOTE** A filter is a program that reads from the standard input and writes to the standard output. Either input or output or both can be redirected to files.

pr has options for "printing" titled, paginated, multicolumn reports with optional line numbers, tab expansion, and a host of other tricks. (Try man pr to see the full story.) The default options for pr give the following format:

- 66-line pages with page number, date, time, and file name at the top of each page
- 5-line header and trailer
- Single-column layout
- Single-line spacing

(Unix has more sophisticated text formatters, but pr is adequate for simple listings.)

I will use the following option arguments to vary these defaults:

- −d Uses double-line spacing
- −t Suppresses the header and trailer and stops after last line of file without spacing to next page

The object is to take a text file, say itext, format it, and display the result on the screen. Our command line will have the following pattern:

```
pr options <itext
```

Note carefully the layout: the options must immediately follow the command. pr will read its input from itext because of the < symbol. The output has not been redirected, so pr writes to the screen. To capture the output of pr in a file, you simply redirect the output by adding a > symbol and a file name. It may appear strange at first but the general format combining both input and output redirection is as follows:

```
pr options <itext >otext
```

Note the sequence carefully. You can picture the output "emerging" from the command `pr options <itext` and going into `otext`. You can practice with the following example:

```
$ pr -t-d <poem >d.poem
$ cat d.poem

Mary had a little lamb,

Its feet were white as snow;
And everywhere that Mary went,

The lamb was sure to go.
$ _
```

Comparing Redirection and Pipelines

You met the pipe symbol | in Chapter 2, where we used `cal | more` to gain a pause between each screen-load of calendric data. The output of `cal` becomes the input of the filter `more`, and the output from `more` is directed to the default standard output, your screen. Compare this example with

```
$ date >today.test
$ _
```

in which the output of `date` is sent to a file.

The two actions are closely related, but you must not confuse the pipeline action of | with the redirection achieved using > and <. All three symbols affect the way the shell deals with input and output. Both > and | effectively take the output of a command and "divert" it from the default `stdout`, namely your screen. The big difference is that | must be followed by the name of a special program, known as a *filter*, whereas > is followed by a file name.

Filters are special in that they take their input from `stdin` and send their output to `stdout`. You can often simulate the action of a filter by using > and < with a temporary file acting as a bridge. For example,

```
$ ls >temp
$ pr -t<temp
```

```
lp0
poem
poem.1
poem.2
$ rm temp
$ _
```

can be more elegantly performed with

```
$ ls | pr -t
lp0
poem
poem.1
poem.2
$ _
```

In the first example, we created an intermediate file called `temp`. To illustrate that this file was of no further use to us, we use `rm temp` to erase it. What the user maketh, the user can taketh away! This command needs a section!

Erasing Files with rm

The `rm` (remove) command (in man section C) is a vital but potentially dangerous command that deletes, kills, zaps, and removes.

```
$ lc file*
file1     file2     file3
$ rm file1 file2 file3
$ cat file1
cat: cannot open file1
$ lc file*
file* not found
$ _
```

They've all gone!

```
$ ls tmp*
tmp1
tmp6
tmp89
$ rm tmp?
$ ls tmp*
tmp89
$ _
```

Still one left!

rm is therefore a rapid, irrevocable way of getting rid of many files and their contents. rm just quietly removes the files with no fuss or feedback.

There are some safeguards, however, which depend on what *write permissions* you have for the directory and the files involved. These permissions are intended to prevent you from erasing the files of others without their prior consent (a practice that people tend to frown on). Usually, you do have these write permissions on your own files, but care is still needed.

A useful trick is to use the −i (inquire) option. With rm −i file*, say, you are asked to confirm the deletion of each matching file. You can answer n or N to preserve the file, or y or Y to remove it.

A dangerous option is −r (recursive), which takes a directory as argument. rm −r stan, where stan is a directory, would erase the directory stan, every file in stan, every subdirectory of stan *and* their files, and so down the hierarchy. The part of the file tree branching from stan downwards is utterly zapped. (This is called *recursive* because rm keeps calling itself with subdirectory arguments.) Clearly this is powerful stuff, but occasionally useful when severe pruning is called for. Happily, you can control the felling of your tree by combining the i and r options: rm −ir stan will seek confirmation before each deletion.

- Use rm with care!
- rm −i is safer.
- rm with * and ? needs extreme care! Use ls first, and ask: do I need any of these files?
- rm −i * and rm −i ??*x*? is safer.
- rm −r *directory* is highly dangerous!
- rm −ir *directory* is less dangerous!

You met rmdir in Chapter 3. This is a milder way of removing directories: if the directory stan has any extant files in it, rmdir stan will not delete stan.

In addition to the dangers of losing files completely (name and contents) with the careless use of rm, indirection can lose you the contents of a file, which is really just as frustrating, possibly more so. The file seems to be there, at least by name, but the data within may not be as planned. So let's return to redirection and filters for a few more insights.

Indirection with Input, Output, and Pipelines

In `cal | more`, the output from `cal` provides the input to `more`, which processes (filters) it, then passes it on. The output *from* `more` is therefore available for further processing. In our example, the output from `more` is simply passed on to `stdout`, but you are free to add further pipe symbols and filters. The output of the final filter of such a chain can go to `stdout`, or it can be redirected to a file.

With `date >today.test`, the output from `date`, on the other hand, is written into the file `today.test`. Examine the following dialogue:

```
$ date | today.test
today.test: execute permission denied
$ _
```

Unix has been asked to treat `today.test` as an executable filter, and is unable to oblige. You'll see later how Unix determines which files are data files and which are executable programs.

Try to guess what would happen with

```
$ date >more
```

Well, you have now created a file called `more` in your current directory! Sorry about that. A previously existing file called `more` would now be overwritten with the date. The next section explains how possibly dangerous overwrites can be avoided.

Appending Output to Your Files

The danger of > overwriting an existing file, with the possible loss of valuable data, may be worrying you. Unix offers a simple remedy. You can *append* data using the special redirection operator >> (two adjacent > symbols with no intervening spaces). By append, I mean adding the redirected data to the end of an existing file without disturbing the existing data. Appending to a nonexistent file works just like >, that is, Unix creates a new, empty file first. Try the following:

```
$ who >who.dat
$ cat who.dat
iwonka tty1a Apr3 10:04
stan   tty2a Apr3 10:32
$ date >>who.dat
$ cat who.dat
```

```
iwonka tty1a Apr3 10:04
stan    tty2a Apr3 10:32
Mon Apr 3 17:33:28 PDT 1995
```

The first line creates or overwrites who.dat. The second line confirms the contents of who.dat. The fifth line appends the output from date to the previous contents of who.dat. The following cat confirms our prediction.

Reversing the append symbols (to give <<) provides a special feature called *in-line input*. You'll see this in action when I cover advanced shell programming.

Standard Errors

In addition to stdin and stdout there is a third standard file created by Unix called standard error, or stderr for short. This is for displaying error or diagnostic messages. Like stdout, stderr is opened and linked to your screen whenever a command starts executing. In the following example

```
$ cat pandora.box >junk
cat: cannot open pandora.box
$ cat junk
$ _
```

the error message is actually sent to the default stderr, namely your screen, and not to the file junk. In fact, junk is empty, as shown by the second cat command. The key point is that if you redirect stdout to a file, stderr remains linked to the screen: you do not want the file picking up a strange mix of good data and error diagnostics.

Summary

In this wide-ranging chapter I covered the following topics:

- Standard input (keyboard)
- Standard output (screen)
- Redirection of output with >*filename*
- The ls command for listing your files
- The wildcards *, ?, and [ ]

- Hidden files such as `.profile`
- The online manual and the `man` command
- How to read a syntax listing
- Single and multiple options: `-l`, `-a-l`, and `-al`
- Use of `cat` for typing file contents, concatenating files, and entering text into files
- The `lc` command for columnar listings
- The `wc` command for counting lines, words, and characters
- The `pr` command for simple formatting of text
- Deleting files and directories with `rm` and `rmdir`, the dangers thereof, and the use of the `-i` (inquire) option
- Appending data to files with `>>`
- The standard error file, the default of which is your screen

CHAPTER

FIVE

Electronic Mail

- Superusers unite!

- The mailperson cometh—`mail`

- Reading, printing, saving, and deleting mail

- Sending mail

- Using other email programs

Unix lets you exchange messages with other users on your machine and, with the proper connections, users on other Unix systems. Indeed, many of the world's largest intercomputer networks are those running under various Unix protocols using uucp (Unix-to-Unix copy) and similar commands (to be discussed in Chapter 17). I'll use the general term *email* (short for electronic mail) to cover the many different user-to-user telecommunications methods available, including not only the traditional mailing of letters and memos but also the transfer of text and binary files.

Before you tackle the details of email under Unix, you need to know a little more about access rights and privileges.

Superusers Unite!

Normally, Unix shields you and your terminal from other active users, and vice versa. However, the system administrator, or anyone else blessed with the password to the special login name root, has the awesome ability to bypass this protective barrier of read, write, and execute permissions. For this reason, any user privileged to log in as root is also called a *superuser*. A superuser can peek into and erase any of your files and directories, interrupt your work at any time with warning messages, kill any or all of your running jobs, ban you from the system by changing or removing your logins and passwords without prior consultation, and generally play God or Devil as the mood takes her or him.

Superusers even boast a special prompt symbol. Rather than seeing the everyday $ or % prompts for the Bourne or C shell, when you log in successfully as root, you see a #. This distinctive root or superuser prompt, #, reminds you that you have gained special access to the system. Of course, all the normal user commands and options can be used; what distinguishes the superuser is the additional arsenal of commands and options that Unix withholds from non-superusers. For obvious reasons, therefore, the root password must be guarded closely and changed regularly. Being admitted to the inner circle brings both power and responsibility. In fact, abuse by a superuser is rare, and when it does happen, it is more likely to be the result of human error than a deliberate assault. As you'll see in Chapter 18, many quite mundane but necessary chores can only be achieved by root, including backing up, changing peripherals, adding users, software updates, and gracefully closing down the system.

Although you cannot protect yourself against intrusions from superusers, you can decide whether you want to exchange messages with other normal users. If you are a natural recluse, you can simply refuse to read your email. You can also put up an electronic equivalent to the Do Not Disturb sign.

Unix offers two commands that permit users to send and receive messages. The `mail` command (in man section C) gives you a sophisticated store-and-forward mailbox. The simpler `write` command (in man section C) lets you send messages directly to any user who is willing to be interrupted. I'll discuss the `write` method first.

You Haven't Written to Me Lately

The `write login` command sends a message from your keyboard to the screen of the user whose login you specify, provided that the target user is active and is "open" to receiving messages. Every user starts life in this receptive state, but at any time you can use the `mesg` command to close the door—or perhaps taking your phone off the hook is a better metaphor:

```
$ mesg n
$ _
```

The argument n means no messages accepted—Go Away!—¡No molestar! If you change your mind later on, you can reverse your choice as follows:

```
$ mesg y
$ _
```

The y, for yes, tells the world that you are now *writable,* that is, willing to accept incoming messages from anybody's `write` commands. As I mentioned, you are normally in the writable state when you first log in, so `mesg y` is only needed to undo an earlier `mesg n`. You (or the system administrator) can arrange matters so that you default to `mesg n` when you log in—I'll show you how in Chapter 6. If you are ever in doubt as to your writable status, just enter `mesg` without an argument and Unix will tell you:

```
$ mesg
mesg is y
```

NOTE Yes, as you may have guessed, a superuser can disturb anyone with a write or wall command regardless of writability. In an emergency, the system administrator may need to grab everybody's attention: I'm halting system in 30 secs! Virus detected!

Commands such as mesg that can both alter and report the status of something are quite common in Unix. Used with an argument they set or change some parameter; used without an argument they tell you the current value. But recall the important exception: cd without an argument changes the current directory to your home directory.

Suppose you are logged in as mary and want to send user stan a message. The first sensible thing to do is to check if stan is online and active. To do this, enter

```
$ who -u
jane     tty03 Mar 14 12:34
joe      tty12 Mar 15 10:09 1:12 169 store
mary     tty02 Mar 15 09:03 .     110 r&d
stan     tty01 Mar 15 11:09 .     170 engineering
stan     tty34 Mar 15 11:15 0:30 172 engineering
$ _
```

The familiar who command with the –u option tells you a little more than the plain who you've used so far. Each section, or column, is usually called a *field*. The fields shown are as follows:

Login name	Name of active user.
Terminal	Name of terminal or line.
Date/time	When user logged in.
Activity	Hours:minutes since line was last used. A period indicates some activity within the last minute, that is, the user is probably at work right now.
pid	Process id number: unique number assigned by Unix to each running process or task. Ignore this for now.
Comment	Optional information often used to identify a terminal's location.

The two occurrences of stan may seem strange, but there's no cause for alarm. Stan is perfectly free to log in as stan on as many terminals as he wishes. Stan may even have several different login names (for accounting and auditing purposes, for example). who shows you all currently logged-in users, so you now know that stan is logged in on both tty01 and tty34. Furthermore, the symbol in the activity field is a period, so you know that stan has been doing something on tty01 within the last minute but tty34 has been idle for a while. Joe, it seems, has left his terminal unattended for over an hour—let's hope he has a good excuse.

If stan were active and writable on only one terminal, you could just enter

```
$ write stan
```

and Unix would figure out the destination. Since stan is active on two terminals, we must tell Unix which one to write to by adding the terminal name as a second argument. If you try

```
$ write stan tty34
permission denied
$ _
```

Unix quickly tells you that stan on tty34 is incommunicado (not writable). So let's try

```
$ write stan tty01

_
```

The absence of the permission denied message is your clue that Stan is writable. The prompt is also absent, but the cursor indicates that Unix is ready for your message. You could immediately start typing your message on this and subsequent lines, but you'll see in a moment that this can be confusing and even wasteful—Stan may respond before you have finished. Both parties need to follow an agreed protocol to avoid those maddening mix ups you get on delayed long distance phone calls. So wait after the write command until you receive an acknowledgment from Stan. Supposing that he was in the middle of something, his screen display would be rudely interrupted mid-job with a warning message and bleep:

```
$ cat poem
Mary had a little la
      Message from mary (tty02) [Tue Apr 13 01:32:15]
mb
...
...
$ _
```

Some formatting commands such as `pr` and `nroff` have a built-in protection against such interruptions, since they can cause havoc with your layout.

If Stan wishes to engage in badinage with Mary, he enters

```
$ write mary
      Mary! Stan here, what's up? o
```

He knows for sure that Mary is active and on tty02, but it is possible that Mary has inadvertently left herself *unwritable*. Note that you can issue `write` commands without being writable! It's not a sensible thing to do, but many dumb things are legal in Unix as in other walks of life. It may also be the case that Mary is logged in on terminals other than tty02, in which case Stan could play safe by adding the argument tty02: `write mary tty02`. This is the terminal where Mary is awaiting your reply. The message following this command appears on Mary's screen as follows:

```
$
      Message from stan (tt01) [Tue Apr 13 01:13:42]
Mary! Stan here, what's up? o

_
```

The two terminals are now "connected" and will remain so until both users enter Ctrl-D (the usual way of terminating a program). More precisely, if Stan presses Ctrl-D, he terminates his write connection to Mary but will continue to receive Mary's messages until she uses Ctrl-D. When you terminate with Ctrl-D, your screen will say (end of message); you press Enter to get back to prompt level.

Returning to the exchange of messages, notice the final letter o in Stan's first response. This means "over" and tells Mary that Stan is ready for her message. She, in turn, will end her reply with an o, then wait for Stan's rejoinder. Typing back before you see this o can lead to strange clutter on the recipient's screen. To signal that you have no more to say, you end your last line with oo meaning "over, out."

When Mary sees the o in Stan's acknowledgment, she types

```
It's your turn to make the coffee! o
```

Stan now types

```
OK, over in ten minutes. oo
```

Mary now knows from the oo that Stan has no more to say. Mary has the last word:

```
Fine, Stan, see you here soon, Mary. oo
```

Both parties can now safely press Ctrl-D and Enter to return to their normal prompts.

I should stress that o and oo are merely common conventions between Unix users: the symbols have no programming significance.

If you do not have a colleague willing to let you play with the write command, you can always write to yourself:

```
$ mesg
mesg is y
$ mesg n
$ mesg
mesg is n
$ write your_login
permission denied
$ mesg y; write your_login
Hello to myself o
Hello to myself o
Must fly oo
Must fly oo
```

Press Ctrl-D and Enter to return to the prompt.

Note the two-command line using a semicolon separator. Note also that each line you write to yourself is repeated immediately. One of the miracles of modern computer science, but admittedly the novelty soon wears off.

Off the Wall

I mentioned that the system administrator can override the mesg n setting of any user. If you are logged in as root, you can send an urgent message to every active user with one invocation of the wall command (in man section ADM). wall stands for "write all." As with write, wall reads your standard input, so you can either type your global warnings, as in

```
# wall
Closing down the system at 5:00pm sharp
```

and then press Ctrl-D and Enter, or redirect your warnings with `wall < warn1.msg`, where `warn1.msg` is a pre-prepared text file. When sending a file message, you do not have to terminate with Ctrl-D, since the file generates an EOF (end-of-file) automatically. Recipients of a `wall` message are interrupted with the warning

```
Broadcast Message from root [Tue Apr 13 01:35:02]
Closing down the system at 5:00pm sharp
```

The `wall` command, unlike `write`, is not intended to set up a dialogue, so the o and oo conventions are not observed. Some implementations of `wall` ensure that even inactive users will get the message when they log in.

Final Warning

I leave this topic with a brief but firm warning not to abuse the `write` command. You would normally need an excellent reason for writing to a complete stranger's screen—`Your printer is on fire` might suffice, but not `Hi, welcome aboard! My name is Joe, and I work down the hall from you....`

> **NOTE** Don't play the fool with `write` and `wall`! Use `mail` unless your message requires immediate attention.

For more organized and civilized intercommunication, you need the `mail` command. Even with this, certain conventions and good habits must be observed for success. Unlike `write`, `mail` lets you send messages to both active and inactive users, whether they like it or not. Whether they read your mail is another matter! And whether they respond is yet another kettle of fish.

The Mailperson Cometh

Contrary to its public image, Unix has always been popular in certain office automation applications. The first Unix application was, in fact, multiuser document preparation at AT&T Bell Labs. The need for interuser communication soon

sparked the development of an email system. The growing team of Unix programmers also found it essential to share messages, so the mail program has grown like Topsy, acquiring many features (some more useful than others).

As a result, the options offered by the mail command, and the names used for a given function, now vary considerably among different Unix implementations. The phrase *blatant featurism* is sometimes used to describe the situation. An emerging solution is to offer all the existing synonyms for a given function, so you may find that ignore and discard, different names for the same function, are both accepted.

mail is a complex command that controls both the receiving, sending, and saving of mailed messages. In addition to text messages, mail can send and receive files of any kind. I'll concentrate on the core features that should be available on most systems, possibly with minor variations in syntax.

Read Your Mail!

Whenever you log in, Unix checks a central repository, a sort of electronic post office called the system mailbox, to see if there is any mail there addressed to you. The system mailbox maintains files for each user in a special directory called /usr/spool/mail, so that Mary's mail is held in the file /usr/spool/mail/mary and so on. Do not confuse this directory with Mary's home directory, /usr/mary. Mail can be received and held for Mary even if her home directory is erased for any reason.

If mail is found for you, you will see the message You have mail before your prompt appears. Some systems will also give you a You have mail message if mail arrives during a session.

To read your mail, you simply enter the command mail. If there is no mail, a no messages response is invoked. For the user with login iwonka, a typical mail-reading session might proceed as follows:

```
$ mail
SCO UNIX System V Release 3.2 Type ? for help.
"/usr/spool/mail/iwonka": 2 messages 1 new 2 unread
>N 2 stan@kelly.UUCP Tue Apr 13 02:01 13/2446 Hello
 U 1 stan@kelly.UUCP Tue Apr 13 01:30 27/1306
? _
```

This response tells you the name of your system mailbox, in this case `/usr/spool/mail/iwonka`, and the number and types of messages waiting for you. Next you are shown the *header* information, summarizing each piece of your mail in reverse chronological order, that is, the most recent mail comes first. You may also see a list of users who have been sent copies of a particular message. The `mail` command now awaits your further instructions. The **?** beside the cursor is a special prompt indicating that you are in *command* (or mail-reading) mode. (Later on, you'll encounter another mode called *input* mode, used when you are sending mail.)

What you type in command mode will determine how your mail is displayed, printed, stored, and/or erased. Each message has a header followed by a *body* that carries the meaty text of the message. `mail` has commands that display either header, body, or both. The command options are extensive and differ between different versions of Unix. Most of the commands have long and short versions—with some exceptions, you need only enough letters of the command to ensure uniqueness. For example, h gives you `header`, `hel` is equivalent to `help`, and so on.

Many of the default values taken by `mail` can be preset by placing an appropriate value in an *environment variable*. In fact, this approach is common for most Unix commands. This makes life extremely flexible for the user, but it complicates matters for Unix book authors! What a command actually does is often up to you and/or your system administrator. Certain global, or system-wide, defaults are set by the system administrator, while each user may have the power to override these locally. Chapter 6 deals with the various ways you can personalize your system, including the setting of environment variables. In this chapter I will occasionally mention the effect of a certain environment variable. This will alert you to the fact that your `mail` command may not work exactly as stated.

The header display says `Type ? for help`. So why not start by entering

    ? ?

You can also type the equivalent commands `help` or `hel`. You'll get quite a list of available commands and optional arguments. The command `list` or `li` also gives you a list of available commands but with no explanation. This is a useful aid when you're on an unfamiliar system.

I'll concentrate on the simple, everyday commands that let you read and save your mail. Be aware that some of the commands used inside `mail` look very much like normal Unix commands, but the options and defaults often differ.

Many system administrators kindly send you a welcome message to greet you when you first log in. If so, you have an early opportunity to gain familiarity with the `mail` command. If not, you should ask a colleague to send you some test messages. Failing that, you can write to yourself (see "Sending Mail" later in this chapter).

The absolutely simplest entry you can make at the ? prompt is to press Enter! This is equivalent to typing p (for print, meaning display) or t (for type, also meaning display). Enter, p, and t all produce the same effect: They display the *current* message, after which the ? prompt reappears. The next message in the header list now becomes the current message. By just pressing Enter, you can quickly scan your mail until a no next message appears followed by the ? prompt. Rather than pressing Enter after each message, you can try

    ? *

which displays all messages, with a pause after each screenful. Messages displayed on your monitor are piped by default through the more filter, so you'll get the familiar pause if a long message fills your screen. You can specify your own filter for fancier displays, but more is usually more than adequate. If not, ask your system administrator to check the PAGER setting. This defaults to more, but can be set to give more elaborate mail display formatting.

Leaving the mail Program

You can leave the mail program by typing ex, exit, or x. This style of departure leaves your mail undisturbed—you can return to mail and find all your messages still in your system mailbox. In fact, the You have mail reminder will still appear whenever you log in until you have cleared the system mailbox (you'll see how soon).

You can also leave the mail program with a quit or q, but this deletes from the system mailbox any message you have read during this session. However, such deleted messages are saved automatically in a special default file in your home directory called mbox. Saving in mbox is done by *prepending* (that is, adding to the start of the file) rather than by appending or overwriting. Prepending ensures that mbox retains your read mail in the same most-recent-first order as the system mailbox. mail allows you to read and delete messages in your mbox, so you don't have to keep mail there forever.

There are ways of varying this default behavior, as you'll soon discover. You can save mail in files other than mbox, and you can delete (and undelete) selected messages during a session. But for now, the key lesson is that exit leaves the system mailbox as is, while quit prunes all read mail, leaving a local copy in /usr/*your_login*/mbox. After reading all your mail and departing with a quit, you will not be bothered with a You have mail greeting until some new mail pours in.

Note again that the file /usr/spool/mail/stan is part of Unix's central system mailbox, from which mail pulls your mail by default. Your local, user mailbox for storing selected mail that you may want to keep is called /usr/*your_login*/mbox.

Having seen the simple, default approach to reading your mail, we'll look at some useful variants in the following sections.

Printing Your Mail Messages

lpr or l (line printer) entered in command mode (after the ? prompt, remember) will print the current message on your default printer. lpr * or l * will print all your messages, one after the other. Here, print really means print—real, black-on-white, ink-and-paper printing! The name lpr suggests another Unix anachronism, stemming from the days when all hardcopy printers were tabulators or line printers. mail will usually be set up to print your messages prettily with page numbers. If this is not the case, your system administrator will be able to help. I'll have a lot more to say about printing in Chapter 10.

Message Headers

The fields in the header need to be understood to exploit the more advanced mail facilities. Take another look at the headers you first encountered in the "Read Your Mail" section:

```
>N 2 stan@kelly.UUCP Tue Apr 13 02:01 13/2446 Hello
 U 1 stan@kelly.UUCP Tue Apr 13 01:30 27/1306
```

The > symbol in column 1 indicates the current message. This is the message that will be displayed by default if you do not specify a message identifier argument in certain commands. Each message header is tagged with a letter in column 2: N means a new message since you last read your mail; U means unread mail; O means old, and so on. mail keeps track of what you are doing, so these status letters are

updated during each session. Each message is numbered in column 3, with higher numbers signifying more recent mail.

The remaining fields are fairly obvious. They tell you the sender, date and time sent, size (lines/characters), and optional subject matter. The latter appears only if the sender entered a line giving the subject title when composing the message. Such titles, as in traditional interoffice memos, can be useful on a heavily used email system. An added benefit is that mail lets you select messages by searching the subject field for a given string. For example, you could display all mail with Urgent anywhere in the subject field. You can also select just the mail from a given user.

If you are not connected to other Unix systems, the sender field may just show the sender's login name. The above example shows the sender as stan@kelly.UUCP meaning user stan on the Unix system (or node) called kelly. Your own site may have such a name. It allows users at other sites to exchange mail with you and your colleagues. I'll discuss this in much more detail in Chapter 17.

Message Selection

You can also display or print each message by selecting the message number. If the headers reveal a letter from the boss at the bottom of the pile, you may feel inclined to read this first before wading through all the valentines. To display message number 9, for instance, you can type p 9, t 9, or just 9. Again, note that display is the default.

```
? p 9
From: boss Tue Apr 13 09:03:23 1995
To:    iwonka
Subject: Layoffs
It has come to my attention that...
...
? _
```

To print message 6, you would use lpr 6 or l 6. You can also display or print a range of messages as follows:

```
? p 3-7
```

displays messages 3, 4, 5, 6, and 7. Equivalently, you can use ? t 3-7 or simply ? 3-7.

    ? lpr 2-4

prints messages 2, 3, and 4. To display or print all the mail from mary, you can enter
p mary or lpr mary. As before, the p is optional.

Other useful display options are listed below:

? p ^	Displays first undeleted message
? p $	Displays last message
? p *	Displays all messages
? p /string	Displays all messages with the specified character string *string* in the subject line (also matches *String*, *STRING*, and so on)
? p :n	Displays all new messages
? p :r	Displays all read messages
? p :o	Displays all old messages
? p :u	Displays all unread messages
? p :d	Displays all deleted messages

You can replace the p with a t, or omit it altogether. The print versions use lpr or
l in place of p.

Sometimes you may want to read the first few lines of messages before deciding
where your priorities lie. The top command, or to for short, used with the usual
message arguments, displays the first five lines of selected messages:

    ? top *

displays the first five lines of all messages.

    ? to 1-3

displays the first five lines of messages 1 through 3.

    ? top mary

displays the first five lines of all messages from Mary.

If you have a heavy mailbag, the following header commands are handy for rechecking message numbers, senders, and subjects:

? =   Displays current message number

? h   Displays screenful of current headers

? h *n*   Displays header for message number *n* (You can also use a range of message numbers here.)

? h+   Displays next screenful of headers

? h−   Displays previous screenful of headers

The number of headers per screenful is yet another value that can be preset in an environment variable; in this case you set a value in the screen variable. You'll see how in the next chapter.

Alternatively, once you know your target messages, you may wish to avoid screen clutter by skipping past the headers. The command for this is ignore or ig for short.

Saving and Deleting Messages

You saw earlier that using quit deletes read messages from the system mailbox and saves them in your mbox. Here are some commands that allow you to save and mark particular messages for deletion during a mail session whether read or not:

? **save**

saves the current header and message in mbox and flags the message for deletion from your mailbox.

? **s**

does the same as save.

? **save tempbox**

saves the current header and message in a file named tempbox and flags the message for deletion from your mailbox.

? **save 1-3 tempbox**

saves headers and messages 1–3 in a file named tempbox and flags messages 1–3 for deletion from your mailbox.

If you use write or w in place of save or s, the action is the same except that the headers are not saved, just the message bodies. A variant of save called Save (a capital "S" makes the difference) lets you save selected messages in a file named for the sender found in the header. Assuming you are stan, the Save command, or S for short, works as follows:

    ? Save mary

saves all messages from Mary in /usr/stan/mary and flags all messages for deletion from your mailbox.

    ? S 1-3

saves messages 1–3 in /usr/stan/*author-of-message-1* and flags messages 1–3 for deletion from your mailbox.

If you want saved messages to go to a directory other than your default, home directory, there is an environment variable called folder you can preset.

All the messages you save using the save, write, or Save commands are flagged so that when you enter quit, they will be deleted from the system mailbox. A command called copy, or c for short, lets you save messages in mbox or a designated file without losing them from the system mailbox when you enter quit. In other words, copy saves without flagging the message(s) for deletion. A variant of copy naturally exists called Copy (or C), which works like Save but does not incur deletion when you quit. You can also delete a message directly from the system mailbox, whether saved or not, by using the delete or d command. The message list arguments follow the established pattern:

    ? delete

deletes the current message from the mailbox without saving it in mbox. The next undeleted message becomes the current message.

    ? d 3-4

deletes messages 3 and 4 from the mailbox without saving them in mbox. The next undeleted message after message 4 becomes the current message.

    ? d boss

Danger! This deletes from the mailbox all messages from boss without saving them in mbox. The next undeleted message becomes the current message.

```
? d *
```

Danger! This deletes all messages from the mailbox without saving them in mbox.

A useful composite command, dp or dt, lets you delete the current message then display the following undeleted message.

WARNING — Once you leave the mail program, you cannot undelete a deleted message.

If you rashly delete messages and want to undo your mistake, you can restore them using the undelete command (u for short) provided you do not leave the mail session:

```
? undelete
```

undeletes the current message. The next undeleted message becomes the current message.

```
? u 3-4
```

undeletes messages 3 and 4. The next undeleted message after message 4 becomes the current message.

```
? u *
```

undeletes all messages.

Reading Mail from Another Source

All my examples have assumed that mail will read from the standard system mailbox. If you want to read mail from some other file, you use the -f option as follows:

```
mail -f mail_filename
```

A common application would be reading mail saved in your mbox, since this file has the same format as the system mailbox. *mail_filename* can have a path; otherwise your current directory is assumed. You can also use -f in those instances when you have saved mail by sender name with Save and you want to study it and respond to it later. Which leads us to the next topic: how to send mail.

Sending Mail

You've been busy reading, printing, saving, and deleting incoming mail in command mode. It's time to return the favor by sending mail to other users. Once again, the options are numerous, so I'll concentrate on the basics. The simplest approach is to use mail with a user name as argument:

```
$ mail mary
Subject: Backups
Thanks for your memo on backups. Let's meet after work.
Regards, Stan
```

Pressing Ctrl-D brings up the $ prompt.

As you can see, mail determines from the user-name argument that you are in *compose* (or input or send) mode, and responds by asking you to enter a single-line subject. This is optional, so you can just press Enter if you have no subject in mind. It's good form to supply a pithy, relevant subject—it can provide a useful searching tool as your mailbag grows.

After the subject line, you simply type away until your message is complete. You then bring the cursor to the start of an empty line and press Ctrl-D (or type a period on some systems). Your missive now wends its speedy way to Mary's system mailbox. Mary will receive a You have mail notice and can do all the good things with your message that I discussed earlier.

If the message cannot be delivered for any reason, mail attempts to return it to your system mailbox with a suitable explanation. In the event of some interruption during transmission, partial messages are saved in the file dead.letter in your home directory.

If you want to send the same message to several users, all you need is to list their names after mail:

```
$ mail mary joe fred iwonka
Subject: Party Time!
My place at 6:00pm tonight.
Regards, Stan
```

Pressing Ctrl-D sends the message and brings up the $ prompt. All four users will receive the same message in their respective system mailboxes.

It is important to distinguish *command* mode (reading mail) from *compose* mode (sending mail). The commands and options are quite different. To complicate matters, while you are in command mode, you can switch to compose mode in order to respond to mail that you have just read. For example:

```
$ mail
```

puts you in command mode in the mail program.

```
? p
```

allows you to read the first letter. Let's say that Joe sent you this letter. To respond to his mail message right away, you would enter

```
? mail joe
```

This puts you in compose mode. Type your subject line and message; then press Ctrl-D to send your missive and return to command mode.

As you can see, mail is a valid command from within mail! A neat variant is Mail (capital "M"). If you had used Mail joe in the above example, Unix would save *your* message in a file named joe (rather like the Save command explained earlier).

There is an even quicker way of responding to the current message. After the ? prompt, you can enter reply, respond, or r for short. For example, let's say you have just read the first letter in your mailbox. Entering r after the ? prompt puts you in compose mode, adds the subject of the first letter to your subject line, and treats the sender of the first letter as the recipient of your letter. The r trick saves you entering the recipient's name and the subject line.

Returning to the original task of writing to Mary, you might prefer to compose your letter using a text editor, especially if it is a long message needing careful thought. While you are keyboarding mail directly, you can only correct errors on the current line—not too helpful for precise composition. There are two approaches. First, you can use redirection as follows:

```
$ mail mary < mary.lett1
$ mail joe fred < memo.3
$ _
```

where `mary.lett1` and `memo.3` are prepared text files. `mail` will read from these files as explained in Chapter 4. The message is terminated by the EOF (end-of-file), so you don't need a manual Ctrl-D. If you want to add a subject line, use the −s option:

```
$ mail −sHello mary < mary.lett1
$ mail −sPayday joe fred < memo.3
$ _
```

As an alternative to the redirection of a pre-edited file, you can invoke and use a text editor while composing a message. But if you are in compose mode, how can `mail` distinguish your commands from real message characters in your letter? The solution requires the use of a special *escape* character to warn `mail` that what follows is not message text, but a command entry. The default escape character for `mail` is the ~ (tilde). To invoke the `vi` editor, for example, you would type ~v; and to get the `ed` editor, you would enter ~e. (Environment variables can be set to give you other editors, but these are the defaults.) You can call the editor at any time to edit a partial message.

Here are two more examples of tilde escape commands:

```
$ mail joe
~c mary bill
~b boss
```

After entering these tilde escape commands, you type and send your letter as usual. The ~c command adds the names `mary` and `bill` to the *carbon copy* or *Cc* list in your message header. Your message will go to them, as well as to `joe`, and all recipients will know that Mary and Joe were "copied" on this message. The header will appear as follows:

```
To: joe
Cc: mary bill
```

The ~b command is a little sneaky. It sends a *blind copy* to `boss`! Only you and `boss` know of this furtive maneuver: the header does not reveal the recipients of blind copies.

While in compose mode you can use the ~! combination to execute a shell command:

```
$ mail joe
~!ls
poem mbox memo.3
```

After the list appears, you are returned to compose mode. See Table 5.1 for a summary of the main `mail` commands.

TABLE 5.1: Summary of mail Commands

mail Command at ? Prompt	Action
Enter	Displays the current message
p	Displays the current message
t	Displays the current message
*	Displays all messages
p *	Displays all messages
t *	Displays all messages
n	Displays message number *n*
p *n*	Displays message number *n*
t *n*	Displays message number *n*
m–n	Displays messages number *m* to *n*
p *m–n*	Displays messages number *m* to *n*
t *m–n*	Displays messages number *m* to *n*
lpr *n*	Prints message number *n*
l *n*	Prints message number *n*
lpr *m–n*	Prints messages number *m* to *n*
l *m–n*	Prints messages number *m* to *n*
user_name	Displays all messages from *user_name*
p *user_name*	Displays all messages from *user_name*
t *user_name*	Displays all messages from *user_name*
lpr *user_name*	Prints all messages from *user_name*
l *user_name*	Prints all messages from *user_name*
p /*pattern*	Displays all messages matching *pattern* in subject line
p :n	Displays all new messages
p :r	Displays only messages already read
p :o	Displays all old messages
p :u	Displays all unread messages
p :d	Displays all deleted messages
to[p] *	Displays top (first 5 lines) of all messages
=	Displays current message number

TABLE 5.1: Summary of `mail` Commands (continued)

mail Command at ? Prompt	Action
h	Displays screenful of current headers
h *n*	Displays header for message number *n*
h+	Displays next screenful of headers
h−	Displays previous screenful of headers
ig[nore]	Bypasses headers
s[ave]	Saves current header and message in mbox and flags for deletion
c[opy]	Saves the current header and message in mbox but does not flag for deletion
S[ave]	Same as save, but saves in special mbox file using sender's login name
C[opy]	Same as copy, but copies to special mbox file using the sender's login name
s[ave] *filename*	Saves current header and message in *filename* and flags for deletion
w[rite]	Same as save, except headers are not saved
q[uit]	Exits mail and deletes all messages flagged for deletion
d[elete] [*arg*]	Deletes current message by default (*arg* can specify * (delete all); *name* (delete all messages from *name*); or a range of message numbers)
dp	Deletes the current message then displays the next
dt	Deletes the current message then displays the next
u[ndelete] [*arg*]	Undeletes current message by default (*arg* as in delete command)
mail *name*	Sets you into compose mode for sending a message to *name*
mail −s *subname*	Same as mail *name*, but adds a subject line
r[eply]	Puts you into compose mode to reply to the current message sender
r[espond]	Puts you into compose mode to reply to the current message sender

Using Other Email Programs

There are many other Unix email programs available, and I'll briefly describe some of them in this final section.

mailx is based on an earlier program called Mail (note the initial capital "M"), and offers many commands for mail preparation and for replying to mail. mailx is similar to mail, but uses tilde (~) escape sequences to separate special commands from the regular text of a message. When you use a tilde escape, it must be the first character on the line. The ~? command displays a summary of all the tilde escape commands. And to add a confusing note, on some Unix systems, mailx has been renamed as mail.

> **NOTE** The mail programs that you work with directly are known as *mail user agents*, and most of them use more primitive mailers called *mail transport agents* such as sendmail to handle the actual mail transmission.

The MH message handling system, developed by Bruce Borden, Stockton Gaines, and Norman Shapiro, with later versions by Marshall Rose and John Romine, uses a very different approach from mail and mailx, in that it provides a set of separate programs for specific mail functions that you can call from an ordinary shell prompt.

The elm mailer, written and placed in the public domain by Dave Taylor, is screen-oriented rather than line-oriented like the other mailers covered in this chapter. It allows you to reply to a message; forward, delete, or move a message; group messages together; and create aliases for the mail addresses you use most often.

Finally, the emacs editor also includes its own mailer, known as rmail. The format of emacs mail files is incompatible with the standard Unix mail-file format, but emacs provides commands for converting between the two.

There are also several excellent email packages available from independent software vendors, in addition to the email components of popular graphical user interfaces such as SCO's Open Desktop or the DeskSet from Solaris.

Chapter 17 offers more information on mailing to remote computers.

Summary

Chapter 5 covered the following topics:

- Unix offers elaborate email facilities between users on the same installation and (with uucp) at other collaborating sites. Chapter 17 covers email to other sites.

- The write command lets you send a message directly to another user's screen provided that user is writable. The mesg command is used to turn your "writability" on and off. The root (or superuser) can write to all active users regardless of their writable status. Use who -u to check who is active. Use write sparingly and with the locally adopted conventions (such as o for "over" and oo for "over, out").

- Root can use wall < message to send a global (write all) warning to every user.

- The syntax for mail command mode is

  [*command*] [*msglst*] [*arguments*]

  (Recall that [ ] means an optional entry, so the above scheme allows the use of the Enter key only! The default command is p or t for display and the default msglst is the current message number.)

- The mail command has many dialectal variations. If you get the You have mail message, use mail to read, search, save, print, delete, and answer your mail.

- While running mail in read mode, you get the prompt ?. For help, you type another ? (or type help). In compose (sending) mode there is no prompt.

- Use mail *name* to send mail to user *name*. The message can be typed via keyboard or redirected from a file.

- While in compose mode, the tilde, ~, acts as an escape character. For example, ~v and ~e will invoke the vi and ed editors respectively. ~c *name-list* will send copies of your message to each user in *name-list*. The legend Cc *name-list* will appear on each message. To send blind copies (no Cc list), use ~b *name-list*.

In this chapter, I've given you plenty of tools and examples to engage in some serious email. In the next chapter, you'll learn how to personalize your Unix environment by setting defaults that will make your life easier.

CHAPTER

SIX

Your Own Personalized Unix

- Changing your password

- Choosing your shell

- Login profiles

- Creating your own login profile

- Using shell variables and metacharacters

Unix is unique in the way it lets you create your own tools and working conditions. In this chapter I'll show you some of the ways you can tailor Unix to suit your particular hardware and work profile. Your system administrator will establish certain overall conditions, but as you become more experienced, you will want to modify the way Unix behaves when you log in. In the current jargon, you will be creating your own personal *environment*. Along the way, you'll learn quite a few new relevant facts about passwords, shells and shell variables, paths, and login profiles.

Changing Your Password

One of the first personal touches you may wish to apply is to change your password. In Chapter 1, I assumed that the system administrator had given you your login name and initial password. At most sites, this initial password is a temporary one that you are expected to change as soon as possible. At other sites, they may start you off with no password at all, leaving you to assign a password if you so desire. The procedures for changing old passwords and assigning new passwords both use the passwd command, as I'll explain in the following section. Until you do have a password, most systems will not bother you with the password: prompt. Some systems will prompt you for a password whether you have a password or not. If you have no password, pressing Enter at the password prompt is the only acceptable response!

For single-user Unix systems, of course, the whole question of passwords and security may be irrelevant—only you can decide whether they are worthwhile. Even if your present situation does not call for password protection, you should still become familiar with the simple passwd command.

For obvious security reasons, passwords should be changed from time to time whether you suspect intruders or not. Clearly, if you have reason to suppose that someone has been using your account illegally, you should immediately contact your system administrator rather than simply changing your password. The system administrator may prefer to give you a fresh login name and password and then set some traps for the intruder on your old login name and password.

Password administration varies widely between different sites. Exactly when passwords need to be changed and by whom can be mandated in different ways depending on the security level of the installation. Some sites specify a maximum

lifetime for each password. If so, you will be prompted to change your password periodically, and you may be locked out if you fail to respond. There may also be a minimum change time for a password, in which case you will be warned if you try to change your password too often.

Furthermore, at some sites, password changes are made only by the system administrator. If your installation is one where individual users are not allowed to change their passwords, the following section will not be relevant.

The passwd Command

The passwd command (in man section C) is used to change a password. It can also be used to establish a password if you do not have one. The following dialog illustrates the procedure:

```
$ pwd
/usr/stan
$ passwd
Changing password for stan
Old password:
```

At this prompt, you type in your old password, or press Enter if you don't have a password. Unix then asks you to type in your new password. Type your new password carefully; then retype it when prompted.

As with passwords entered during login, Unix does not echo passwords keyed in during the passwd procedure. The next thing to note is that you need to know your old password (if any) before you can change it! This is abundantly sensible, of course. Slightly less obvious is the need to type the new password twice. The idea is that with a single, non-echoed entry, you might mistype the intended password and then have great trouble recalling what you typed. If your two new password entries differ, Unix responds with

```
Mismatch - password unchanged
$ _
```

or some similar warning. You must then enter passwd again and repeat the exercise more carefully. You will also get a warning if your old password is entered incorrectly. Note that some systems will not prompt you for the old password if you do not have a password. The absence of warnings tells you that you have successfully changed your password. In the event of a warning, passwd leaves your password unchanged.

Good and Bad Passwords

While on the subject of changing passwords, it is worth recapping the rules for good password construction. A poorly devised password is almost as bad as having none at all, leading to complacency and a false feeling of security. If your system offers automatically generated passwords, you should take advantage of this feature. There has been much research on what constitutes a good password based on measuring the "obviousness" and "ease of guessing" of character strings. Since serious intruders can quickly generate millions of password combinations, you clearly need to avoid short and simple passwords.

A minimum password length can be specified by the system administrator, typically six characters. Passwords should contain at least two alphabetic characters and at least one numeric or special character. You should avoid telephone numbers, birthdays, and car registration numbers. Passwords that correspond to login names (or their anagrams) or to names in a dictionary can be automatically rejected. The system administrator can also set the maximum number of retries when you attempt to enter or change a rejected password (the default is usually three or four).

The latest versions of the `passwd` command provide optional tests for obviousness. In addition, SCO UNIX offers a command called `goodpw` (in man section ADM) that subjects a proposed password to a variety of sophisticated tests.

The /etc/passwd File

Passwords are stored in an ASCII file called `/etc/passwd`, not to be confused with the executable file `/bin/passwd`. The directory `/etc`, by the way, is pronounced "et-see" rather than "et cetera." It contains various administrative data files and programs. Try `ls /etc` for a quick look at their names. In addition to the file `passwd` you'll also see the file `motd` (message of the day) that I mentioned in Chapter 1.

The file Command

The existence of two files of different types, both called `passwd`, may prompt you to ask if there's a quick way to determine the type of a file. The directory name often gives you a clue: `/bin/passwd` is likely to be a program (binary) file. Certain file-naming conventions also help: the file `qsort.c` is likely to be the source code of a C language program, and so on. However, these clues are not wholly reliable, since any directory can store any kind of file, and users need not abide by file-naming

conventions. A useful command called `file` (in man section C) comes to the rescue. `file` takes one or more file (or directory) name arguments and tells you what kind of file each one is likely to be.

```
# file /etc /bin/passwd /etc/passwd /usr/src/qsort.c
/etc:       directory
/bin/passwd:   pure executable
/etc/passwd:   ascii
/usr/src/qsort.c:   c program text
# _
```

Note that `file` cannot always determine the file type exactly. It reads the first few lines looking for clues, but recall that Unix files have no preordained structure other than that determined by users and their programs.

/etc/passwd lists all active users including `root` and `bin`. Each user entry occupies a separate line with seven fields separated by colons. Many routines, including those used by the login program, need to read the /etc/passwd file. Only `root` can write to the /etc/passwd file directly, but changes are usually made indirectly via special commands, some of which are available to ordinary users. For example, the `passwd` command outlined previously works by changing a field in /etc/passwd.

An emerging trend is the provision of menu-driven system administration, reducing the need to know the quirks of individual commands. SCO UNIX, for example, provides `sysadmsh` (system administration shell), an easy-to-use, menu-based interface that `root` can run to set up and change almost every system parameter, including user passwords. This is the ideal solution for small Unix sites without a full-time system administrator.

WARNING   It is dangerous to even *think* about editing the /etc/passwd file directly! You can peek but don't poke!

Any user can examine the contents of /etc/passwd by using `cat`:

```
$ cat /etc/passwd
root:gf54JQxxZ32Fd:0:1::/:/bin/sh
...
stan:oIg65rfRdffn8:24:12:Stan Kelly-Bootle:/usr/stan/:/bin/sh
```

```
fred:qEsgs3324Fcc2:25:12:FrederickLemaitre:/usr/fred/:/bin/csh
joe::27:14:Joseph Lussac:/usr/joe:
...
$ _
```

Your listing will be different, but the seven fields (separated by six colons) should be recognizable. Two adjacent colons indicate an empty (or null) field. The field after the final colon may also be empty, as in the case of Joe's entry above.

All seven fields in /etc/passwd are listed in Table 6.1 for reference. Their full significance will emerge later in this chapter.

TABLE 6.1: /etc/passwd Fields

Field Number	Field Name	Description
1	login name	Name assigned to each user.
2	encrypted password	User's password as encrypted by Unix (shown as an * in many Unix versions).
3	uid	Unique user identification number assigned to a user (root is 0).
4	group id	Number indicating the user's group.
5	miscellaneous	Field usually used for additional user information, for example, full name, telephone number, etc. The finger command is used to display this field.
6	login dir	The home directory that the user is logged into automatically after login.
7	default shell	The name of the shell that will run for this user after login.

Every user, you will recall, is allocated a home directory, usually a subdirectory of /usr. It is field 6 of /etc/passwd that determines your home directory when you first log in.

Field 3, the user id (uid), also deserves a mention here. Your login name is used by the login routines to determine your numerical uid. Thereafter, Unix uses only your uid for the internal checking of your identity. It is possible for two login names to share the same uid (and therefore be effectively the one user), but two different uids cannot have the same login name.

Field 2, if nonempty, is deliberately peculiar! When I said that /etc/passwd was an ASCII file visible to all users and that it contained each user's password (including root's), you may have guessed there would be a catch somewhere! The jumble of characters in the second field of stan's entry is an *encrypted* version of Stan's password.

The encryption mechanism works as follows: if your password is, for example, mazkywu, then the Unix encryption algorithm might produce a6Fc76HGGdsS1. In this direction, encryption is fast, simple, and gives a unique mapping. In other words, distinct passwords cannot produce the same encrypted result. So when you log in and type a password, the system does not check your entry against your current password; rather, Unix encrypts your entry and compares the result with the encrypted version found in /etc/passwd.

Since the encrypted password is "public," you may wonder if the original password can be determined. In theory the answer is yes; in practice, to recover mazkywu from a6Fc76HGGdsS1 requires computing resources far beyond those in most nongovernment agencies. Note that even the superuser cannot decrypt your password. If you forget your password, the superuser (and no one else) can erase your password and provide you with a new one.

If decryption takes your run-of-the-mill supercomputer more than, say, a hundred years, it is fair to say that your password is safe! Of course, no encryption scheme is 100 percent satisfactory for all circumstances, and as computing price/performance ratios improve, encryption algorithms need to respond. For this reason, some Unix systems no longer store the encrypted passwords in the accessible /etc/passwd file. In place of the encrypted password, you may find a * symbol. Documentation about high-security systems is naturally hard to come by!

In the above example, note that Joe's password field is empty, possibly indicating that he or she has no password at present. This means that other users (and spies) are aware of Joe's vulnerability. The moral is clear! Get yourself a password as soon as possible.

The crypt Command

While on the subject of security, I should mention that Unix provides a crypt command (in man section C) that lets you encrypt entire files. The same command is used to decrypt encrypted files. You select a string of characters known as your *encryption key*. This key controls the conversion of your readable text (known in the spy trade as the *plain* or *clear* text) into the encrypted or enciphered version. The latter,

of course, is pure gibberish and only those knowing the key can use the `crypt` command to decrypt (or decipher) this gibberish back to the original plain text. If you keep your key to yourself, nobody (not even the superuser) will be able to read your encrypted secrets. Again, one must add the proviso that a suitably determined spy equipped with CIA/NSA computer power may be able to crack your code. (Incidentally, the U.S. government regulates the distribution of the Unix encryption utilities, so they are not normally available to unauthorized sites overseas.)

A typical encryption/decryption session might look as follows:

```
$ crypt <plain >encrypted
Enter key:
```

At this prompt, you type your key. (The screen will not echo the string you enter.) Enter the following command:

```
$ rm plain
$ _
```

The text in the file `plain` is now enciphered in the file `encrypted`, and to be safe you have erased the original! Note the redirections, needed because `crypt` reads from your standard input and writes to your standard output. Decryption requires the entry of the same key (so better not forget it) and a natural reversal of redirection:

```
$ crypt <encrypted >plain
Enter key:
$ _
```

At this prompt, you enter your key to decrypt the text in `encrypted` and redirect the decrypted text to `plain`.

It is worth mentioning here that the Unix tradition has never been overly paranoid regarding security. The original intent was to protect individual users without hindering the cooperation needed for joint program development. You'll see presently how groups of users can be defined, able to share access to certain directories and files while keeping out other users.

Choosing Your Shell

As I explained in Chapters 1 and 2, most of your work with Unix is performed in cooperation with a shell. You will recall that a shell is a special program that interprets

your commands and provides a programming interface to the kernel. Until fairly recently, the choice of shells was limited; however, the current trend is towards implementations giving you a choice of shells. (Chapter 20 discusses the evolution of Unix in more detail.) Some sites offer the Korn shell in addition to the Bourne and C shells. An early decision you (or your system administrator) can make is which shell should be your default shell, that is, the shell that is activated when you log in. Of course, this choice does not prevent you from switching shells during a session.

Your default shell is determined by the last field of the file you have just been studying, /etc/passwd. Look again at the example I gave earlier:

```
stan:65rfRdffn8:24:12:Stan Kelly-Bootle:/usr/stan/:/bin/sh
fred:qEs324Fcc2:25:12:Frederick Lemaitre:/usr/fred/:/bin/csh
joe:RDff43SXz3:27:14:Joseph Lussac:/usr/joe:
```

The field after the final colon, if not empty, is the full file name of the default shell program for each user. Such programs are usually in the bin subdirectory of root. The name bin stands for *binary*. You may recall from Chapter 2 that binary (executable) files, as opposed to text files, contain executable programs or commands in a special format—you may not be able to display their contents with cat, but the kernel knows how to interpret them as instructions. If you run ls /bin, you can list the names of a large number of Unix commands stored in /bin. Some of these will be familiar. Most of the general Unix commands reside in the /bin directory. To appreciate the significance of the /bin directory, a small digression is needed to discuss PATHs.

The Path to Success

Each user has an individual sequence of directories called a PATH that tells Unix where to look for an entered command. When you enter date, for example, the shell will first search for the program date in your *current* directory. If it's not there, a search is made in each of the PATH directories and the first date file encountered will be executed. (I assume here that the permissions set for date and its directory allow you to access and run it—I'll have more to say about such permissions in Chapter 7.)

If date is not found, of course, you'll get a command-unknown message. Such a message does not necessarily mean that there is no date program on your system; it may simply mean that there is no date program in your current directory, nor in any of the directories specified by your PATH. I'll show you soon how to check and change your PATH. For now, it should be clear that /bin, where all the common

commands reside, must be one of the directories in your PATH. If not, you are in for a frustrating time! Another directory that holds commonly used commands is called /usr/bin, so this is also normally found in PATH.

Your *current* directory, by the way, is usually in your PATH by default or by design (you'll see how later). The PATH mechanism conveniently lets you run programs that reside in directories other than your current directory (the one given by pwd). Of course, if you know that prog resides in the directory */xxx/yyy/zzz*, you can (provided the permissions are right) run it by entering the full path name, */xxx/yyy/zzz/prog*, regardless of your PATH and your current position in the file tree.

The name bin crops up frequently in Unix in different contexts, causing possible confusion to the unwary. There is the login name bin, representing a user who has some but not all of the privileges of root. You also have several bin directories such as /bin and /usr/bin available to all users. In addition, each user normally has a personal bin directory, such as /usr/stan/bin.

When you come to create your own programs and commands, they will usually be for your own private use, so they would not normally reside in /bin or /usr/bin. They could go into your home directory, but rather than clutter that up, it is helpful to have your own binary directory of executable programs. If you are mary, for instance, you would create a directory called /usr/mary/bin. By adding this directory to your PATH, you ensure that you can run your personal programs from any directory.

With this PATH digression behind us, let's return to the default shells.

The Names of the Shells

The Bourne shell is an executable file called sh. Since it resides in the /bin directory, its full name is /bin/sh. Assuming that /bin is in your PATH, and you have no other program called sh in an earlier directory of your PATH sequence, then the Bourne shell can be invoked with sh or, as you'll see later, with optional arguments: sh *args*.

Similarly, the C shell is stored in the file /bin/csh and the Korn shell in /bin/ksh. There is also a /bin/rsh available on many Unix versions. This is a *restricted* version of the Bourne shell that the system administrator may mandate in order to limit a user's access to certain commands. You should try ls /bin/*sh to check which shells you have on your system.

The last entry in your line of /etc/passwd will be /bin/sh if your default shell is the Bourne shell, or /bin/csh if your default is the C shell. Similarly, the Korn shell is indicated by the entry /bin/ksh. No entry after the final colon usually means that your default shell is the Bourne shell. In the /etc/passwd example, users stan and joe will default to the Bourne shell, while fred defaults to the C shell.

Later on, when you start looking at shell scripts, I will point out some of the differences between these shells. Until then, simply accept the default shell that your system has provided. The differences will not affect your work significantly until you reach more advanced operations.

Since shells can be run like normal programs, you can enter the commands sh, csh, or ksh to run the Bourne, C, or Korn shells respectively. However, note that there can be differences between the way the C shell is invoked automatically during login compared with invoking it manually with a command. These differences will be clarified in the next section where I discuss the login profile.

Login Profiles

There are usually several site conventions determined by your system administrator. These provide what might be called global actions, or defaults affecting all users. They are placed in a special file known as the *global login profile*. The shell executes the commands in this file whenever you log in.

NOTE   Unix login profiles are similar to the AUTOEXEC.BAT files of DOS. Various parameters can be set and commands can be executed automatically when you "start" the system. AUTOEXEC.BAT is executed when you boot DOS, but Unix login profiles are executed each time you log in.

You can elect to modify some or all of these defaults either temporarily during a given session, or permanently for all sessions. The general idea is that you can run commands of your own choosing to modify your environment during a given session: such changes will last until you log out. Or, you can place these commands in a special file in your home directory known as your *personal login profile*. When you log in, the shell will first execute the global login profile (if one is found), and then execute your personal login profile (if one is found). The net result of executing these two sets of commands gives you your "permanent" startup environment each time you log in.

Since you can change your personal login profile at any time, it is not quite correct to use the word *permanent*. As you gain familiarity with Unix, however, your login profile will settle down to reflect your usual needs. Note the tremendous flexibility of having a global profile for everyone followed by personalized profiles for each user.

The profile names and mechanisms vary between the Bourne and C shells as outlined in the following sections.

Bourne Shell Login Profiles

When you log into the Bourne shell, it looks for a file called /etc/profile. This is the global (or system-wide) login profile. If found, all the commands in /etc/profile are executed. Next, the shell looks for a file called .profile in your home directory. This is your personal login profile. If found, the shell executes all the commands in .profile. Then the prompt appears to signal the start of your session. The normal Bourne shell prompt is $, but this can be modified by login profile commands, as you'll see presently.

C Shell Login Profiles

Whenever you run the C shell, it first looks for a file called /etc/cshrc. This is the C shell equivalent to the Bourne global login profile. If found, all the commands in /etc/cshrc are executed. Next, the shell looks for the file called .cshrc in your home directory. This is your personal C shell run command file. If found, the shell executes all the commands in .cshrc. If the C shell is being run at login time, an additional login profile called .login is sought in your home directory. If found, the commands in .login are executed. Finally, the prompt appears to signal the start of your session. Usually the C shell prompt is %, but this can be changed by commands in any of the three profiles listed above.

Typically, the global login profile calculates and displays disk usage information, displays the motd (message of the day), checks your mailbox and tells you if you have any mail, and displays any news bulletins. It also usually sets a umask that determines the default permissions for any files and directories you may create. More on this in Chapter 7.

For the moment, I'll concentrate on setting personal profiles for the Bourne shell. Apart from the profile name differences, there are several differences in the commands available in the C shell and how certain parameters are set. Appendix A lists the key differences between the Bourne and C shells.

Your Own Login Profile

What sort of commands can you usefully run from a login profile? Well, you can display the date and time (with date), call for a daily aphorism from the fortune cookie jar (with usr/games/fortune), check who else is logged in (with who), invoke a personal memo service (with calendar), modify your prompt symbol, and a host of other useful tasks. Your profile can contain any sequence of commands with appropriate arguments and pipes, and the effect is the same as if you were to key these commands each time you logged in. In addition to running any of the standard utility commands available, or commands that you have created yourself, many of the tricks performed by your profile depend on setting values in *shell variables*.

Shell Variables—An Introduction

Shell variables are rather like the variables used in conventional programming languages such as BASIC. Remember that Unix shells are not only command interpreters but also offer many features of a programming language. The shell variable is your first gentle exposure to shell programming. The key notion of a variable is that you can provide a name, or *variable identifier*, for some entity, such as PATH or doc. Variable names with capital letters are usually reserved for standard variables with predetermined Unix meanings, as listed in Table 6.2. You have already met the PATH mechanism. Now you know how the PATH sequence of directories is stored: in a shell variable, conveniently named PATH!

TABLE 6.2: Built-in Bourne Shell Variables

Variable	Description
CDPATH	Search path for the cd command
PATH	Search path for user commands
MAIL	Name of the mail file that the shell will check to see if you have mail
MAILCHECK	Frequency with which the shell checks for new mail
MAILPATH	List of mail files to be checked by shell, together with optional messages to be displayed (default is "You have mail")
PS1	Primary prompt symbol (default is "$ ")
PS2	Secondary prompt symbol (default is "> ")
IFS	Internal field separators (default is space, tab, newline)
SHACCT	Name of file used for accounting purposes
TERM	Your terminal name
HOME	Your home directory

NOTE The shell variables discussed here are for the Bourne shell only. The C shell has its own predefined variables that are similar but different. Appendix A lists these differences.

Your own personal variables should have names with small letters. This rule is simply a useful convention, by the way. As long as you avoid using the built-in variable names for your own variables, you can use any names you like. However, keeping to the Unix traditions will make your shell scripts more legible.

The value of a shell variable can be set by means of an assignment statement. For example,

```
PATH=:/bin:/usr/bin:/usr/stan/bin
doc=/usr/stan/document
PS1= 'Enter your command: '
```

sets the variable PATH to the expression :/bin:/usr/bin/:usr/stan/bin; similarly, doc and PS1 are given the values /usr/stan/document and 'Enter your command: ' respectively. Note carefully that the direction of assignment is from

right to left. The initial : in PATH indicates your current directory and is equivalent to writing dot colon(. :).

There are no $ prompts shown in the above snippet. Each line is part of a *shell script*, rather than a sequence of manually entered commands. When a script is executed, each of the above lines would be interpreted exactly as if you had typed them in yourself. However, there is no prompt or pause, unless the script specifically requests input. You can picture a script as an invisible typist, rapidly entering a sequence of commands. There's a good deal more to shell scripts, of course, but the first essential concept is that of simulating a sequence of manual commands.

NOTE   **Spaces aren't allowed before or after the = assignment operator.**

Setting PS1 to any character string will change your primary prompt. You can even set your prompt to #, the usual superuser prompt. Please resist the temptation—it will not increase your powers and will certainly cause much angst and confusion.

In the last example, your prompt would be changed from '$ ' to 'Enter your command: '. Note the use of single forward quotes when setting PS1; these ensure that the spaces within the new prompt string are transferred to PS1. Great care is needed to distinguish forward quotes from backquotes. Unix is quite picky about these two symbols: entering the wrong quotes can have disconcerting effects! (More on this in Chapters 13 and 16.) Note also the space at the end of the prompt string for added legibility:

```
$ PS1='Enter your command: '
Enter your command: _
```

Later on, you'll see other reasons for placing quotes around certain characters. The general idea is that the shell treats some characters, known as *metacharacters*, in a special way (recall the use of * and ? as file-name wildcards, for example), but when such characters are *quoted* (that is, surrounded by single or possibly double quotation marks), the shell treats them literally.

Once set, any variable name, prefixed by a $, can be used in expressions. The leading $ symbol (not to be confused with the default prompt symbol) tells the shell to

convert the name to its current value before performing an operation. For example,

```
Enter your command: cd $doc
Enter your command: pwd
/usr/stan/document
Enter your command: echo PATH
PATH
Enter your command: echo $PATH
:/bin:/usr/bin:/usr/stan/bin
Enter your command: echo '$'PATH
$PATH
Enter your command: echo PS1
PS1
Enter your command: echo $PS1
Enter your command:
Enter your command: PS1='$'
$ _
```

The effect of cd $doc is exactly the same as cd /usr/stan/document since $doc evaluates to the expression assigned to doc earlier. One immediate advantage of such personal variables is to save typing! Once doc is assigned, you can use $doc as a convenient abbreviation.

The echo PATH example illustrates the importance of the $ prefix. The echo command (in man section C) simply echoes its arguments by sending them to your standard output. echo PATH therefore displays PATH quite literally, but with echo $PATH, the shell evaluates the variable PATH and echoes the value stored therein, namely :/bin:/usr/bin:/usr/stan/bin. Putting forward quotes around the $, you'll notice, removes the special interpretation of the $ as a variable evaluator, so that '$'PATH echoes as $PATH. Similarly, note how the metacharacter $ changes the result of echoing PS1 and $PS1.

The echo command is more useful than at first meets the eye! As the PATH example shows, echo lets you examine the contents of a variable, a useful operation when debugging a program. Even with nonvariables, echo is useful when you want a shell script to display a message:

```
echo 'Please enter Y or N '
```

Another useful application for echo is to send a fixed string to a file using redirection:

```
$ echo ' ** Hello Mary! ** ' >junk
$ cat junk
```

```
** Hello Mary! **
$ _
```

We'll make use of this trick occasionally to create small files without bothering with a text editor. The result is similar to the `cat >>poem.1` trick you used in Chapter 4.

You can include newlines in a quoted string as follows:

```
$ echo 'Workers of the
> World, Unite!'
Workers of the
World, Unite!
$ _
```

After pressing Enter (newline) at the end of the first line, the shell displays its *secondary prompt*, in this case a > symbol, and waits for more input. After the final quote and newline, the shell knows that the command is complete, so it echoes the complete string, including the embedded newline, then displays its primary prompt, $. The secondary prompt is stored in the predefined shell variable PS2. By default, PS2 contains ´>´, but you can set it to any string using the assignment operation:

```
$ PS2='More input:'
$ _
```

As you saw in the case of PS1 earlier, a variable can be assigned another value at any time, hence the origin of the term "variable."

Variable names are usually chosen to indicate the type of value stored. As in the case of file names, you should avoid certain characters that may confuse the shell, such as spaces, > < * ? $ " ´ ` and \. Remember, too, to avoid using any of the predefined shell variables listed in Table 6.2.

A common command found in login profiles is `stty` (in man section C), a command that lets you customize your terminal in various ways. This is especially useful if you are using a dumb terminal with limited features.

Setting Terminal Options with stty

The command `stty` stands for "setting options for your teletypewriter," a reminder of the ancient origins of Unix! As the number and complexity of terminals has continued to blossom since the early 1970s, the `stty` command has grown in size to

match. I will simply list some of the common `stty` options. The simplified syntax is

```
stty [-a] [options]
```

Using `stty` with no arguments will simply display a list of certain current settings. With the `-a` argument, `stty` displays all the current option settings. To set options, you use `stty` with various mnemonics as arguments. For example,

```
$ stty -tabs
$ _
```

will cause any tab codes to be converted to spaces when outputted to your terminal. This is useful if your terminal does not handle tab codes automatically. Similarly, you can vary the keystrokes used for erasing characters and killing lines:

```
$ stty erase[backspace] kill @
$ _
```

Here, the notation `[backspace]` means you press the Backspace key, since it is difficult to show you this action on the printed page! Alternatively, you could enter `$ stty erase '^h'` since Unix interprets '^h' as Ctrl-H, the ASCII code for backspace. The net result of this command is to assign the backspace key to the character erase function, and the @ key to the line delete function. A Berkeley version of `stty` called `tset` may be available on your system. The syntax is different but the same options are generally available.

Viewing Your .profile File

Until you have developed some editing skills (see Chapters 8, 11, and 12), you will not be able to play around with your login profile. However, you can list your current profiles and see what they are doing for you by entering

```
$ cat .profile
```

For example, you'll probably find entries similar to the following in your `.profile` file:

```
PATH=:/bin:/usr/bin:$HOME/bin:
MAIL=/usr/spool/mail/ `logname`
export PATH MAIL
umask 077
```

Note that $HOME will be converted to your home directory, say `/usr/stan`, resulting in a PATH set to `:/bin:/usr/bin:/usr/stan/bin:`.

The second line illustrates an important use of the backquote mark ` (also known as the *grave* accent), not to be confused with the single forward quote ´. Expressions within backquotes are taken as commands to be run by the shell, and the resulting value of the executed command replaces the backquoted expression. Easy for me to say! To see what this means, consider what happens when the shell encounters the backquoted expression `logname`. The shell pauses to run the command logname, a simple command that returns your login name, say stan. Magically, the line

```
MAIL=/usr/spool/mail/`logname`
```

is transformed to

```
MAIL=/usr/spool/mail/stan
```

This line then establishes the name of the file that will be examined periodically to see if mail has arrived (see Table 6.2). The ability to invoke commands within commands, as it were, takes some getting used to, but it gives Unix shell scripts considerable power and elegance (not found in DOS BAT files, for example!). More on this in Chapters 13 and 16.

The export command tells the shell that the following list of variables, PATH and MAIL, will be needed in other programs. To understand this technicality requires an understanding of how shells can spawn subshells, so I'll spare you the details until Chapter 13. The umask (short for "user mask") line sets a default for permissions on files and directories that you may create. (More on this in Chapter 7.) With this background, you should be able to get some idea of what your own .profile is up to. Similarly, you can examine /etc/profile to see what global settings have been arranged for all users.

In the next chapter I move on to another vital aspect of personalizing your Unix: setting up your own directories and files.

Summary

In this chapter, you learned about some of the features in Unix that you can change to suit your needs. In this discussion, we covered the following:

- Password control varies from site to site depending on the degree of security needed. Users can change their passwords with the passwd command.

- Some of the rules for devising good passwords were discussed; for example, you should avoid short, obvious, alpha-only strings.

- The `file` command tells you the type of a particular file: ASCII, shell script, language source code, pure executable, or directory.

- Passwords are stored in encrypted form in the `etc/passwd` file along with user name, user id, group id, miscellaneous user details, home directory, and default login shell.

- The `crypt` command lets you encipher and decipher your files using an encryption key.

- Your default shell is usually either the Bourne shell, `/bin/sh`, or the C shell, `/bin/csh`. Other shells are the Korn shell, `/bin/ksh`, and the restricted Bourne shell, `/bin/rsh`.

- Your PATH is a sequence of directories. When searching for a file to execute, the shell looks in your current directory, then in each directory in your PATH. Most normal commands are files in `/bin` or `/usr/bin`. Your own commands are usually placed in `/usr/yourname/bin`.

- Login profiles offer a means of customizing your Unix environment. These files contain commands that are executed automatically whenever you log in. Global login profiles set defaults for all users. Your personal login profile can determine your own preferred defaults as well as running selected commands when you log in.

- Shell variables can be assigned values to personalize various aspects of your work. `PS1` and `PS2` can be assigned strings to serve as your primary and secondary prompts. The `PATH` variable can be changed to include directories of your own choosing. Private variables are useful for reducing typing: `doc=/usr/stan/document`.

- The `echo` command is useful for

    Displaying the values of variables: `echo $PATH`

    Displaying fixed messages

    Creating small files

- Certain characters (metacharacters) have special meanings to the shell unless enclosed in single or double quotes.

- The `stty` and `tset` commands can set terminal options, usually in a login profile. You can vary the keystrokes used for character and line deletions. `stty -tabs` converts tabs to spaces on output.

- Backquoted expressions are executed *in situ* by the shell.

CHAPTER

SEVEN

Your Own File System

- Your home directory

- Permissions

- Changing owners and groups

- Changing permissions

■'ve mentioned several times that Unix presents you with certain global resources under the general care and nourishment of the system administrator, while at the same time giving you your own home directory where you are, more or less, sovereign. Your home directory is your normal starting point in the Unix file hierarchy. From this node you are free to grow your own branches by sprouting subdirectories and files of your own choosing. Furthermore, you can determine with great precision who can access your home territory: you can prevent outside access to particular files or to whole directories. This chapter, therefore, covers both the creation of your own file system and the setting of permissions.

These are major steps in getting Unix on your side. Unix revolves around files, so you need to create a tree of directories with names that help you to organize your files. Many beginners simply let their files build up in their home directory. This is as chaotic as shoving all your papers into one big folder: storage effort is reduced at the expense of retrieval effort. As a simple suggestion, you could organize your files as follows:

/usr/stan	Home directory
/usr/stan/bin	Subdirectory for private programs
/usr/stan/memo	Memo subdirectory
/usr/stan/memo/fred	Directory for all memos to/from Fred
/usr/stan/memo/mary	Directory for all memos to/from Mary

The files representing your correspondence with Fred, say, can now have helpful names with a subject and date, such as inv091290. Since they are in the fred directory, the file names do not have to be saddled with references to Fred. Your freedom to create files and directories is absolute in your own home!

Home Rule

If you are user stan logged into /usr/stan, for instance, you can create a new file called /usr/stan/copy.poem or a new empty subdirectory called /usr/stan/memo ready to hold more files and subsubdirectories:

```
$ cd
$ pwd
```

```
/usr/stan
$ cp poem copy.poem
$ mkdir memo
$ cd memo
$ pwd
/usr/stan/memo
$ cp ../poem copy2.poem
$ mkdir fred
$ cd fred
$ pwd
/usr/stan/memo/fred
$ _
```

Remember that cd with no arguments puts you into your home directory.

NOTE Remember, every directory holds two special directory "names": . (dot) means the directory itself, and .. (dot-dot) means the parent directory.

cp (in man section C) is the copy command. Used here in its simplest format, it copies the first named file (known as the *source*) to the second named file (known as the *destination*), overwriting the latter if it already exists. The source file for cp must exist; the destination file may or may not exist. Unless you specify otherwise, cp assumes that the files are in your current directory. Notice that in the second use of cp in the last example, I want to copy /usr/stan/poem. Since the current directory was /usr/stan/memo, I had to "step back" a level to the parent, using the .. notation. Of course, I could have typed the full path name:

```
$ cp /usr/stan/poem copy2.poem
```

but the ../ trick is simpler once you get used to it.

You have already met mkdir, which tries to create a subdirectory given by its argument. mkdir can fail for various reasons, for example, if the subdirectory already exists. The parent of the newly created directory is your current directory. Note that mkdir does *not* change your current directory. After mkdir memo, you are still in /usr/stan. Beginners often forget to change (cd) to the new directory before trying to use it. Result: puzzlement and frustration.

If you tried to cd to someone else's home directory to perform the above sequence of commands, the chances are that Unix would object with a permission denied

message or similar brick wall. Unless you are logged into `root` as a superuser, the right to mess around outside your home directory and its children is under the control of others. In the same way, you have the power to admit or keep out any nonroot users. I have mentioned permissions several times in a general context. It is time to explore this crucial topic in greater detail.

Permissions

There are, in fact, eighteen different permission classes, so you are facing an area of Unix which most beginners find confusing at first assault. The different types of permissions fall into three categories, and the permission classes arise from the possible combinations of permissions from these categories:

- File and directory permissions
- Read, write, and execute permissions
- Owner, group, and public (or others) permissions

Before I list them exhaustively, let's review the basic concepts.

The Owner

Every file and directory has a designated *owner*, usually the original creator. Let's consider first a file that you own. You can grant or withhold its three permissions (read, write, and execute) in any way you wish. These three, also known as *access modes*, are quite independent. You can set these three permission levels differently for three sets of users: yourself, members of your group, and others.

Naturally, you grant yourself, as owner, read and write permissions (in fact, you usually get these two permissions by default). Where appropriate, you can give yourself execute permission with a single `chmod` command, as you'll see later.

File Permissions

Read permission means you can list the contents of your own files with `cat` or `pr` or any other command that accesses the bytes inside your file. Write permission means that you can change the contents of a file, using any editor or command that

writes new values to the bytes inside your file. If the file is executable (either a binary program or a shell script), execute permission means that you can run it as a program. Note that as a safety precaution, you may want to withhold write permission from some of your own important files. This is rather like removing the plastic tag on an audio or video tape. If the need arises to alter such files, you can always restore the write permission. You'll meet the chmod (change mode) command soon that allows you to vary the permission levels at any time.

You can now decide who else should have these access rights. If you belong to a group (assigned by the system administrator), group members may enjoy any or all or none of the three permissions. This can be decided on a file-by-file basis. Finally, all other users outside your group can be granted any or all or none of the three permissions. Permissions granted outside the group and owner are sometimes called *public* permissions.

Directory Permissions

The three permissions can also be applied to directories, although the meaning of read, write, and execute has to be interpreted slightly differently. I'll explain these subtle differences in several ways to ensure that you understand their significance.

Read and write directory permissions are fairly obvious. You need read permission to determine the *contents* of a directory with ls or a similar command. ls has to read the various fields in a directory in order to give you the *names* of its files and subdirectories. This is quite different from the act of reading the contents of a file or subdirectory. Directory read permission is quite independent of, and must not be confused with, any of the permissions set on the files and subdirectories themselves. If you grant others read permission on your directory, but withhold read/write permissions on your files, then other users will be able to see all your file names but unable to access or change your files. Conversely, you could (in theory) withhold directory read permission but grant file read and/or write permissions. If so, other users would not be able to determine your file names with ls, yet if they somehow managed to learn the name of one of your files, they might be able to read and/or change it.

Directory write permission lets you alter the contents of a directory. Without such permission, therefore, you cannot add or remove files or subdirectories.

Directory execute permission is often called directory *search* permission. Without this permission, a user cannot access any file or subdirectory, since such access calls for a search of the directory in order to locate that file or subdirectory.

In order to cd into a directory, you also need directory execute permission in that directory; and even with this permission, you would further require write permission in that directory in order to alter its contents, that is, create and erase files, or create and erase its subdirectories.

Stan was able to create the subdirectory memo and create and access files therein because he has read, write, and execute permissions in his own home directory, /usr/stan, and its children. Yes, each user acquires these and similar permissions on their own directories and files as a sort of birthright, and only root can take them away. (You, as the owner, could also remove some or all of these permissions from yourself, or even relinquish your ownership, but that might border on the suicidal!)

Whether you have permission to cd into /usr/mary, and having got there, mess up her files, is entirely up to mary and root. To reduce verbiage, I will refrain from mentioning the exceptional powers of root unless they merit special attention.

Mary may well grant group members and/or others execute permission on her home directory but withhold other permissions. If so, such users could cd to /usr/mary, but without directory write permission, would not be free to create files and subdirectories there. Stan could not even list the files in /usr/mary unless Mary grants them directory read permission there. Note that if you happened to know the name of a program file in usr/mary and she gave you execute permissions on both the directory and the program, you could run it without needing directory read permission. If you find this confusing, be patient. All will be clear soon.

If Mary had a file called poem, other users could not read or copy it unless Mary grants them file read permission for that file. Nor could they write over or change a file in /usr/mary without specific file write permission on that file. When write permission is withheld on a file, we say that the file is *write protected,* and similarly for reading permission, we use the phrase *read protected.*

Once again, under normal circumstances, you can have full read, write, and execute permissions (as appropriate) on the files and subdirectories that you create in your home directory (and its branches), but outside this, other users can withhold or modify these permissions. To change the contents of a directory you must have *write* permission on that directory. This includes making, erasing, and renaming files, and creating subdirectories with mkdir. To copy a file with cp, you need to have *read* permission on the source file and *write* permission on the destination file, if it exists. If the destination file does not exist, you must have *write* permission on the directory.

It's time to classify all these permissions and then see how you can set and change them.

Permissions for Owner, Group, and Others

Like Caesar's Gallia, Unix offers three divisions of access permissions:

Owner   Permissions granted to the current *owner* of a file or directory. The owner is usually the original creator of the file or directory, but ownership may be alterable using the chown (change owner) command (discussed later in this chapter).

Group   Permissions granted to a set of consenting users forming a group. Groups are given a group name by the system administrator, who also arranges for individual users to join or leave each group.

Public   Permissions granted to all users. Public file and directory permissions apply to any legal user.

In each of these divisions, there are three types of permission available: *read, write,* and *execute.* The terms, coded as r, w, and x, are reasonably intuitive, but you must be aware that they each mean slightly different things when applied to files and directories. There are therefore six types of permission to digest: file read, directory read; file write, directory write; file execute, directory execute.

As I mentioned earlier, the last combination looks peculiar, since one does not normally think of directories as being executable. Shell scripts and program files are executable, but surely a directory such as /usr/stan cannot be "run" like a program? The answer is that the "execute" in the directory execute category has a special interpretation, sometimes known as directory search permission.

A Unix directory, as you may have noticed, is very much like a file: both have names and both store data. The difference, of course, is that the data inside a directory is a list of file and subdirectory names together with certain control information to help Unix locate them on your disk. To discover the file and subdirectory names in a directory, using ls for instance, requires *read* permission on that directory. To add or remove files or subdirectories requires *write* permission on the directory. Even to rename a file, you must have *write* permission on the directory. And to access a file

requires *execute* permission: when a file name is a command argument, for example, the directory must be searched before the file can be located on your disk.

By withholding directory execute (or search) permission, you can prevent access to any file in that directory, since accessing a file requires a search of its directory.

Note carefully a point that confuses many beginners: provided you have write permission on a directory, you can remove one of its files even when the file is *write protected*. Write protection of a file protects only its contents; the file itself is vulnerable unless its directory is write protected.

The following listing should clarify the situation:

Permission	Symbol	Meaning
no permission	-	Permission withheld.
read	r	Read permission on a file allows access to its contents.
		Read permission on a directory allows the determination of the names of its files and subdirectories, for example, with ls.
write	w	Write permission on a file allows change to its contents.
		Write permission on a directory allows change to the contents of that directory by adding or deleting files and subdirectories.
execute	x	Execute permission on a file allows use of that file as a command.
		Execute permission on a directory allows a search of that directory for a file.

The four symbols r, w, x, and - (no permission) are used to specify the permission rights for each file and directory. To examine file permission rights, you use the ls -l command. The -l argument means "long" or "full" listing. For directories, you use ls -ld, where the combined -ld argument means long directory listings. Here are some examples:

```
$ ls -l openhouse
-rwxrwxrwx 1 stan prog 245 May 20 10:15 openhouse
```

The leftmost field of ten symbols is the permissions field. The first symbol indicates the type of file as follows:

Symbol	Type of file
–	Ordinary file
d	Directory
b	Block I/O device
c	Character I/O device

For the moment, you can ignore the I/O device files. My examples will be limited to ordinary files and directories.

The remaining nine symbols show the three sets of three permissions for owner, group, and others. In the example above, the display shows the following permission field:

- The first symbol, -, means openhouse is a *file* (a d here would indicate a directory).
- The first rwx means that the owner, stan, has read, write, and execute permissions.
- The second rwx means that all members of stan's group have read, write, and execute permissions.
- The third rwx means that all others have read, write, and execute permissions. (This group is also called the public permissions group.)

As you can see, openhouse is accessible to everybody. All can read, change, and run this file as a program or command provided that its directory has execute permission for all.

Without too much diversion from our study of permissions, let's look briefly at the other fields displayed by ls -l.

Field	Description
1	The file has only one link. This means that the file is known only as openhouse. A 2 here would mean that the file can be accessed via two different names (or links).
stan	The file is owned by stan.
prog	The file belongs to the group called prog.
245	The file has 245 bytes.
May 20 10:15	The file was last modified at this date/time.
openhouse	The file name is openhouse.

Here's another example:

```
$ ls -l myprog
-rwxr-x--- 1 stan prog 645 May 21 12:15 myprog
```

The owner of myprog, namely stan, enjoys rwx permissions, so he can read, write, and execute this file. Members of the prog group, however, can only read and execute myprog, as indicated by the group permissions r-x. The lack of write permission means that group members cannot modify myprog. Their ability to erase myprog will depend on permissions in the directory. All others are given permissions of ---, namely no permissions at all! Outsiders cannot read, change, or execute myprog. Attempts to do any of these operations will invoke the message

```
myprog: permission denied.
```

To allow members of the prog group to check file names and access files in /usr/stan, the directory permissions must be set appropriately:

```
$ ls -ld /usr/stan
drwxr-x--- 5 stan prog 780 May 19 09:25 /usr/stan
```

Note the initial d indicating a directory. The owner has rwx permissions, allowing stan to read, write, and search /usr/stan. Group members are denied directory write permission, so they cannot create or erase files and subdirectories in /usr/stan. However, they have read permission, so they can use ls to discover all the file names. They also have execute permission, so they can access the files they want to read and run.

Default Permissions

When you acquire your home directory, it normally comes with the following default permissions set by the system administrator:

```
drwx------
```

These permissions will also be acquired by any subdirectories you create. They imply that, initially, you have sole control over your directories. Only you can read, write, and search them. Nobody else can cd to your directories, alter their contents by adding or removing your files or subdirectories, or search them to access your files.

Any files you create will usually default to

```
-rw-------
```

Once again, nobody can interfere in any way (except root, of course). Note, however, that your script files do not acquire execute permission by default. If you create shell scripts and wish to run them, you must set execute permission yourself. (Binary program files become executable automatically when you compile and link them.) You'll see how to do this in the next section.

WARNING   It's a good idea to create a file and a directory and check their
permissions with ls. This will reveal the current defaults.

These initial permission defaults can be varied by you and/or the system administrator by changing a parameter known as the umask (or user mask). This requires a knowledge of the octal numbering system used to encode the rwx pattern of each permission set, so I'll spare you the details until later.

Changing Owners and Groups

The key point to note is that only you, the owner, and the omnipotent root can vary your permissions. Likewise, you cannot go around changing anyone else's permissions! You can, however, relinquish ownership of a file (subject to the system administrator's approval). You use the chown (change owner id) command (in man section C) as follows:

```
$ chown mary poem memo
$ _
```

Provided that poem and memo are found and you are their owner, the above line will change the ownerships to Mary. You can list as many file names as you wish, separated by spaces. The second argument can be any valid login name, or you can use the corresponding numerical uid (user id). The file is still in your directory, so Mary may not be able to do much with her new possession. One thing she can now do as the new owner is to change the permissions of these files, if she so desires.

A similar command, chgrp (change group id—also in man section C), lets you change the group id of a file.

```
$ chgrp systems poem memo
$ _
```

will change the group of the two files to systems. Providing that the directory permissions allow, members of the systems group acquire new access rights on these two files.

Changing Permissions

The chmod command (in man section C) is used by the owner of a file or directory (or by root) to change its access permissions.

There are two distinct ways of using chmod, best described by a few examples. The first method is called the *absolute* method because it changes all of the permission settings:

```
$ ls -l myprog
-rwxr-x--- 1 stan prog 645 May 21 12:15 myprog
$ chmod 0777 myprog
$ ls -l myprog
-rwxrwxrwx 1 stan prog 645 May 21 12:15 myprog
```

The first argument of chmod is called the *mode*. Here, a mode of 0777 has somehow managed to set the permissions to -rwxrwxrwx (that is, read, write, execute for owner, group, and public). The trick works as follows:

Permission	Numeric Value
-	0
r	4
w	2
x	1

For each of the three sets, you add up the numbers corresponding to the permission required:

rwx = 4 + 2 + 1 = 7

rwx = 4 + 2 + 1 = 7

rwx = 4 + 2 + 1 = 7

This gives you the mode argument of 777 (the leading 0 is optional).

If you are familiar with the octal and binary notations, the mode argument in chmod is easy to figure. Each rwx group is expressed as an octal number. Write each octal number in binary, for example:

```
777 = (111)(111)(111) = (rwx)(rwx)(rwx)
666 = (110)(110)(110) = (rw-)(rw-)(rw-)
542 = (101)(100)(010) = (r-x)(r--)(-w-)
```

1 means permission granted; 0 means permission denied.

A few more examples may help:

Mode	Permission
0600	-rw-------
0666	-rw-rw-rw-
0222	--w--w--w-
0555	-r-xr-xr-x
0744	-rwxr--r--

The other chmod method is called the *relative* or *symbolic* method. Here, you select just the permissions to be changed; the other permissions are unaltered. The syntax is

chmod [*who*] [+|-|=] [*permissions*] *filename*

The optional first argument, *who*, can be any of the following symbols (or combinations of them):

Who	Meaning
a	All users (the default)
g	Group

Who	Meaning
o	Others (public)
u	User (owner)

The second argument can be either + (to add a permission), - (to remove a permission), or = (to assign a given permission and remove any others that might be there). Note the syntax: | is read as OR (exclusive).

The third argument, *permissions*, can be any combination of the familiar r, w, and x symbols.

The final argument is the name of the target file or directory. As you can guess, the total number of variants is astronomical, but here are a few simple examples:

```
$ ls -l myprog
-rwxr-x--- 1 stan prog 645 May 21 12:15 myprog
$ chmod o+x myprog
$ ls -l myprog
-rwxr-x--x 1 stan prog 645 May 21 12:15 myprog
$ chmod ug-r myprog
$ ls -l myprog
--wx--x--x 1 stan prog 645 May 21 12:15 myprog
$ chmod a+r myprog
$ ls -l myprog
-rwxr-xr-x 1 stan prog 645 May 21 12:15 myprog
$ chmod u=r myprog
$ ls -l myprog
-r-------- 1 stan prog 645 May 21 12:15 myprog
```

As you can see, o+x adds execute permission to others (leaving the rest unchanged); ug-r removes read permission from user (owner) and group; and a+r adds read permission to owner, group, and others. Note that +r would give the same effect as a+r since a is the default. To combine a series of permissions, separate each with a comma, for example,

```
$ chmod o+x, ug-r myprog
```

The u=r example sets read permission to user (owner), but *clears* all other permissions. Use this format with care! Play around with chmod to get the feel for it. In spite of the apparent complexities, it soon becomes natural. There are just a handful of common combinations. Two you'll be using a lot when we discuss shell programming later are

```
chmod u+x filename
```

and

```
chmod +x filename
```

The first format makes *filename* executable by you (the user); the second version makes *filename* executable by everyone!

Summary

Chapter 7 covered the following topics:

- Your HOME directory is the starting point of your own file system.

- Create subdirectories with mkdir to help organize your files.

- Use cp *file1* *file2* to copy the contents of *file1* into (a possibly new) *file2*.

- Use cd *target_dir* to navigate around your directories. Use pwd to check where you are.

- Separate access permissions apply to directories and files; read, write, and execute; and owner, group, and others. Eighteen permission combinations are therefore possible: $2 \times 3 \times 3$.

- You are the owner, by default, of your HOME directory, and of all the files and subdirectories that you create.

- As the owner, you can vary the access permissions for group and others. Permissions for others are also known as public permissions.

- Use ls -l and ls -ld to determine the access permissions of files and directories respectively.

- The symbols r, w, and x indicate read, write, and execute permissions. The symbol – means "permission withheld."

- Three groups of three symbols (combinations of r, w, x, and –) indicate the permissions for owner, group, and others.

- For files, execute permission means you can run (execute) the file as a program (binary object file or shell script text).

- For directories, execute permission means search permission.

- Use chown to change the ownership of a file or directory. Use chgrp to change group ownerships of a file or directory. Only the owner and root can change ownerships, and even the owner's right can be withheld by the system administrator.

- Use chmod to change permissions on a file or directory.

- chmod has two syntaxes:

Absolute	chmod octal_number filename	Changes all permissions
Relative	chmod [who][+|−|=] [permissions]filename	Changes only selected permissions

- The octal_number is built from − = 0; r = 4; w = 2; x = 1 for each of owner, group, and others. Hence 777 means rwxrwxrwx. The optional who argument is a = all users (the default); g = group; o = others; u = user (owner). Omitting who defaults to a. Use + to add a permission; − to remove a permission; = to assign a permission while removing any others that might exist. The permissions argument can be any mix of r, w, and x.

- A combination you'll meet quite frequently is

chmod u+x filename

which is needed to make filename executable by you. The argument a+x (same effect as +x) extends execution rights to all users.

CHAPTER

EIGHT

Light Editing with ed

- Unix text editors

- Starting with ed

- Adding more text

- Changing your text

- Regular expressions

- Miscellaneous commands and switches

You've seen how to create simple text files by redirecting keyboard entries. Using the append operator, >>, you can add further lines at the end of such files, but to correct or change your file requires a program called a *text editor*. The job of preparing, editing, formatting, and printing text, of course, has become a major computer application, generating a wide base of specialized word processing and desktop publishing technologies. Unix itself was co-opted into the document preparation game very early on, helping the Bell Labs clerical departments to create and format technical manuals and office documents.

On the question of terminology, it is daily becoming more difficult to separate the categories known as text editor, word processor (WP), text formatter, and desktop publisher (DTP). There are certainly extremes that can be identified, but in between, word processors are now offering sophisticated features, such as graphics and multiple fonts, formerly reserved for text formatters and DTP packages. The advent of the low-cost laser printer has expanded the very meaning of WP.

It is, perhaps, wiser to ignore the label on the box, and just examine the feature list. The common complaint is "raging featurism": that word processors are becoming bloated with features that are rarely needed for the average letter writer or even for the novelist and technical writer. In a highly competitive field, the marketeers have clearly decided that "features sell," and if the price is right, users can simply ignore the unused 2Mb's worth of bells and whistles occupying their disks.

There is no doubt where ed sits in this fuzzy taxonomy: ed is a pleasantly primitive *line editor* at the bottom of the heap with no pretensions beyond its humble station. A line editor is so called because the unit of change is one line of text at a time. Its origin is the early Unix teletypewriter, the only available terminal at the time.

Contrast this with a *screen editor,* such as vi, where you control one screenful of your text at a time. You can scroll up and down, move to any character in any line in any page, and see directly the effect of your changes.

Unix Text Editors

Several text editors are now usually bundled with Unix: ed, ex, and vi (written at UC Berkeley by Bill Joy, who went on to help start Sun Microsystems). You may also have restricted or learner's versions of these called red, edit, view, and vedit. In addition, Unix often comes with the troff text-formatting program (written by

Joseph Ossanna) or one of its many variants. troff (pronounced tee-roff) and its successor nroff (pronounced en-roff) are programmable formatters that convert text files to a format suitable for typesetting machines. They are the forerunners of the DTP revolution in the PC market.

Outside vendors offer a variety of text editors, word processors, and DTP packages that provide progressively more features than the equivalent bundled offerings. The most popular text editor (certainly among programmers, whose needs are rather peculiar) is emacs, originally devised by Richard Stallman and ported to Unix by James Gosling, available in commercial versions from CCA and Unipress. There is now a "free" GNU version of emacs available from Stallman's FSF (Free Software Foundation)—you pay only for the cost of the medium. (The acronym GNU, by the way, is recursive: **G**nu is **N**ot **U**nix.)

Several of the popular PC word processors have also been ported to Unix. SCO offers Microsoft Word 5.0 and the Lyrix word processor, both geared for multiuser applications.

Why ed?

> **NOTE** The Unix ed bears some resemblance to the DOS edlin editor.

If your site offers one of the modern text editors or WP systems mentioned above, you may wonder if this chapter on the old-fashioned ed is going to be worthwhile. I can offer four reasons why you should at least know the rudiments of ed:

- Wherever you go in the Unix world, dear old reliable ed will be found, working in the same way for the Bourne, C, and Korn shells without regional dialectal variations.

- It is easy to learn and retain the basic steps of ed for those simple file creations and quick-fixes that crop up—short shell scripts and login profiles, for example.

- ed introduces the joys of the *regular expression*, a construct that has applications in other Unix areas such as grep (a pattern-searching utility) and sed (a versatile stream editor), both useful in shell programming and other applications.

- ed forms the basis of other editors, so the commands are useful elsewhere (in vi for example).

Starting with ed

Before we delve into the syntax, let's see a simple ed session:

```
$ cd
$ ed richard.iii
?richard.iii
a
Now is the winter of our discontent
Made glorious summer by this sun of York,
.
w
78
q
$ _
```

We now check the effect of the above sequence.

```
$ ls -l richard.iii
-rw------- 1 stan group 78 Jun 17 17:35 richard.iii
$ wc richard.iii
richard.iii 2 15 78
$ cat richard.iii
Now is the winter of our discontent
Made glorious summer by this sun of York,
$ _
```

Let's review this session line by line. The cd command ensures that you are in your home directory before you start creating and editing files.

When you enter ed followed by a space and a file name that does *not* exist, the screen echoes the name preceded by a query, ?, leaving the cursor on the next line. The ? is ed's standard way of saying, "What's that? I don't understand." Typing an h after an ed query will invoke a short explanation, such as "cannot open input file."

I chose the file name richard.iii on the reasonable assumption that you would not have such a file in your home directory. Invoking ed with no file name or with an existing file gives slightly different results, as you'll see in a moment.

After entering this file name, the cursor waits on the next line underneath the ?. There is no $ prompt. You are now running ed and ed is quite taciturn—the cursor is your only prompt.

You start in *command mode,* with ed awaiting a command. Typing a (lowercase is essential), followed by Enter, invokes the *text-entry* command. In text-entry mode (also known as *input* or *append* mode), any text you type (in our case, the two lines of Shakespeare) is added to a special buffer file. You are actually editing a temporary copy of your original file in a file named, with good reason, buffer. Your original file is not immediately affected, a fact that will gain in significance as we proceed. There is only one buffer file, by the way, so ed can only edit one file at a time.

After pressing Enter on the final line, you type a period and then press Enter again. A text line with a solitary, leading period tells ed that you have finished entering text and wish to terminate the append mode. The cursor now awaits your next command. You type w, meaning *write,* and ed writes the text in your buffer to a new file, richard.iii. This action is often referred to as *saving* your edits. The number 78 that appears tells you how many bytes (including newlines) have been written (saved) to disk. The cursor again prompts you for another command.

Typing a q (for the quit command) ends the session. You exit ed and return to your normal shell prompt.

You can now confirm that the file richard.iii does indeed exist and contains the text you typed. The ls -l command establishes that you have read and write permission. wc gives you line, word, and character counts. (Note that the 78 in both the ls and wc responses matches the byte count given after the write command.) The cat command provides the ultimate proof that ed works!

There are several important lessons in this simple ed application. The text in your buffer will be lost if you enter q (quit) before w (write). ed will warn you with a cryptic ? if you have changed your buffer and try to quit before saving your edits. If you really want to jettison your edits, you enter q again to quit.

If you haven't changed your buffer, ed will let you quit without hindrance. (If you quit with a Q, though, any changes will be lost without warning.) On balance, it's better not to take chances: develop the habit of saving your buffer before quitting. With a long text entry it is customary to write to disk regularly in case a malfunction ruins your buffer.

On the plus side, the buffered approach lets you *undo* your most recent edit. Pressing u nullifies your last editing action.

ed is what is known as a *modal* editor. When you type an a in command mode, the effect is different from typing an a in text-entry mode. The command mode a simply switches modes: it puts you into text-entry (append) mode without sending the character "a" to the buffer. Once you are in text-entry mode, typing a sends "a" to the buffer without affecting the mode. Staying alert of your current mode takes some practice, since ed is not overly informative. If you inadvertently type normal text while you are in command mode, ed will respond with ? after the newline, since the text line is unlikely to be a recognizable command (most ed commands are very short). However, if you forgetfully try to enter commands while in text-entry mode, the buffer will gladly accept single-line entries of "a", "w", and "q" as though they were text, and your resulting file will be weird. A single period at the start of a fresh line is the only way to exit text-entry mode and return to command mode.

Your first ed session simply created a file from keyboard entries, a task that could be equally accomplished with cat or echo and redirection. In the next session, you will see how to display and change individual lines in a file.

Your Lines Are Numbered

ed internally assigns consecutive line numbers to your text buffer. The first line is numbered 1, a statement that beginners may find stunningly obvious—however, in Unix and C, many sequences start at 0, so you must never jump to conclusions!

You use these line numbers in many editing situations. When in command mode, the command *n*p will display the *n*th line if it exists. If *n* is greater than the last line, ed responds with a ?. You can even omit the p, so that typing the command 2 defaults to 2p, which will display the second line. (Note that the abbreviation p for print is a remnant from the early Unix days when terminals produced hard copy.) You can also display ranges of lines as follows:

1,3p	Displays lines 1 to 3 inclusively
4,12p	Displays lines 4 to 12 inclusively
5,5p	Displays line 5 (same as 5p or 5)

and so on. The number before the comma must be less than or equal to the number after the comma. If you try 7,6p, for instance, you'll get the familiar ? response.

The symbol $ has the special meaning "last line" in ed's command mode. So even if you are not certain how many lines you have in the buffer, you can display the following:

$p   Displays the last line

1,$p   Displays all lines (from first to last)

4,$p   Displays from line 4 to the last line

and so on. A useful variant on the p command is the n (numbering) command. It works like p but also displays the line number on the left:

```
$ ed richard.iii
78
1,$p
Now is the winter of our discontent
Made glorious summer by this sun of York,
1,$n
1    Now is the winter of our discontent
2    Made glorious summer by this sun of York,
$,1p
?
_
```

The line numbers and the symbol $ are known as *addresses,* for obvious reasons. The general form of many ed commands can be written as follows:

[*address,address*][*command_letter(s)*] [*filename*]

where the default command letter is usually p for display. The default address(es) vary according to the command. For example, for the w command used in the first session, the default address argument is 1,$, meaning that w and 1,$w are equivalent: both forms write all lines to disk. The file name is used only with read and write commands. The default is the *currently remembered* file name, usually the file being edited. I'll elaborate shortly.

The first address range argument can also appear as a search expression, but for the moment I'll concentrate on the simpler line number form of addressing.

w   Writes all lines from buffer to "current" disk file

1,$w   Same as w above

    2,2w newdat   Writes line 2 to disk file newdat

    3,6w   Writes lines 3 to 6 to "current" disk file

Specifying nonexistent lines or illegal ranges invokes the ? response, as in the previous example, and no data is written. If the specified file does not exist, it will be created. If it already exists, it will be overwritten, so take care!

No spaces are allowed between the address part and the command letter. The rule is that depending on the command letter you enter (a, p, w, and so on), the action will be applied to the line(s) specified (or implied by default) in the address part, or perhaps to the line(s) following the current address, as explained in the following section.

Your Current Address

Next comes the tricky bit! At any stage in your ed session, a special pointer called the *current address* keeps track of which line number your editing has reached. Usually this is the line most recently read or changed. It is vital to know where your current address is since many commands, by default, affect the buffer at the line immediately following the current address.

Full-screen editors let you move the cursor to the point of change, but with ed you cannot directly see the cursor's position relative to the text buffer. Also, most commands change the current address either directly or indirectly, so care and practice are needed. Luckily, it is quite easy to display the current line or its number, or both.

The current address is always represented by the period symbol (not to be confused with the period used to terminate text-entry mode). You can use the period, always pronounced as *dot*, in any of the address arguments as though it were a line number. So, you can use any of the following commands to display the current line:

    .p

    .,.p

    .,. (default is p)

    . (default is p)

    p (default is .,.)

The most convenient of the five "display current line" variants is the single dot. Likewise, you can combine the dot with other addresses to display a range of lines. For instance, to display all lines from the current line to the last line, enter

    .,$p

To display all lines from the current line to line 5 (assuming that the current line comes before line 5), enter

    .,5p

The address pairs 1,$ and .,$ are so common that the following shorthand notations are allowed:

    ,p is the same as 1,$p, which displays the first to last lines.

    ;p is the same as .,$p, which displays the current to last lines.

All the display variants change the current address to whichever line displays last. After .,5p, for example, the current address becomes 5. A common Unix idiom for this is "the dot value is 5."

You can check your dot value using the = command:

    [address]=

displays the line address of the address argument. With no address argument, = defaults to $=, which displays the address of the last line. The command .= displays the address of your current line. The default to $= is rather unusual: difficult to justify, and easy to overlook. The usual ed address default is dot, the current line, but with = you have a quirky exception. Sorry about that.

The command 1= is legal but hardly useful: it returns a 1, the same address as the argument! So, = (meaning $=) and .= are the two most useful address location commands. (Later, in the "Patterns and Searches" section, you'll see some other applications.) Note carefully that = does not change the current dot value. Try the following example:

```
$ ed richard.iii
78
.=
2
1,$p
```

```
Now is the winter of our discontent
Made glorious summer by this sun of York,
,p
Now is the winter of our discontent
Made glorious summer by this sun of York,
.=
2
1p
Now is the winter of our discontent
.=
1
$=
2
=
2
.=
1
q
$ _
```

Immediately afer loading a file with ed, the current address is set to the last line loaded, namely line 2. This explains why the first .= gives 2. When you display line 1 with the 1p command, the current address becomes line 1. The = command with no address gives the same result as $=, namely line 2, the address of the last line.

Adding More Text

Let's try the a (append) command to add some lines to the Duke of Gloucester's soliloquy. The syntax is

[*address*]a

followed by your typed additions, then a period when you want to return to command mode. This sequence adds your typed text to the line following *address*, the default being the current line (the dot value). The combination *n*a will add text after line *n*, while a or the equivalent .a will add lines after the current line. In all cases, any lines that get "pushed down" will be renumbered. Before using a, therefore, you should make sure you know where you are and where you want your insertions to go.

You may have spotted a catch. What if you want to add text *before* the first line? 1a will not help, because that starts the insertion after line 1. The answer is to use a "fictitious" address: 0a is interpreted as "append text before line 1."

Here's a sequence to give you some practice with these new commands:

```
$ ed richard.iii
78
.=
2
a
And all the clouds that loured upon our house
In the deep bosom of the ocean buried.
.
w
163
.=
4
1,$n
1       Now is the winter of our discontent
2       Made glorious summer by this sun of York,
3       And all the clouds that loured upon our house
4       In the deep bosom of the ocean buried.
-1p
And all the clouds that loured upon our house
.=
3
0a
Enter Richard, Duke of Gloucester, solus

RICHARD

.
w
214
1,$n
1       Enter Richard, Duke of Gloucester, solus
2
3       RICHARD
4
5       Now is the winter of our discontent
6       Made glorious summer by this sun of York,
7       And all the clouds that loured upon our house
8       In the deep bosom of the ocean buried.
.=
```

```
8
-1p
And all the clouds that loured upon our house
.=
7
q
$ _
```

The first append, a (meaning .a), adds text after the current line, as confirmed by the numbered listing. The second append, 0a, inserts new text before the first line, causing the lines to be renumbered. I used w immediately after each addition to illustrate the good habit of saving your work as you go along.

I've slipped in another address variant: -1p will display the line before the current one, and (naturally) resets the dot value to the line just displayed. The following are entirely equivalent because of the various address and command defaults:

```
.-1p
.-1
-1
-p
-
```

As you become familiar with these defaults, you'll find yourself using the shortest format in common situations.

The same trick works for + and - with other numbers and addresses:

.+1p   Displays the line after the current line. Same as .+1, .+

.+5p   Displays the line that is 5 lines beyond the current line. Same as .+5 and +5

.-6p   Displays the line that is 6 lines before the current one. Same as .-6 and -6.

$-7   Displays the line that is 7 lines from the end.

Changing Your Text

Now that you have gained some familiarity with the ed address arguments for appending and displaying, you'll find the following commands easy to use. They all

perform the various tasks associated with text editing: inserting, deleting, moving, copying, changing, and collating selected portions of your text.

Patterns and Searches

A major concern when changing text with a "blind" line editor is determining where you are. ed has a simple search facility that lets you locate the occurrence of a given pattern. For example, /sun/p or /sun/ will search forward from the line following the current line and print (display) the first line containing the string "sun":

```
/sun/p
Made glorious summer by this sun of York,
```

Note that the p is optional, being the default. Also, the match is case-sensitive, so "Sun" will not be found—later, you'll see how to vary this behavior. Even the second / is optional provided nothing else appears after the pattern.

To determine on which line the match occurred, you can use /sun/=, which displays the number of the matched line. If the search reaches the end of the buffer without a match, the search wraps around to the start and continues to the current line. If no match is found, ed complains with a ?. If a match *is* found, the dot value is set to the matching line. This means that you can repeat the forward search by repeating the entry /sun/ (or /sun/p). A shortcut is to use // to repeat a search. ed takes // to mean "the most recently used pattern" (more on this later).

To search backwards from the line preceding the current line towards the start of the buffer, you enter ?sun?p. You can repeat a backwards search with ??. As with forward searches, ed wraps around the search to ensure that the whole buffer can be scanned.

Note that /sun/ will match any occurrence of "sun" including "Datsun" and "sunshine". To limit the search to whole words, you can include spaces in the pattern: / sun /.

Using *regular expressions* in the search pattern permits more complex matching of strings, as you'll see later.

The line addresses you reach with a search can provide the address argument(s) for any ed command:

    1,/sun/p   Displays from line 1 to next line with "sun" match

/sun/,$p	Displays from next "sun" line to end
/sun/,/moon/p	Displays from next "sun" line to next "moon" line

I'll return to this theme when you've seen a few more commands at work.

Inserting Text

The i (insert) command works like a but inserts the following text immediately *before* the given address. Use the following syntax for this command:

[*address*]i

You must type a solitary period to exit input mode. The default address is dot (.), the current line. 1i and 0a have the same effect: insertion occurs before the first line. Subsequent lines in your buffer are renumbered. The value of dot is set to the last line number inserted.

A useful variant is the ip command, which works like i but also displays the new current line. In fact, p can be tagged on to many other commands; the result is that after the normal command action, a .p command is performed.

You can use i with the pattern search mentioned earlier: if you enter /Yours etc/i, and follow this command with text, then a dot, that text will be inserted immediately before the first line that contains the string "Yours etc".

Deleting Lines of Text

The d (delete) command deletes the line(s) specified in the address(es) argument. The syntax for this command is as follows:

[*address*,*address*]d

The default is

.,.

which deletes the current line. Subsequent lines are renumbered and the value of dot is set to the line following the line deleted. A natural exception to this rule is when you delete the last line: the current line becomes the new last line in the buffer. For example, 1d deletes the first line; the former second line becomes the new first line. 1,$d has the dramatic effect of deleting every line in your buffer. Of course, if

you change your mind, you can use the u (undo) command. In any case, your original file is still intact unless you used w after clearing the buffer.

Using the search pattern trick is very popular:

/sun/d   Deletes the next line with a "sun" match

?sun?d   Deletes the first line before the current line that contains "sun"

The dp variant deletes the current line (just like d), then displays the new current line (the one after the deleted line).

Moving Lines of Text

The m (move) command moves one or more lines of text to a fresh position in the buffer (renumbering the lines accordingly). This command uses the following syntax:

[s1_address,s2_address]md_address

You specify the address range of the lines to be moved using *s1_address* for the starting address and *s2_address* for the ending address. To move a single line, you can use either *s1_address,s1_address*, or save time with the one argument, *s1_address*. The default is . , . or equivalently, . (this moves the current line). After the m, you specify a single destination line number, *d_address*. The lines being moved will be inserted *after* the *d_address*. Note that 0 is a valid *d_address*—it moves the target lines to the beginning of the buffer.

Here are a few examples using the move command:

1,2m4   Moves lines 1 and 2 to just after present line 4. Previous line 3 becomes line 1, previous line 1 becomes line 3, and so on. The new current line is line 3.

1,1m6   Moves line 1 to just after the present line 6.

1m6   Same as 1,1m6.

4m0   Moves line 4 ahead of present line 1.

m+   Switches the current line with the following line. (This works because the defaults are . , .m.+1).

m$ Moves the current line to the end.

m0   Moves the current line to the beginning.

After the move, the dot value is set to the new address of the last line that was moved.

There is an important restriction on the value of *d_address*: it must not fall within the *s1_address*, *s2_address* range. So 1,4m3 is not allowed.

Moving is equivalent to a deletion followed by an addition of text. The mp variant is useful: it moves the selected lines, then displays the last line that was moved.

Copying Text with the Transfer Command

The t (transfer) command transfers (copies) one or more lines of text to a fresh position in the buffer (renumbering the lines accordingly). It works just like m, using the same syntax, but leaves the s1–s2 lines *in situ*.

You specify the address range of the lines to be copied in *s1_address*, *s2_address*. As with m, you need only specify one address to copy a single line. The default is .,. or . (which copies the current line). After the t you specify a single destination line number, *d_address*. The lines being copied will be inserted *after* the *d_address*. Note that 0 is a valid *d_address*—it copies the target lines to the beginning of the buffer.

There is an important restriction on the value of *d_address*: it must not fall within the *s1_address*, *s2_address* range. So 2,5t3 is not allowed.

The dot value is set to the new address of the last line that was copied.

Common transfer combinations include

t.   Duplicates the current line

t$ Copies the current line at the end of the buffer

1,t Duplicates the whole buffer at the end

The tp variant should be noted: it copies the selected lines, then displays the last line that was copied.

You may wonder why t was chosen for copy mode. By a quirk of the English language, c also stands for change, as explained in the next section.

Deleting and Inserting Text with the Change Command

The c (for change) command deletes the line(s) given by the argument address range, then replaces them with typed text. The c command takes this syntax:

```
[s1_address,s2_address]c
```

followed by the text you want to insert, and a single-line period to exit text-entry mode. It is equivalent to a deletion followed by an insertion of text. The default address is . , . (which deletes the current line and inserts text). Remember always that the address arguments can be line numbers, symbols such as dot and $, or search strings such as /sun/ and ?sun?, or any reasonable combination of these.

After the change, the current line (dot value) becomes the address of the last line you entered. As with any edit that rearranges the lines in your buffer, c renumbers all affected lines.

The combination cp is allowed—it changes then displays the current line. (Do not confuse this command with the Unix cp (copy) command!) This is a good place to recall the u (undo) command. Immediately after an ill-advised change, you can restore the status quo with a u. Even better, you can use up and reassuringly display the restored line:

```
.=
21

.
This is text line 21
c
I'm changing line 21
.
up
This is text line 21
```

Deleting and Inserting Text with the Substitute Command

The c command is fine when a line needs extensive modification. When you want to alter just a few words, however, retyping the whole line is counterproductive. ed offers the versatile—and therefore quite complex!—s (substitute) command, which allows you to replace selected parts of a line. The full syntax is daunting at first sight, but I'll break it down into manageable sections as I proceed:

    [s1_address,s2_address]s/find_exp/repl_exp/[g|N]

> **NOTE**   Remember, g | N means "either g or N but not both."

The s command lets you make changes without having to delete and revamp a whole line. Occurrences of the "find" string *find_exp* can be replaced with the replacement string *repl_exp* in various ways dictated by the arguments you supply. For the moment, I'll assume that *find_exp* is a normal text string that you want to change. Later on, when I cover *regular expressions,* you'll see how more complex searches and replacements can be made.

The first argument is the familiar address range; this range specifies those parts of the file in which you wish the substitutions to be made. The default address is

    . , .

so that by default you will be replacing strings in the current line only. Thus the command s/sun/moon/ will replace the *first* (leftmost) occurrence of "sun" in the current line with the word "moon". Note carefully that if you had more than one "sun" in the current line, only the first one would be changed.

To continue with the replacement, you can type /sun/s/sun/moon/. This entry searches forward from the previous match to the next "sun" and, if one is found, it will be changed to "moon". As I explained in the "Patterns and Searches" section, you need to picture the first /sun/ as a kind of address argument. To reduce keystrokes, you can repeat the replacement as follows:

    /sun/s//moon/

The empty // expression is taken as the most recently used search pattern—in other words, // "remembers" the pattern /sun/.

You can also change all occurrences of "sun" in the current line, by using the g (global) suffix as follows:

```
s/sun/moon/g
```

Similarly,

```
1,$s/sun/moon/
```

will go through the whole file replacing the *first* occurrence of "sun" on each line to "moon", while

```
1,$s/sun/moon/g
```

would do a complete "sun" to "moon" switch for *all* occurrences throughout the file. This last format gives what is usually called a *global* replacement in current WP jargon. The ed meaning of global is much less expansive: the g suffix means "line global" not "file global." The address range argument controls how many lines are affected; the g suffix controls whether more than one occurrence of the find string in each target line will be replaced. (You'll meet another use of g as a global command later.)

Note that the p suffix can be usefully added to display the last line in which a replacement occurred:

```
1,$s/sun/moon/gp
```

The value of dot, by the way, is set to the last line for which a match and replacement was made. If no match is found, the dot value is unchanged, and ed will report an error with the customary ?.

Yet more flexibility is provided for those occasions when you want to replace just the second or third (or whatever) occurrence of a string in one or more lines. If there are four "sun" strings in the current line, s/sun/moon/3 will replace the third "sun" with "moon". The final number can range from 1 to 512, the default being 1 (first occurrence).

You should be aware that ed's replacement strategy is quite implacable: the "sun" in "sunny" would be matched, giving you a possibly spurious "moonny". To avoid such calamities, you can include spaces in either or both strings:

```
s/ sun / moon /
```

Another useful trick is the special shorthand character & in the replacement string. This is interpreted by ed as the current find string. For instance,

```
s/ sun/ & and moon/
```

would replace " sun" with " sun and moon". To turn off this special meaning of & when you want to insert real ampersands, you use the traditional Unix escape route—the backslash \:

```
1,$s/ and / \& /g
```

This replaces every " and " with " & " throughout the file.

I'll show you several more elaborate substitution tricks later on when I explain the use of regular expressions.

Joining Two or More Lines of Text

The j (join) command combines a group of adjacent lines by stripping out the intervening newline characters. The result is one "long" line containing the characters taken from the lines given by the argument address range. This command will (naturally) ignore a single address: you need at least two lines for "join" to make sense, as shown in the following syntax line:

```
address1,address2j
```

The default argument is interesting: ., .+1j joins the current line with the following line, as does simply entering j. The current line (dot value) ends up as the address of the newly joined line. Subsequent lines (if any) are renumbered.

You can use the jp combination to join and display the newly formed line.

The List Command

The l (for list) command is very much like the p command. Even the syntax is the same:

```
[address1,address2]l
```

These are the only differences:

- Characters that do not normally appear onscreen, such as tab, backspace, and control codes, are given unambiguous visible symbols.

- Lines too long for your screen are *folded,* or, in other words, clipped and shown on separate lines.

As with p, you can combine the l command with many other edit commands, al, cl, il, and so on, with obvious results.

Labeling a Line with the Mark Command

The k (mar*k*) command assigns a single-letter *x* as a mark (or label) to the line given by *address*. The command uses this syntax:

[*address*]k*x*

The default .k marks the current line. The letter *x* must be lowercase. The current line (dot value) is unchanged. Once you have marked a line, you use the expression '*x* at any time as an address argument without having to know its line number. For example, entering kz marks the current line as z. Even after extensive editing, the command 'z,$p will display text from the marked line to the end. Using an unassigned mark or a mark assigned to a subsequently deleted line will invoke the dreaded ? signal.

Marking is especially useful when handling large portions of text (compare the "block marking" features of most WP packages):

/sun/ka	Marks "sun" line as a
/moon/kb	Marks "moon" line as b
'a,'bp	Displays the marked block
'a,'bm$	Moves the block to the end
'a,'bd	Deletes the block
u	Restores the block

Reading Files

There are many editing situations where you want to collate two existing files. The r (for read) command lets you read from any file and insert its contents into the

current edit buffer immediately following the given argument address. The command follows this syntax:

[*address*]r [*filename*]

The default here is $r, which adds the contents of *filename* to the end of your buffer. The dot value is set to the last line read into the buffer.

The familiar 0 address format, 0r, is used for adding file data at the beginning of the buffer. Assuming the file name is found and read successfully, ed responds with the number of bytes added to your buffer:

r footnote	Appends contents of file footnote at end of buffer (same as $r footnote)
78	Confirms 78 bytes added
w	Saves buffer
254	Confirms total bytes saved

If you do not supply a file name, ed uses the *currently remembered* file name, if such exists. The general idea is that ed keeps track of previous file names used and offers them as useful defaults. The f (for file-name) command can be used either to discover or to alter the currently remembered file name:

```
f
stan.data
f footnote
f
footnote
```

The r and w commands both default to the currently remembered file name, if any. You'll get an error, of course, if you try to default to a nonexistent file name.

If you invoke ed without a file name, the first file name you use in any command becomes the currently remembered file name. Thereafter, though, r and w commands do not change the currently remembered file name. For example, if you entered the following commands

```
$ ed
f
```

no file name appears, since there is no file name for ed to remember. However, if you next enter the command r footnote, invoking f results in the file name foot-note appearing onscreen; footnote becomes the currently remembered file name. Say you make changes to the text of the footnote file. If you enter the command w, your changes will be saved to footnote, since the default file name argument to w is the currently remembered file name. Remember, if you want to save the edited text to a different file, say temp.save, you enter the command

```
w temp.save
```

Entering f after this operation still brings up the file name footnote, since you have not changed the currently remembered file name.

In addition to f there is another command, e (for edit), that changes the currently remembered file name. The next section discusses this command.

The e Command

The e and E (edit) commands let you switch the file you are editing during an ed session without leaving and reinvoking ed. Use the following syntax with these commands:

```
e [filename]
E [filename]
```

e deletes your current buffer and reloads it with the given file name. If you have changed your buffer without saving your changes (shame on you), ed warns you with a ?. With E, you get no such warning, but otherwise the two forms, e and E, work the same.

The default file name that you load is the currently remembered file name, as explained in the previous section. You'll get an error if no such default has been previously established. Recall that you can always use the f (file-name) command to check the current default and change it if necessary. However, unlike r and w, when you use e with a real file name argument, that file name becomes the currently remembered file name. Take a look at the following example:

```
$ ed stan.data
654
a
```

Text is added to the file `stan.data`; then the following commands are entered:

```
.
w
750
f
stan.data
```

ed remembers this file name, as it was invoked with the ed command at the start of the editing session. Entering e now would default to e `stan.data`. However, if you enter a new file name after e, that file name becomes the currently remembered file name:

```
e new.data
365
f
new.data
```

Regular Expressions

Regular expressions are special strings of characters that you create in order to locate *matching* pieces of text. The principle extends (and modifies) the familiar idea of wildcard symbols to include quite complex matching possibilities.

A regular expression is a sequence of ordinary (or nonspecial) characters and special characters (also known as metacharacters). The earlier searches you made with `/sun/` were, in fact, simple examples of regular expressions with no special characters (apart from the delimiters). Nonspecial characters just match themselves, so that `/sun/` simply matches "sun."

You have already seen how the shell treats certain characters such as *, ?, and > as special. However, ed's special characters have their own special flavor, so some care is needed. For example, some characters are special to ed only in certain contexts, and the meaning of a special character can vary according to its context!

The characters that ed's regular expressions may treat as special are \ ^ $. [ ] * and &, plus the pairs \(\) \{ \} and [: :].

You use these characters in combination with ordinary text strings in order to search your files for matches. When a match is found, ed allows you to perform any number of editing functions using the g (global) command. Before I show you the

g command in action, I need to show you how to construct a regular expression. The best approach is to study some annotated examples:

Dear   Matches "Dear" anywhere in the file

^Dear   Matches "Dear" only at the *start* of any line

The ^ has two special meanings. As the first symbol inside [ ], it means NOT (that is, it reverses the sense of the match)—more on this usage anon. If the ^ symbol appears anywhere after the first position inside [ ], it has no special meaning. Used outside [ ], ^ means "try to match the following text at the beginning of a line." If you need to search for a literal ^, you can "turn off" (or *escape*) the special meaning with the escape symbol \: \^Dear matches "^Dear" anywhere in the file. This is a general rule: a special symbol placed immediately after \ loses its special meaning. This rule is particularly important because of the large number of special characters used in ed. Later examples will clarify this point.

Similarly, $ means "match the preceding text at the end of line." For instance, sincerely$ matches "sincerely" only at the *end* of any line. Again, note that $ loses its special "end-of-line match" meaning when used inside [ ], or when escaped: sincerely\$ matches "sincerely$" anywhere in the file.

You can combine ^ and $ as follows: ^contents$ matches any line containing only the string "contents". In other words, a match is sought with "contents" at both the start and end of a line. A useful variant is ^$, which matches any empty line (one with a newline only). There is, by the way, no regular expression that matches a newline character.

The next two examples show the escape mechanism at work:

\^\$ Matches "^$"

\\   Matches "\"

The period has yet another meaning in ed! In regular expressions, a period outside [ ] matches any single character:

i.m   Matches "iAm", "ibm", "i m", and so on, but NOT "i<newline>m"

i\.m   Matches "i.m" only

i?m   Matches "i?m" only

Note carefully that the wildcard ?, used by the shell to match any single character, has a different application in ed's regular expressions. The period in ed's regular expressions works just like the ? in shell commands. ed uses the ? either as a normal character or to control backward searches (as you saw earlier).

The behavior of the wildcard asterisk, *, is also different when you move from shell commands to ed's regular expressions. First, note that ed's * is only treated as a special character when it is used outside [ ]. Second, recall that the shell matches a * with any string including the empty string (but excluding file names beginning with a period).

However, with ed, the regular expression *x** (where *x* is any single-character regular expression) matches any number of occurrences of *x* including *none*. In other words, *x** matches the empty string, *x*, *xx*, *xxx*, and so on. This takes some getting used to, especially if you've spent too many years with MS-DOS. Note the following example: HEL* matches "HE", "HEL", "HELL", "HELLL", and so on. The first match seems weird! But HEL* matches "HE" followed by *no* occurrences of "L". With MS-DOS, HEL* would not match "HE". DOS would certainly match "HEL", "HELL", and so on, but, unlike ed, it would also match "HELP", "HELxyz", and so on.

To obtain a DOS-like * match, you need the following combination:

    .*

matches any string not containing a newline (so it also matches the empty string). The dot will match any single character, but with the modifying *, the match is with any number of any characters, including none. In this example, a.*S matches "aS", "aRubbishS", and so on. The only character between "a" and "S" that would escape a match is a newline. ed, recall, is a line-based editor, so a regular expression never "straddles" a line.

I've mentioned that ^ $. and * have special meanings only when used outside [ ] and without a preceding \. The reason is that characters inside [ ] are interpreted differently. Consider the following examples:

[35Z]   Matches "3", "5", or "Z"

X-[180]   Matches "X-1", "X-8", or "X-0"

Q[.21]p   Matches "Q.p", "Q2p", or "Q1p"

[m^*$]   Matches "m", "^", "*", or "$"

The idea is that a match is made with any *one* of the characters found inside the square brackets. A period or $ anywhere inside [ ] are taken as normal symbols. ^ and * are also taken literally *unless* they are the *first* characters after the [. When these two symbols occur first inside [ ], the search is logically inverted:

i[^b]m   Matches "iam", "i9m", and so on but does not match "ibm"

i[*b]m   Same as i[^b]m

i[^bc]m   Matches all "ixm" combinations *except* "ibm" and "icm"

If you are seeking a match with a range of ASCII characters, you can spell them out in full, or to save keystrokes, you can use the dash (–) to form a *range:*

[123456]   Matches "1", "2", … or "6"

[1–6]   Matches "1", "2", … or "6"

The dash trick only works with symbols in ascending ASCII sequence:

[a–z]   Matches any lowercase letter

[a–A]   Illegal, since "a" follows "A" in ASCII value

[9–<]   Matches "9", ":", "=", and "<"

You can include any number of ranges within [ ], and you can also combine ranges with the ^ symbol:

[A–C0–2]   Matches any string starting with "A", "B", "C", "0", "1", or "2"

[^0123456789]   Matches any nondigit

[^0–9]   Same as [^0123456789]

But, I hear you cry, what if I want to search for -, [, or] in a range of characters? The following examples should explain the possibilities:

`[ ]0-2]`	Matches "]", "0", "1", or "2". (The first] immediately after the opening [is treated as nonspecial.)
`A[-0-2]`	Matches "A-", "A0", "A1", or "A2". (The - immediately after [loses its special meaning.)
`A[^-0-2]`	Matches "A" followed by any character other than "-", "0", "1", "2", or newline. (The - immediately after [^ loses its special meaning.)
`array[02-4]\[[^0-3]\]`	Matches "array0[6]", "array4[Z]", and so on. (The second [and third] are taken literally because of \.)
`^["(][Tt].*["")]$`	Matches any line that starts with a quote mark or an open parenthesis followed by a "T" or "t", and ends with a quote mark or a close parenthesis.

Having seen how regular expressions are formed and how they match text strings, it's time to apply them in typical editing situations. First, let's look again at the s (substitute) command.

Substitute Command Revisited

Recall the syntax of the s command:

`[s1_address,s2_address]s/find_exp/repl_exp/[g|N]`

In our first explanation, *find_exp* was a simple piece of text that needed replacement; for instance, `1,$s/sun/moon/g` replaces all occurrences of "sun" with "moon" in all lines.

I can now confirm that s works with regular expressions in the *find_exp* fields. The find string "sun" is in fact a regular expression, howbeit of the simplest variety with no special effects. The replacement string, *repl_exp*, however, cannot be a regular

expression. *repl_exp* does allow the special use of &, as explained earlier. Let's look at the following example:

```
1,$s/sun/& and moon/g
```

This replaces all occurrences of "sun" with "sun and moon" in all lines. The & in this command line is set to equal the matched *find_exp*. The &, of course, is not that useful in the above example, since we know in advance that it will set to "sun" if any matches occur. But, suppose you had this command line:

```
1,$s/Ch[1-9]/& Appendix/g
```

This replaces "Ch*n*" with "Ch*n* Appendix" for *n* = 1–9. Here the & string assumes different (and appropriate) values for each match. The regular expression [1-9] matches any one numeral from 1 to 9. With this and similar tricks, you can make quite sophisticated, selective text substitutions.

Even more flexibility is available using the g and G (global) commands, and their "inverses" v and V. Read on.

Global Commands

The g (global) command has the following syntax:

```
[s1_address,s2_address]g/reg_exp/[command_list]
```

Briefly, the command means: "Find each line that contains a match for *reg_exp*, and perform *command_list* on it."

Unlike the s command (which defaults to . , .), the default address range argument for g is 1 , $—the whole buffer. The g command, like s, searches the address range (from low to high line numbers) seeking matches with the regular expression given in *reg_exp*. For each line providing a match, the dot value is set to that line; then g performs whatever ed commands are listed in the final argument, *command_list*. If you omit this list, a p (display) command is assumed.

The direction of search is controlled by the choice of the character (known as the *delimiter*) used to surround the *reg_exp*. In the last example, we used / to give us a *forward* search from the line following the current line towards the end of the file; if required by the address range, the search will wrap around to the start of the buffer

and continue to the current line. This ensures that a 1,$ search, for example, will scan the whole buffer. For a backwards search, you use ? in place of /:

```
[s1_address,s2_address]g?reg_exp?[command_list]
```

Here, the search starts with the line preceding the current line, moves to the start of the buffer, then wraps around to the end (if necessary) to complete its scan at the current line.

In a typical application, the *command_list* would contain p, d, m, t, or s commands, so that displays, deletions, moves, transfers, and substitutions are made only on lines that meet certain criteria determined by *reg_exp*. For example, g/^Para/s/;/:/gp will replace every ";" with ":" on every line that begins with "Para". The p ensures that you see what is going on.

A useful construct, similar to the & used in the *repl_exp*, is the special (and rather strange) *null* regular expression, //. As you saw briefly in the "Patterns and Searches" section, this is interpreted as the most recently "remembered" matching pattern. For complex regular expressions, this can be a great time-saver:

```
g/^Para[0-9]$/s//New Heading/p
```

The substitution find expression will be taken as /^Para[0-9]$/. You must not confuse the regular expression // with the empty replacement string //:

```
g/^Para[0-9]$/s///p
```

Here we are replacing the matched lines ("Para0", "Para1",..., or "Para9" on a single line) with empty lines.

The g command *command_list* can contain any number of ed commands, including a, i, and c but excluding !, g, G, v, and V. Each command except the last one has to end with a \ (here used as the traditional Unix command line "extender"—you can picture it as "escaping" the following newline character):

```
g/^Para[0-9]$/d\
```

deletes matching lines.

```
r file1\
```

reads in a file.

```
a\
```

appends text; then after text is entered, followed by a dot,

```
p
```

displays the last line read.

The G version of the global command works like g with one essential difference: after finding a match, the command waits for a command to be entered via the keyboard. G is therefore called the *interactive* global command. Only one manual command may be entered, but (unlike g) a, i, and c are not allowed. You can interrupt the G command with the Del key.

Inverse Global Commands

The v and V commands work like g and G but with the pattern-matching logic reversed. Let's look at an example:

```
v/^Para[0-9]$/s/Old Heading/New Heading/p
```

Here the substitution would be made on every line that did *not* match /^Para[0-9]$/. As you can guess, some care is needed with this one! Apart from the inverted matching search, the same rules and restrictions noted for g and G apply.

Miscellaneous Commands and Switches

I end this skirmish with ed by listing a few miscellaneous commands and switches.

The Prompt Command

The P (prompt) command changes the ed prompt to *. Toggle P to remove and restore the * prompt.

```
$ ed stan.mail
78
P
*_
```

```
P
_
```

The Prompt Switch

The -p (prompt string) command, followed by a string of characters, changes the ed prompt to that string:

```
$ ed -p# stan.dat
345
# _
```

The Minus Switch

Invoking ed with a minus sign suppresses the display of byte counts when using e, r, and w commands:

```
$ ed -stan.dat

_
```

First Line Formatting

You can include a special string in the first line of your ed file that will set tab stops and a maximum line length:

```
$ ed stan.dat
345
a
<:t,4,9,13s75:>
```

This sets tabs at positions 4, 9, and 13, and sets your line length to 75 before you begin editing it. For this feature to work, your terminal must be in stty -tabs or stty tab3 mode, as explained in Chapter 6.

Escaping to the Shell with !

Without leaving ed, you can run other shell commands by using the exclamation (or *bang*) command !. For example, while in ed command mode, !date will temporarily switch you to the shell, execute the date command, display the date, then return to ed. One of the restrictions placed on red, the reduced version of ed, is that

it does not allow the ! escape trick. In the command following the !, the following special characters can be used:

% means the last remembered file name (see the f command).

! means the last used command, so that ! ! repeats the last command.

Ctype Matching

Several special sequences, called *ctype classes,* can be used in regular expressions to match general categories or ranges of characters. They all follow the general format

[:*ctype_name*:]

where *ctype_name* has any of the values listed below:

ctype	Matches
[:alpha:]	Alphabetic characters
[:upper:]	Uppercase characters
[:lower:]	Lowercase characters
[:digit:]	Digits
[:alnum:]	Alphanumeric characters
[:space:]	Spaces and tabs (whitespace)
[:print:]	Printable characters
[:punct:]	Punctuation marks
[:graph:]	Graphical characters
[:cntrl:]	Control characters

Multiple Occurrence Matching

If you follow a single-character regular expression with \{m\}, where m is an integer between 0 and 254, the match is made with *exactly m* occurrences of the single-character pattern. \{m,\} (note the comma) matches *at least m* occurrences. A

further variant is \{m, n\}, which matches any number of occurrences between m and n, inclusively. For example:

`[A-Z]\{12\}`	Matches any sequence of exactly 12 capital letters
`[0-9]\{7,\}`	Matches any sequence of at least 7 digits
`x\{3,5\}`	Matches "xxx", "xxxx", or "xxxxx"
`[:cntrl:]\{2\}`	Matches any two contiguous control codes

Summary

I've taken you quite quickly through the chief ed commands. There are several more advanced tricks that you may wish to look up in the man pages. How much you need will depend on your particular work profile. For simple changes to your profile file, you will probably need only the a, i, c, s, and d commands.

I also explained how regular expressions help you to search files for simple and complex patterns. Regular expressions will prove useful later on when I cover the text editor vi and the utilities grep and sed.

CHAPTER

NINE

Processes and Multitasking

- Unix images and processes

- Background processes using &

- Killing processes

- Checking your processes with ps

- Have a nice process

- Multicommand lines

- The sleep command

- Scheduling processes

In this chapter, I'll explore the significance of Unix's multitasking capabilities, clarify the somewhat murky terminology, and show you how you can exploit multitasking in your daily devotions.

Multijargon

Before I explain multitasking, you should be aware of two older, related terms. *Multiuser* simply means that the system can simultaneously service more than one online terminal, while *multiprogramming* implies that the system can run several programs at the same time. A multiprogramming system is not necessarily multiuser (take a single-user PC under OS/2, for example), but a multiuser system certainly needs multiprogramming. Unix, of course, is both a multiprogramming and a multiuser operating system. Naturally, to cope with several concurrent users, Unix must be installed on a system with the necessary multichannel I/O (input/output) boards.

Note that multiprogramming includes the situation where 300 users are each running `date`, as well as the situation where one user is running `date`, `who`, and `lp` at the same time.

Some computers, known as *multiprocessing* systems, achieve multiprogrammimg by using several processors (either running independently or tightly coupled), but we will be concerned with multiprogramming on a single-processor system with the aid of a suitable operating system. A multiprocessor system can literally run several programs simultaneously; with a single processor, multiprogramming is, in fact, a clever illusion. Deep down inside a single-processor system, only one machine instruction can be executed at any instant. A sufficiently powerful central processing unit (CPU), however, can devote a *time slice* to one program, then switch to service another, and so on, giving the appearance of simultaneity.

Multiprogramming Operating Systems

The multiprogramming operating system must be designed to perform a delicate juggling trick. It must allocate *resources*, such as CPU cycles and memory, and assign priorities so that each program receives adequate attention. Urgent jobs must be

granted larger and/or more frequent CPU time slices without unduly neglecting lesser jobs. Also, jobs differ in their requirements. Number-crunching programs tend to be CPU intensive, while many business applications are I/O bound, with relatively little computation. The operating system needs to handle mixes of such jobs as efficiently as possible.

A program that is waiting for user input, for example, can be safely suspended regardless of priority. Remember that between each of your tentative keystrokes, your 100 MHz CPU is capable of many millions of useful cycles.

A program that is actually executing must have a copy of some or all of its *object code* (also known as the machine code, binary code, or executable binary image) loaded in RAM (Random Access Memory, also known as primary memory) so that the CPU can access the program instructions. For this reason, RAM is an important resource that needs to be allocated and husbanded by the operating system. At any particular moment, your RAM will hold not only the object code of the active program but also the object code for a certain number of suspended programs, together with various data areas holding the intermediate results of these programs. Most if not all of the operating system kernel must also be resident in RAM. As far as the CPU is concerned, the kernel is simply a set of programs that needs to be executed on demand. Since the kernel is in charge, of course, the kernel is not just another program: it maintains its own priorities to avoid being upstaged by user programs.

How many programs can coexist in primary memory naturally depends on the amount of RAM and the object code sizes. Yet another teaser for the poor operating system!

Some suspended programs and their data (or selected portions of these) may have to be *swapped* out from RAM to disk to make room for the next scheduled program. Later, when the operating system selects them for execution, the swapped items must be restored from disk to RAM. Much research has been devoted to the art of scheduling and swapping, since the immediate effect of excessive swapping is performance degradation. Disk I/O is relatively much slower than RAM reads and writes. And remember that the CPU itself gets involved in the swapping activity. An extreme case known as *thrashing* can bring the system to a snail's pace: the system is so preoccupied with swapping in and out that little or no productive processing takes place.

The inner detail of these gymnastics is happily hidden from the average user, but having a general feel engenders some sympathy for the folk who design operating

systems. Also, in practical terms, it explains the old adage that you can never have too much RAM.

The situation is further complicated by the need to remember which programs are suspended, when, and for what reason. The operating system needs to store the *context* of each suspended program so that execution can resume at the right point with the same values prevailing at the time of suspension. Contexts are really snapshots of the CPU's program counter and registers, and contexts are being saved and restored regularly by the operating system as programs are switched.

Multitasking

The more modern term *multitasking* includes the idea of multiprogramming but extends the concept to include the ability to run different parts of the same program (also known as *threads*) simultaneously. The basic idea is that most programs can be treated as a sequence of smaller elements called *tasks*. Sometimes these tasks must be run *synchronously*, that is, executed and completed in order, one at a time, since task 2, say, may need the results from task 1 before it can proceed. On other occasions, some or all of the tasks in a program can be usefully tackled independently (or *asynchronously*). And, of course, you encounter mixed situations where task 1, task 2, and task 3 can be run independently, but task 4 must await their completion.

Another element in the jigsaw is that many peripherals, such as tape and disk drives, can operate asynchronously. An I/O task (such as reading from a disk) can be triggered by a system call in program A and left to run independently while the operating system prepares to run another task or program. The operating system scans a table of suspended jobs and determines which of those that are "runnable" has the highest priority, say program B. The context of program A is then stored together with a flag indicating its wait status (waiting for a disk read). The previously saved context of program B is then restored and program B starts executing. But how will the suspended program A ever get restarted? Well, the I/O device needs to signal that its operation is complete, and this is done by a *device interrupt*. As the name implies, an interrupt can occur at any time, and the kernel must take note of it even if no immediate restart of program A is possible. The kernel's reaction to the interrupt in this case would be to change the status of program A from "waiting for disk read" to "runable." This restores program A as a candidate for execution, and eventually, depending on its relative priority, program A will regain its place in the sun.

Peeling off these deeply nested onion layers is a complex business—the key is to have an overall picture and lots of faith. Luckily, Unix offers you some simple commands that let you run as many programs as you wish and keep track of their progress. But first, more jargon!

Unix Images and Processes

The terms *program* and *task* are rather vague: a piece of code can be divided in many ways, both conceptually and practically. A programmer can construct a program by compiling and linking many smaller programs or modules. During execution, such programs can invoke other programs and subroutines, some of which may be *system calls.* These are basic service routines provided by the operating system. So at one level of discussion, a program is a source code text prepared by a programmer; at another level, a program is a compiled, binary file on a disk; at yet another level, a program is a piece of binary code sitting in your RAM waiting to be *dispatched* (that is, executed) or possibly temporarily swapped out to disk through lack of lebensRAM.

To reduce this ambiguity, Unix uses two precise terms, *image* and *process.* To set the scene before precision strikes, repeat the following mantra: The process is the execution of the image.

WARNING The terms *process* and *processor* are still a tad confusing. A multi-processor system has several CPUs, but a single-processor Unix system can process several Unix processes! Also, the term *process control* can refer to real-time systems at chemical and other plants, as well as to the part of the kernel that controls Unix processes.

More technically, the image represents the executable program in binary form (mis-leadingly called the *text segment*), together with various data structures holding the context of the program, and two work areas (called the *data segment* and the *stack*). Figure 9.1 shows a simplified version of a Unix image. All you need to know for now is that the text segment in RAM is strictly read-only: the kernel ensures that it

FIGURE 9.1:

Image Layout

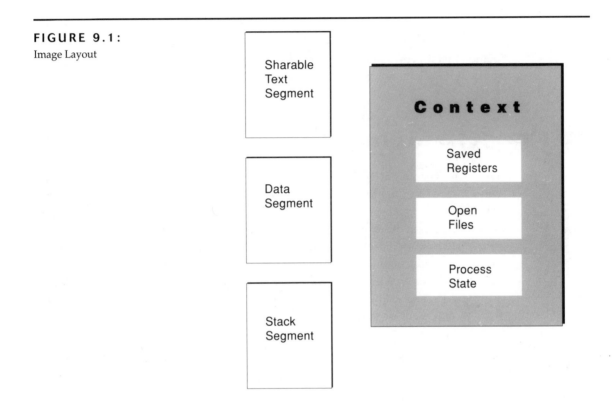

cannot be written over or changed during execution. The other areas can be freely accessed *and* changed during execution. The image must be resident in RAM while its process is executing.

Process Biography

When you invoke the wc (word count) command, for example, the shell (via calls to the kernel) loads an image and starts a new process with a unique numerical *pid* (process identifier). All subsequent references to this process (both by users and other processes) are made via its pid rather than by the name of the original command. You met a similar situation with user and group identifiers, and the theme appears in many other Unix situations. The pid's 0 and 1, by the way, are reserved for special processes created when Unix first boots.

If another user invokes the wc command, a fresh process is created with a different pid. (A completely new image, by the way, is not always needed with a new process, since processes are able to share the text segment of an image when running the same program.)

You could even invoke wc again while your first wc is still running (you'll see how soon), and the second wc would create a separate process with its own pid. The point to stress is that programs and processes are distinct entities. There can be many processes independently executing the same program.

Each runnable process will be selected for execution according to its priority (later you'll see how priorities are set and altered). The state of a process can change many times during its lifetime. It may be put in a *sleeping* state, meaning that it is suspended temporarily for various reasons, such as waiting for I/O or for other processes to finish. Usually, a process will run to completion and then disappear from the scene. A process may also terminate through some error condition or as a result of a signal (such as kill) from the user or from another process. However it is terminated, a completed process is removed from the table of processes, and the RAM it occupied is freed for new processes.

Forks and Spawns

While a process A is running, it may *spawn* another process, B. B is said to be the *child* of A, and A is called the *parent* of B. Spawning is achieved by a system call known as fork, so we often talk about processes being forked. A child process can itself spawn children, and so on ad infinitum. A detailed understanding of the spawning mechanism is not essential for your day-to-day Unix operation, but the following brief summary will give you a helpful background.

Initially, the child and parent processes are virtually identical. They each start with independent, identical copies of the original RAM image but, being separate processes, they do have distinct pid's. The child also has access to any files that the parent has opened. Processes can also share special I/O channels called *pipes* that behave rather like files, as you saw in Chapter 4 (more on this soon).

The child then calls exec using the command name and its arguments (if any) inherited from the parent. exec is a system call that revamps the child's image so that the child process starts executing the inherited command. Child and parent processes are now free to go their own way and do their own things by executing their

now different images. Because they can both access the same open files and pipes, though, there are opportunities for *interprocess* communication and cooperation.

The pipes and filters you saw in Chapter 4, in fact, were simple examples of two co-operating processes. In ls | wc, for example, the ls process writes to the pipe while the wc process reads from the pipe. The kernel buffers and synchronizes this activity, and will delay the reading process if the buffer is empty. Similarly, the writing process is held up if the buffer is full.

The parent process also has an important option: it can choose to *wait* for its child to terminate. The parent makes this choice by invoking the system call wait, which is so arranged that the parent is informed when the child process has terminated and the reason for termination. Since a parent may spawn several children before going into a wait state, wait also tells the parent which of the child processes has terminated. The full relevance of this parental "wait for the kids" privilege will emerge in future sections when you see how the shell process spawns children.

The fork is a fundamental operation in Unix: when you first boot Unix, there are just two basic processes created called swapper (or sched) and init, with pid's 0 and 1 respectively. All other user processes are spawned by calls to fork! For example, init forks several background processes called *daemons* (more on these later) and a set of getty processes that monitor each terminal looking for user logins.

In some ways, the hierarchy of processes, from parents to children, to grandchildren, is comparable with the file hierarchy outlined in previous chapters. Before I enlarge on this theme, there is an important parent process to consider—one you have been quietly using since Chapter 1!

The Shell as a Process

Although I did not make a splash about it, you have already been exposed to Unix processes and their forks. Whenever you type a command, the shell spawns a process that executes that command. Running the shell itself, as you may have guessed, is a process.

The shell process can run some commands under its own steam, but more often than not it spawns a child process to execute the programs and commands you enter.

Being a patient parent, the shell usually waits for this child process to complete, after which the shell displays its prompt, inviting a new command.

But what if you could tell the shell *not* to wait for the child process to finish? What if you could get the prompt back immediately, while the child process continued on its own? Clearly, you could then run another command while the child process was running in the *background*. Unix offers a simple way of achieving this desirable feat. In fact, you can easily set up as many commands as you wish, all running "simultaneously."

Some processes do not lend themselves to background execution, of course. Text editors such as ed require constant keyboard and screen interaction, and must be run in the *foreground*. Similarly, commands producing screen displays can cause chaos if run in parallel. Some jobs that seem to be ideal for background processing are in fact handled correctly by Unix without special user intervention. For example, you'll see that Unix can automatically *spool* printing jobs. Spooling means that all print requests are queued up centrally so that you don't have to wait for the printer to print your job before you execute another command.

Of course, there may be a limit to the number of background commands you can have at one time, depending on RAM size, the complexity of the commands, and what other users are up to. With many Unix systems now using demand-paged virtual memory (which extends the effective RAM size by using available disk space as if it were addressable RAM), the only practical limit may be that response becomes unacceptable because of excessive swapping.

With these provisos in mind, let's return to the keyboard and do some single-processor multiprocessing!

Background Processes Using &

The simplest way to create simultaneous processes is with the & command terminator. When you terminate a command with & (followed by Enter), the shell spawns a child process as usual, but does not wait for the child to terminate. Rather, the

shell displays the pid (process identifier) of the new process, then immediately displays the prompt for another command:

```
$ wc chapter*  >chap.count &
2676
$ ed stan.data
?stan.data
a

_
```

The number 2676 indicates the unique pid of the process spawned to execute the image loaded by the shell in response to the wc command. This process, counting the lines, words, and characters in all the files matching chapter*, will run in the background while you are busy editing stan.data in the foreground. The output of the wc process is redirected to the file chap.count. Can you see why this redirection is necessary? Yes—without redirection, the results of the count would go to your standard output, and strange numbers would appear mixed up with your ed displays!

The above example can be extended:

```
$ wc chapter* >chap.count &
2676
$ ls -1 accounts/inv* >invfiles &
3125
$ ed stan.data
345
a

_
```

You now have two background processes running while you do some more text editing. Note that the 345 is *not* a pid, but the number of characters in stan.data!

There are many candidates for background processing. Long sorts, spreadsheet recalculations, and formatting runs, for instance. For programmers, lengthy compilations and links can putter along out of sight while new code is being edited in the foreground.

The wait Command

What if you initiate one or more background processes with & and then decide that you need to wait until they have all terminated? For example, you may realize that you need the results of the word count process in order to start the next job.

One answer is to use the wait command (in man section C). The wait command takes no arguments. If the prompt appears immediately after entering wait, you can be sure that all your background processes are complete. Otherwise, there must be background processes still running, and you and your screen must simply wait for the prompt! Alert readers may wonder if wait is executed in the normal way by a child process spawned by the shell. The answer is no! wait must be executed by the shell itself by using the system call (also called wait) and exercising the parental "wait for the children" privilege I discussed earlier.

What if you initiate a long background process and change your mind? Or supposing a process gets into that bane of all programmers, an endless loop or some other kind of wild state? (It is remarkably easy to write a shell script that will run forever without achieving anything useful.) The next section reveals the essential but lethal kill command.

Killing Processes

You can kill any or all of *your own* processes with the kill command, so caution is urged. The superuser, as you might guess, can kill any user's processes, and sometimes has to exercise this power in emergencies (viral or trojan horse invasions, for instance).

A killed process just disappears: its image is cleared and it ceases to qualify for scheduling by the kernel. Killing your own processes, though, is not quite as fatal as zapping the wrong file. If you inadvertently kill a background process running a long wc, for example, you can simply reissue the command and only time has been lost. Nevertheless, killing the wrong process can be a nuisance.

The kill command, for historical reasons, is rather misleadingly named. kill actually sends a *signal* to a process. Some of these signals do, in fact, request or enforce process termination, but other signals sent by kill have no connection with killing at all! Some defence for the name is that, by default, if no signal is specified, kill does send a signal requesting process termination; for most users, this is the only situation where kill is ever used. Let's look at the kill syntax to clarify matters:

```
kill [-signo] pid1 [pid2 ...pidn]
```

WARNING If you forget the - in front of *signo*, the *signo* will be interpreted as a pid!

The kill command sends the signal given by the optional *signo* argument to each process indicated in the list of process identifiers. You must indicate at least one pid. The special value 0 can be used for *pid1*, in which case the signal is sent to all processes created from your current login, excluding your shell process.

The default signo happens to be 15—this is the request-process-termination signal. So,

```
$ kill 2676
```

is the same as kill -15 2676, which sends a termination request to the process with pid 2676. In our earlier example this pid was running wc, so you may wonder why Unix does not allow a simple kill wc format. The reason is that you may have several processes running wc jobs, whereas the pid is unique.

To check the success of your kill request, you need to run the ps (process status) command, the subject of a later section. Under most circumstances, kill *pid* will actually kill the process, but there are exceptions. First, a process can be run under the nohup (no hangup) regimen. This deserves a small digression.

Hello, I Must Be Going!

Suppose you want to start a mammoth job, log out, switch off your terminal, head home, and crack an ice-cold Fosters. You can do all this and leave your job running. You simply type nohup and a space, followed by your command and its arguments (if any), ending with & to create a background process:

```
$ nohup bigjob args &
3421
$ logout
```

The process running bigjob carries on in the background at low priority, but if someone logs in on your terminal, the process is immune from an accidental or

intentional `kill 3421`. Likewise, you yourself cannot use `kill 3421`. Apart from `nohup` jobs, there may be some pathological cases where the process staggers on unheeding and ignores simple kill attempts. Is there no way, then, of terminating such processes? Yes, Unix provides a big blaster signal that guarantees sudden death to both running-wild and `nohup` processes:

```
$ kill -9 3421
```

So, *signo* value 9 is the real killer.

Similarly,

```
$ kill -9 0
```

is a rather heavy-handed way of stopping all your active processes, excluding the parent shell.

The system administrator, as mentioned earlier, can kill any or all processes, regardless of "ownership." There is a special *signo* used only by the superuser to curtail all user activity, reducing the system to a single-user state prior to making major system changes or closing down for the night.

```
# kill -1 1
```

The `signo` value 1 means *hangup*, and is only used after issuing a prior warning (for example, `wall`) to all active users. (Some systems have a `killall` command, for use by `root` only, which also kills all active processes, with the exception of those processes involved in the shutdown procedure.) (More on this in Chapter 18.)

The other values for `signo` are for advanced users, but you may want to take a peek at the `man` pages for `kill`.

Before moving on to the `ps` command, one more piece of process jargon is needed. Your shell process is considered to be the group *leader* of all the spawned processes you may be running. In more complex situations, there may be other group leaders, possibly other shells running under your shell with their own children. Recall the `!` command in `ed` (Chapter 8) that "escapes" you temporarily to the shell. In fact, `!` spawns a fresh copy of `sh`. When you exit this shell, you return to its parent, namely `ed`; when you exit `ed` you return to its parent, the original `sh`. The group concept lets you consider just those processes running from a certain parent (usually your shell) without the confusion of any earlier generation of processes.

Checking Your Processes with ps

To keep track of what processes are active, you use the ps (process status) command (in man section C). The ps command is one of those that has attracted many dialectal variants, so your version may differ from mine. The prevalent syntax is as follows:

```
ps [options]
```

The most common options are

None	Lists processes of your terminal only in short format
-d	Lists all processes except process group leaders
-e	Lists all processes
-a	Lists all terminal processes except group leaders and nonterminal processes
-t *tlist*	Restricts list to the terminals in *tlist*
-p *plist*	Restricts list to the pid's in *plist*
-g *glist*	Restricts list to the pid's in the groups given by *glist*
-u *ulist*	Restricts list to pid's belonging to uid's in *ulist*
-f	Provides full listing
-l	Provides long listing

Some options determine *which* processes will be displayed; other options determine *how much* information you'll get. You can combine some of these options, or rely on the various defaults. Consider the following example:

```
% ps
PID    TTY    TIME    CMD
1801   tty3   0:04    csh
2452   tty3   0:04    ps
% _
```

For a change of scenery, I've switched from my SCO UNIX to a dialup BSD (Berkeley Software Distribution—see Chapter 20) system called basis. Note the C shell prompt.

There are two processes active on my terminal: pid 1801 is running csh, the C shell, and pid 2452 is running ps. The latter, of course, is the selfsame ps command that is reporting the state of my processes! The other fields shown are quite obvious: TTY tells you the name of the controlling terminal; TIME gives the accumulated execution time in minutes:seconds.

ps with no options confines its attention to processes running from your own terminal and gives a short listing. This is by far the most common format you will need. Usually, you will invoke ps simply to find a pid for the kill command or to verify that a kill has been successful. The TIME field is also useful for checking on possible endlessly looped processes.

For a fuller account of your own processes, use the −f option:

```
% ps −f
UID      PID PPID  C   STIME     TTY  TIME CMD
bin     8371 5386  127 16:14:35 tty3 0:03 ps −f
polemic 5386   1    5 03:06:56 tty3 0:04 −csh
% _
```

The CMD field is now a bit more informative: it shows not only the command name but the arguments and options used when it was called. The additional fields are as follows:

UID	The login name of the process owner
PPID	The pid of the parent process
C	The processor utilization for scheduling
STIME	The starting time for the process

In the above example, the PPID (the pid of the parent) of ps is given as 5386, which can be confirmed by checking the reported pid of csh, also 5386.

To see what the system itself and the other users are up to, you can use the −a option:

```
% ps −a
PID     TTY    TIME  CMD
100     co     0:03  timehack
 79     co     6:34  dqueuer
 81     co     6:34  cron
 83     co    16:53  update
5386    tty3   0:04  ps
% _
```

Note first that co, the systems console, is running several mysterious processes that are none of your business! Unless you are a superuser, of course, you are not allowed to kill any process you do not own, so do not try.

The process called cron is an example of a *daemon* process. The spelling indicates that such processes are amiable spirits rather than evil *demons*. Daemons run ceaselessly in the background performing various essential tasks. cron is the clock daemon responsible for scheduling other processes (more on this when you meet the at and batch commands later in this chapter). The update process is another daemon, responsible for updating the disk system at specified intervals. (The daemon names vary according to Unix version.)

The above ps –a display seems to have forgotten the csh shell process. The reason is that the a option excludes group leader processes such as your shell. You should experiment with other option combinations: –ag will extend the a listing above by showing you the shell processes and other group leaders; –alg will tell you more than you might care to know about all processes.

The l option adds status and state fields to the ps listing, interpreted as follows:

Process Status Bit	Meaning
01	Process image is in RAM.
02	System (internal) process.
04	Process image is locked in RAM.
10	Process is being swapped.
20	Process is being traced (waited upon) by another process.

The value displayed is the sum of these bits, so that 06 means the process is a system process (02) and is locked in RAM (04). Certain processes, such as those for physical I/O, may need to be locked in RAM to prevent the kernel from swapping them out to disk at an injudicious moment.

Process State Field	Meaning
0	Nonexistent
S	Sleeping
R	Running
I	Intermediate
Z	Terminated
T	Stopped
B	Waiting

The long l listing also tells you the priority assigned to each process. The higher the number, the lower the priority. The default priorities for all processes are set and adjusted by the system administrator. You can *lower* the priorities on your own processes individually when you run commands, but only the superuser can *increase* them. The nice command is used to adjust scheduling priorities. Read on.

Have a nice Process

When the system tries to run too many high-priority jobs at the same time, response deteriorates and everybody suffers. The prevailing Unix philosophy is to be kind and gentle and reduce the need for system administrator intervention by lowering the priorities on long-winded, not-so-urgent jobs. Be nice to other users, and they'll be nice to you—thus the name for the nice command. The nice syntax is

```
nice [-inc] command [args]
```

This will run the given *command* with its optional *args* at a priority level determined by the optional number *inc*. A terminating & is quite common to put the process in the background but is not part of the nice syntax. To understand the impact of the *inc* argument, you need to know that each process has a *nice number* in

the range 0–39, from which the kernel calculates the actual scheduling priority. The value 0 represents the highest priority, 39 the lowest. The default nice number is 20, right down the middle. To lower your priority, you have to increase the nice number, hence the name *inc* I've given to the option. The number you supply for *inc* increases the current nice number by *inc* up to a maximum of 39. The default value for *inc* is 10, so that

```
$ nice -10 wc inv* >count.inv &
2654
$ _
```

and

```
$ nice wc inv* >count.inv &
2654
$ _
```

both increase the nice number by 10 (usually from 20 to 30), thereby lowering the priority assigned to the wc process. The ps -l (long format) command, by the way, tells you the current nice number. The nohup command, introduced earlier, automatically adds 10 to its process's nice number, so nohup jobs always run at a lower priority (the price you pay to avoid termination).

A not-so-nice property of nice, however, is that the superuser can also use *negative* values of *inc* in order to lower the nice number and increase the priority of any process:

```
# nice --15 bigjob &
5431
# _
```

This entry makes bigjob run with a nice number of (20–15) = 5. Note that ordinary users are not allowed negative values of *inc*, whereas superusers can use positive or negative values.

If you or the system administrator use *inc* values that try to push the nice number outside the range 0–39, the shell quietly adjusts a negative result to 0, and a result greater than 39 is reduced to 39.

In the final sections of this chapter, I'll cover some useful command-line variants and introduce the tee, sleep, at, crontab, and batch commands.

Multicommand Lines

It is important to distinguish the multicommand line from the background command line. The following entry:

```
$ wc chapter* ; who
      123   677  3488 chapter1
      223 1090   4560 chapter2
      ...
      stan tty1 Oct 13 00:34
      mary tty2 Oct 13 10:24
      ...
$ _
```

has two commands separated by a semicolon. The shell executes each command in the foreground and in sequence as though you had entered them on separate lines. Consider next the following situation:

```
$ wc chapter* ; who | wc
      123   677  3488 chapter1
      223 1090   4560 chapter2
      ...
      2 10 46
$ _
```

The pipe symbol | acts only on the who command. However, if you want to analyze the output from *both* commands, you can add parentheses as follows:

```
$ (wc chapter* ; who) | wc
      983 7140 36545
$ _
```

The two commands still execute in the foreground, one after the other, but their output is combined as far as the filter is concerned.

This seems a natural place to show you the tee command. The name comes from the t-pipe familiar to all plumbers and gardeners. In Unix parlance, a t-pipe has one input and two identical outputs (unlike the plumbing version where each output carries a fraction of the input flow). Placing a tee in a pipe allows two copies of the input data to be tapped. One output must go to a file; the identical output carries on down through the filter. Figure 9.2 illustrates the following example:

```
$ who | tee save.it | wc
      2 10 46
```

```
$ cat save.it
    stan tty1 Oct 13 00:34
    mary tty2 Oct 13 10:24
    ...
$ wc <save.it
    2 10 46
$ _
```

As you can see, tee sends the output from who to the file save.it, and also to the pipe to wc.

FIGURE 9.2:

tee Command T-pipe

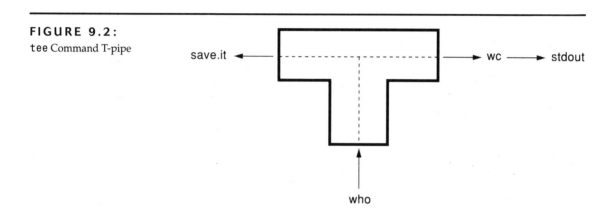

Returning to background processes, you can set up several background processes on the one line by repeating the &:

```
$ wc chapter* >chap & ls -1 acc/inv* >invfiles &
2676
3125
$ ed stan.data
345

_
```

You can also mix background and foreground jobs as follows:

```
$ who >whodat & date
5421
Fri July 21 13:01 PST 1995
$ cat whodat
```

```
stan tty1 July 21 00:34
mary tty2 July 21 10:24
...
$ _
```

Here, who runs in the background while date is a foreground process. With tiny jobs like these, of course, the difference is somewhat metaphysical.

You can see now that there are three command terminators:

Newline (Enter)	Process foreground, prompt on next command line
;	Process foreground, but stay on command line (no prompt)
&	Process background, prompt on next command line

The sleep Command

Sometimes you may want to put a sequence of commands in the background. An instructive example uses the sleep command (in man section C). sleep n simply cycles idly for n seconds (not exceeding 65,535 seconds) and can be most useful in shell scripts where you want to slow down a sequence of displays:

```
echo Hope you have time to read this line
sleep 5
echo before I show you this line
```

Now play with the following example, using different numbers for the sleep argument:

```
$ (sleep 10; date) & date
6734
Fri July 21 13:01 PST 1995
$ Fri July 21 13:11 PST 1995
```

The process, with pid 6734, will first execute sleep and then execute date, both in the background. The second date command is in the foreground, so it displays right away followed by the prompt. Approximately ten seconds later, the second date displays. The timing can be slightly wrong depending on how busy the system is—remember that processes receive time slices according to their priorities.

Notice that the output from the second `date` simply appears wherever the cursor happens to be at the time. In this example, no harm is done, but recall my earlier warning about background processes that may ruin your screen layout.

The `sleep` command can be used to create a primitive alarm system:

```
$ (sleep 3600; echo Jeopardy on TV!) &
$ _
```

After approximately one hour, the screen will display the chosen message. If you embed one or more Ctrl-G characters in the message string, you will ring the bell on your terminal. Remember that the message may appear anywhere on the screen, mixed up with any foreground displays you may be generating at the time.

Scheduling Processes

A related command called `at` (in man section C) lets you schedule jobs to run at some future date:

```
$ at 4:30am tomorrow
wc chapter* >chap.count
```

You next enter Ctrl-D to terminate your input. Once you enter Ctrl-D, `at` assigns a job id, such as 6A, and displays it together with the date scheduled to run the list of commands you have submitted:

```
6A 04:30 Jan 23 1995
$ _
```

If you decide to cancel the request, you enter

```
at -r job-id
```

You can cancel only your own scheduled jobs unless you are the superuser.

The `at` command syntax for scheduling future jobs is

```
at time [date] [increment]
```

The list of commands will be executed at the time and date arguments supplied (as modified by the optional increment). These arguments can take many forms, best illustrated by the following examples. Unix makes sensible assumptions as to when

the jobs should run. If you enter **8** or **8:00am** with no day specified, you'll be scheduled for today if possible (that is, if it's not yet 8:00 a.m.); otherwise the jobs will run at 8:00 a.m. the following day. Similarly with months and years!

Without a colon between hours and minutes, time must be 1, 2, or 4 digits. A 24-hour military format is assumed unless you add the optional am or pm. 1- and 2-digit entries are taken as hours; 4-digit times are taken as hours and minutes. (A 3-digit entry is clearly ambiguous.) at also accepts words such as `tomorrow` and `next` as well as day and month names.

If you entered any one of the following as the time argument:

```
8
08
0800
8:0
08:0
8am
8:0am
08:00am
```

your scheduled jobs will be executed at 8:00 a.m. today if you entered the at command before 8:00 a.m., or at 8:00 a.m. tomorrow if the at command was entered at 8:00 a.m. or later. Similarly, the following time arguments will cause your scheduled jobs to run the next time the clock strikes 11:00 p.m.:

```
22
2200
1100pm
11:00pm
```

You can also use these special time arguments with at: `now`, `noon`, and `midnight`.

The optional *date* argument takes any one of the following formats to specify the day you want the scheduled jobs to run:

```
Feb 23
today
tomorrow
Sunday
```

You can even specify the year you want the scheduled jobs executed:

```
Feb 23, 1997
```

will run your jobs on February 23, 1997.

To use an optional increment, enter a + followed by a number and one of the following unit arguments:

```
minute(s)
hour(s)
day(s)
week(s)
month(s)
year(s)
```

Combining these gives you an enormous battery of scheduling schemes. Here are a few suggestions:

```
at 0800 Feb 12
at now +2 days
at tomorrow +3 hours
at 11:00am Monday next week
at 5:00pm Sep 15 next year
```

The cron daemon that you met earlier has the task of keeping tabs on all the at jobs in the works, and dispatching them when their due date/time arrives.

The system administrator has the power to select which users are permitted to use the at facility.

Redirection in both directions is useful with the at command. at takes its input from stdin, so if you set up a file with a list of your jobs (one command per line), you can simply enter

```
$ at now +1 month <command.file
23S 08:34am Jan 23 1999
$ _
```

The scheduled times of waiting jobs can be displayed using at with the -l option:

```
at -l [job-id1 job-id2 ...]
```

If you omit the *job-id* arguments, you get a list of all the jobs currently scheduled; otherwise you get just the jobs requested.

Jobs scheduled with at are not background processes in the strictest sense: they are simply earmarked for future processing and when the scheduled date/time arrives, they are entered for execution (background or foreground) as though you had just typed their commands yourself.

You can even write a shell script that will schedule itself to run at regular intervals. The following line embedded in a shell-script file called `myshell` will generate a request to run itself at 8:00 a.m. every Monday:

```
echo "myshell" | at 0800 Mon next week
```

You'll learn more of these tricks in Chapter 13.

More elaborate methods of scheduling recurring jobs are possible with `crontab`. The details are beyond our immediate scope, but briefly, `crontab` lets you set up a list of commands in a file called /usr/spool/cron/crontab/*username*. Each line in this file specifies a command, and the time and interval for execution. The `cron` daemon then scans this file regularly and schedules the jobs as required. The superuser can control which users are allowed to use this facility.

The `batch` command (providing the superuser gives you permission) is a much simpler scheduling mechanism that lets you set up big jobs to be run whenever the system loading permits:

```
$ batch
bigjob >bigjob.stats
```

Pressing Ctrl-D enters the command line and returns you to the system prompt. Unlike `at`, `batch` does not specify a scheduling date/time. All you know is that `bigjob` will run as soon as conditions allow.

Summary

Chapter 9 has covered many fundamental aspects of Unix: how it manages to handle many processes "concurrently," and some of the important commands that let you and/or the superuser exploit and control multitasking. The key concepts and commands are summarized as follows:

- A parent process creates child processes by spawning (forking) a copy process which is then modified.
- The shell (parent) spawns a child to execute your commands. The parent can either wait for the child to finish, or immediately prompt for further commands.

- Using the & command terminator puts the command process into the background, letting you perform other commands in the foreground (or background).

- Processes have a unique numerical process identifier (pid) used in commands such as `kill` to terminate the process.

- You met the following commands:

`wait`	The shell waits until all background processes have terminated.
`sleep n`	Do nothing for *n* seconds; then exit.
`at`	Schedule a process for a future date/time.
`crontab`	Set jobs for regular processing.
`batch`	Schedule jobs when system load allows.
`tee`	Divert output to a file and send a copy to a pipe.
`ps`	Display status of all or selected processes.
`nice`	Adjust the scheduling priority of a process. Users can lower priorities; superusers can lower or raise priorities.
`nohup`	Run a process at low priority but prevent hangups from `kill [-15]` commands.

- Multiline commands can be entered using ; and &.

- Commands can be grouped using (`command1; command2`).

In Chapter 10, I'll show you how to handle all those printing jobs that form the basis of the new automated, paperless office!

CHAPTER

TEN

Printing and Spooling

- Central and local printers

- Overcoming the printer jungle

- The `lp` command

- The `lpstat` command

- Changing print requests with `lp -i`

- The `lprint` command

- Simple formatting with `pr`

The subject of printing has cropped up several times in previous chapters—usually in the context of *displaying* information on the screen. In this chapter, I'll be using the word "print" in its normal sense: the act of putting permanent characters on paper.

As I warned you, Unix clings to the confusing anachronism of the term "print" to mean "output to terminal." This is a vestige of times past when terminals were teleprinters that produced user input and system responses in the form of printed paper, known as *hard copy*, to distinguish it from more volatile representations. It was even worse than that: teleprinters clattered along serially at 7 characters or less per second on cheap rolls of unperforated paper! The word teletypewriter was usually abbreviated to TTY (pronounced "tit'ee"), and this has survived into the 20th century: the general terminal interface is known as dev/tty, hence the current Unix joke: What do you call a $20,000 high-resolution, 30-inch, 3-D color monitor? Answer: tty01!

When CRTs were introduced they were promptly dubbed "glass tit'ees." The commands and mnemonics for sending output to the new terminals, CRTs, retained their old "printing" associations. As you saw in Chapter 8, for example, ed still uses the p command for display. In normal conversation, too, the word "print" often means "display," depending on the context. In passing, note another annoying ambiguity: "blank" means "space" rather than "null" or "empty."

The early "real" printers for lengthy listings were usually *line printers* based on punched card tabulators that printed a line at a time, at speeds ranging from 100 to 600 lines per minute, and with very limited, uppercase fonts. For this reason, you find that many Unix hardcopy print-control commands include the mnemonic lp (line print) even if you are using character-serial (one character at a time) printers or page-based laser printers. So you'll meet commands such as lpstat, lprint, lpadmin, lpfilter, lpsched, and so on, as well as lp itself used as a command and a subdirectory.

Central and Local Printers

The cost of high-speed line and page printers often dictates that a central pool of such devices be shared by many users. At the same time, many terminals have *printer ports* that permit the attachment of slower, cheaper printers as a dedicated

local service. You'll see that Unix supports both configurations. The central printer approach, of course, requires special arrangements so that printing jobs can be prioritized and scheduled if several users request a printout at the same time. This is achieved by *spooling*, whereby copies of the print image are stored (queued) temporarily until the printer is ready. "Spooling" is yet another anachronism stemming from the predisk days when all but the tiniest files were stored on reels (or spools) of magnetic tape. SPOOL as a fancy acronym of Simultaneous Peripheral Operation On-Line is a piece of reverse engineering! Tape drives, of course, are still with us, but are now mainly used as high-volume data backup devices, agents for transferring data between alien systems, and distribution media for software.

Spooling means that you do not have to wait for your print request to be completed. Your print command and options are placed in a queue, leaving your terminal free for other jobs. The queue is scanned periodically by a system daemon, known as the *LP request scheduler,* running in the background.

Each site has a default printer to which print requests are sent in the absence of contrary instructions. Larger sites may have clusters of similar printers, called *classes,* that can share the load—a request will be handled by whichever printer in the class becomes available first. Printers can also be addressed by name, and Unix offers flexible control when you have printers that are loaded with preprinted forms, such as invoices or checks.

Save a Tree

I've delayed dealing with the topic of real printing in a vain effort to preserve our dwindling forests. Ironically, unless you tell Unix otherwise, the typical printing defaults can be quite wasteful for small runs: you are likely to get extra *banner* pages at the front of your listings telling you all about your print request. I should not have to urge caution in the overproduction of hard copy. The early dream of the paperless office has become the nightmare of huge piles of unread (unreadable) reports. When a listing *is* essential, avoid the temptation of producing that "spare" copy.

Overcoming the Printer Jungle

You are probably aware of the bewildering diversity of printing devices. As with the CRT market, attempts at standardization are bedeviled by rapid technological progress. The result is that Unix has a great deal of irksome but essential baggage devoted to handling the hundreds of different printer models currently available. It is the job of the system administrator, aided possibly by the printer vendor if the model is peculiar, to set up a central printer service.

Briefly, this involves allocating an appropriate port (serial or parallel) and ensuring that this port is disabled from normal terminal logins. After physically attaching the printer to this port, the device can be accessed as /dev/tty n, where n is the number of the serial port. Parallel ports (usually attached to Centronics-compatible printers) are accessed via /dev/lp0.

The directory /dev contains special files which represent your peripherals: terminals, printers, disk drives, and so on. Unix, as I mentioned earlier in this book, treats many different objects as though they were files. The ordinary disk files you've been using have this essential property: sequences of characters (bytes) can be read from them and written to them. Since you can also send and receive streams of bytes to and from peripheral devices, Unix gives each I/O device a special file-like interface. This elegant idea was another Unix innovation subsequently adopted by DOS and other operating systems. The advantage is that the input and output of many commands can be redirected not only to standard output (screen) and from standard input (keyboard) but also to and from other devices on your system.

Of course, devices differ considerably in how they physically handle input and output. Each type of peripheral must have its own software interface, called a *device driver*, linked into the kernel, to translate its individual quirks. The driver absolves both the kernel and the user from having to know too much about the device's internal nuts and bolts. The result is that normal file operations such as opening, closing, reading, and writing can be equally applied to devices. (Of course, not all such operations make equal sense with all devices: reading data from a printer, for example, is restricted to receiving handshaking signals such as "ready," "paper low," "paper jammed," and so on.)

Output can be redirected to a cooperative special file using the normal > operator. If you are `root`, a simple test of the newly installed printer's physical connections can therefore be made as follows:

```
# who >/dev/tty3a
# _
```

for serial ports, or

```
# who >/dev/lp0
# _
```

for parallel ports. The exact `/dev` argument, of course, will depend on the port number and type selected.

This simple redirection bypasses the Unix print services such as spooling, so it is not recommended for normal production printing jobs. The characters from who (or any other command that produces output) will print "as is" with no formatting, page jumps, or page numbers. Worse still, there is no protection against the printer receiving data from other users. The collision could be messy!

To establish proper service, the system administrator has several additional chores to perform. The printer must be given a name, optionally assigned to a class, and provided with an interface program. Details of the printer's characteristics must be placed in the `terminfo` file if not already there. There may also be a need to define or change one or more *filter* programs. I'll discuss filters in more detail later. For now, look on them as programs that can adjust the output files of applications to match and exploit the features of particular printer models. Filters can also help in detecting and reporting printer errors. Unix comes with several standard filters, but new applications and printer models may require special versions. These are often provided by the printer or application vendor.

If you lack an experienced system administrator, nearby guru, or helpful vendor, you may be lucky enough to have a Unix implementation with a friendly system administration shell. The SCO Unix System V/386, for example, has `sysadmsh`, which offers simple menus for adding and configuring printers (and many other tasks, of course). The menus avoid the need to master the intricacies of the `/usr/lib/lpadmin` command (in man section ADM).

Assuming you do have an established printer service, let's look at the commands available to exploit it.

The lp Command

The lp command (in man section C) submits a request to the print service. The syntax is

```
lp [options] [file1 file2 ... fileN]
```

Without the options, this command will spool and then print the given files on the default printer. In the absence of any file names, lp takes its input from your keyboard—giving you a rather expensive typewriter! The following entry will print the contents of stan.data on the default printer:

```
$ lp stan.data
request id laser-24 (1 file)
$ _
```

The command responds by assigning and displaying a *print request id,* showing the printer name, a unique number that increments with each request, and the number of files in the spool. The print request id can be used in subsequent commands to identify and control the printing in various ways. You may recognize similarities here with the process id explained in the previous chapter. Because the request is spooled, the prompt immediately returns, and you can enter more commands.

If you have more than one printer and do not want to print on the default printer, you can use the -d option:

```
$ lp -ddaisy stan.data
request id daisy -26 (1 file)
$ _
```

Here, I've elected to print on a printer called daisy. The printer name follows the -d with no intervening white space. Note that with some installations the name after the -d may refer to a class—that is, a cluster of identical printers. In this case, the request will be serviced by whichever printer in the class first becomes free.

Wildcard file-name arguments are useful with lp:

```
$ lp chapter.*
request id laser-34 (12 files)
$ _
```

will request the printing of any files in your current directory that match chapter.*. You can also print several files by listing their names with spaces as separators:

```
$ lp chapter.1 chapter.5
request id laser-36 (2 files)
$ _
```

If you use continuous sprocket-fed stationery, you will, by default, get a form feed after chapter.1 has printed.

Printer Options

Before studying the lp options, you should print a few small files to see what global defaults may have been established for your system. An /etc/default/lpd file set up by the system administrator controls certain options that interact with the options you enter with an lp command. For example, the usual global default for printing banner pages will give you an extra page in front of the listing proper. Banner pages summarize the print request, showing the date, user id, the request id, and the file names being printed. In large installations with a central printing facility, the banner pages serve the essential function of identifying who gets what. In smaller sites, you may want to inhibit the banner pages:

```
$ lp -onobanner chapter.1 chapter.5
request id laser-36 (2 files)
$ _
```

The lp options vary from site to site, so check your local manual. The options shown here are available on SCO Version V and similar versions. The -o option is followed by the nobanner suboption. Other -o suboptions are listed below:

Suboption	Description
-onofilebreak	Omits the form feed between file listings
-olength=n	Sets page length to n lines
-olength=ni	Sets page length to n inches
-olength=nc	Sets page length to n centimeters
-owidth=ni	Sets page width to n inches
-owidth=nc	Sets page width to n centimeters

Suboption	Description
-olpi=*n*	Set line pitch to *n* lines per inch
-ocpi=*n*	Sets printer to *n* character(s) per inch
-ocpi=pica	Sets printer to 10 characters per inch
-ocpi=elite	Sets printer to 12 characters per inch
-ocpi=compressed	Sets printer to maximum possible characters per inch

Some printers, of course, cannot respond to all of these options. A single font printer with fixed character size, for example, could not honor certain pitch-changing options.

You can enter as many separate –o suboptions as you wish provided you repeat the –o:

```
$ lp -onobanner -ocpi= elite chapter.1
request id laser -38 (1 file)
$ _
```

Other useful lp options are as follows:

Option	Description
lp -n[*number*]	Prints *number* copies of each file requested. The default is 1 copy.
lp -m	Sends a mail message to you when the printing is complete.
lp -w	Displays a message on your terminal when the printing is complete. If you happen to be logged out when this message arrives, it will be diverted to your mailbox.
lp -q[*priority*]	Sets a priority level for your print request. The default is set by the system administrator. Zero is the highest priority, 39 is the lowest.
lp -s	Suppresses the normal "request id" message.
lp -R	Erases the file(s) when they have been printed. Use this with care, of course!

Option	Description
lp -L	Uses the local printer attached to your terminal. See also the lprint command described later.

A Simple Shell Script

As you can see, combining various lp options can lead to hideously complex commands. If you are loath to type such long-winded commands on a regular basis, Unix offers the shell script, which merits a brief detour. You'll see shell scripts and procedures in more detail in Chapters 13 and 16, but this is a good opportunity to show you a simple but practical example. You can readily devise your own myprint procedure, say, so that myprint chapter.1 performs a complex command with less typing effort.

Using ed or cat >myprint, create a file called myprint containing the single line

```
lp -onobanner -ocpi=elite $1
```

The expression $1 (familiar to DOS batch file programmers) is called a *positional parameter*. If you invoke myprint with the argument chapter.1, the shell replaces $1 with chapter.1, giving you the same effect as the longer lp command and its options. There are two ways of invoking your new command. With the first method, the following command

```
$ sh myprint chapter.1
```

spawns a Bourne shell that reads the file myprint, replaces $1 with the argument chapter.1, then executes the resulting command:

```
lp -onobanner -ocpi=elite chapter.1
```

The second method involves first making myprint directly executable by changing its mode with chmod:

```
$ chmod u+x myprint
```

Thereafter, myprint can be invoked without the need for sh:

```
$ myprint chapter.1
```

Your current shell now does the work, but the end result is the same as in method 1.

The u+x option in chmod gives you alone, as the owner, execution permission for myprint, as explained in Chapter 7. If you want to grant all users permission to use myprint, you would vary the chmod option as follows:

```
$ chmod a+x myprint
```

or equivalently,

```
$ chmod +x myprint
```

since a (all users) is the default. Alternatively, you may wish to limit usage to members of your group with

```
$ chmod g+x myprint
```

After using chmod, you should run ls -1 myprint to check that it has the correct x fields for your purposes.

Shell scripts are available for both the Bourne and C shells, although the syntax and available features are different (see Appendix A). Peculiar to the C shell, though, is another keystroke-saving ploy called the alias command. Let's make another detour before we return to the printing commands.

The C Shell alias Command

The C shell alias command is rather like a *macro* in other languages. You save keystrokes by replacing a long command string with a shorter one:

```
% alias myprint lp -onobanner -ocpi=elite
% _
```

Thereafter, until you leave the shell, myprint acts as a synonym or alias (hence the name) for the command and options entered above. The C shell replaces myprint with

```
lp -onobanner -ocpi=elite
```

so that myprint can take additional options as well as the usual file arguments:

```
% myprint -olength= 55 chapter.2
request id laser-39 (1 file)
% _
```

has the same impact as entering

```
% lp -onobanner -ocpi=elite -olength=55 chapter.2
request id laser-39 (1 file)
% _
```

Your aliases are not "remembered" from one session to the next, so if you want to use them regularly, the appropriate alias commands must be placed in your .cshrc file. You'll recall from Chapter 6 that .cshrc, the C shell read command file, is read each time a new subshell is created. You could place your list of aliases in your .login file, but this is read only once, when you first log in. Any subshells spawned during a session would not know about these aliases unless they were also present in .cshrc.

If you forget which aliases have been set up, alias with no arguments will tell you:

```
% alias
bye     clear;logout
c       clear
dir     ls -al
g       grep
gb      set gb=`/bin/pwd`; cd $gt;set gt=$gb
gt      set gt=`/bin/pwd`; cd !^
h       history
la      ls -F
ll      ls -l
m       more
motd    more /etc/motd
p       ps -ef
reserv  taper
rm      rm -i
rot13   tr "[A-M][N-Z][a-m][n-z]" "[N-Z][A-M][n-z][a-m]"
myprint lp -onobanner -ocpi =elite
mytemp  cd /usr/stan/tmp
% _
```

(See Appendix A for details.) Some of the above aliases, by the way, are supplied globally by the system administrator. They are so common in the C shell world that they assume the character of "standard" commands. It can be a tad confusing for beginners who look up dir, say, in the man pages and find it missing. Well-run sites, though, will have local man pages that document all aliases and other local quirks.

Note especially the rm alias. By aliasing an *existing* command you are effectively overriding its standard definition. Naturally, great caution is needed! You would

not want cd to remove all your files, would you? In the case of rm, the alias is a common safety ploy: the -i argument warns you before erasing files.

Note also that you can alias a group of commands as in bye, which will invoke clear followed by logout.

You can examine a particular alias as follows:

```
% alias mytemp
mytemp  cd /usr/stan/tmp
% _
```

You can kill off an alias by using unalias followed by the name of the alias:

```
% unalias mytemp
% mytemp
mytemp: Command not found
% _
```

Of course, if mytemp is aliased in your .cshrc, it will be revived the next time you spawn a new shell.

The unalias command also accepts wildcards, so unalias * will remove all existing aliases, and unalias ??print will kill off myprint as well as skprint, and so on.

The full power of alias emerges when you combine several commands, possibly including previously defined aliases, under the one alias:

```
% alias pjob mytemp; myprint
% _
```

It's time to return to the lp command.

The -c Copy Option

Since print requests are queued (spooled), you may wonder what happens if you reedit or erase a file before the print service has had a chance to extract the file from the queue and print it. The answer is that under normal circumstances the printout reflects the latest state of your file. If you erase it too soon, you'll lose the listing! If you edit it before the print is complete, the results can be unpredictable: you may be editing a part of the file that has already been printed, or not, as the case may be. There are two solutions: leave the file alone until it's fully printed; or use the -c (copy) option.

You can check the status of your print requests using the lpstat command. You'll see how in the next section.

The –c option tells the shell to make immediate copies of all the files in the lp command. It is these copies that will eventually print regardless of what you do with the original files. The –c option, like the other lp options, can be placed in any order in the options sequence. The following commands will work the same—both send a copy of chapter.2 to the print service:

```
$ lp -onobanner -c -ocpi=elite -olength=55 chapter.2
$ lp -onobanner -ocpi=elite -olength=55 -c chapter.2
```

You can now edit (or erase!) chapter.2 without affecting the listing.

The lpstat Command

Whenever processes are pushed into the background, you need some way of following their progress. Just as ps and pstat tell you the status of processes in general, lpstat (in man section C) keeps you informed regarding the fate of your print requests. As with pstat there are options that affect the amount of information to be displayed. You can check individual or groups of print requests by user name or id, request id, and/or printer name or class. The default is to report on all your requests that are still in the queue.

```
$ lpstat
laser-36   stan 4567 Aug 23 15:56 on laser
laser-40   stan  678 Aug 23 16:08
laser-45   stan 1243 Aug 23 16:23
$ _
```

The display tells you when each request was submitted, by whom, and the size in bytes of each file. The legend "on laser" indicates that request laser-36 is currently printing a file of 4,567 bytes on the printer called laser.

The most common options are listed below. The options can be combined in any sequence. You can actually type all as a list argument, but since this is the normal default list, there is no pressing reason to do so.

lpstat Option	Meaning	Description
-a[*list*]	Acceptance	Displays status of printer or class names in optional list. Default is all printers and classes. The list can be entered as laser,daisy or laser daisy.
-c[*list*]	Class	Lists class names and their members. Default is all classes.
-d	Default	Displays the name of the default printer.
-o[*list*][*l*]	Output	Displays status of requests in *list* (default option is all). The list can be any mix of printer/class names and request ids. The l (long) option gives a more complete display.
-r	Request	Displays the status of the LP request scheduler, for example, Scheduler is running. If the scheduler is not running for any reason, the spooling service is not available, and you will need to print directly using cat >dev/*xxx*.
-s	Summary	Displays a complete summary of the printer service: default printer, class lists, character sets, and so on.
-t	Total	Gives a complete LP status display: all users and all printers.
-u[*list*]	User	Displays status for the users in list (default is all users).
-v[*list*]	Device	Displays printer names and dev/*xxx* paths for printers named in list (default is all printers).

Changing Print Requests with lp -i

The lp -i command lets you change the options on a print request after it has been submitted—provided, of course, that you act before the printing is complete. You'll need to know the print request id, so if you haven't made a note of this, you'll need to run lpstat first. If the printing has started but has not finished, the printing will halt and a new request with the revised options will be submitted, that is, you start again from the beginning of the file. You use the -i option as follows:

```
lp -i print_id new_options
```

The new_options arguments can be any valid lp print options, and they replace the original options to form a revised request. The designated files are not changed.

The cancel Command

You use the cancel command to cancel any printer requests. The syntax is

```
cancel [id1 id2 id3...idn] [prname1 prname2...prnamex]
```

Specifying the optional id arguments will cancel requests with those id numbers. Specifying the optional printer names will cancel requests made on particular printers. If a file is currently printing, cancel stops it in its tracks. If you specified several files in the same request, any not yet printed will not be printed.

The Iprint Command

Many terminals nowadays have a built-in port allowing you to connect a printer. These are called *local* printers to distinguish them from the central *spool* printer(s). As an alternative to the lp -L option mentioned earlier, you can print a file on your local printer with the lprint command (in man section C). There are two formats:

```
lprint -
```

will print the following keyboard entries (until you enter Ctrl-D).

```
lprint filename
```

will print the argument file. Your etc/termcap file must be set correctly with your terminal and printer parameters.

Simple Formatting with pr

The pr command (in man section C) can be used to format your listings in various ways. pr sends formatted text to the standard output by default, so you need to pipe this to lp to get formatted hardcopy printouts:

```
$ pr chapter.1 | lp
request id laser-69 (1 file)
$ _
```

In the absence of pr options, the above prints chapter.1 with simple page breaks, with each page numbered, dated, and headed by the file name. The following options are available:

Option	Description
+k	Starts printing at page k (default is page 1).
-k	Prints in k columns (default is single column).
-d	Prints in double-line spacing.
-e[k]	Expands tab codes in file to give tabs at character positions $k+1, 2\times(k+1),\ldots$. The default gives tabs at every 8th position.
-n[k]	Adds k-digit line numbers. Default is 5, that is, line numbers up to 99999.
-w[k]	Sets line width to k. Default is 72.
-o[k]	Offsets (indents) each line by k character spaces. Default is 0.
-l[k]	Sets page length to k lines. Default is 66.

Option	Description
-h[*header*]	Replaces file-name header by the string *header* at top of each page.
-p	Screen only: pauses after each page.

As you can see, some of the pr options match similar options available in the lp command, so you need to avoid unnecessary duplications. Setting the options in pr (and possibly creating a shell script or alias) has the merit that you can have a screen preview before piping out to lp. The -p (page pause) option is useful here. A typical pr example might be:

```
$ pr +10 -e9 -d -h"Chapter 1" chapter.1 | lp
```

This would print the header Chapter 1 on each page, starting at page 10 of the chapter.1 file. Tabs would be ten character positions apart, and the printout would be double-line spacing.

Summary

In this chapter you saw how printers can be physically attached to the system using serial or parallel ports. Each printer type has to be identified via entries in the /dev directory and controlled via specific device drivers linked to the kernel. Devices in /dev behave rather like conventional files, so Unix can redirect output to them using the > operator. Each printer needs an entry in the terminfo file defining its characteristics, and filter programs may be needed to translate file data prior to printing.

Requests to print are spooled using the lp command. These trigger background processes that can be monitored with the lpstat command and cancelled with the cancel command.

To reduce the typing of complex command options, I introduced the idea of shell scripts and explained how chmod is used to make a command file executable. For the C shell, I suggested the alternative of using the alias command.

Local printers (attached to terminals) can be fed using the lprint command.

The pr filter offers simple printer formatting.

CHAPTER

ELEVEN

The vi Family of Editors

- Basic commands

- vi modes and submodes

- Creating a file with vi

- Text entry

- Cursor movement

If you survived Chapter 8 on the ed editor, this chapter should be plain sailing. It covers several evolutionary stages in Unix text editing after the distinctly plumpen, line-based philosophy of ed. vi (pronounced "vee-eye") stands for "visual," and this points to its most visible feature: you get to see a whole screenful of the text you are editing. vi was originally developed by Bill Joy (who also designed the C shell) for the BSD (Berkeley Software Distribution) versions of Unix. If your system claims "Berkeley extensions," this usually means that you have vi and csh (the C shell) available. The standard Unix (System V) also includes vi, so it's almost certain that you will find it on your system.

The vi family of editors inherits most of the concepts found in ed. In particular, both ed and vi are modal editors with *text-entry* and *command* modes. They also offer the same elaborate text searching methods based on *regular expressions*. The historical reason for this overlap is that vi makes use of a line editor called ex, which in turn is an enhancement (superset) of ed. In fact, vi is really ex with a fancy, screen-oriented user interface. You'll see later that from within vi you can use the colon (:) escape command to switch to ex command-line mode. In this mode, the familiar ed commands found in ex are all available!

Some users still prefer to use ex (or a simplified version of ex called edit) as a sort of supercharged ed, but the visible screen interface has made vi the editor of choice at most Unix sites. Programmers in particular like the *autoindent* feature that helps create structured, legible source code. They also relish the ability to create wild macros and the opportunity of escaping temporarily to the shell in order to test the program being edited. vi bristles with options and legerdemain but is easily customized so that it fires up with your personal preferences preset as defaults. Those who persevere and master vi achieve remarkable editing feats at high speed and will brook no criticism of vi, however mild.

I have tried to make this chapter as self-contained as possible for the benefit of readers who skimped on Chapter 8. The pace, however, will be brisker since by now you should be familiar with editing terminology and Unix command syntax. vi is a large, complex program to which entire books have been dedicated (as well as posters, coffee mugs, and reference cards; some sources are listed in Appendix C: Unix Resources), so I make no claim to a comprehensive treatment. The vi man pages (all thirty-eight of them in section C) should be consulted for the less common options.

Preliminaries

vi uses some special key combinations for cursor and display control, so you need to make sure that Unix knows about your terminal and all its quirks. You may have heard of the *connector conspiracy.* This is the theory that the physical characteristics (size, pinout, and gender) of connectors are deliberately doctored at regular intervals in order to prevent the interoperability of systems and peripherals. Even when you beat this conspiracy, you find that each terminal model has its own peculiar software interface with the outside world. The output codes generated by, say, the Delete key or by combinations such as Ctrl-U are far from standard. Similarly, the input code sequences needed to clear the screen or delete to the end of a line vary among manufacturers (and often between monitors from the same manufacturer). Your terminal, therefore, must be correctly identified to the Unix system before the vi-specific keystrokes will work as planned. vi makes use of the following special keys (the actions are described briefly and may depend on the current mode as indicated; I'll elaborate later):

NOTE   Keyboards do vary greatly, so you should check the given mappings of keystroke-to-action on your own system and make the necessary adjustments to this chapter's instructions.

Name	Action
Esc	Returns you to command mode or cancels commands. Also terminates an ex command.
Return	Terminates an ex command or starts a newline in text-entry mode. (Return is sometimes labeled Enter or ⏎.)
Interrupt	Aborts a command (often labeled Del, Delete, or Rubout).
Bksp	*Text-entry mode:* Backspaces the cursor by one character on the current line. Removes the previously typed character from the edit buffer, but does not remove it

Name	Action
	from the display (sometimes labeled as Left Arrow). The current line is defined as the line containing the cursor.
	Command mode: Backspaces cursor without deletion (can take a preceding *count* parameter).
Ctrl-D	*Command mode:* Scrolls down a half-screen.
Ctrl-F	*Command mode:* Scrolls page forward.
Ctrl-B	*Command mode:* Scrolls page backward.
Ctrl-N	*Command mode:* Moves cursor down one line (alternative to cursor arrow key).
Ctrl-P	*Command mode:* Moves cursor up one line (alternative to cursor arrow key).
Bell or Ctrl-G	*Command mode:* Displays vi status.
Ctrl-R or Ctrl-L	*Command mode:* Redraws the screen (choice depends on terminal type).
Ctrl-U	*Text-entry mode:* Restores cursor to the first character inserted on the current line (further insertions can then be made from that point).
	Command mode: Scrolls up a half-screen.
Ctrl-V	*Text-entry mode:* Used to insert control characters into the text by suspending the normal action of that control character (some exceptions).
Ctrl-W	*Text-entry mode:* Moves the cursor to the first character of the last inserted word.
Ctrl-T	*Text-entry mode:* If autoindent is on, gives an indent of shiftwidth spaces from left-hand margin. (Shiftwidth can be preset or varied by vi commands.)
Ctrl-@	*Text-entry mode:* When entered as first character of an insertion, vi replaces Ctrl-@ with the last piece of text inserted (unless this exceeds 128 characters). Similar to . (dot) in command mode.

Because keys can be labeled in so many different ways, I'll use the vi generic names that appear in the left-hand column.

The secret to getting these vi special keys to work as shown lies in having an entry in the file /etc/termcap that provides Unix with details of your terminal's capabilities (hence the name termcap). The /etc/termcap file is a database describing all the terminals in your system (and possibly some ancient ones that have long since vanished). To speed access to this large database, a condensed (compiled) version of termcap is created in the usr/lib/terminfo directory.

termcap is a text file that you can view, print, and (God forbid) edit. My alarm here stems from the potential Catch-22: how to edit a file that may need editing before you can edit a file! Happily, editors such as ed are fairly undemanding, so there are usually "generic" termcap entries that give you sufficient features to create a termcap entry that will support vi.

Each termcap entry can take from one line for simple terminals to as many as thirty lines for more complex models. With the advent of color and graphics, the situation is growing even more complicated. Each entry starts with a two-character abbreviation followed by a set of alternative names (separated by |). Next comes a sequence of highly cryptic, comma-delimited entries representing that terminal's characteristics.

NOTE If vi does not know your terminal type, you may get garbled screens or a message saying "Using open mode." In either case, exit with :q! and check your termcap file and TERM variable setting, as explained below.

To add a new terminal to termcap, you try to find an existing entry for a similar terminal, then copy and edit that entry. The man pages for termcap are in section F (for files). Listed there are several hundred coded capabilities that you can add to a termcap entry. To give you the merest flavor, consider the entry

```
cl| adm3| 3| lsi adm3:bs:am:li#24:co#80:cl=^Z
```

This is for the Lear Siegler ADM-3 terminal, known to Unix as either cl, adm3, 3, or lsi adm3—hence the first four entries separated by | (| is read as "or"). For historical reasons, the first terminal name is always two characters, while the second name is the most common abbreviation for that terminal. vi always uses the second name, in this case, adm3. As you'll see, this is also the name that is usually set in your

shell variable, TERM. The final name is a fuller description intended solely as a visual aid to humans, so spaces are allowed.

Following the name fields, there are as many capability fields as required. You use the backslash at the end of a line if you need to continue your entry on the next line. The above example has five capability fields: bs for backspace/erase; am for automargin (also known as wraparound); li#24 and co#80 to indicate a 24-line × 80-column screen. vi needs to know your screen size, of course, so it can scroll and position the cursor correctly. Finally, the cl=^Z field means that Ctrl-Z will clear the ADM-3 screen. Note that not every program requires that every available capability of your terminal be set in termcap. For example, you could run ed without having the clear screen capability defined. Usually, though, Unix will come with a generous termcap selection, and your terminal will be fully described somewhere in the list. The point is that if vi appears to work fine on your terminal, then the termcap fairy has blessed you already. If vi works erratically, the chances are that termcap needs attention. Other applications, such as Lyrix and Multiplan, also refer to /etc/termcap, so sooner or later you should get your terminal in the database.

NOTE Before vi can be used, your terminal must be correctly registered in /etc/termcap and /usr/lib/terminfo, and your shell variable TERM must be set with your terminal name.

From now on, I will assume that your system administrator, supplier, or local guru has established a suitable termcap entry for your terminal.

It is also necessary to set the shell variable TERM to the terminal name used in termcap (usually the popular name found in the second name field). This is normally achieved by an entry in your .profile (Bourne shell) or .login (C shell) file, as explained in Chapter 6. If you are using the Lear Siegler ADM-3 terminal, a typical .profile entry might be

```
TERM=adm3
export TERM
```

for the Bourne shell, or

```
setenv TERM adm3
```

for the C shell (more on these differences in Appendix A).

Meet the Family

There are three editors in the vi family: view, vedit, and vi itself. They all offer full, navigable screen displays of your text. Gone are the traps of "hidden" line addresses that vary as you edit your files (although you can use line addresses if you wish by escaping to ex mode). With vi and her siblings, you are closer to the modern WYSIWYG (What You See Is What You Get, pronounced "wiziwig") school of editing. With this added power, of course, comes a heavy baggage of commands and features. However, as I preached in Chapter 8, you can get by with just a handful of basic commands. And, since the effects of your actions are more immediately visible than with ed, the learning curve is that much easier.

Before you start worrying about whether you have three distinct sets of commands to learn for each member of the vi family (which cynics might say is par for the Unix course), let me reassure you that view and vedit are simple subsets or variants of vi—they all share the same command structure. The differences are as follows:

view   The "read-only" version of vi. Allows a file to be displayed, scrolled, and searched but not altered in any way.

vedit   The "novice" version of vi. It offers the *showmode* feature by default, provides more help, and reduces the complexity of certain operations.

All three editors are invoked using the same syntax:

```
vi [-option...] [command...] [filename...]
view [-option...] [command...] [filename...]
vedit [-option...] [command...] [filename...]
```

Later in this chapter I'll explain the various options and command sequences available. Many of them will not make much sense until you've seen how vi works. Unless stated specifically, you can assume that all three editors treat these options and commands in the same way.

In many ways, you can look on view and vedit as invocations of vi with certain default options and settings built in. For example,

```
view filename
```

is entirely equivalent to

```
vi -R filename
```

since the -R option specifies read-only mode, that is, you can look at the contents of a file, but you can't make any edits.

The vedit variant runs vi in novice mode with certain options set on or off by default as shown in the list below. How and where you can vary these options with the set command will be covered later; for now, note that there are *switch* options and *string* options. The ex and vi convention is that each switch option has an "on" version and an "off" version distinguished by the prefix no. For example, to set magic on, you use set magic; to turn it off, you use set nomagic. By contrast, string options are set to specific values, for example, set report=6. Each string option has a default value that it assumes in the absence of an explicit set assignment. The vedit defaults are listed below:

no magic	Reduces the number of special characters allowed in regular expressions.
report=1	Sets the report threshold to 1. This means that any command that changes more than one line will invoke a visual report after the command. The normal vi default is report=5. The idea is that beginners are warned immediately after modifying two or more lines so they can use undo promptly to cure any inadvertent editing errors. Experienced users can set the threshold higher.
showmode	The legends INSERT, APPEND, CHANGE, or OPEN MODE will be displayed whenever you activate one of the text-entry modes.
redraw	If you have a dumb terminal, the editor will vary its display output to simulate an intelligent terminal. This option is becoming less useful as dumb terminals become extinct.

You can turn novice mode off and on from within vedit with set nonovice and set novice, but you cannot directly control novice mode from within vi (or ex). What you can do from within vi (or ex) is to set or unset any or all of the above options.

Beginners are advised to use vedit with novice set on (the default), or use vi with showmode set on. The latter (assumed in this chapter) requires the following steps:

1. When vi first fires up, you are in command mode.

2. Type : (colon)—do not press Return.

3. A colon appears on the status line, with the cursor immediately following. You are now in ex mode.

4. Type set showmode followed by Return.

5. You are now back in vi command mode.

6. vi will now display the appropriate text-entry legend (INSERT, APPEND, and so on) whenever you switch to insert, append, change, or open modes.

vi remains in showmode for this session only. You can make showmode or any other selectable option permanent by putting suitable commands in a file called .exrc (ex resource). We'll see how in a moment.

Another example of setting defaults is the mesg option. While using vi, it is most unpleasant to receive messages from other users. You can control email write permission (as explained in Chapter 5) during vi sessions only, with the commands set mesg and set nomesg (the default is nomesg). These choices override your current writeability only while vi is being used.

The six steps listed above may not be immediately intelligible, so let's look closer at the various modes mentioned so far.

The Three+Four Modes

You have already seen that ed is a *modal* editor. Well, vi is modal too, and even more so! vi has three main operational modes: *text-entry, command,* and *ex escape.* In addition, the text-entry mode can be further divided into *insert, append, change,* and *open* submodes. To recap what modalism means: the interpretation of your keystrokes depends vitally on which mode vi is in at the time.

WARNING Watch out for some ambiguity in the literature: text-entry mode is often referred to as text-insert mode (or just insert mode). It is less confusing to think of text-entry mode having four submodes: insert, append, change, and open (as indicated with showmode on).

The following list summarizes the differences between the three main modes and provides some audio-visual clues that may help you to distinguish them:

Text-entry mode
Typed characters go to a temporary file known as the editing buffer (and eventually to a permanent file if the buffer is saved). Visual clues: printable characters that you type will appear on the screen. If showmode is on, the appropriate legend INSERT, APPEND, CHANGE, or OPEN MODE will be displayed at the bottom right of the screen. Audible clue: pressing Esc will exit text-entry mode without bleeping.

Command mode
Keystrokes are interpreted as vi editing commands. Each command is usually a single or double keystroke (with possible modifiers), performing such operations as cursor movement, screen scrolling, text deletion, change and movement, string searching, and switching to the other modes. Visual clues: the typed commands do not immediately show on the screen. If showmode is on, the absence of the mode legends is significant! Audible clues: typing a character that does not correspond to a command will sound a bleep. Pressing Esc will always bleep (and you remain in command mode).

ex Escape mode
Your input is interpreted as an ex command. Visual clues: the ex command prompt : (colon) will be displayed at the beginning of the status line. The cursor appears after the colon. ex commands are displayed as you type them but have no effect until you press Return or Esc.

I'll call this third mode the ex mode to avoid verbiage. The ex mode is always visually apparent: a colon prompt is displayed on a line known as the status line. This

is where you will enter any ex commands followed by the Return or Esc keys. After completing an ex command, you usually return to command mode. Note that ex commands include most of the ed commands discussed in Chapter 8.

The showmode feature controls a helpful display on the right-hand side of the status line that tells you when you are in text-entry mode. In fact, you are told the sub-mode: INSERT, APPEND, CHANGE, or OPEN. Initially, you'll find it useful to have a visual "mode reminder," but before long, you'll be quite proud to shed this shaming crutch (or at least switch it off if your colleagues are kibitzing).

Mode Navigation

You normally fire up in command mode. You need to learn the following set of simplified mode-switching maneuvers (I'll elaborate later):

NOTE   **Alphabetic commands are case-sensitive.**

From Mode	To Mode	Command, Key, or Action Needed
Command	Text-entry	i, I (insert)
		a, A (append)
		o, O (open new line)
		s, S (substitute)
		c, C (change)
		r, R (replace)
Text-entry	Command	Esc
Command	ex	: (colon)
ex	Command	Return or Esc after ex command
Text-entry	ex	Must go via command mode with Esc, then : (colon)

From Mode	To Mode	Command, Key, or Action Needed
ex	Text-entry	Must go via command mode with Return or Esc after ex command, followed by a text-entry switch

After this general background, it's time to use vi on some simple texts. The first example illustrates simple text entry, cursor movement, and file saving. The only way to learn vi is by constant practice. It is not easy to describe all the vi features using words alone. What may take several long sentences to explain precisely is often immediately apparent when you experiment with vi.

Creating a Text with vi

First, we'll create a special trash directory to keep our vi experiments out of harm's way. You should set up vi to give you showmode on, as described earlier.

```
$ cd
$ pwd
/usr/stan
$ mkdir trash
$ cd trash
$ vi test.data
```

As you can see in Figure 11.1, the screen will now show twenty-three tildes, one in the extreme left-hand column (column 1) of each line, from line 2 to line 24. The cursor will appear in column 1 of line 1. Line 25, the status line, will say "test.data" [New file]. Line 25 is reserved for status messages and for entering ex commands.

I am assuming an 80-column × 25-line screen, of course. vi looks at the terminfo file to determine each terminal's screen size, and displays are adjusted accordingly.

The tildes are simply place markers indicating empty lines. They are not text characters to be saved in a file, and they will disappear one by one as you enter text on successive lines.

If test.data is an existing file, vi test.data will initially display some or all of its contents depending on the file size and your screen size. If the text requires less than a screenful, tildes will indicate the unused lines. If the text exceeds the capacity

FIGURE 11.1:

The Opening vi Screen

```
⊤
-
-
~
~
~
~
~
~
~
~
~
~
~
~
~
~
~
~
~
~

"test.data" [New file]
```

of the screen, you initially see the top "screen's worth" (no tildes) and you will have to scroll down to reveal the rest of the file. vi provides many scrolling and searching commands (up and down, by line, half-page, full-page, multiple pages, and so on) for rapid scanning of large files.

The status line is used not only to report various conditions, but for entering ex commands. You can clear this line at any time, provided you are in command mode, by pressing Ctrl-L. (On some terminals, you must use Ctrl-R.) This useful command is known as *screen refresh* or *screen redraw*. You can also use it to remove any spurious rubbish from the screen, such as those random characters that arise from glitches in a communications line, or unwanted, unstoppable messages from root! Remember that you can block other users from writing to you, either permanently or just when you are using vi.

Pressing Ctrl-G (or Bell, if you have such a key) when in command mode will display a status message giving you the name of the file you are editing, whether or not it has been modified since the last save, and a number representing the percentage of the amount of the file (measured in lines) that lies in front of the current character (that is, the character at the current cursor position). Ctrl-G is therefore called the *status* command.

NOTE   The innocent word *blank* is not always used consistently in Unix literature. It can mean empty when describing the "line" between successive end-of-line characters. It can also mean spaces or tabs.

The cursor is initially placed under the first nonblank character found in the first line, so status would show 100%. If the first line is completely blank, the cursor appears in column 1. The cursor position plays a vital role in vi editing. It controls where your entered text will be positioned in the target file.

Text Entry

The editor fires up in command mode. Before you can enter, change, or rearrange text, you must switch from command mode to one of the text-entry modes. Adding fresh text is done in either append mode (the a command) or insert mode (the i command). These modes differ only in where the text is added: you append *after* the current character but insert *before* the current character. In some situations, such as initially when the buffer is empty, this distinction is irrelevant. On other occasions, the difference is vital. For example, to add text at the end of a line, you must use append mode (you'll see shortly that some cursor movement commands do not allow the cursor to be moved beyond the last character of a line).

1. Type a (lowercase) without a Return. The "a" will not appear—show no surprise!

2. You are now in text-entry mode. In particular, you are in append mode, and the APPEND MODE legend should appear on the right side of the status line, line 25. (If not, perhaps you are using vi with the showmode off? To fix this, type Esc, colon, then type set showmode followed by Return. Now repeat from step 1.)

3. Type the following text with Returns at the end of each line:

   ```
   At last, I am using vi, the visual editor. I am in append
   mode, so my keystrokes are being stored (appended) into the
   editing buffer. Later on, after further editing, I will save
   this text by writing from the buffer to the file test.data.
   ```

I have entered a final newline (Enter) and two spaces after each period to match the definition of a sentence in vi. Certain vi commands rely on this convention when moving the cursor one sentence at a time.

Notice how the tildes have disappeared from lines 2 to 6, but on the unused lines, 7 to 24, there are still tildes in column 1. If you make any typing errors, ignore them for the moment. I'll explain how to make corrections after you've learned some cursor movement commands.

The above text is stored in the editing buffer. Until you write it out to disk, the file test.data remains empty. During long editing sessions, it is sound practice to save the buffer at regular intervals. To do this, follow these steps:

1. Press Esc to leave append mode and return to command mode.

2. Type a colon. You are now in ex mode. The status line will echo this colon. It serves as the ex mode prompt.

3. Type w (the ex write command) followed by Return. This writes the editing buffer to disk. Since you did not specify a file name, the buffer is written to the current file, namely test.data. You are now back in command mode.

You can save the buffer in any directory/file name combination for which you have write permission. For example, if the file test.temp does not exist, :w test.temp will create such a file and then write the buffer to it. If test.temp exists, the :w command will *not* overwrite it, but you can force an overwrite with :w! test.temp. The current file name is not changed by the :w command, so subsequent writes would still default to test.data in the absence of a file name argument. A useful variant is :w>>*filename*, which appends the vi buffer to *filename*. There are three convenient ways to write and exit vi:

:wq(Return)	Same as :w(Return) followed by :q(Return).
:x(Return)	Same effect as above.
ZZ	Same effect as above, but note that you do not need to type the colon or press Return. When you are in command mode, as opposed to ex mode, no Return is needed after a command: your input takes effect immediately once the command is completed. The status line will confirm your write operation:

```
"test.data" [New file] 5 lines, 237 characters
```

From now on, the above sequence will be described as "type :w" or simply :w, as though it were a single command. Such commands are sometimes called colon commands—they consist of the colon escape to ex mode, then an ex command followed by a Return (or Esc), which executes the ex command and usually returns you to command mode. I say "usually" because there are colon commands that exit vi or escape temporarily to the shell. With such commands, you will receive clear visible clues (the shell prompt, for instance) that you are *not* back in vi command mode.

> **NOTE**   If you want to abort a partially entered ex command, press the Interrupt key (either Del, Delete, or Rubout on most terminals).

Now that you are back in command mode, you'll notice that the APPEND MODE display has disappeared. There is no explicit COMMAND MODE legend, but there's a simple trick available to confirm your command-mode status (especially useful if showmode is off). Just press Esc again, and you will hear a beep. If you are already in command mode, Esc is an invalid selection. And if you weren't in command mode, you are now! Some find this Esc probing a viable substitute for the showmode feature. We can summarize the preceding session as

```
a[text]Esc[:w<Return>]
```

It started in command mode, switched to text-entry (append) mode, escaped to command mode, detoured to ex mode, then returned to command mode. The clue to mastering vi is gaining fluency with such sequences to the point where you move between the modes without thinking about them. You even reach the stage where vi seems eminently intuitive!

Finally, let's exit vi. Since you have just saved your work, a simple :q (quit) will bring you back to the shell from which vi was invoked. If you try :q before all current changes have been saved, you will be warned and vi will not exit until you either write your changes or tell vi to discard them. You overrule the warning with :q! (quit and discard recent changes without complaint). As noted earlier, you can write and quit in one fell swoop using :wq, :x, or ZZ.

If you now invoke vi with test.data, the text will appear and the status line will announce

```
"test.data" 5 lines, 237 characters
```

Note that the legend [New file] is now missing.

Cursor Movement

It's time to explore the major cursor movement commands, which are listed below. Note carefully that many vi commands are case-sensitive (for example, 1 and L perform different functions):

Command	Action
1 or spacebar or →	Moves cursor to the right, but not beyond the end of a line (note the warning beep). The spacebar does *not* blank out any characters being traversed.
h or Bksp or ←	Moves cursor to the left, but not beyond the start of the current line (a beep sounds). (The current line is the line containing the cursor.)
+ or Return	Moves cursor to the start of the next line. Beeps if no next line.
j or Ctrl-N or Ctrl-J or LF or ↓	Moves cursor down one line in same column. (Note: LF is the Line Feed key found on older terminals). Beeps if no next line. If column in the lower line is beyond the end of the line, the cursor will move to the last character of that line. The cursor will never move down to an empty position beyond the end of a line.
k or Ctrl-P or ↑	Moves cursor up one line in the same column. Beeps if you are on the first line. If column in the upper line is beyond the end of the line, the cursor will move to the last character of that line. The cursor will never move up to an empty position beyond the end of a line.

Command	Action
-	Moves cursor up to the start of the previous line. Beeps if no previous line.
^	Moves cursor to the first nonblank character of the current line.
0 (zero)	Moves cursor to column 1 of the current line (whether blank or not).
$	Moves cursor to the last character of the current line.
w	Moves cursor forward to the start of the next word. Words are taken to be strings separated by whitespace (newlines, spaces, or tabs) or punctuation symbols, so "heavy,metal,rock" and "heavy metal rock" both count as three words. Repeated application will scan words on next line (if any).
W	As for w, but words are taken as strings separated by whitespace (punctuation alone does not count). If you were scanning forward with W, "heavy,metal,rock" would be skipped as one word. "Heavy, metal, rock" would need three Ws to skip. Repeated application will scan words on next line (if any).
b	Works like w, but moves cursor backwards to the start of the previous word.
B	Works like W, but moves cursor backwards to the start of the previous word.
e	Works like w, but cursor stops under the last character of the next word. If the cursor is already inside a word, it will stop at the end of that word.
E	Works like W, but cursor stops under the last character of the next word. If cursor is already inside a word, it will stop at the end of that word.

Command	Action
(	Moves cursor to the start of the current sentence, or to the start of the previous sentence if the cursor is already at the beginning of a sentence.
)	Moves cursor to the start of the next sentence. vi looks upon a sentence as any string terminating with a period, question mark, or exclamation mark that is followed by either two spaces or a newline. The two-space requirement is a nuisance for those who prefer single spacing between sentences.
H	Moves cursor to home, sweet home, namely column 1 of the top line of the screen.
L	Moves cursor to the bottom line of the screen.

Using test.data, practice these cursor movements until you feel comfortable with them. In the next chapter we'll start some serious vi editing.

Summary

You've now had your first taste of the vi family of visual editors: vi, view, and vedit. You've seen the three modes of vi in action: text-entry, command, and escape/ex. After a pause for breath, we'll explore vi in more detail in the next chapter.

CHAPTER

TWELVE

Advanced vi Techniques

- Screen controls

- More on text-entry modes

- Deleting, changing, and searching text

- The ex command mode

- Miscellaneous ex commands

- Entering and leaving vi

Three aspects of v i affect the learning curve. First, the commands you type do not appear on the screen, so you lack the familiar, direct visual confirmation of your keystroke. (Did I type "b" or "B"?) Of course, you do see the result of the command, and with time, the blind keystroke and the resulting cursor movement meld in a natural way. Second, the habit of keying a command followed by a Return must be broken: in command mode, the valid command keys are "instant" and a spurious Return can be a nuisance. Finally, the different actions arising from a case shift are not consistent or memorable. Invalid commands always beep, so expect some noise during your apprenticeship. However, note that most keys have some command assignment, so the danger of errors is quite high.

NOTE Unclear on the concept! People often complain about *steep* learning curves. In fact, steep means easy! See Fig 12.1.

FIGURE 12.1:
Comparison of learning curves

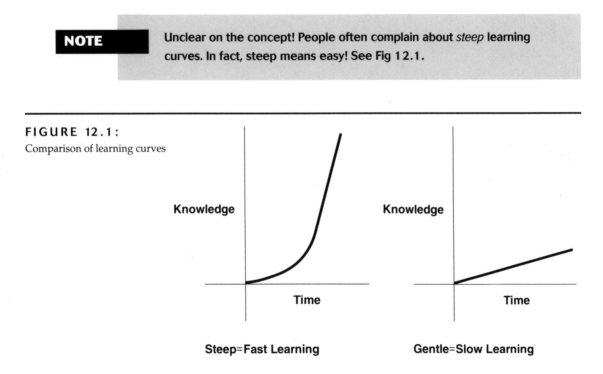

Some of these commands are usefully mnemonic, but others not so: the lowercase l for cursor right is particularly inappropriate. (Yet such is the quirk of human

memory that this soon becomes unforgettable!) Once you have played with these, you are ready to jazz up the action by adding a *count* number in front of the cursor movement command. Whenever it makes sense you can multiply the movement as follows:

3l   Moves 3 characters right (if possible—the end of the current line is the limit).

6h   Moves 6 characters left (but never beyond the start of the current line).

2+   Moves down 2 lines, ending at the start of the line. Beeps if move is impossible.

4$ Moves to end of the line that is 3 lines beyond the current line. (The 4 is needed because moving to the end of the current line counts as one move.)

The full syntax of the cursor-movement commands is therefore

[*count*] *command*

with a default *count* of 1. The *count* option is the general rule, so I will only mention it when it does not apply or when the meaning is unusual.

Screen Controls

With the small text entered so far, the screen-control commands, such as scrolling and paging, are singularly unimpressive. So let's use a nice vi trick to increase the file size. Position the cursor under the final period of the last line of the `test.data` example in Chapter 11. Press Esc to ensure that you are in command mode; then type a (append) followed by Return to put you on line 6. Now type

```
This line is being added to test.data.
```

and then press Return to bring the cursor to line 7.

Now press Esc to return to command mode and simply type a period (the repeat command). The text of line 6 will be repeated on line 7:

```
At last, I am using vi, the visual editor.  I am in append mode, so
my keystrokes are being stored (appended) into the editing buffer.
Later on, after further editing, I will save this text by writing
```

```
from the buffer to the file test.data.
This line is being added to test.data.
This line is being added to test.data.
```

The rule is that a period typed in command mode repeats your last insert (or delete) command.

Next try the u (undo) command. Line 7 clears. Press u again. Line 7 reappears! So, u tells vi to undo the effects of the *previous* command. If the previous command was a u, u undoes the effect of that undo, thereby restoring the previous file state. Three successive u's are the same as one u; four u's effectively do nothing, and so on. (Contrast this with the nested undo command found in some editors that can progressively restore each previous state.) The vi undo command allows you to toggle between two states. This can be useful after a text change. You can quickly compare the old and new versions, and retain the one that appeals.

Use the period again and again to repeat the last inserted line, and notice how the screen scrolls up when you reach line 24. You can now usefully explore the following screen-control commands:

Command	Action
[*n*]Ctrl-U	Scrolls the screen up *n* lines. The default gives a half-screen scroll up.
[*n*]Ctrl-D	Scrolls the screen down *n* lines. The default gives a half-screen scroll down.
[*count*]Ctrl-F	Pages the screen forward, leaving two lines between pages for continuity, if possible. Note that *count* gives the number of *pages*, with a default of 1.
[*count*]Ctrl-B	Pages the screen backward, leaving two lines between pages for continuity, if possible. Note that *count* gives the number of *pages*, with a default of 1.
Ctrl-G or Bell	Displays the status line.
z<Return>	"Zeroes" the screen by redrawing the display with the current line placed at the top of the screen. This is an apparent exception to the "no Return" rule. In fact, the z command can be followed by a Return, ., or - with different effects (see below).

Command	Action
z.	As z\<Return>, but places the current line in the middle of the screen.
z−	As z\<Return>, but places the current line at the bottom of the screen.
Ctrl-R or Ctrl-L	Refreshes the screen, clearing any spurious displays; also clears the status line message. Test to see which variant works on your terminal.

More on Text-Entry Modes

Once you can move the cursor about, you are ready to practice the four basic text-entry modes: append, insert, open, and change. You have already used the a (append) command, so the following variants should be straightforward. Remember that the following commands switch you to text-entry mode, so after typing the required text, you need to press Esc to return to command mode.

Command	Action
a[*text*]	Appends *text* after cursor
A[*text*]	Appends *text* at end of current line no matter where the cursor is
i[*text*]	Inserts *text* before cursor
I[*text*]	Inserts *text* in front of current line no matter where the cursor is
o[*text*]	Opens a new line below the current line and inserts *text*
O[*text*]	Opens a new line above the current line and inserts *text*

Note especially the lowercase and uppercase variants. In addition to these commands, you can use the J (join) command, which joins (combines) the current line with the line following, but does not switch you to text-entry mode.

Text Deletion

You can delete characters from the screen and/or the buffer in text-entry and command modes, but the methods used in command mode are far more flexible. In text-entry mode, you can use the Backspace key to erase immediately noticed errors. Each Backspace you press moves the cursor to the left, erasing one character from the buffer but not from the screen. This can be disconcerting at first (and even at second or third). The screen is refreshed when you press Esc and return to command mode. Using Ctrl-R or Ctrl-L (refresh) also tidies up the screen. The following command-mode deletion methods have the merit of keeping the display and buffer in synch. Note that delete commands do *not* switch you to text-entry mode. After a command-mode delete, you are still in command mode.

Command	Action
x	Deletes the character at the cursor
[*count*]x	Deletes *count* characters forward starting at the cursor
X	Deletes the character ahead of the cursor
[*count*]X	Deletes *count* characters backward starting at the one ahead of the cursor
dd	Deletes the current line
D	Deletes from the cursor to the end of the current line
d<*cursor_movement*>	Deletes from cursor or from current line to a point determined by the *cursor_movement* argument

The d<*cursor_movement*> method is best explained by some examples. Before you try these, keep the u key in mind in case things get out of hand: you can undo (restore the damage of) any deletion immediately with u. If you mess up a line beyond repair by u, the U variant can be used: U restores all the changes you may have made on a line since you first moved the cursor there. Also, vi has special delete buffers that save deleted text, so you can also recover your most recent nine deletions, as

I'll explain shortly. The cursor-movement command following the d determines the extent of the deletion as listed below:

Command	Deletion
dw	From the cursor to the end of the word
db	From the cursor to the beginning of the word
d<Return>	Current line and *the following line*
d0	From the cursor to the beginning of line
d^	From the cursor to the first printable character of line
d$	From the cursor to the end of line
d)	From the cursor to the end of sentence
d(	From the cursor to the start of sentence
dL	From the cursor to the end of screen
dH	From the cursor to the start of screen

On top of these powerful monsters, you can add a count argument:

Command	Deletion
d4w	Four words forward
d3b	Three words backwards

You may be puzzled by the placement of the *count* argument, but vi is logical here. The cursor-movement format is 4w to skip four words, so d4w will delete four words.

Changing Text

Change-text commands work rather like delete commands with two major differences: they mark the area of text to be changed, and they switch you to insert mode so you can enter the replacement text. The way vi marks your text is by displaying a $ sign in place of the last character of the block to be changed. For example, if you place the cursor on the first character of "visual" in test.data, and enter cw (change word), the screen will show visua$. The c command, as you may guess, can take any of the cursor-movement arguments (and the usual count arguments

as well). You are now in text-insert mode. If you type "exciting", these characters will replace visua$ on the screen (and in the buffer). So the general syntax is

    c[count]<cursor_movement>[text]<Esc>

which brings you back to command mode. (The < > symbols are used to improve legibility; they are not to be typed when they surround a typical entry.) Here are some common variants.

NOTE | With r and R the buffer is not updated until you leave insert mode.

Command	Action
[count]r<char>	Overstrikes the character at cursor with count copies of another character you specify, char, while remaining in command mode (default is 1)
[count]R<text><Esc>	Overstrikes the current line with count copies of text (default is 1)
cc<text><Esc> or C<text><Esc>	Changes current line and replaces it with text
s<text><Esc>	Substitutes current character with text
[count]s<text><Esc>	Substitutes count characters with text
S<text><Esc>	Substitutes current line with text
[count]S<text><Esc>	Substitutes count lines with text
><cursor_movement>	Shifts all lines determined by cursor_movement to the right by shiftwidth spaces (8 by default)
<<cursor_movement>	Shifts all lines determined by cursor_movement to the left by shiftwidth spaces (8 by default). You can change the default with a set command (see Table 12.1 later in this chapter).

Command	Action
>>	As for >, but shifts current line only
<<	As for <, but shifts current line only

> **NOTE** A general rule is that doubled operators affect the current line, for example, dd (delete line), cc (change line), << (shift line to left), and so on.

Yanking and Putting Text

vi offers several auxiliary buffers that help you to "cut and paste," that is, move text fragments from one part of the file to another (or even between different files). There are twenty-six named buffers known as *a, b,...z* and nine delete buffers labeled 1–9. In addition there is an *unnamed* buffer that serves two roles: it acts as the default buffer in many operations, and it serves as the receptacle for the most recently deleted piece of text. For this reason it is often referred to as delete buffer 0.

You can *yank* text from the editing buffer into one of the twenty-six named buffers, or into the unnamed buffer, as follows:

    ["*<letter>*]y<*cursor_movement*>

If you specify a letter, text will be yanked into that named buffer. Using a lowercase letter gives you a destructive yank (known as a *General Sherman*), whereby previous buffer contents are overwritten; using the uppercase letter leads to an appending yank (or *Lincoln*), where the yanked text is added to the buffer.

By default, the unnamed buffer is used. The amount of text saved is determined by the *cursor_movement* argument. For example, "ayw will yank the current word into buffer a, replacing a's previous contents. "Ay(will yank and append a sentence to buffer a. The following variants will not surprise you:

    ["*<letter>*]yy

or, equivalently,

    ["*<letter>*]Y

will yank the current line.

Each time you delete text, it is moved automatically to the unnamed buffer and also loaded onto the stack of delete buffers 1–9. The nine most recent deletions are therefore accessible by number just as the yanked texts are accessible by letter.

To transplant the yanked or deleted text, you use the p (put) command. This moves the contents of a buffer to the editing buffer at the current cursor position. The syntax is

```
["<letter\number>]p
```

or

```
["<letter\number>]P
```

where, as before, the default buffer is the unnamed buffer. For example, "3p will put the contents of delete buffer 3 into the edit buffer, while "sp will put in the contents of buffer s. Exactly where the recovered text will appear in your final document depends on whether the yanked or deleted text contains a partial line or not. Also, the choice of p or P has an effect. The p form will place the buffer text below the current line or after the cursor, while P places it above the current line or before the cursor. A little experimentation will clarify these differences.

Because of the defaults, a common cut-and-paste strategy is to delete, move the cursor, then retrieve the buffer contents with a p.

An important point to note is that these buffers retain their contents until you exit vi. Since you can switch files during a vi session, it is possible to cut from one file and paste to another.

Searching Text

Searching in vi is similar to the approach you saw in the ed editor. The syntax has four basic formats:

```
/[pattern]/[offset]<Return>
/[pattern]<Return>
```

or

```
?[pattern]?[offset]<Return>
?[pattern]<Return>
```

The / symbol gives forward searches, while ? gives backward searches. The pattern argument can be any regular expression (re-read Chapter 8 if you need a refresher

on these). If no pattern is given, vi uses the previously entered pattern (if none exists, you get an error beep). *offset* is a positive or negative number that modifies your search as follows:

/sun/+2

will stop two lines after the line having the first occurrence of "sun" after the current cursor.

?sun?-4

will stop four lines prior to the line having the first match with "sun" during a backward search from the current cursor.

You can use the set ignorecase (or set ic is also acceptable) ex command if you want a case-insensitive search. In this case, /sun/ will match "Sun", "SUN", and so on. The default setting is noic, which results in case-sensitive searches.

Having located a match, a simple n repeats the last search command in the same direction. Use N to repeat a search in the opposite direction.

To search for a given character in the current line, you can use

f<*character*>

for a forward search, and

F<*character*>

for a backward search. Useful shorthands let you use a semicolon to repeat the last character search, while a comma repeats the search in the opposite direction.

A slight variation on f and F will move the cursor to the character just before a match:

t<*character*>

for a forward search, and

T<*character*>

for a backward search. As with f, you can use a semicolon to repeat the last character search, while a comma repeats the previous search in the opposite direction.

Another trick associated with searching is the ability to *mark* text. With large files, you may want to place "bookmarks" or "place markers" to speed up future references. The m (mark) command has the following syntax:

m<*lowercase_letter*>

The current cursor is associated with the given letter. The letter marks give you twenty-six placeholders (not to be confused with the named buffers). Later on, after editing elsewhere, you can revisit a marked place in the edit buffer by using the ′ (forward quote) or ` (backquote) commands:

```
'<lowercase_letter>
```

will move the cursor to the start of the line containing the position previously marked with the argument letter. The backquote variant takes you to the exact spot previously marked. An error beep will greet attempts to find a nonexistent mark. vi treats ′<letter> and `<letter> as valid cursor-movement commands, so, with due care, you could combine them with d (delete) commands.

The ex Command Mode

When you enter a colon in command mode, you pass to ex command mode. Subsequent commands appear after the colon prompt on the status line. As explained earlier, ex is a line-oriented editor derived from ed. As a first approximation, you can use the ed commands detailed in Chapter 8. However, in practice, ex command mode is usually reserved for those jobs that cannot be done easily in vi command mode. Text insertions, changes, and searches are best done with the vi visual interface. ex is better employed with file manipulations (reading and writing), setting global options, and temporary escapes to the shell. I'll concentrate on these.

Using the Shell within vi

You can run any Unix command without leaving vi. The syntax is

```
:!<unix_command> <Return>
```

In the unix_command argument you can use % as a shorthand for the name of the current file, # for the name of the last edited file, and ! for the previous command. For example, if you entered

```
:!cp # stan.temp<Return>
```

this would copy your last edited file to stan.temp. Then later on, you could repeat this command with

    :!!

Note, though, that since you can switch files during a vi session, the meaning of # (the last edited file) can change!

You can also spawn a shell and run any number of Unix jobs, then return to vi where you left it with the following command:

    :sh

When you have finished your shell excursions, Ctrl-D returns you to the previous vi session.

When you escape to the shell, vi will warn you if you have changed your edit buffer since the last write:

    [No write since last change]

You can avoid this constant nagging with

    :set nowarn

and turn it back on with

    :set warn

The idea behind the warning is that many unforeseen events can occur during a temporary escape to the shell. Also, if you want to make use of the file being edited, it is clearly sensible to make sure that the file is updated. When you are "out in the shell," you cannot usually access the vi buffer, but you can access the edited file on the disk.

Misc ex Commands

The following sections discuss some useful miscellaneous vi features available in ex mode. If you are in command mode, you'll recall, you need to prefix these commands with a colon.

Abbreviations

The abbr (or ab for short) command lets you set up time-saving abbreviations. If you find yourself typing "SCO UNIX" frequently, you can enter the command:

    :abbr scx SCO UNIX

or

    :ab scx SCO UNIX

Now you need only type "scx" to bring up the full phrase. Some care is naturally needed: using an abbreviation such as "SCO" might misfire if you use "SCO" in other contexts. You usually enter all your standard abbreviations in the .exrc file (ex resource or startup file) that I mentioned in Chapter 11. I'll discuss .exrc in detail at the end of this chapter. You can remove an abbreviation with the unab (or equivalently, una) command:

    :una scx

Macros with the map and map! Commands

The two map commands are rather similar to abbr. They let you set up *macros* to speed your input. A macro, as far as the map command is concerned, is a *single* printable or control character (excluding digits, Esc, and Enter) that triggers a whole sequence of commands or characters. The map command sets up macros that work in command mode, while the map! variant is used for text-entry macros. As with abbr, your macro assignments can be temporary (all or part of the current session) or "permanent" (set up in .exrc and effective during each session unless temporarily turned off).

Suppose you find yourself frequently using the :!who shell escape sequence to see who else is logged in. You can map (or assign) any nondigit keyboard or control character (excluding Esc and Enter) to achieve this job with one keystroke rather than five. If you assign a key that already has a vi meaning, expect some confusion! Your newly mapped macro will override the normal vi function assigned to that character. Since the vi commands have commandeered most of the printing keys, the choice is rather limited. Of course, it's your call: you may find a better use for a letter than the standard function assigned by vi. The most promising unassigned

printing keys are g, q, v, K, V, and Z together with the punctuation symbols [,], @, #, and *. Of the control combinations, you should avoid (or use with care) the following in vi macros, since they have special meanings in one or more modes:

Ctrl-B	Ctrl-R	Ctrl-L	Ctrl-W
Ctrl-D	Ctrl-S	Ctrl-M	Ctrl-]
Ctrl-F	Ctrl-U	Ctrl-N	Ctrl-@
Ctrl-G	Ctrl-V	Ctrl-Q	

A simple but instructive map example is

```
:map V xp
```

The colon is not needed if you are already in ex command mode. Typing V in command mode will trigger the command sequence xp. The x will delete the character at the cursor, and the p (put) command will display the deleted character (from the unnamed buffer where deletions are stored) after the new cursor position. The net result is to reverse two characters: the original cursor character and the one to its right. You have only saved one keystroke, but the V is mnemonically superior to px. Some users even map a lowercase letter to a single uppercase letter command in order to save a shift!

As a more complex example, we'll assign Ctrl-Z to the !who sequence as follows:

```
:map <Ctrl-Z> :!who<Ctrl-M>
```

Before I show you how to do this, let's examine the results. Thereafter, pressing Ctrl-Z in command mode will have the same effect as entering : !who. Note that the Ctrl-M provides the Return keystroke needed to complete the command—without the Ctrl-M, the system would sit there waiting silently for an Enter. The Ctrl-M was not required in the xp example since the x and p commands do not need the Return key. With all mapping applications you must carefully match the actual keystrokes needed for each macro in the appropriate modes. If your macro is invoked in command mode and contains an i, for example, the following macro keystrokes will be interpreted in text-insert mode until an Esc is reached.

To insert the two control codes in the above sequence, you need a special trick: just pressing Ctrl and Z or Ctrl and M will *not* work! You must first enter Ctrl-V followed by the appropriate control combination. Ctrl-V is vi's control code escape character. It warns vi that the next entered character is to be taken literally with no special interpretation. (There are a few exceptions: Ctrl-Q and Ctrl-S are always trapped by Unix before vi sees them. They are used to "pause" and "restart" certain processes, so it is wise to avoid using Ctrl-Q and Ctrl-S in macros.) The actual keystrokes needed to achieve the mapping are therefore

```
:map <Ctrl-V><Ctrl-Z> :!who<Ctrl-V><Ctrl-M>
```

followed by Return. Your screen will show:

```
:map ^Z :!who^M
```

since vi translates the Ctrl-V to ^ (caret), the traditional visible symbol for the Ctrl key.

As an alternative to entering <Ctrl-V><Ctrl-M>, you can try <Ctrl-V><Return>—if this works on your system, vi will also echo the string ^M.

If your macro needs the Esc key, you'll need the same Ctrl-V trick to enter it as a map argument. vi will echo ^[on the screen to confirm your entry.

The macro you set up need not be a complete command. You can map part of a command and enter the balance manually. For example,

```
:map Y "ay
```

maps part of the yank-into-buffer-*a* command. After entering Y, you need to complete the command with a cursor-action command specifying how much text is to be yanked. Typing Y) will expand to "ay), which yanks from the cursor to the start of the next sentence. But, I hear you cry, Y is already a valid vi command: it usually yanks the current line. However, overriding a standard command is quite reasonable here since there is a synonym for Y, namely yy—both usually yank the current line. So with the new macro in place, typing Yy will give you "ayy with no loss of features or keystrokes.

You make your macros permanent by entering them into your .exrc file along with your favorite abbreviations.

If you want to remove a macro during a session, you use the unmap command. The following commands will remove the V and Ctrl-Z macros we set up earlier:

```
:unmap V
:unmap <Ctrl-V><Ctrl-Z>
```

If they are in your .exrc file, of course, they will be reestablished when you next fire up vi. There is another way of storing any permanent vi settings. The environment variable EXINIT can be assigned abbreviations, maps, and set commands:

```
EXINIT='set nowarn|abbr SKB Stanley|map V xp'
```

Note the single quote marks and the separator | between successive commands. You may recall meeting environment variables such as HOME, MAIL, and PATH, and how they are assigned, in Chapter 6. Such assignments are usually placed in your .profile file, followed by

```
export HOME MAIL PATH EXINIT
```

so they become effective when you log in, and available to your Bourne shell and any child shells. Recall that the C shell uses the setenv command in the .cshrc file. I'll have more to say on this subject in the next chapter.

The version of map used so far gives you macros that work only in command mode. For example, you could not expect the V macro to work in text-entry mode! For macros that work in text-entry mode, you need the map! variant, but otherwise the syntax and philosophy is the same. The map! variant is really an alternative to abbr. As with map and abbr, be very careful that the macros you assign do not impede normal typing—the characters you map lose their normal significance. There is an unmap! variant for unmapping map! type macros.

To see what macros and abbreviations are in force, you simply enter :map, :map!, or :ab with no arguments.

The set Command

You've met several attributes that you can turn on and off, or assign values to, with the set command. There are many more of varying degrees of importance depending on the type of editing you are engaged in. Recall that set works only in ex command mode, so you need to type :set if you are in command mode, or < Esc>:set if you are in text-entry mode. Table 12.1 gives a list of the more common arguments

TABLE 12.1: Common set Arguments

set Argument	Default	Action or Property
autoindent, ai	noai	Each line you create is indented to match the indent of the previous line. To back up to the preceding tab stop, enter Ctrl-D. Tabbing is controlled by the value of shiftwidth (see set shiftwidth below).
autoprint, ap	ap	Displays the current line number after certain ex commands. Equivalent to adding a p after such commands.
autowrite, aw	noaw	Writes the buffer to disk after certain commands if the buffer has changed.
beautify, bf	nobf	Discards all control characters except tab
directory, dir	dir=/tmp	set dir=*path* specifies the directory for the edit buffer.
errorbells, eb	noeb	Rings the bell before an error message.
ignorecase, ic	noic	Case is ignored when matching regular expressions.
list	nolist	Displays tabs as ^I and end-of-lines as $.
magic	magic	set nomagic reduces the number of metacharacters available in regular expressions so that only ^, \, and $ have special significance.
mesg	nomesg	set nomesg turns off email write permission during vi sessions.
number, n	nonumber	All output lines will display with their line numbers.
report	report=5	set report=*n* will provide a warning if your command modifies more than *n* lines.
scroll	scroll=1/2 window	Sets the number of lines scrolled when Ctrl-D is received in command mode. Also sets the number of lines displayed by the z command to twice the value of scroll. The default is *W*/2 where *W* is the value used in set window=*W*.
shell, sh	sh=/bin/sh	set sh=*pathname* sets the path name of the shell to be spawned by the ! and shell commands. If the SHELL variable is present, this gives the default, otherwise /bin/sh is assumed.

TABLE 12.1: Common set Arguments (continued)

set Argument	Default	Action or Property
shiftwidth, sw	sw=8	set sw=*n* sets tab width to *n* spaces (see set autoindent).
showmatch, sm	nosm	When) or } is typed, the cursor will move to the previous matching (or { for one second. Useful when editing source code where matching pairs of nested ( ) and { } are important.
showmode	noshowmode	Displays the text-insert mode, for instance, INSERT, APPEND, CHANGE, OPEN.
term	term=TERM	set term=*XXX* changes the terminal type of the output device to *XXX*.
terse	noterse	Reduces the amount of error diagnostics for the experienced user.
warn	warn	set nowarn removes the [No write since last change] warning when you escape to the shell.
window	Default varies	set window=*n* sets the number of displayed text lines to *n*. The default depends on the speed and screen size of your terminal: typically 8 for slow terminals, 16 for medium speed terminals, and (max-1) for fast terminals. Most modern terminals will default to 24 lines of text with line 25 reserved for ex commands and messages. The default value for set scroll is half the set window value (see set scroll).
wrapscan, ws	ws	Regular expression searches will wrap around past the end of the file and back to the start of the file. set nows will prevent search wrap around.
wrapmargin, wm	wm=0	set wm=*n* will set the margin to *n* spaces during automatic newline insertion while in text-entry mode.
writeany, wa	nowa	Suspends the normal checks made before a write command, so that provided you have permission, you can write to any file.

you can use with set together with their defaults. Some attributes, known as *switch* options, default to either off or on. Others, known as *string* options, default to certain values.

For example, unless you set autoindent, vi assumes that autoindent is off, and unless you set noautoprint, vi assumes that autoprint is on. For switch options, you use set *argument* to turn on the property, and set no *argument* to turn it off. String options use the syntax

```
set argument=value
```

I list the default values that vi assumes in the absence of contrary instructions. Some arguments can be abbreviated as indicated. You'll find that any reasonable abbreviation will work provided there is no ambiguity.

You can use set with no arguments to get a list of all current settings. Recall, also, that vedit invokes vi with various novice options already preset.

The .exrc File

In most cases, the defaults will be adequate while you are learning vi. When you want to personalize your editing, you can start adjusting these options in the .exrc file—a wonderful way to try out your vi skills in fact! This file is always scanned (if present) when vi (or ex) is fired up. You can look on .exrc as a sort of .profile or .cshrc file for vi sessions.

A typical .exrc file might contain lines such as

```
set nowarn
set eb
set report=3
abbr SKB Stan Kelly-Bootle
map V xp
map Y "ay
map T "ap
```

Entering and Leaving vi

There are several useful options you can add when you invoke vi with an existing file. If you type vi *filename* and *filename* exists, you fire up ready to start editing

at the first line of the file. Often it saves time to enter vi with the cursor at some more convenient point, for instance, the end of the file, or at the last sentence you were working on.

The syntax for invoking vi allows the following variants:

```
vi + filename
```

This loads *filename* as usual but displays the last screenful with the cursor at the end of the file.

```
vi +n filename
```

places the cursor at the start of the *n*th line.

```
vi +/pattern filename
```

takes you to the start of the line holding the first occurrence of *pattern* in the file. If *pattern* contains spaces, you must surround it with double quotes:

```
vi +/"Yours faithfully" myletter.skb
```

Once vi has located a match, you can use the n command for repeat forward searches and then use N for repeat backward searches.

You can switch files without leaving vi by using the :e for edit command (just like the e command in ex and ed). Suppose you have edited and saved myletter.skb with :w, and want to edit poem. You simply type

```
:e poem
```

and you start with the cursor at the beginning of poem, which now becomes your new default file name. You can also use the variants

```
:e + poem
:e +/winter poem
```

or

```
:e +20 poem
```

to place the cursor in your preferred starting point.

For more advanced cursor location when editing multiple files, vi offers a tag system. This is beyond the scope of this book, but you may wish to consult the man vi section for details. I also recommend *A Guide to vi* by Dan Sonnenschein (Prentice-Hall, 1987) and *Learning the vi Editor*, Fifth Edition, by Linda Lamb (O'Reilly & Associates, 1990).

Summary

The key to mastering vi, as with any complex editor, is diligent practice. You soon reach the point where you can instinctively navigate between the three modes (text-entry, command, and escape/ex). Although the myriad of commands seems daunting, look on each single-letter command as "fast" rather than "cryptic." The commands are only "cryptic" until you get to know them!

CHAPTER

THIRTEEN

Exploiting the Shell

- Shell scripts

- Shell and subshell variables

- How shell scripts work

- Familiar quotations

- More on metacharacters

- The inner workings of the shell

The Unix operating system was designed by programmers for programmers. More precisely, the very first version of Unix was devised by Ken Thompson (joined later by Dennis Ritchie), who was "dissatisfied with the available computer facilities, discovered a little-used PDP–7 [an early DEC mini-computer], and set out to create a more hospitable [programming] environment." This background helps to explain the unique flavor of Unix. The limited hardware resources demanded a compact, efficient kernel and a flexible file-handling system. Starting, as it were, with a clean, nonpropriety slate, Thompson was free to combine "a carefully selected set of fertile ideas" with no immediate commercial or marketing considerations. The sole predefined objective was a system that was programmer-friendly.

Programmers are by nature independent and creative souls. They are seldom content to use a fixed set of tools to achieve a given result. Programmers are usually fascinated by the tools themselves rather than by the applications thereof. They want to forge and reforge the tools, so they welcome an operating system that offers freedom to those smart enough to "hack" it. The word "hacking," by the way, originally referred to this benign propensity to tinker with programs, prizing clever and even arcane tricks above the needs of the "despised user." The hacker as network intruder and criminal is a recent and unfortunate semantic deterioration. Unix therefore evolved initially as a tool-making tool for programmers with few concessions to the end user at the bottom of the DP food chain.

Where does all this leave the non-programmer with payrolls to run, debts to collect, and disks to back up at the end of the day? The irony is that because programmers have little interest in users' requirements, the Unix designers made no dogmatic assumptions as to what the ideal user interface should look like. Rather, they came up with a set of tools that allowed, *inter alia,* the creation of shells.

Shells are the outer, intercessory layers between user and Unix. They parse your command line, perform wonderful transformations on command arguments, and locate and interpret your commands. But the shell is also a powerful programming language providing the tool-making facility I referred to. With the shell, you can create your own commands and even build a completely new environment.

To many users, the Bourne or C shell *is* Unix: the familiar prompt for character-based commands with cryptic, inconsistent syntaxes. Yet as you've seen in previous chapters, a shell is "just" another Unix program rather than an integral part of the operating system. The "real" Unix is the kernel, and via system commands (usually

accessed via C or assembly language), programmers can tap the power of Unix without using the standard shells.

A popular in-joke among programmers is "If you don't like the Unix interface, write your own shell." In fact, you can control your interface without delving directly into the kernel. The available shells, sh, csh, and ksh, are sufficiently powerful and flexible to allow you to build more friendly interfaces using shell scripts. These interfaces will still be character-oriented, but they can present menus, simple windows, and even point-and-select features using a mouse. For the more elaborate GUIs (graphical user interfaces) with icons, resizable windows, dialog boxes, and the other trimmings associated with the Apple Macintosh, new, complex shells are needed. And, in fact, this is exactly what has been happening since Unix migrated from the labs to the world of business, where the needs and desires of ordinary users attract more respect; see Chapter 19 for more information.

There are now thousands of sites where the non-programmer is seldom, if ever, prompted by a $ or % symbol. The new interfaces range from simple shell script menus to elaborate GUIs such as SCO's Open Desktop (based on OSF/Motif), Apple's A/UX 2.0, AT&T's Open Look, and many others. Some of these are more like separate operating-system layers on top of Unix than traditional shells. Others simply exploit the facilities offered by one of the standard shells. The thrust of this chapter is to show you how shell scripts can, paradoxically, protect you from the rigors of the shell and provide your own personalized user interface.

Shell Scripts

As the name indicates, a shell script is a text file that guides and coaxes the shell into performing a sequence of actions. A script can hold any series of commands (both internal shell commands and external Unix commands, with or without arguments), programs, or even other previously written scripts. Scripts can use redirections and pipes, allowing you to write your own *filters*. You might compare this concept to a movie script, where each action, speech, and camera angle is carefully listed. As you study a shell script, you try to imagine how the shell will react to each piece of text, as though you were entering the script on the keyboard. If you've been exposed to DOS, the analogy with .BAT (batch) files will be helpful, except that Unix shell scripts have a much richer armory of features.

There are, alas, small but nagging differences between the Bourne and C shells and these affect the shell script syntaxes and available features. (Appendix A covers the main shell variants.) This chapter will deal with Bourne shell scripts for several sound reasons. First, the Bourne shell, /bin/sh, is the father of all the Unix shells and is available on most, if not all, Unix installations. Further, Bourne shell scripts will "run" under the C shell, /bin/csh. What happens, in fact, is that the C shell can recognize a Bourne shell script and invoke the Bourne shell to execute it. Bourne shell scripts will also run under the Korn shell (/bin/ksh). The latter combines most of the features of the Bourne and C shells, and is now bundled with the popular SCO UNIX and other implementations. There are also utilities available that can translate shell scripts from one shell format to another.

/bin/sh is a complex program and many large books have been devoted to its features (see Appendix C: Unix Resources). I will tackle the most important aspects in the next two chapters. This chapter will give you an overall grasp of shell scripting, offering a host of simple but effective strategies for improving your life without incurring the pain of the arcane shell programming features. In Chapter 16, I'll delve a little deeper with more advanced shell scripts.

You have already encountered examples of shell scripts. The .profile and .login files I discussed in Chapter 6 are all shell scripts, used to preset various parameters and perform other set up tasks.

Shell scripts can prompt for input and take different actions depending on the keyed response. Similarly, commands can be triggered with user-supplied arguments and, depending on the results of such commands, select the appropriate steps from your script. This concept of selective or conditional execution, common to all programming languages, is known as *flow control*. Some of your simple shell scripts will just carry out a fixed sequence of operations, serving rather as a keystroke-saving macro, while others can guide you through a maze of choices. Recall that a shell script can invoke other programs and shell scripts, so there is, in fact, no limit to what you can achieve.

Shell scripts, once written and debugged, actually reduce your shell-shock by replacing complicated command lines with simpler entries of your own choosing. If you are new to programming, shell scripts offer a reasonably gentle introduction to the art. There is no compilation phase: the shell immediately interprets your scripts, and you can develop them progressively, testing and debugging section by section.

Your First Shell Script

As a first, somewhat naive illustration, suppose you regularly wanted to show the date, list the current logged-in users, and check their status. You could, of course, enter the commands `date` and `who` (with suitable arguments) each time, but why not make the shell do the work with a script file? Simply create a file called `dw` (using `vi` or `ed`) containing the five following lines (the first three of which are optional, cosmetic, but highly recommended):

```
:
# @(#)dw -- show date and users -- SKB 11/13/95
#
date
who -u
```

Anatomy of dw

The initial solitary colon is not essential, but rather a long-established convention indicating that the text that follows is a Bourne shell script. The colon is treated as a NOP (no operation) by the Bourne shell—in nonjargon terms, the colon is successfully ignored by the Bourne shell. The C shell *does* make use of the first character found in a script. An initial # (also known as the *comment* character) tells the C shell that the following text is intended as a C shell script. Any initial symbol other than # will cause the C shell to invoke the Bourne shell to execute (or try to execute) your script as a Bourne shell script.

> **WARNING** The two worst things you can do are to start a Bourne shell script with a # and to omit the # at the start of a C shell script! For maximum portability, always start your Bourne scripts with a colon. C shells must start with a #.

Of all the non-# symbols available to start your Bourne script, the most sensible (and therefore the hallowed tradition) is the harmless NOP (colon). This gives both humans and C shells a clear warning of the nature of your script. Avoid blank lines at the start of your scripts: an initial newline is certainly a valid non-# character but it does not provide a strong visible clue.

The next two lines are optional comments signaled by a leading #. (The # is quite safe now that we are past the initial character in the file.) The Bourne shell ignores any word starting with # and also ignores all subsequent characters up to the next newline. You use comments to annotate your scripts (author, date, version number, and so on). I'll have more to say later about the need to develop good commenting habits. The @(#) string is a useful trick used by the what command to extract the title and purpose of a script. what scans an argument file and displays information from any commented section containing the sequence @(#):

```
$ what dw
    dw:
    dw -- show date and users -- SKB 11/13/95
$ _
```

For this reason, @(#) is often known as the *what string*. After a what string, you should enter a succinct description of the script, preferably with version date and author. You can use as many what strings as you wish at any part of your script. The what command will display all such marked legends.

The third line, a single #, is just for improved legibility. A blank line here would be equally acceptable. The fourth and fifth lines do the real work by invoking date and who. The who -u option provides additional user data as explained in Chapter 5.

The Naming Problem

The name you give the file needs some thought because that name will be used to invoke the script file. You should avoid existing command names, of course, and you should, in the Unix tradition, keep your script names as succinct as possible! Calling the script date_and_who, for example, makes its intentions clear, but errs in the direction of volubility—after all, the idea is save typing effort. I therefore elected to call the file dw which provides some clue to its purpose. We'll first check the contents of dw:

```
$ cat dw
:
# @(#)dw -- show date and users -- SKB 11/13/95
#
date
who -u
```

Exploiting dw

There are several ways of exploiting the dw file. Since sh, the Bourne shell, is a program that accepts input from its standard input (usually your keyboard), you can simply redirect input as follows:

```
$ sh <dw
Mon Nov 13 15:33:50 PDT 1995
root    tty02   Nov 13 11.08         .  168
stan    tty01   Nov 13 14:45         .  169
iwonka  tty06   Nov 13 12:32      0:02 170
$ _
```

The result is quite intuitive: sh accepts the commands from the dw file (ignoring : and skipping the comments), just as though you had keyed date; who -u. A tad less intuitive is the following variation:

```
$ sh dw
Mon Nov 13 15:33:51 PDT 1995
root    tty02   Nov 13 11.08         .  168
stan    tty01   Nov 13 14:45         .  169
iwonka  tty06   Nov 13 12:32      0:03 170
$ _
```

Even without the redirection, sh has accepted dw as an argument, extracted from it the two commands, and executed them with identical results. The program sh (like many other Unix programs) can take its input from a file named as an argument whether you use < for redirection or not. Although these two examples give the same result, there is a technical difference. In the sh dw example, the shell retains your keyboard as standard input; with sh <dw, the standard input has been redirected to the file dw.

The Bourne shell, as I've mentioned several times, is a program called sh, so you can invoke it at any time by entering sh with or without arguments. The fact that your login shell, usually sh too, is now asked to "run" sh seems a little spooky at first encounter. If you recall the discussion in Chapter 9 on parent and child processes, the situation should not worry you unduly. The sh that processes dw is a child process forked by your login (or home) shell that also happens to be an sh process. When one shell forks another shell, the child is called a *subshell*. The full implications of this situation will emerge as I proceed. For the moment, accept on faith that the subshell you have invoked with sh dw takes the characters from dw rather than from the keyboard. The result is what you might expect from actually typing the commands you stored in dw.

Executing dw Directly

After showing you two ways of exploiting dw, I must now spring a surprise on you. dw is not yet a proper shell script. A shell script, by definition, is an *executable* text file that can be run like a normal command. Having to invoke dw with an explicit sh is rather a nuisance. Yet, if you try dw from the shell prompt, you'll get an exe-cute permission denied message. Before you (or anyone else) can run your new dw script as a regular command you *must* make the file executable. You'll recall that the usual default permissions for the files you create are simply read/write for you, the owner. Let's check this fact:

```
$ ls -l dw
-rw------- 1 stan other 13 Nov 13 13:32 dw
$ _
```

(Depending on the ruling default permissions, you may find differences in the first field. Some systems may be set to give, say, read/write permissions to you and read permission to your group, for example, -rw-r-----. Other sites may default to -rw-r--r--, offering read permission to every user. You can even set your umask to override these defaults either temporarily or permanently.)

The easiest way to add execution permission for you as user-owner is

```
$ chmod u+x dw
$ _
```

as explained in Chapter 7. Check again, and you'll find that you now have read/write/execute permissions:

```
$ ls -l dw
-rwx------ 1 stan other 13 Nov 13 13:40 dw
$ _
```

You may wish to extend execution rights to your group by changing the first chmod argument from u+x to ug+x. Or you can be generous and give everyone execution rights (whether they want them or not) by using a+x. (Just +x will also work since the default here is a). Of course, dw is currently in your home directory, so accessi-bility by others may be limited. Your new command may be more convenient in a more general directory, either /bin for everyone (if the system administrator agrees) or your own /bin directory (such as usr/stan/bin, or usr/mary/bin, the most natural place for personal executables). Some sites have a usr/local/bin for miscellaneous local commands.

Now you can test dw. It works like a simple command—just enter the script file name:

```
$ dw
Mon Nov 13 15:33:50 PDT 1995
root    tty02   Nov 13 11.08      .  168
stan    tty01   Nov 13 14:45      .  169
iwonka tty06    Nov 13 12:32   0:02 170
$ _
```

In the above invocation, the login shell recognizes that dw is a shell script (because dw is an executable text file rather than a compiled binary file) and immediately spawns a subshell to read and execute the commands in the dw file. (The subshell does many other things that need not divert us just now.) The parent shell waits for the subshell to finish its work. The end-of-file signal, generated when dw has given its all, kills the subshell process, just as if you had keyed Ctrl-D. The parent shell now revives and shows the prompt. Quite a neat scenario!

Shell Script Summary

Let's pause to summarize the six basic shell-scripting steps:

1. Plan the command sequences and test them on the keyboard.

2. Choose a good, nonclashing name for your script.

3. Create the script file with your favorite editor.

4. Start the file with a colon and add pithy comments.

5. Make the file executable with chmod.

6. If necessary, mv the script to its proper directory.

Script Debugging

One can scarcely talk about *debugging* at this early stage with such a minimal script as dw. But it is conceivably possible that your dw may not work! If you get a command not found or similar message, use pwd and ls to check that you are still in your home directory and that dw was created there. If you get an execute permission denied message, perhaps you forgot to chmod. Less common, but worth keeping in mind, is that another command of the same name exists in a directory listed ahead of your current directory in your PATH variable. Check your PATH with echo $PATH. For script testing, it is useful to have both the current and home directories

in your PATH variable. Remember that `date` and `who` are in the `/bin` directory, so `/bin` must be in your PATH. Finally, make sure that `dw` contains the correct text. Recall that even if your PATH does not contain the directory holding a particular command (or script), you can still run it (permissions permitting!) by using the full path name `/usr/stan/dw`. The general rule is that when you invoke a command with a prefixed path starting with `/`, the shell does not bother to check the paths set in the PATH variable.

For more advanced debugging, you can include the command

```
set -v
```

in your script. This turns on the *verbose* mode in which each line of the script is echoed on the screen as it is read by the shell. The feature is turned off with

```
set +v
```

The verbose mode can also be switched on with

```
$ sh -v dw
```

which saves you editing the `dw` file. You can also use

```
set -xv
```

This reduces the verbosity by displaying only the executable lines—comments are not displayed.

Special Commands

The `set` command used above (not to be confused with the `ex` command of the same name that you saw in Chapter 12) is an example of a *special command* for the Bourne shell. Special commands are built into `sh` and can be executed efficiently without invoking a child process. (The C shell has its own set of special commands.) You have already met two special commands, `echo` and `cd`. In the interests of efficiency, these two common commands are implemented inside the shell. There's an added practical reason for executing `cd` within the shell without creating a new process. When a shell script changes a directory with the `cd` command, the new directory must prevail until the script encounters another `cd` or until the subshell terminates.

New Commands from Old

Meager though it is, dw is a *new* command that you've added to the hundreds that came from your Unix vendor. Some of the supplied utilities are, in fact, shell scripts, so dw need not have an inferiority complex. And, as you'll see, you can include dw in other scripts, and these scripts in other scripts, and so on, to produce more elaborate commands.

Since dw acts like a normal command, you can use all the tricks you've learned that are appropriate for a command that sends data to the standard output:

```
$ dw >datewho.dat
$ cat datewho.dat
Mon Nov 13 15:33:51 PDT 1995
root    tty02    Nov 13 11.08       .  168
stan    tty01    Nov 13 14:45       .  169
iwonka  tty06    Nov 13 12:32   0:03 170
$ _
```

You could even generate a background process with

```
$ dw >datewho.dat &
44
$ _
```

The display of a process id (44 in my example) indicates that the & has worked in the usual way.

You can also filter the results of dw as follows:

```
$ dw | grep 'iwonka'
iwonka tty06    Nov 13 12:32 0:03 170
$ _
```

Here, we use grep (man section C) to search the output of dw for occurrences of the string "iwonka". grep means global-find regular expressions and print. grep *<re>* will display all lines containing the regular expression *<re>*. The regular expressions recognized by grep are the ones I described in Chapter 8. grep itself will be discussed in Chapter 15.

The single forward quotes around iwonka are optional here but recommended for safety: the grep family (grep, egrep, and fgrep) has many flags and options! When

grepping for phrases or characters separated by spaces, by the way, the single quotes *are* essential:

```
$ dw | grep 'Nov 13'
root    tty02    Nov 13 11.08    . 168
stan    tty01    Nov 13 14:45    . 169
$ _
```

Even at this simple level, you can start to see how useful shell scripts can be developed by combining existing Unix tools. Let's write another shell script called `prau` (print active user):

```
:
# @(#)prau -- print active user -- SKB 11/13/95
#
dw | grep '.'
```

Here you see the script `dw` embedded in a new script. Once you have used `chmod u+x prau`, the new command is ready for testing:

```
$ prau
iwonka tty06    Nov 13 12:32    . 170
stan    tty01    Nov 13 14:45    . 169
$_
```

The `prau` command lists all lines with a dot in the output of `dw`. This will pick up all users who have been recently active, since the activity field from `dw` will be a dot. Of course, there *may* be other periods in the output of `dw`, and these will also be displayed. In Chapters 15 and 16, you'll see techniques for limiting the search to particular fields. The process can be continued: you could use `prau` inside a larger script to display other useful information about users.

The Dot Command

Yet another way of invoking `dw` exists using the Bourne shell *dot* command:

```
$ . dw
Mon Nov 13 15:33:53 PDT 1995
root    tty02    Nov 13 11.08    .    168
stan    tty01    Nov 13 14:45    .    169
iwonka tty06    Nov 13 12:32   0:06 170
$ _
```

> **NOTE**   The dot command is available in the Bourne and Korn shells, but not in the C shell.

Here the login shell itself reads and executes the commands found in the file dw—there is no subshell involved. Once again, the displayed results are the same as for sh <dw, sh dw, and dw. The technical differences will emerge later. Briefly, when a subshell runs a command, any changes that the command makes to your environment (variable assignments, changes of directory, and so on) affect only that subshell. When you return to the parent shell, the original environment is restored. Since the dot command executes its argument command in the current shell, any changes made are retained when the command exits.

As an illustration, your .profile file is (almost) a normal shell script (it has one nonstandard quirk: it can be run without execution permission) that is executed whenever you log in. If you edit your .profile file, the changes will have no effect until your *next* login. However, by running .profile with the dot command, you can immediately reinitialize the environmental variables in your current shell without having to log out and in again:

```
$ . .profile
$ _
```

Shell and Subshell Variables

You encountered shell variables (sometimes called shell parameters) in Chapter 6. They play a vital role in shell programming. You saw some of the many predefined *environment* variables such as TERM, PS1, PS2, HOME, and PATH, usually set in .profile:

```
TERM=ansi
HOME=/usr/$LOGNAME
PATH=:/bin:/usr/bin:$HOME:$HOME/bin
...
export TERM HOME LOGNAME PATH ...
```

The shell itself gives default values to PATH, PS1, PS2, and IFS. The defaults are usually as follows:

PATH   :/bin:/usr/bin:$HOME

PS1 $

PS2   >

IFS   Space, tab, newline (These are the standard internal field separators, used by the shell when parsing the command line.)

IFS is not usually tampered with, but the other defaults are often overridden in .profile and other scripts. The HOME default is set by login (which reads the HOME field in /etc/passwd) to /usr/$LOGNAME—it can be reassigned but rarely is. An existing variable can be used when reassigning another variable, as indicated above. The $ prefix and the export special command will be explained soon.

The initial colon in PATH represents a difficult-to-see null path. A null path is interpreted by the shell as your current directory, so this is the first directory to be searched by the shell for the invoked command. You may sometimes see a PATH defined as

PATH=/bin::/usr/bin:$HOME:$HOME/bin

Here, the null path is more "visible" as the empty entry between two consecutive colons. Your current directory would now be the second place to be examined, after /bin, in the command search sequence.

The env command, with no arguments, will display all the environment variables with their current settings:

```
# env
HOME=/
HZ=100
LOGNAME=root
PATH=/bin:/usr/bin:/etc
SHELL=/bin/sh
TERM=ansi
TZ=PST8PDT
# _
```

For a change, I show you the values used by root. Run env in your home directory and note the settings. The variables HOME, LOGNAME, PATH, and TERM are all obvious. The remaining variables are explained below.

HZ   Hertz: the number of clock interrupts per second. This hardware dependent value is stored in /etc/default/login and should not be tampered with.

SHELL   The path name of the default shell. In the absence of an explicit entry in the last field of /etc/passwd, SHELL provides your default shell. If there is an "r" in the file part of the name, the restricted form of the shell, for example /bin/rsh, will be used. rsh gives the system administrator more control over the commands available to a user.

TZ   Time zone information used by commands such as date to display the time appropriate to your zone, including automatic adjustment for summer daylight saving time. A special shell script called etc/tz is used by root during installation to set TZ, so you will not normally want to play with this value.

The importance of the environment (and other) variables is that your scripts can be more generic by accessing values that are not known when you write your scripts. If your script aims to write a file in the user's home directory, for example, the value $HOME is guaranteed to hold this value no matter who is running your script.

WARNING   No spaces are allowed between = and the adjacent expressions when assigning values to variables.

You also learned in Chapter 6 how to devise your own variable names (known as *user variables*) and assign useful values to them:

```
$ SKBLIB=/usr/stan/lib
$ echo SKBLIB
SKBLIB
$ echo $SKBLIB
/usr/stan/lib
$ echo "$SKBLIB"
```

```
/usr/stan/lib
$ cd $SKBLIB
$ _
```

The above sequence, performed at the keyboard, could equally be embedded in a shell script, of course. Note carefully the use of the $ character: it "converts" a variable name to the value contained in the variable. Forgetting this fact will cause you much grief, so don't forget! As the above example shows, SKBLIB without the $ echoes literally. I've also thrown in an example to show that $ retains its transforming power even when double-quoted. When I come to metacharacters and quoting, you'll see the importance of this property.

The rules for naming user variables are quite simple. They must start with a letter or an underscore. Following this can be any sequence of letters, digits, or underscores. Unix is case-sensitive. Upper- and lowercase letters are considered to be different: NEXT and NeXT are distinct variables! And, naturally, you should make your names usefully mnemonic and avoid incorporating any of the predefined environment variable names.

Variables can be combined in various ways. Consider the following examples:

```
$ CH="Chapter "
$ ch=1
$ echo $CH$ch
Chapter 1
$ echo $CHch

$ _
<newline only--CHch is an unknown variable>
$ echo ${CH}ch
Chapter ch
$ echo $CH{ch}
Chapter {ch}
$ echo ${CH}${ch}
Chapter 1
$ CH1=$CH$ch
$ echo $CH1
Chapter 1
$ echo CH1
CH1
$ echo "$CH"ch
Chapter ch
$ _
```

For convenience, I show these as keyboard conversations with the helpful echo command. Within a shell script, the combined names may well be arguments to other commands.

Note the use of braces and quotes to avoid a sequence that the shell might otherwise consider a valid variable name.

Setting and Unsetting Variables

The act of naming a variable in an assignment statement such as SKBLIB=/usr/stan/lib serves both to define (or set or declare) it and give it a value. There are occasions when you want to remove a variable name from the list. The unset special command can do this. Alternatively, you can simply assign a null value to a variable without actually removing it from the shell's list.

```
$ ANYVAR=
<assign nothing at all!>
$ echo $ANYVAR

$ _
<newline--null value>
$ unset SKBLIB
$ echo $ SKBLIB

$ _
<newline--not known>
$ _
```

The line ANYVAR= can equally be written ANYVAR="" since the empty string "" is as null as possible. Note that the environment variables PATH, PS1, PS2, MAILCHECK, and IFS *cannot* be unset (and quite rightly so). Although the two variables ANYVAR and SKBLIB echo in the same way, there is a subtle but important technical difference between a variable being unset (no longer defined) and a variable having a null value (but still remaining defined). This may seem rather Zen, but some clever shell-programming tricks depend on this difference.

Several expressions using $ and { } can be used to test whether a variable is defined-but-null or simply undefined, and depending on the result of the test, other values can be assigned. Table 13.1 later in this chapter lists these expressions, but they will not be used until the next chapter.

In this and the next chapters, you'll also meet some special shell variables that are set *automatically* by the shell. Some of these specials cannot be changed by the user. Both types are tabulated below for reference, with the $ prefixed, ready for action; their full significance will be clarified as we proceed.

Variable	Meaning
$n	The *n*th positional parameter:
	$0 is the invoking command name.
	$1 is the name of the first argument.
	$2 is the name of the second argument.
	$9 is the name of the ninth argument.
	The special command shift is used to access more than nine arguments. If only *M* arguments are used, $n is empty for values of *n* greater than *M*. The set command can be used to change the values of $1 to $9.
$*	Holds all the argument positional parameters (starting with $1 and separated by spaces) in the command line. Not limited to nine arguments.
$@	Same as $* except when quoted as "$@". "$@" is "$1", "$2"... but "$*" is "$1 $2...".
$#	The total number of positional parameters excluding $0 (the command name).
$-	The option flags used in the command line.
$?	The exit value (decimal) returned by the command. Cannot be changed by user assignment. The usual convention followed by most commands is: a zero value indicates a successful command, a nonzero value indicates failure, and the nonzero value gives the reason for the failure. The exit values depend on how the command has been programmed, so there is no absolute guarantee that 0 means success.

Variable	Meaning
$$	The process id of the current shell. Cannot be changed by user assignment. (Warning: the name of the variable is $, so you need $$ to access its value!) Since the process id is a unique number, $$ is often used to construct a unique name for temporary file. For example: *any_command*>>$HOME/tmp/data.$$
$!	The process id of the last background command (invoked with the & operator). Cannot be changed by user assignment.

Exporting Variables

Any variable "known" to a shell can be used in a shell script running under that shell. A variable can be inspected (to extract its value), compared with other variables, used in arithmetical operations, and (apart from the exceptions listed above) have new values reassigned or reset in a shell script; indeed, the use of variables is one of the features that makes the shell a "proper" programming language.

Unless you take specific steps, the names and values of variables are *local* (confined) to the shell in which they are declared. If a parent shell names a variable, that variable will not be known to any child processes (such as subshells) unless you *export* it using the export command.

```
$ GREET=Hello
$ echo $GREET
Hello
$ sh
<now running subshell>
$ echo $GREET

$ _ <newline response: GREET unknown in subshell>
<Ctrl-D back to parent shell>
$ export GREET
$ sh
<run a subshell again>
$ echo $GREET
Hello
<GREET is now known to subshell>
$ GREET=Saludos
```

```
<reassign GREET>
$ echo $GREET
Saludos
$ _
<Ctrl-D back to parent shell>
$ echo $GREET
Hello
<parent shell retains original value of GREET>
```

There are two important lessons here. First, you need to export a variable name before the subshell knows of its existence. Second, even when the name is exported, any new assignments made within the subshell remain local to the child process. If you examine your .profile file, you'll find that the environmental and user variables are all exported so that they are available, with their assigned values, to all processes spawned by the login shell. If you assign new values to, say, HOME or PATH in a subshell, such changes will be temporary.

The set command you met earlier can be used to display all the variables known to the current shell, together with their values. Simply use set with no arguments:

```
$ set
PATH      :/bin:/usr/bin:/usr/stan
PS1       $
PS2       >
SKBLIB    /use/stan/lib
...
```

The rule that a subshell cannot alter the values of variables set in its parent shell is of fundamental importance. It is related to the concept of *local* and *global* variables found in most programming languages. In languages with global variables, nasty side effects are a constant danger, especially in large programs, because changes made in one module can unwittingly affect distant modules. Unix shell variables are global in the sense that their scope (or visibility) and initial values can be extended (via export) from parent to children. However, the side effect problem is solved by preventing child processes from affecting the parent environment. export simply provides *copies* of variables for child processes—the originals cannot be molested.

As you develop more complex shell scripts you'll come to appreciate this arrangement. Your script commands can be incorporated into other script commands, possibly by complete strangers many years from now, so there is no telling what variable names may be floating around at different process levels. Unrestricted global variables would greatly complicate the shell-programming process.

Another vital and related aspect of locality is that when you change a directory with a `cd` call in a shell script, you affect only the subshell environment. The current directory as seen by the parent is not changed. Consider the following skeleton script:

```
:
# @(#) tcd -- test cd in a shell -- SKB 11/27/95
#
SKBLIB=/usr/stan/lib
echo 'Starting directory='
pwd
cd $SKBLIB
echo 'After cd, subshell directory now='
pwd
```

Assuming `tcd` has been made executable with `chmod`, let's test it as follows:

```
$ cd
$ pwd
/usr/stan
$ tcd
Starting directory=
/usr/stan
After cd, subshell directory now=
/usr/stan/lib
$ pwd
/usr/stan
$ _
```

When we return to the parent shell, we are still in our starting directory in spite of the `cd` performed within the subshell.

How Shell Scripts Work

What really happens when you enter `dw` at the prompt? The full story is quite complex, but some of the subtleties need to be appreciated in order to master the art of shell scripting. Here's a brief walkthrough to give you a feel for the sequence and to establish some essential shell jargon.

The first hurdle for your parent `sh` shell (the login shell displaying the $) is *parsing* your command line. Parsing means that the command line is broken into *tokens* (or *words*) to determine the name(s) of the command(s) and the nature of the options

and arguments, if any. During this parsing, certain special symbols (known as *metacharacters*) may trigger a variety of transformations to the arguments (such as command substitutions, parameter substitutions, blank interpretation, and filename generation, of which more later).

To do all this, the shell must scan the environment to pick up the values assigned to environment variables. The shell also sets the special variables with useful values such as $#, the number of arguments, and the positional parameters ($0, $1, and so on), encountered during the parse. Next, the shell will set up any explicit redirections indicated by the > and < symbols.

Eventually, the dreaded moment of execution draws nigh. There may be several commands in the command line (you've met examples such as *xxx* | *yyy* and *xxx*; *yyy*), but let's concentrate on the situation where a single command such as dw has been invoked. The shell needs to locate the file dw (using the directory search sequence in PATH) and check the directory and file permissions. If the file is not found, the command is aborted. We talk about an *exit* from a process back to its parent.

This is a convenient point to introduce another vital chore performed by the shell. The shell always passes to the parent process a parameter $? known as the *exit status* (also called the *condition code* or *return code*). By convention, a zero value indicates a successful command execution; a nonzero value indicates failure *and* its value tells you the reason for failure. All the standard commands follow this convention but be aware that the values depend on the programmer following certain rules. Many shell programming features make use of the exit status. When you test the result of certain operations in order to control the execution flow of the script, a zero exit status is taken as *true*, while a nonzero exit status is taken as *false*. I'll amplify this aspect of shell programming in subsequent chapters. You can perform commands conditionally as follows:

```
comm1 && comm2
comm3 || comm4
```

If comm1 executes successfully, returning an exit status of 0, then comm2 will be executed; if comm1 fails, returning a nonzero exit status, comm2 will be ignored. Actually, comm1 and comm2 can each be compound expressions representing a whole slew of commands such as *x*; *y*; *z* or *x* | *y* | *z*. The second line reverses the logic: comm4 will only execute if comm3 is unsuccessful.

Your script can actually force a command to fail! The special command exit *n* causes the processing shell to abort with an exit status of *n*, so that user-detected error conditions can be "passed on" to other shell scripts that include your script.

Having located dw and checked the permissions, the shell must analyze the type of the dw file. If it is a compiled, binary program, a dw process is spawned to execute it. If dw is an executable text file, a subshell is spawned that will read the commands from the file. During this process, further parsing and substitutions will occur depending on the text encountered. For example, occurrences of positional parameters will be replaced by the appropriate values. If $0 occurs in the shell script, it will be replaced by the invoking command name. Each occurrence of $0 to $9 is replaced with the corresponding command argument, and $* is set with a string representing all the command's arguments separated by spaces. Similarly, each occurrence of $# will be replaced with a value representing the number of arguments used in the command line.

As each line of the script "unfolds," further processes and subshells may be spawned to any number of levels down the process chain, depending on the type of commands encountered. Any special commands such as echo and cd will be executed "within" the current shell. It is not rewarding to dwell obsessively on all this activity. Eventually, child processes and subshells succeed and die, the script's end-of-file is reached, and control reverts back to the original login shell.

Yes, it is possible to overload the system with too many processes and subshells. Both your login shell and the system as a whole have limits set by the size of the process table in the kernel. The error message Fork failed–too many processes or similar is Unix telling you to cool down (or buy a larger system!).

The Positional Parameters

So far, our dw script has been invoked without arguments. To endow your scripts with the same flexibility as normal Unix commands, you need to understand the positional parameters alluded to in the previous section. A simple, impractical example will illustrate the way a shell script "knows" how it was called: the number and names of its arguments. Consider the silly script called ssc:

```
:
# @(#) ssc: Silly Script -- SKB 11/24/95
# This daft program illustrates the use of positional parameters
# and the shift command
# usage: enter ssc followed by at least one argument
echo 'Command='
echo $0
echo 'Number of args='
```

```
echo $#
echo 'The original arg list='
echo $*
shift
echo 'The arg list after a shift='
echo $*
```

Create and chmod this file as usual; then test it with various arguments:

```
$ ssc -a b cd efg
Command=
ssc
Number of args=
4
The original arg list=
-a b cd efg
The arg list after a shift=
b cd efg
$ _
```

The invoking command is ssc, as confirmed by the value echoed from $0. The number of arguments is 4, the value in $#. The first echo $* output displays each of the four arguments, $1, $2, $3, and $4. After the shift special command, $1 takes the value of the original $2, $2 takes the value of the original $3, and so on. Try ssc with ten or more arguments. Notice that $* holds all the arguments, even if their number exceeds nine. Since there is no positional parameter called $10, one of the applications of the shift command is to access the tenth or higher argument. Try quoting some or all of the arguments, and see how the shell strips the quotes. The number of arguments in

```
$ ssc "-a b" cd efg
```

is three, not four, because the space between -a and b has been *quoted*, that is to say *hidden*, from the shell.

Try ssc with no arguments. The first $* correctly reports an empty list of arguments, but you'll get an error on the shift command—there is nothing to shift!

An example that may puzzle you is

```
$ ssc x y x >misc.tmp
$ cat misc.tmp
Command=
ssc
Number of args=
```

```
3
The original arg list=
x y z
The arg list after a shift=
y z
$ _
```

No, the redirection expression >misc.tmp is *not* considered a command argument. Before we explore more complex scripts, let's spruce up dw to illustrate a few more basic principles. Use vi or ed to amend dw as follows:

```
:
# @(#)dw -- show date and users -- v 2.0 SKB 11/13/95
#
echo 'Today is:'
date
echo '
The following users have logged in:'
who -u
```

Running the new version produces the more legible display:

```
$ dw
Today is:
Mon Nov 13 17:33:50 PDT 1995

The following users have logged in:
stan    tty01   Nov 13 01:45   0:01    169
iwonka tty06   Nov 13 00:32     .      170
```

To help explain this enhanced script, a brief diversion on echo and quoted characters will be useful.

echo and the Shell Metacharacters

The echo command (introduced in Chapter 6) lets you display texts and variables so that you can annotate and tabulate the output of commands embedded in your scripts. echo by itself will give you a newline; otherwise it echoes each of its arguments. The arguments of echo are groups of characters separated by one or more spaces or tabs. It is vital to remember that these arguments are handled by the shell before being "echoed," so many strange transformations are possible: you do not always get back exactly the string of characters shown in the arguments.

After echoing the final (possibly transformed) argument, echo gives a concluding newline. You can suppress this newline in two ways: use the –n switch or the special '\c' escape sequence. (Not all versions support both of these features, but at least one of them should be available.) For example,

```
$ echo Enter your Name:
Enter your Name:
$ _
```

But,

```
$ echo  -n Enter your Name:
Enter your Name:$ _
```

and

```
$ echo Enter your Name:'\c'
Enter your name:$ _
```

The last variant can also be written as

```
$ echo 'Hear this:\c'
Hear this:$ _
```

or as

```
$ echo "Hear this:\c"
Hear this:$ _
```

WARNING Don't confuse a single forward quote (´) with a backquote (`).
Don't confuse two single forward quotes (´´) with a double quote (").
Don't confuse two backquotes (``) with a double quote (").

The \c pair is known as an *escape sequence* since the character following the backslash "escapes" its normal interpretation by the shell. You met this concept in ed and vi, where regular expressions made use of \ as the escape character. In the case of \c, however, note that you must also use single or double quotes: '\c' or "\c" (more on quoting soon).

echo also allows the following useful escape sequences (your terminal may not recognize all of them, though):

'\b'	Backspace
'\f'	Formfeed
'\n'	Newline
'\r'	Carriage Return
'\t'	Tab
'\v'	Vertical Tab
'*oct*'	The ASCII code represented by the octal number *oct*. For example, echo '\07' is equivalent to sending BELL (or Ctrl-G) to the terminal. Armed with a list of octal codes for special graphics symbols, you can give your scripts jazzy windows and boxes. Octal numbers must start with a zero.

Familiar Quotations

Going back to the enhanced dw example, note the use of single forward quotes around the legends. These *hide*, or *escape*, or *quote* the spaces, newlines, and other special characters from the shell. The three words are not quite synonymous, but they are often used to describe any of the various tricks available to modify the shell's normal actions. I'll use the verb "quote" to cover all such methods.

Space and tab, normally used as argument separators (or *delimiters*), can be quoted using single forward quotes. The two commands

```
$ echo Today is:
Today is:
$ _
```

and

```
$ echo 'Today is:'
Today is:
$ _
```

produce the same display, but for slightly different reasons. In the first version, echo has two arguments, Today and is:, which are echoed one after the other. In the second example, echo "sees" only one argument, the string 'Today is:'. In fact, the shell strips off the quotes and passes the sequence Today is: as one argument to echo. Try this with several spaces between Today and is: to confirm my story.

Similarly, in the entry,

```
echo '
The following users have logged in:'
```

we are quoting the newline after the first quote, so a newline will be echoed before the text (notice the extra line in the display). The following alternative achieves the same result:

```
echo
echo 'The following users have logged in:'
```

Even when not essential, using single forward quotes around text for display is a good habit to develop. The complete rules for forward quotes, double quotes, and backquotes are quite tricky. Here, and in the next section, I provide examples to give you a feel for the subject. I'll present the formal rules later. Note that for convenience I give the examples as direct keyboard interactions with the shell; they can, of course, also be translated as lines in a shell script.

```
$ echo 'What does "quote" mean?'
What does "quote" mean?
$ echo "What does 'quote' mean?"
What does 'quote' mean?
$ _
```

Backquotes

The backquotes play a leading role in shell programs. The general idea is that when the shell encounters `command`, it executes (or tries to execute) *command* and replaces the whole expression `command` with the output (if any) from that execution. The backquoted *command* expression can contain any legal switches, options or arguments—it may even be a compound expression holding several commands. Clearly, it is not usually fruitful to use backquotes with commands that do not produce any output. The term *command substitution* is used to describe the shell's action

when a backquoted command (possibly with arguments) is found in a command line. Command substitution provides a powerful method for generating arguments, setting values in shell variables, and other tricks:

```
$ echo Today is `date`
Today is Tue Nov 14 17:33:50 PDT 1995
$ _
```

The above provides an alternative way of creating the dw script file, by the way. The following example will come as no surprise:

```
$ echo 'Today is `date`'
Today is `date`
$ _
```

Single quotes hide the backquotes from the shell, so no command substitution takes place. However, the following example *may* shock you:

```
$ echo "Today is `date`"
Today is Tue Nov 14 17:33:50 PDT 1995
$ _
```

What is going on? Well, rules are rules, and an important Unix shell rule is that double quotes do *not* hide backquotes. Double quotes (unlike single forward quotes) allow the shell to "see" backquotes, so the date command is invoked. You'll meet another double quote exception, the $ symbol. There are excellent reasons for these exceptions between single forward quote and double quote hiding. They allow you to control when and where the shell makes certain types of substitutions—you'll meet many such situations as the saga unfolds. Here's another use of backquotes:

```
$ pwd
/usr/stan/lib/misc
$ HERE=`pwd`
$ echo $HERE
/usr/stan/lib/misc
$ cd
<do things in /usr/stan>
$ cd $HERE
<return to /usr/stan/lib/misc>
```

The output from pwd is saved in the shell variable HERE. You can subsequently use $HERE to return to a previous directory. Examples like these are common in scripts where you may have no prior knowledge from which directory the script starts running.

In the following example, the backquoted command has an argument:

```
$ mail `cat mailshot` <memo
```

If `mailshot` contains a list of recipients, the `cat` command will "output" these names to provide an argument to the `mail` command. Each recipient will be sent the contents of the `memo` file. The `mailshot` file can be formatted as

```
stan
mary
boss
```

or as

```
stan mary boss
```

The first layout works because the command substitution mechanism interprets newlines as word delimiters and passes each name forward as a separate argument to `mail`.

More on Metacharacters

As you've seen, the shell can treat a large number of *metacharacters* in a nonliteral sense. For instance, the shell will expand * to match file names, so echo * will not display an asterisk! What you'll get is a list of file names (all those in your current directory not starting with a dot, in fact). The shell action with *, ?, and regular expressions, is known as *name generation*. The full list of potential metacharacters (depending on the context) is quite daunting: < > ( ) {} [] ; | ? / \ $ " ´ ` # & space, tab, and newline. You need to learn gradually when and where each symbol can have a special meaning, how the shell treats them, and how to inhibit (or delay) their special effects.

In the following sections I'll explain the more common metacharacters, glossing over some of the complexities until later. Since some of the metacharacters interact with each other, there will be some repetitions in these sections.

Escaping with \

The metacharacter \ (backslash) lets you quote any single metacharacter, including \ itself.

```
$ echo \*
*
$ echo \\\?
\?
$ echo `date`
Mon Nov 14 17:33:50 PDT 1994
$ echo \`date\`
`date`
$ echo "\`date\`"
`date`
$ _
```

The \ is also used to generate ASCII control codes, as explained earlier: '\t' for tab, '\0n' where n is the octal value of an ASCII character, and so on. The special sequence '\c' is used to suppress the newline you normally get from echo:

```
$ echo 'Enter Name: \c'
Enter Name: $ _
```

Note also the common use of \ at the end of a command line too long to fit on your screen.

```
:
# @(#): longline -- show use of \ as line extension
#
echo This line seems to be far, far, far, far too long \
to fit on one line.
```

This script would display as follows:

```
$ longline
This line seems to be far, far, far, far too long to fit on one
line.
$ _
```

The layout would depend on the width and wraparound properties of your screen. The newline immediately after \ is hidden from the shell.

The Comment Character

is used to indicate comments in your shell script. Comments are annotations that appear in printed listings, telling you of such things as the author, revision dates, and reasons for certain lines. Such comments are ignored by the shell and are for

human consumption only. As your scripts become more complex, pithy comments become essential both to you and your next of kin (i.e., those who may have to decipher and maintain your code when you have moved on).

Any word that starts with a # leads to the rest of the line being ignored. You can test the effect of # using echo:

```
$ echo Enter your Name: # added in version 2.0 11/14/95
Enter your Name:
$ echo Enter your Employee '#':
Enter your Employee #:
$ echo 'Enter your Employee #:'
Enter your Employee #:
$ echo abc#def
abc#def
$ echo abc #def
abc
$ _
```

In the first line, the # and all following characters are ignored. In the next two examples, the # is quoted so that its special meaning is lost: you get a literal # displayed. The previous examples illustrate the fact that # is also taken literally when it is not the first symbol of a word. You can also use the backslash:

```
$ echo abc \#def
abc #def
$ echo abc \\ #def
abc \
$ echo abc \\\#def
abc \#def
$ _
```

Note again the double \ \ needed to display a single \.

Double Quotes

Double quotes can be used to quote *most* metacharacters: the exceptions are $ ` " and \. Apart from these, double quotes can be used in place of single forward quotes. The $ metacharacter is used for *parameter substitution;* the ` is used for *command substitution.* Both kinds of substitutions occur within double-quoted arguments encountered by the shell.

```
$ echo abc "#"def
abc #def
```

```
$ echo "abc #def"
abc #def
$ echo $HOME
/usr/stan
$ echo '$HOME'
$HOME
$ echo "$HOME"
/usr/stan
$ echo "\$HOME"
$HOME
$ echo "`date`"
Tue Nov 14 17:33:50 PDT 1995
$ echo ""

$ _
<empty string-newline response>
$ """
> Bye
> So long"
Bye
So long
<keeps prompting until matching " supplied>
$ echo "\""
"
$ echo "\\"
\
$ echo '\\'
\\
```

Before proceeding make sure you understand why these examples work the way they do.

Metacharacter Sequences

To simplify the quoting of sequences of metacharacters, you can enclose them all in single forward quotes (or double quotes with the noted exceptions). For example, '$*' is equivalent to both '$"*' and \$*. However, since $ is *not* quoted by double quotes, the shell would treat "$*" as $"*" with possibly peculiar results.

The double quotes and single forward quotes will not affect normal characters, so if a metacharacter occurs in the middle of normal text, you can quote the whole string:

```
$ echo The '*' in your eye
The * in your eye
$ _
```

can also be written as

```
$ echo 'The * in your eye'
The * in your eye
$ _
```

Care is needed to display ' and ", as you may have guessed. Look at the following:

```
$ echo Have you read "War and Peace?"
Have you read War and Peace?
$ echo 'Have you read "War and Peace?"'
Have you read "War and Peace?"
$ echo "Have you read 'War and Peace?'"
Have you read 'War and Peace?'
$ _
```

Now try the following examples, and see if you can explain the results:

```
$ echo \
> Hello
Hello
$ _
```

The \ has hidden the following newline from the shell, so you get the PS2 (secondary prompt), usually the symbol >. In other words, echo is still waiting for an argument. Once you enter Hello and newline, echo will echo as shown.

In the following exercises you'll see examples of *file-name generation* and how it can be suppressed if not needed. Words containing unquoted occurrences of *, ?, and characters enclosed in the pair [ ] are treated by the shell as patterns. The shell generates a sorted list of file names (including directory names) that match the pattern. If this list is empty, i.e., no matches are found, the word is left unchanged. Otherwise, the list of matching file names *replaces* the word. The patterns recognized are not quite as complex as the regular expressions you met in ed and vi. The syntax is also just ever so slightly different. The Bourne and C shells also have minor differences. I'll concentrate on the Bourne shell here. (See Appendix A for shell variants.)

*	Matches any string including the empty (null) string, but excluding *dot* file names, that is, file names starting with a period. (In ed and vi, *x** matches *zero* or more occurrences of *x*.)

?   Matches any single character except the initial period of a
            dot file name. (In ed and vi, the period is used for single-
            character matches, including the period itself but excluding
            newline.)

[xyz...]   Matches any one of the characters within the brackets.

[a-x]   Matches any character in the range.

A ! (pronounced *bang*) immediately following the [reverses the sense of the match.
Thus:

[!xyz]   Matches any character *not* inside the brackets.

[!a-x]   Matches any character *not* in the range. (In ed and vi, the
            caret (^) rather than ! reverses the match.)

These elements can be combined to provide more complex patterns. For example:

```
$ echo [a-c]??[x-z]
ashy atoz b.sy busy clox
$ echo [d-e]*[!a-z]
decimal2 easy5 easy.3
$ _
```

A key point that can mislead the unwary is that file name generation does *not* take
place when no matches occur. Consider this example:

```
$ echo ?
?
```

You would normally expect to use '?' or "?" to echo a metacharacter such as ?. But
here the shell happened to find no single-character file names in the current directory! Hence the "word" ? was passed on unchanged. Obviously, the safest way to
echo a literal ? is to escape or quote it since we can never be certain that no single-
character file names will be found.

```
$ echo \?
?
$ echo '?'
?
$ echo "?"
?
```

Compare these examples with the following:

```
$ echo /bin/??
/bin/ed /bin/dw /bin/vi
$ echo ???
bin tom tmp usr
$ echo \*
*
$ echo '*'
*
$ echo "*"
*
$ echo *
<lists all file names except those with leading dot>
$ echo .*
<lists all file names with leading dot>
# echo *+*
lost+found
$ echo wx*yz
wx*yz
<no matches were found>
$ echo 'wx*yz'
wx*yz
$ echo   'What's that?'
> OK
> OK'
What's that?
OK
OK
$ _
```

Notice the mismatched ' in the last example: with a missing ', the shell expects more input, and will keep prompting until you supply a final quote.

I conclude this section with a brief summary of the Bourne shell's metacharacters, shown in Table 13.1. Use quotes or \ to inhibit their action. Some of these metacharacters have already been discussed. Others are listed here for completeness and will be the subject of further elucidation in Chapter 16.

This is a good moment to recap some basic facts about the role of the shell. A clear picture of "who does what" is essential to good shell scripting. The correct use of shell variables, special commands, and metacharacters depends on a knowledge of how shells and subshells interact.

TABLE 13.1: Metacharacter Summary

Symbol	Meaning
>	*command* >*file* redirects stdout to *file*.
>>	*command* >>*file* appends stdout to *file*.
<	*command* <*file* redirects stdin from *file*.
|	comm1 | comm2 pipeline: stdout from comm1 directed to stdin of comm2 asynchronously.
<<*delim*	Takes data (known as a *here document*) embedded in a shell script and redirects it to a command's stdin. The data is redirected until the string specified in *delim* is reached.
*	Wildcard matches all strings including null but excluding dot file names.
?	Wildcard matches all single characters except initial dot of a dot file name.
[*char_list*]	Matches any single character in *char_list*.
[*!char_list*]	Matches any single character *not* in *char_list*.
[*r1–r2*]	Matches any single character in range *r1* to *r2*.
[*!r1–r2*]	Matches any single character *not* in range *r1* to *r2*.
&	comm1 & comm2 executes comm1 in background. comm2 does not wait for comm1 to finish (asynchronous execution).
;	comm1;comm2 executes comm1 then comm2 (sequential execution).
;;	Used as command terminator in case commands.
\`*commlist*\`	The command(s) in *commlist* are executed and the output of the final command replaces the backquoted expression (command substitution).
(*commlist*)	The command(s) in *commlist* are run in a subshell.
{*commlist*}	The command(s) in *commlist* are run in the current shell.
$*n*	The parameter $0 is set to the command name; the parameters $1–$9 are set to the first nine arguments.
$*	Holds *all* the positional parameters starting with $1.
$@	Same as $* except when quoted as "$@". The parameter "$@" is "$1" "$2"... but "$*" is "$1 $2...".
$#	The total number of positional parameters excluding $0 (the command name).

TABLE 13.1: Metacharacter Summary (continued)

Symbol	Meaning
$-	The option flags used in the command line.
$?	The exit status value (decimal). A zero value usually indicates a successful command. A nonzero value usually indicates failure.
$$	The process id of the current shell.
$!	The process id of the last background command.
$VAR	The value of the variable VAR. Empty if VAR not defined.
${VAR}str	The value of VAR is prepended to literal string str.
${VAR:-str}	$VAR if VAR is defined and non-null; otherwise str. $VAR remains unchanged.
${VAR:=str}	$VAR if VAR is defined and non-null; otherwise str. If VAR is undefined or null, str is assigned to $VAR.
${VAR:?mstr}	$VAR if VAR is defined and non-null; otherwise displays the message mstr and exits the shell. Default message if mstr empty is VAR: parameter null or not set.
${VAR:+str}	str if VAR is defined and non-null; otherwise makes no substitution. Without the :, the expressions work the same, but shell only checks whether VAR is defined (null or not).
\char	Takes char literally (escape).
'str'	Takes string str literally (single quote).
"str"	Takes string str literally *after* interpreting $, \`commlist\`, and \.
#	Comment character: ignores words starting with # and ignores all subsequent words up to next newline. (The Bourne shell also treats any line starting with a semicolon or space as a comment.)
VAR=str	Assigns str as new value of VAR.
VAR=	Assigns null value to VAR. Contrasts with unset VAR, which undefines VAR.
commlist1 && commlist2	Executes commands in commlist2 only if the commands in commlist1 have executed successfully (i.e., have returned an exit status of zero).
commlist1 || commlist2	Executes commands in commlist2 only if the commands in commlist1 have executed unsuccessfully (i.e., have returned a nonzero exit status).

The Shell Game

To put the traditional shell as a command interpreter in perspective, consider what happens when Unix first boots up. I'll simplify the details to avoid obscuring the key events. The sequence of events before your terminal is ready for action can be summarized as a succession of four major processes:

```
init-getty-login-shell
```

init acts as a general process spawner. (You may wish to reread Chapter 9 to refresh your understanding of how a parent process forks, or spawns child processes.) In the process hierarchy, the first init created during a Unix boot plays a similar role to that of root in the file hierarchy. Just as the root directory is mother to its subdirectories (and so on to other generations), the first init gives birth to offspring subprocesses (which in turn beget subsubprocesses). The big difference between processes and directories is that processes can spawn *subinstances* of themselves. In particular, init can spawn init children, which inherit fully their parent's procreative powers. root, however, cannot generate another root—it is the uniquely named parent of all subsequent subdirectories.

init works in conjunction with a file called /etc/initab (short for initialization table). Briefly, initab specifies which processes can be spawned by init in each of eight possible *run levels*. A run level represents a particular system configuration, for example, single-user mode or multiuser mode.

We often refer to process *paths* by analogy with directory paths. You can trace a path from the first init process down through a series of spawned child and grandchild processes. As each terminal logs off and each child terminates, Unix moves back up the path to the original init process.

After certain booting initialization phases are complete, and provided you are in multiuser mode, the original, Big Daddy init spawns separate child init processes for each connected terminal, then waits patiently for the drama to unfold. It is one of these init children that opens the standard input, output, and error files for your terminal, and then calls getty. getty sets the terminal type, speed and line protocol, and displays the login message seeking your login name. getty reads your login name and passes it as an argument to the login process.

login prompts for your password (if necessary) and checks it against the entry found in the /etc/passwd file. If this check fails, login will prompt you again.

There may be limits to the number of login attempts or to the time allowed to complete them. Note that these prompts are being performed at system level by the login process—no shell is yet involved. If the login eventually fails for any reason, the process path will revert to the startup init which is aware of the fate of all its children. If you pass the password hurdle, login performs the following chores (not necessarily in the order indicated):

- Updates certain accounting files so that your presence as a logged-in user is known. Commands such as who and finger need to know who logged on, where, and when.

- Checks and notifies you if you have mail.

- Displays any motd (message of the day).

- Executes the startup files, if any, (.profile for the Bourne shell, or .login for the C shell, as indicated in /etc/passwd), to set various environment variables, such as TERM (terminal type), PS1 (primary prompt symbol), and PS2 (secondary prompt symbol). You can also set up other tasks to be performed here (see later).

- Consults the file /etc/default/login (if present) to establish other environment variables, such as TZ (time zone), HZ (interrupt-clock frequency in Hertz [cycles per second]), and ALTSHELL (alternative shell).

- cd's to your working directory (HOME).

- Gets the user and group ids from /etc/passwd. (These are needed by the shell to determine your access rights to directories and files ouside your HOME base.)

- Sets the permissions umask to octal 022. (This establishes default permissions for your own files and directories.)

- Executes the login shell named in the last field of /etc/passwd. (If the last field is empty, executes the default shell, usually /bin/sh, the Bourne shell.)

But, and this is a significant "but," the program name sitting at the end of etc/passwd can represent any suitable executable file name your system administrator decrees. He or she can reduce you to a restricted shell (such as rsh), a nonstandard, vendor-supplied shell, or can even invoke a particular application with no direct shell access at all. Recall that only the superuser can edit the /etc/passwd file, so the startup shell or program cannot be set or changed without suitable authority.

For the moment, though, let's assume that /etc/passwd gives you the Bourne shell, /bin/sh. Unless you have redefined the variable PS1 (the primary prompt symbol), you now see the $ prompt. The sh process now running and waiting to interpret your commands is your *parent* shell. You can picture the parent shell accepting input from your standard input (usually the keyboard unless redirected) until it receives an end-of-file sequence (Ctrl-D). Terminating the shell will normally wake up the process that spawned the shell, namely login. This explains why the login message reappears.

When you enter a command line, the shell has several jobs to do:

- Parse the command line to distinguish command names from options and arguments (remember that a command line may contain many commands together with redirections, pipes, and other operators).
- Expand any wildcard symbols.
- Convert any variable names encountered to their assigned values.
- Locate the file indicated by the first command name to be executed (using the PATH variable as explained in Chapter 6).
- Check that you have execute permission(s).

(There are a host of other details which I'll gloss over for the moment.)

If the file cannot be found, or if access and/or execute permissions are denied, the shell issues a warning message and redisplays the prompt. The shell will also reject your command line if the syntax is faulty.

If all is well, the next steps depend on the type of file located by the shell. You may recall the file command from Chapter 7, used to determine file types. The two file types of interest here are as follows:

- Executable program (also known as binary) files. These come in many flavors depending on the language and compiler used in their generation.
- Executable ASCII text or shell script (also known as *command text)*.

In the first case, where the command file is a compiled, executable program, your login (or parent) sh process spawns a child process to execute the command. Any command arguments and options are passed to this process. What happens next

depends on whether the & operator appears after the command entry. If the & operator has been used, the parent process (your login shell) will not wait for the child process to finish, so the prompt will appear immediately and the child process proceeds independently in the background. With no & operator, the parent waits for the child process to terminate, after which the process path returns to the login shell and the prompt reappears. You have seen both these variants in previous chapters. To avoid mental strain, you should, for the moment, ignore the fact that the process running the executable program can, and probably will, spawn its own child processes, and so on... but eventually, barring accidents, your login shell "regains" control.

The case where the file is a shell script (executable text file) has a very important difference. Your parent login shell has to spawn a fresh shell, known as a subshell, to handle the situation. The subshell is an sh process (the spitting image of its parent) but instead of reading commands from the keyboard, it reads and obeys the commands in the shell script.

With this background, you are getting nearer to understanding the Unix shell. In the next two chapters I introduce some of the most common tools used in shell scripts. Then we can start writing useful scripts to automate your daily chores.

Summary

The main thrust of this chapter was to explain the importance of the shell as a programmable interface. You saw how shell scripts can create new commands from existing commands. Some simple scripts were devised to illustrate the different ways a script file can be executed. You also saw how the shell interprets various metacharacters, and how these interpretations can be altered by "quoting." I showed you how to use the predefined shell variables and how to define, use, and export your own shell variables. I introduced the positional variables $0-$9 that allow your script access to command arguments. The chapter ended with an overview of how Unix boots up via the init-getty-login-shell sequence of processes, and how the shell spawns subshells to execute your scripts.

CHAPTER

FOURTEEN

Dipping in the Toolbox

- The sort command

- The uniq command

- The head and tail commands

- The split command

- The cut and paste commands

- The find command

- The tr, translate, and dd commands

Before delving deeper into shell programming, I want to introduce a few commands that are particularly useful in shell scripts. I will confine the discussion to the most common options and applications for these commands. I suggest you skim through these commands at first reading to get a feel for their properties, then refer back to a command when it appears in the later shell script exercises.

The sort Command

The sort command (in man section C) is a *filter* that sorts *lines* from your standard input and passes the sorted result to your standard output. By default, the sort will be in *ascending* order (usually determined by the ASCII code sequence, but there are local exceptions) and will sort by comparing whole lines. In most cases, sort is used to sort items in one or more files and pass the result to a file or to another filter for further processing. You'll also see examples where we sort the data emerging from other commands such as who and ls.

A rich fund of options exists to modify the sort ordering and/or to sort by selected fields (usually called *keys*) from each line. Let's start by sorting a naive file called staff containing employee names:

```
$ cat staff
Jones, A. P.
Amis, Q. K.
Brown, S.
Smith, E. M.
Smith, A. L.
$ sort staff
Amis, Q. K.
Brown, S.
Jones, A. P.
Smith, A. L.
Smith, E. M.
$ cat staff
Jones, A. P.
Amis, Q. K.
Brown, S.
Smith, E. M.
Smith, A. L.
$ _
```

The first point to notice is that you can use `sort staff` rather than `sort <staff`. In other words, if `sort` sees an input file name argument, `sort` will read from that file without explicit redirection. In fact, you'll see later that `sort` can accept more than one input file, so that

```
sort staff temps
```

will read both files to give one sorted, composite output. If you don't supply an input file name, or if you name the file – (minus), `sort` reads and sorts your standard input.

The next thing to observe is that `sort` has not altered the sequence in the `staff` file itself: the sorted output simply appears fleetingly on the screen. To obtain a sorted file, you can use redirection as follows:

```
$ sort staff >s_staff
$ cat s_staff
Amis, Q. K.
Brown, S.
Jones, A. P.
Smith, A. L.
Smith, E. M.
$ _
```

You could now use `mv s_staff staff` to copy the sorted data over the original file. What you must *never* do is

```
$ sort staff >staff
```

This will cause havoc to the `staff` file, since Unix has to overwrite the very file it is trying to sort. There is a way to safely sort a file onto itself without using an intermediary file. You use the `-o` (output) option as follows:

```
$ sort staff -o staff
$ cat staff
Amis, Q. K.
Brown, S.
Jones, A. P.
Smith, A. L.
Smith, E. M.
$ _
```

The −o option works with any named output file, so it offers an alternative to redirection:

```
$ sort staff -o s_staff
$ _
```

or

```
$ sort -o s_staff staff
$ _
```

Both of the alternatives above give the same result as

```
sort staff >s_staff
```

Spaces after the −o are optional: `sort staff -os_staff`, and `sort -os_staff staff` work OK, but I prefer the space for legibility. The key point is that the file name following the −o is the output file regardless of its position in the argument list.

You can reverse the sort ordering with the −r (reverse) option:

```
$ sort -r -o r_staff staff
$ cat r_staff
Smith, E. M.
Smith, A. L.
Jones, A. P.
Brown, S.
Amis, Q. K.
$ _
```

The output is now in descending ASCII sequence. Incidentally, if you are unfamiliar with the 7-bit ASCII code, you may encounter some surprises when using `sort`. If you refer to Appendix B (ASCII Tables), you'll see that the uppercase letters have lower numeric values than the lowercase letters! So, a strictly ASCII-ascending sort moves "Z" (value 90) ahead of "a" (value 97), and so on. The ASCII values of the control characters, numerals, tab, space, and punctuation symbols should also be noted: unless you take precautions, `sort` blindly follows these values, often with disconcerting results. Although `sort` usually makes sense only when applied to text files, Unix makes no attempt to enforce sensible usage. You can `sort` binary files without complaint, although the results will not usually be meaningful.

Over There!

Since the Sun never sets on Unix (or vice versa?), there are many foreign language variations that sort (and other utilities) needs to support. Even languages that use the Roman alphabet (some need extended 8-bit ASCII character sets for accented letters and diacritical marks) can present collation headaches. For example, Spanish lexicographers sort "czarina" ahead of "chabacano," while Welsh dictionaries place "llabyddio" after "lwmp." The Cherokee syllabary, with eighty-five distinct single-case symbols, calls for a complete remapping of the ASCII character set. Other languages, such as Chinese and Japanese, demand more dramatic extensions to 16 or higher bit encodings. This fascinating subject is unfortunately beyond the scope of my treatise, but it is vital to avoid the parochial ASCII-only mindset.

To overcome some of the quirks of the ASCII sequence, sort offers many order-overriding options. I summarize these in Table 14.1, prior to explaining each in more detail in the following sections.

TABLE 14.1: Summary of sort Options

sort Option	Action
c	check sort order. Used in conjunction with sort order options. No sort is performed but you get a warning message if the target file(s) are not in the specified sequence.
r	reverse designated ordering
f	fold lowercase letters to uppercase
d	dictionary order
i	ignore nonprintable characters
n	numeric value order
M	Month name order (JAN, FEB,…)
b	Leading blanks ignored (restricted sort keys only)
t*x*	Use *x* as the field separator symbol (the default is space and tab)

The sort f Option

`sort -f` *filename* treats lowercase letters as uppercase when sorting, so that "a" sorts ahead of "Z" in ascending order. (The f stands for "fold": we say that lowercase letters are *folded* into their uppercase equivalents.) Consider the following session:

```
$ cat staff
Jones, A. P.
Amis, Q. K.
deMoivre, Z.
Brown, S.
Smith, E. M.
Smith, A. L.
$ sort staff
Amis, Q. K.
Brown, S.
Jones, A. P.
Smith, A. L.
Smith, E. M.
deMoivre, Z.
$ sort -f staff
Amis, Q. K.
Brown, S.
deMoivre, Z.
Jones, A. P.
Smith, A. L.
Smith, E. M.
$ sort -fr staff
Smith, E. M.
Smith, A. L.
Jones, A. P.
deMoivre, Z.
Brown, S.
Amis, Q. K.
$ _
```

The concise `-fr` format is entirely equivalent to providing the two options `-f` and `-r`. Whenever a combination of `sort` options makes sense, you can save keystrokes by combining the option letters in any sequence after a single `-`.

The sort d Option

sort -d *filename* gives a "dictionary" sort. This means that characters other than letters, digits, spaces, and tabs are ignored when sorting. Dictionary order, as I indicated earlier, is a property that varies with language, and has to be defined in the locale setting.

The sort i Option

sort -i *filename* gives the ignore-nonprintable-character option. (Recall that space and tab are considered to be "printable.") If your file contains control codes, they can cause trouble when sorting since their ASCII values are lower than space. The definition of "nonprintable" also varies from language to language, and has to be defined in the locale setting.

The sort n Option

sort -n *filename* (the number option) lets you sort by arithmetical value. Although the values of the ASCII numerals are in numeric order, there are many situations where a string sort of numeric fields gives the "wrong" result. Consider the following session:

```
$ cat nlist
90
100
200
080
$ sort nlist
080
100
200
90
$ _
```

You can guess why the string "90" comes in last (highest). The ASCII sort simply compares all first characters, all second characters, and so on. The "080" finds its rightful place because it has been padded with a leading zero (a leading space

would also work). The -n option sorts by true numeric value, ignoring leading spaces and spurious zeros:

```
$ sort -n nlist
080
90
100
200
$ _
```

The -n option goes even further by handling negative numbers and decimals. Compare the following two sorts:

```
$ cat num
1.65
-.9
-2
.67
$ sort num
-.9
-2
.69
1.65
$ sort -n num
-2
-.9
.67
1.65
$ _
```

The sort M Option

The sort -M *filename* option sorts alphabetic month names in proper calendric sequence, JAN before FEB, and so on. Consider the following example:

```
$ cat sales
Mar 93 500
Jan 94 780
Oct 93 120
Sep 94 340
Apr 93 560
Jan 93 178
$ sort sales
Apr 93 560
```

```
Jan 93 178
Jan 94 780
Mar 93 500
Oct 93 120
Sep 94 340
$ sort -M sales
Jan 93 178
Jan 94 780
Mar 93 500
Apr 93 560
Sep 94 340
Oct 93 120
$ _
```

Well, we haven't quite achieved a good date ordering, but at least the months are in sequence. When we reach multikey sorts, I'll show you how to sort by month and year. (Incidentally, I support the useful convention of listing dates as YY/MM/DD which simplifies the whole date sorting mess.) The -M option folds the first three letters of the month names to uppercase before comparing them. So, you can use jan, JAN, January, and so on, as the mood takes you. If sort encounters a nonmonth triplet, such as "Sun" or "XXX," it will take this as *lower* than JAN. Yes, you can reverse the month ordering with -Mr or -rM. To obtain a month/year sort, you'll need to know how to sort on *keys* within a line. Our examples so far, by default, have sorted on a single key, namely the whole line.

Sorting Keys and Fields

You specify a sorting key by supplying two additional arguments, +*pos1* and -*pos2*, that define where the key starts (+) and where it ends (-). Omitting the -*pos2* argument means that the key extends to the end of the line. The *pos1* and *pos2* arguments are numeric and specify, in their simplest form, the *fields* that make up the sorting key. A field is any sequence of characters separated by a field separator (by default a blank, that is, a space or a tab) or by a newline. In the sales file of the previous example, there are three fields: month, year, and units sold. If *pos1* is set to 1 and *pos2* is set to 2, the sort will be over the second field, namely the year:

```
$ cat sales
Mar 93 500
Jan 94 780
Oct 93 120
Sep 94 340
Apr 93 560
```

```
Jan 93 178
$ sort +1 -2 sales
Apr 93 560
Jan 93 178
Mar 93 500
Oct 93 780
Jan 94 780
Sep 94 340
$ _
```

Note that fields 1 and 3 play no part in the above sort. If you try `sort +1 sales`, you'll see that the sort key now combines fields 2 and 3, since the absence of *-pos2* extends the key from *pos1* to the end of the line. You should try other combinations such as `sort +2 -3 sales` to get the picture.

You can interpret *+pos1* and *-pos2* as saying: the sort key starts at the beginning of the (*pos1*+1)th field and ends at the end of the (*-pos2*)th field. Some prefer to look at it as follows:

    +pos1   Start sorting after field number *pos1*

    -pos2   Stop sorting after field number *pos2*

For multikey sorts, you simply enter a sequence of *+pos1* and *-pos2* arguments in the order required. The ordering options d, f, i, M, n, and r can be used in two ways: if placed globally before the first *+pos1* argument, they affect all the following key sorts; if placed behind a particular *-pos2* argument, they affect only the preceding key. If a particular key sort order is modified, the modifier overrides any global modifiers that may affect that key sort. Look at the following:

```
$ cat sales
Mar 93 500
Jan 94 780
Oct 93 120
Sep 94 340
Apr 93 560
Jan 93 178
Mar 91 230
$ sort +0 -1M +1 -2 sales
Jan 93 178
Jan 94 780
Mar 91 230
Mar 93 500
```

```
Apr 93 560
Sep 94 340
Oct 93 780
$ _
```

We first sort field 1 by month name, given by +0 -1M; then within each month we sort by year (field 2) in ascending ASCII (the default ordering), given by +1 -2. Try sorting first by year then by month:

```
$ sort +1 -2 +0 -1M sales
Mar 91 230
Jan 93 178
Mar 93 500
Apr 93 560
Oct 93 780
Jan 94 780
Sep 94 340
$ _
```

We now see the file in true historic sequence.

Finally, you could try a sort on three keys. To illustrate the n option, I've modified the sales figures:

```
$ cat sales
Mar 93 -50
Jan 94 780
Oct 93 1206
Sep 94 340
Apr 93 -560
Jan 93 -50
Mar 91 230
Jun 91 -50
$ sort +2nr +1 -2 +0 -1M sales
Oct 93 1206
Jan 94 780
Sep 94 340
Mar 91 230
Jun 91 -50
Jan 93 -50
Mar 93 -50
Apr 93 -560
$ _
```

The +2nr argument could also be written +2 −3nr, but since field 3 is the final field, the −3 is a default that can be omitted. The nr modifier (reverse-numeric sort) therefore follows the +2 (starting field) argument. Notice how subfields are sorted: the three lines with −50 fields appear in year/month order.

Multiple File Sorts

The sort command can also sort several files at the same time. Suppose you had two files, staff1 and staff2, giving names from different departments:

```
$ cat staff1
Herring, A.
Smith, E. M.
Ireland, J.
Jones, A. P.
Amis, Q. K.
$ cat staff2
Smith, E. M.
Smith, A. L.
Brown, S.
$ sort -o all_staff staff1 staff2
$ cat all_staff
Amis, Q. K.
Brown, S.
Herring, A.
Ireland, J.
Jones, A. P.
Smith, A. L.
Smith, E. M.
Smith, E. M.
$ _
```

Again, note that sort staff1 staff2 >all_staff would achieve the same results.

The sort u Option

In the previous example, the name *Smith, E. M.* appears in both files, and naturally shows twice in the sorted file. The sort command offers the −u (unique) option that automatically suppresses duplicates:

```
$ sort -u -o all_staff staff1 staff2
$ cat all_staff
Amis, Q. K.
```

```
Brown, S.
Herring, A.
Ireland, J.
Jones, A. P.
Smith, A. L.
Smith, E. M.
$ _
```

You'll shortly meet a related command called uniq that reports or hides duplicated fields in a sorted file.

The sort b Option

−b is the *ignore* blank option. sort −b +*pos1* −*pos2* *filename* causes the sort to ignore any leading blanks (spaces and tabs) at the beginning of the designated field of *filename*. Normally, in ascending 7-bit ASCII order, blanks sort ahead of all printing characters. This can be a nuisance. Consider the following example:

```
$ cat staff
 Jones, A. P.
Amis, Q. K.
Brown, S.
   Smith, E. M.
Smith, A. L.
$ sort staff
   Smith, E. M.
 Jones, A. P.
Amis, Q. K.
Brown, S.
Smith, A. L.
$ sort −b +0 staff
Amis, Q. K.
Brown, S.
 Jones, A. P.
Smith, A. L.
   Smith, E. M.
$ _
```

but,

```
$ sort −b staff
   Smith, E. M.
 Jones, A. P.
```

```
Amis, Q. K.
Brown, S.
Smith, A. L.
$ _
```

Note carefully that −b affects only leading blanks and only in restricted sort key specifications. Later on, you'll see other uses of the −b option when sorting individual fields in each line. You can also attach the b after the *pos1* argument:

```
$ sort +0b staff
Amis, Q. K.
Brown, S.
 Jones, A. P.
Smith, A. L.
  Smith, E. M.
$ _
```

The uniq Command

The uniq command (man section C) scans a file looking for any *adjacent* lines that happen to be identical. Options let you restrict the comparisons to certain fields and characters in each line. Other options let you select duplicates or nonduplicates. By default, uniq outputs nonduplicates together with one copy of each duplicate (hence the name uniq, pronounced *unique*). Consider the following sequence:

```
$ cat input_file
a
b
b
c
c
c
d
a
$ uniq input_file
a
b
c
d
a
$ _
```

The final "a" is not considered a duplicate since it is not adjacent to the previous occurrence of "a". To ensure that all duplicates are filtered out, you need to sort the file first. A single file-name argument is always taken as the input to uniq, which then sends its output to the standard output (usually your screen). If you supply two file-name arguments, the second argument is taken as the output file. So, the output from uniq can be sent to a file without the need for the redirection symbol >:

```
$ uniq input_file output_file
$ cat output_file
a
b
c
d
a
$ _
```

This gives rise to a slight quirk. What if you want to pass the output of a command to uniq and then send the output of uniq to a file? In this case, the > is needed. Take the following example:

```
$ sort input_file | uniq
a
b
c
d
$ sort input_file | uniq > output_file
$ cat output_file
a
b
c
d
$ _
```

Note first that "a" occurs only once in the output from uniq, since sort has brought the two "a's" together. Remember that uniq's idea of "duplicate" is "adjacent duplicate." Next, observe that if you omitted the >, uniq would "see" a single file-name argument and would therefore consider output_file as its input source with much ensuing confusion.

The general syntax is

```
uniq [-udc [+n] [-n]] [input_file [output_file]]
```

The final four brackets indicate that you can omit both file name arguments or you can omit the output_file argument. You cannot, I explained earlier, drop the

input_file argument and retain the *output_file* argument.

The other options are explained briefly in the listing below, followed by detailed examples.

-u	Output only the nonduplicated lines.
-d	Output one copy of each adjacent duplicated line; do not output nonduplicates.
-c	Precede each line with a count number showing the number of duplicates found. Implies also -ud.
+*n*	Ignore the first *n* characters when testing for duplicates.
-*n*	Ignore the first *n* fields when testing for duplicates.

The default uniq with no options combines the actions of -u and -d. In other words, it displays the nonduplicated lines *and* one copy of each duplicate. The -c option implies and overrides -u and -d to give the default display plus a count on each line. In other words, -cu , -cd , -cdu, and -cud are all equivalent to -c.

```
$ cat input_file
a
b
b
c
c
c
d
a
$ cat -u input_file
a
d
a
$ cat -d input_file
b
c
$ uniq -c input_file
1 a
2 b
3 c
1 d
1 a
$ _
```

The proper use of −*n* requires an understanding of fields. As with the sort command, a field is any sequence of nonspace, nontab characters that has spaces or tabs (or a final newline) separating it from adjacent fields. The −*n* option tells uniq to skip the first *n* fields on each line together with any leading spaces or tabs before determining whether the rest of the line constitutes a duplicate. Here are some examples.

```
$ cat sales
Mar 91 230
Jan 93 178
Mar 93 178
Apr 93 178
Oct 93 780
Jan 94 780
Sep 94 780
$ uniq -1 sales
Mar 91 230
Jan 93 178
Oct 93 780
Jan 94 780
$ uniq -c -1 sales
1 Mar 91 230
3 Jan 93 178
1 Oct 93 780
2 Jan 94 780
$ uniq -2 sales
Mar 91 230
Jan 93 178
Oct 93 780
$ uniq -d -2 sales
Jan 93 178
Oct 93 780
$ _
```

Here, the −1 option tells uniq to ignore the first field, so that the month name takes no part in the process. Lines 2, 3, and 4 now appear as adjacent duplicates, and only the first copy, "Jan 93 178", is output. The other examples show how to combine several options.

The +*n* option skips *n* characters before the comparisons are made. You can combine −*n* and +*m* options. uniq skips the first *n* fields, then skips the first *m* characters of the (*n*+1)th field.

The head Command

The head filter command (in man section C) lets you see the first few lines of one or more files. A similar command called tail that inspects the last few lines of a file is covered in the next section. Together they provide an easy way of answering such questions as "What on earth is this file called memo.misc?"

The head syntax is as follows:

```
head [-count] [file1 file2 ...]
```

where *count* specifies the number of lines you wish to output from each of the file-name arguments. The default *count* value is 10. Being a filter, head takes standard input and gives standard output. It is often used in pipelines. For example, to display the four best sales periods, you could use head with one of our earlier sort examples:

```
$ cat sales
Mar 93 -50
Jan 94 780
Oct 93 1206
Sep 94 340
Apr 93 -560
Jan 93 -50
Mar 91 230
Jun 91 -50
$ sort +2nr +1 -2 +0 -1M sales | head -4
Oct 93 1206
Jan 94 780
Sep 94 340
Mar 91 230
$ _
```

Note that if *count* exceeds the number of lines available, head simply does the best it can. Remember that if you supply a large enough value for *count* without redirecting output to a file, your display will run off the screen unless you pipe via the more filter:

```
$ head -40 mail_list | more
```

The tail Command

The `tail` filter command (in `man` section C) works like `head` but outputs the final *count* lines, blocks, or characters from the argument file. The syntax is a tad more complex, though:

```
tail +|-[count][lbc] [-f] [filename]
```

The l, b, and c options designate lines, blocks, or characters. The default is l for lines. As with `head`, the default *count* is 10, so that

```
tail filename
```

simply displays the last ten lines of *filename*, while

```
tail -c filename
```

would display the last ten characters of the file.

The *count* argument determines the starting point in the file. If you specify a positive argument, *+count*, `tail` will start outputting *count* lines from the beginning of the file. A negative sign, *-count*, means start *count* lines from the end of the file. The default *count* is still 10 if you just supply the + or − with no number. So,

```
tail +b filename
```

displays *filename* from block 10 to the end. Similarly,

```
tail -c filename
```

outputs the last ten characters. The meaning of block, by the way, depends on the implementation, but is usually 512 bytes. `tail` is usually limited by buffer sizes to reporting about 300 lines, but in practice this is no impediment. `tail` and `head` are mainly used to check a few lines of a file to help identify its version and contents.

The −f (for "follow") option is used to check on the progress of a file being built by another process. For example,

```
tail -f filename
```

displays the final ten lines then sleeps for a second before reading the file again. You can therefore see line by line as the file grows.

Before leaving `head` and `tail`, note the quirk that `head` can take several file name arguments, whereas `tail` accepts only a single file name argument.

The split Command

The `split` command (in man section C) splits a given file into smaller files of a given size. You can specify the size and the names of the partial files created by `split`. The syntax is

```
split [-n] [filename [split_name]]
```

This will split *filename* into *n*-line pieces called *split_name*aa, *split_name*ab, *split_name*ac,...,*split_name*az, *split_name*ba, and so on. The number of files produced depends entirely on the size of *filename* and the value of *n*. The last file may contain fewer than *n* lines, of course. The default *n* is 1000 lines, and the default *split_name* is x. So, if you had a 2001-line file called hairs, the command

```
$ split hairs
```

would create three files called xaa, xab, and xac as follows:

File	Contains
xaa	Lines 1-1000 from hairs
xab	Lines 1001-2000
xac	Line 2001

The command

```
$ split -1500 hairs gray
```

would create two files called grayaa and grayab:

File	Contains
grayaa	Lines 1-1500 from hairs
grayab	Lines 1501-2001

The `split` command needs some care when used with pipes. Consider

```
sort hairs | split gray
```

If your aim is to sort hairs before creating the grayaa, grayab split, this will not work! split would take gray as the file name argument, and would try to split it if such a file existed. To make split accept the output from sort (or any similar piped command) as its standard input, you can do one of two things: omit the gray

argument and accept default splits called xaa, xab, and so on. Or, supply a dash (–) as follows:

```
sort hairs | split -gray
```

The dash warns split that the "file" to be split must be taken from the standard input, and that gray is really the *split_name* suffix.

There is a more sophisticated split command called csplit that splits a file into sections determined by markers in the text. You supply a sequence of arguments that locate the markers. These arguments can be line numbers or regular expressions with optional repetition factors. Consult man section C for more details. Splitting a large file into smaller files is useful in many email situations.

The cut Command

The cut command removes selected fields from each line of a set of files and sends the result to the standard output. The syntax is

```
cut -clist [file1 file2 ...]
```

or

```
cut -flist [-dchar] [-s] [file1 file2 ...]
```

WARNING No spaces are allowed between the c (or f) and the *list* argument! Likewise, no spaces are allowed between d and *char*.

The *list* argument is a comma-separated sequence of ranges (*integer–integer*) indicating the fields. With the –c (for column) option, the ranges indicate the character (column) positions you wish to be retained in each line. (Some find the name cut confusing since the range arguments lead to *extraction* rather than elimination. You can alias cut as extract if you feel strongly about this.) Thus,

```
cut -c1-30,35-80 filename
```

would display columns 1-30 inclusive and columns 35-80 inclusive from each line of *filename*. Characters outside these positions are ruthlessly suppressed. You can redirect the output, of course, with

```
>output_filename
```

The range can be a single number meaning "retain just that column position." The range *-n* means the same as *1-n* , while *n-* is equivalent to *n-last_column.* For example,

```
cut -c-30,35- filename
```

would simply suppress columns 31-34 inclusive.

With the *-f* option, the *list* represents field numbers and ranges. Fields are defined by the *-d char* argument. The *char* you supply is taken as the field separator (or delimiter, hence the *-d*). If you do not supply a *-d* argument, *-f* assumed that your fields are delimited by tabs, the most natural default. A common variant is to use *-d:* since many Unix files use the colon as a field delimiter. For instance,

```
$ cut -d: -f1,5 /etc/passwd
root: supervisor
daemon: system daemon
...
stan: Stan Kelly-Bootle
$ _
```

outputs the first and fifth fields of the password file, giving you a list of user id's and names.

The *-d char* trick works only with *-f* and is just like the *-t char* option for defining fields in the sort command. Sorry about the inconsistency! Also note that if your *char* is a character such as space or * that the shell treats specially, you should add single quotes: *-d* ´ ´.

Finally, the *-s* option, used only with *-f*, suppresses all lines that do not have the specified (or default) delimiter. This is useful when your file has headers or comment lines that are not really part of your database. Omitting the *-s* in such cases will lead to unwanted, nondelimited lines passing through.

The paste Command

The paste command works rather like the reverse of cut (whence the well-known text-editing collocation, "cut and paste"). paste merges (or concatenates) lines from a set of files and sends the result to your standard output. The syntax is

```
paste [-s] [-dchar] file1 file2 ...
```

Take the simplest case (no options) first:

```
$ cat items
shoes
socks
pants
$ cat prices
12.90
3.45
19.95
$ paste items prices
shoes    12.90
socks    3.45
pants    19.95
$ cat deliveries
Jan 12 95
Feb  3 95
Dec 25 94
$ paste deliveries items
Jan 12 95    shoes
Feb  3 95    socks
Dec 25 94    pants
$ paste items prices deliveries
shoes    12.90    Jan 12 95
socks    3.45     Feb  3 95
pants    19.95    Dec 25 94
$ _
```

It is easier to see what is happening than to explain the process formally. The merge is done horizontally, treating each line in each file as a column. Corresponding lines from each file are pasted with a tab as the column separator. The effect with two file arguments is a two-column output, three files give three columns, and so on. Compare this with cat where files are merged vertically:

```
$ cat items prices deliveries
shoes
```

```
socks
pants
12.90
3.45
19.95
Jan 12 95
Feb  3 95
Dec 25 94
$ _
```

What happens with the three-column `paste` shown earlier is that each newline in the `items` and `prices` file is translated to tabs, while the newlines in the final file, `deliveries`, are outputted without change. This is the general plan for all multifile pastings: the final file argument "retains" its newlines; the earlier files undergo the newline to tab translation. (Of course, the files themselves are unchanged by `paste`.)

The conversion to tab characters by `paste` is the default. You can set a different insertion character by using the `-d`*char* option. For example:

```
$ paste -d: items prices
shoes:12.90
socks:3.45
pants:19.95
$ paste -d´ ´ items prices
shoes 12.90
socks 3.45
pants 19.95
$ _
```

Again, the final file's newlines get through, but the earlier file's newlines are converted to *char*. As with `cut`, the *char* argument may need to be quoted to prevent misinterpretation by the shell. If in doubt, quote!

The *char* argument can actually contain a sequence of column separator characters, so the option is often written as `-d`*list*. The *list* can include the familiar escape sequences: \n (newline), \t (tab, the default), \ \ (backslash), and \0 (empty string, i.e., no column separation). `paste` will grab a separating code from your `-d`*list* for each column to be merged. If it runs out of separator codes before all the columns are processed, `paste` cycles around the list again. Consider

```
$ paste -d´\t:´ items prices deliveries
shoes    12.90:Jan 12 95
socks     3.45:Feb  3 95
```

```
pants     19.95:Dec 25 94
$ _
```

Note carefully that the final newlines of `deliveries` are *not* involved in the translation. The newlines in `items` pick up ´\t´ (tab); the newlines in `prices` pick up the colon.

The −s (for subsequent) option drastically changes the pasting action and can be used with one or more file arguments. Here are two examples:

```
$ paste -s items
shoes     socks     pants
$ paste -s items prices
shoes     socks     pants     12.90   3.45   19.95
$ _
```

The −s option says paste together the lines from the given file or files. By default, tabs replace every newline except for the final newline of the final line in the final file. That's my final word.

`paste` sends its results to the standard output so redirection *to* a file or filter is very popular. Redirection in the other direction needs some care. Using `paste` on the right hand of a filter raises the same problem you saw with `split`. To get `paste` to accept standard input rather than file input, you must use − (dash) in lieu of a file argument. Consider

```
$ ls | paste - - -
assets.1    basis      bible
crafts.x    dtd.skb    eric.mail
...
$ _
```

Each − invokes a line from the output of `ls` and pastes the result with the default tab. Recall that the normal output from `ls` is a single column listing of the current directory.

The find Command

The `find` command (man section C) turns out to be more versatile and useful than its mundane name might suggest. It certainly finds files and directories that match the usual wildcards (*, ? and [ ]), just like `ls` and its relatives. But `find` can also

search for files that match more complex criteria such as time of last access, ownerships, permission flags settings, and file type. You can also combine such tests using logical NOT, AND, and OR operators. find's other claim to fame is that it can be set to perform arbitrary commands depending on the results of its search. The full syntax is quite complex, but the basic scheme is simple enough:

```
find pathname expression
```

find searches first for files in the directory given by *pathname*. If any subdirectories are encountered, these will also be searched, and so on for any subdirectories found (rather like the ls -R recursive descent option). In other words, the whole subtree from *pathname* downwards is searched. For example,

```
find . expression
```

will search your current directory (represented by the famous dot) together with its subdirectories, and so on down the tree. Replacing the dot with your home directory ($HOME) gives a search over your own neck of the woods: your home directory and everything below it. Using / (root) as the *pathname* argument will invoke a search of the entire hierarchy. You can also list several directories in the *pathname* argument (separated by spaces), and find will do the same "in depth" search of each, one by one.

The *expression* argument tells find what to look for, and what to do when a match is made. The *expression* argument consists of one or more *primary* expressions. Each primary expression returns a Boolean value: *true* for a match, *false* for a mismatch. Some expressions provide "actions" rather than "matches" and always return *true*. The final expression usually represents the action to be taken if the preceding primary expressions combine to give *true*. There are many different primary expressions, each with its own *raison d'être* and syntax. Most of these expressions take arguments, so find combines flexibility and complexity in the true Unix tradition. Here's a simple example:

```
$ pwd
/usr
$ find . -name "poem.?" -print
./stan/poem.1
./stan/poem.3
$ _
```

Here, find is looking for files in (or below) the current directory (which happens to be /usr) that match poem.?. We quote this expression because of the wildcard character: we want find to "see" the ?. If unquoted, the shell would interpret it

first. Remember to quote any file arguments that contain *, ? or [. The expression -print says display (send to the standard output) the path names of all matching files. The expression -name *filename* returns *true* for those files matching *filename*. You can add any number of tests to the list. Each test is logically AND'd in sequence, so the final action is invoked only if all the tests return *true*. No explicit AND operator is needed; you simply use spaces between tests, as shown in the following example:

```
$ find . -name "poem.?" -size +2 -print
./stan/poem.3
$ _
```

This lists only the files matching poem.? that have more than two blocks (a block being 512 bytes on most systems). Here we apply the test -size +2 to each file matching poem.?. The -size expression takes a numerical argument as follows:

size argument	Meaning
n	*True* if file has exactly *n* blocks.
+*n*	*True* if file has more than *n* blocks.
-*n*	*True* if file has fewer than *n* blocks.

Remember this syntax: many other "magnitude" tests use the same trick.

You can redirect or pipe the output of find in the usual way:

```
$ find . -name "poem.?" -size +2 -print >$HOME/temp
$ cat $HOME/temp
./stan/poem.3
$ _
```

Tests can be logically OR'd using the -o operator, or logically reversed with the ! (bang) operator. The three logical operators, OR (-o), AND (implied by space), and NOT (!), can be combined in any way required provided that you observe their built-in precedences. NOT has the highest precedence, followed by AND, followed by OR. (I'll cover the concept of operator precedence in detail in Chapter 15. Briefly: higher precedence operators are applied before lower precedence operators.) To override the precedence rules, or simply as an aid to legibility, you use the *escaped* parentheses \(and \). For example,

```
$ find . \( -name "poem.?" -o -name "ode.?" \) -size +2 -print
./usr/mary/ode.5
```

```
./usr/stan/poem.3
$ _
```

If you don't hide the parentheses, the shell will interpret them in its own fashion, with unexpected effects (usually a syntax error). Recall that (*command_list*) tells the shell to invoke a subshell to perform the commands in *command_list*. If you use unescaped parentheses with find, the shell will try to interpret your Boolean expressions as commands.

If I had run the last example from the /usr/stan directory, the output would have been ./poem.3. In other words, find produces a path name relative to the current directory.

So far, we have simply displayed the matching path names using the -print expression. The -exec *command* [*args*] \; expression lets you execute any command (with any relevant options and arguments) whenever a match is found. The syntax of -exec is a tad quirky, but the power of -exec is ample reward:

- The command must be terminated with a space followed by an escaped semicolon: \;.

- A special argument {} (two braces) is recognized by find as the name of the currently matching file name.

Consider the following example:

```
find / -exec ls -ld {} \;
```

Here we pass each file and directory in the system as an argument to ls -ld to give a long listing of the entire hierarchy. The next example,

```
find / -name "*.junk" -exec rm {} \;
```

removes the entries for *every* file in the system (directory write permissions allowing, of course) that matches *.junk. Each matching file is passed via the symbol pair {} as an argument to the rm command. Note that you are free to supply any valid options for the given command. For example, you could write -exec rm -f {} \;.

A useful variant on -exec is -ok. The syntax and action are identical, but -ok displays the command followed by a query mark, ?, and pauses for confirmation. If

you respond with y, the command is executed; otherwise find moves on to the next file match and again seeks confirmation. For example,

```
$ find / -name "*.junk" -ok rm {} \;
rm ./usr/joe/old.junk ? y
rm ./usr/stan/new.junk ? n
$ _
```

A common use for find is the selective backing up of files. I'll discuss the why's and how's of backing up in Chapter 18. For now, note that find offers the following primary expressions that let you select files that have been accessed, modified, or created since the last backup.

-atime *n*   *True* if the file was last accessed exactly *n* days ago.

-mtime *n*   *True* if the file was last modified exactly *n* days ago.

-ctime *n*   *True* if the file was last changed exactly *n* days ago (changed means created or modified).

Each of these timing tests take a numerical argument representing a number of days. As with -size *n*, you can add a + or – in front of the number to modify the test. +*n* means "more than *n* days ago"; –*n* means "fewer than *n* days ago." If you back up weekly, say, the following command tells you which of your files have been created or modified since the last backup:

```
find $HOME -ctime -7 -print
```

You can restrict this selection to regular files (excluding special files and directories) by adding a -type expression:

```
find $HOME -ctime -7 -type f -print
```

-type takes a single-letter argument, as shown in Table 14.2, later in this chapter. Rather than just list the files or pipe them into some copying command, you can perform the backup within find as follows:

```
find $HOME -ctime -7 -type f -cpio /dev/tape
```

The -cpio expression takes a device argument: the special file representing the backup device where your data and programs are to be saved. This is usually a tape or floppy-disk drive. In Chapter 18 you'll meet the cpio command upon which the -cpio expression is based.

Another expression that's useful when backing up (and in many other situations) is −newer. As the name suggests, this lets you select the more recent version of two files:

```
find . -name "poem.?" -newer "poem.index" -print
```

Any files matching poem.? that have been modified more recently than poem.index will be displayed.

find can also select files that belong to a given user or group:

```
find / -user "stan" -print
find / -user 25 -print
find / -group "sys" -print
```

These lines will display all files owned by stan; all files owned by user id 25; and all files belonging to the group sys. −user takes either a login name or a user id argument. −group takes either a group name or a group id argument. Since it is *possible* (but undesirable) that login and group names can be numeric, find checks all −user and −group arguments against the names stored in /etc/passwd and /etc/group, respectively. If the argument is numeric and not found as a name, find then checks for an id match.

The −perm expression lets you select files that have certain permissions set. The argument used is the octal permission mode that I explained in Chapter 7. The following line,

```
find / -type f -perm 0744 -print
```

will display all regular files that have −rwxr--r-- set in the permissions field. Recall that octal 744 can be written in binary as

```
(111)(100)(100)
```

whence the mapping to

```
(rwx)(r--)(r--)
```

ADVANCED USERS ONLY

A trick is available for testing the full internal mode used to encode the file type, the owner/group/others permissions, and several special modes such as setuid (set user id), setgid (set group id), and file locking and sticky bits. If you write `-perm -mode`, `mode` can include the following values:

```
0010000 fifo special
0020000 character special file
0040000 directory
0060000 block special file
0100000 regular file
0000000 regular file
0004000 set user id on execution
00020#0 set group id on execution if # is 7,
        5, 3, or 1;
        enable mandatory file/record lock if
        # is 6, 4, 2, or 0
0001000 set sticky bit (save text image after
        execution)
```
in addition to the usual 000 to 777 owner/group/others permissions.

Table 14.2 summarizes the more useful primary expressions available with `find`.

TABLE 14.2: Primary Expressions Available with `find`

Expression	Action or Return Value
`-atime n`	*True* if the file was last accessed exactly *n* days ago.
`-atime +n`	*True* if the file was last accessed more than *n* days ago.
`-atime -n`	*True* if the file was last accessed less than *n* days ago.
`-cpio dev`	Back up the current file to the device *dev*. Always returns *true*.
`-ctime n`	*True* if the file was last changed exactly *n* days ago.
`-ctime +n`	*True* if the file was last changed more than *n* days ago (changed means created or modified).
`-ctime -n`	*True* if the file was last changed fewer than *n* days ago (changed means created or modified).

TABLE 14.2: Primary Expressions Available with `find` (continued)

Expression	Action or Return Value
`-exec command \;`	Executes command. Returns *true* if *command* returns a zero exit status (success); otherwise returns *false*.
`-exec command {} \;`	As above, but `{}` is replaced by the matching path name.
`-links n`	*True* if the file has exactly *n* links.
`-links +n`	*True* if the file has more than *n* links.
`-links -n`	*True* if the file has fewer than *n* links.
`-mtime n`	*True* if the file was last modified exactly *n* days ago.
`-mtime +n`	*True* if the file was last modified more than *n* days ago.
`-mtime -n`	*True* if the file was last modified fewer than *n* days ago.
`-newer file`	*True* if the current path name is newer (modified more recently) than *file*.
`-name file`	*True* if *file* matches a file name (wildcard characters must be quoted).
`-ok command \;`	Displays command followed by ?, and awaits confirming y before execution. Returns *true* if *command* returns a zero exit status (success); otherwise returns *false*.
`-ok command {} \;`	As above, but `{}` is replaced by the matching path name.
`-perm oct_mode`	*True* if the permission flags of the current file match the octal mode given by *oct_mode* (see Chapter 7).
`-perm -oct_mode`	*True* if the full internal mode of the current file matches *oct_mode*.
`-print`	Sends current matched path name to standard output. Always returns *true*.
`-size n`	*True* if the file is exactly *n* blocks long ($n \times 512$ bytes).
`-size +n`	*True* if the file is more than *n* blocks long ($n \times 512$ bytes).
`-size -n`	*True* if the file is fewer than *n* blocks long ($n \times 512$ bytes).
`-type t`	*True* if the file type matches the *t* argument. File types are: f regular file d directory b block I/O device file c character I/O device file p named pipe (Note that these letters match the first character in the permissions field, as shown by `ls -l`, apart from f. As you saw in Chapter 4, `ls -l` shows – for a regular file.)

TABLE 14.2: Primary Expressions Available with `find` (continued)

Expression	Action or Return Value
−user *uname*	*True* if file is owned by *uname*. (If *uname* is numeric and does not match a login name in /etc/passwd, find treats it as a user id.)
−group *gname*	*True* if file belongs to group *gname*. (If *gname* is numeric and does not match a group name in /etc/group, find treats it as a group id.)

The tr Command

The tr command (in man section C) is a simple but worthwhile filter for performing a host of character translation routines. The syntax is

```
tr [-cds] [in_string] [out_string]
```

tr reads from the standard input. Any character read that does not match a character in the *in_string* argument is passed unchanged to the standard output. But any character that is matched in the *in_string* is translated into the corresponding character found in the *out_string* before being passed to the standard output. First, two pointless examples:

```
$ cat items
shoes
socks
pants
$ tr s z <items
zhoez
zockz
pantz
$ tr so zx <items
zhxez
zxckz
pantz
$ _
```

In the first session, the *in_string* is the single character s, and the *out_string* is the single character z. The posh way of describing this situation is that tr establishes a 1-to-1 mapping between the two strings. All s's in items (note the redirection) are mapped to z's and passed to the standard output. The mapping is case-sensitive, so that uppercase "S" would not be translated. items itself is unchanged.

In the second test, a two-character in_string of so maps to the *out_string* zx. All "s"'s become "z"'s and all "o"'s become "x"'s.

You can redirect the output of tr to a file or another filter. This should *not* surprise you if you've been paying attention! You should also by now appreciate that some characters need to be protected from the shell:

```
$ cat items
shoes
socks
pants
$ tr o ´ ´ <items
sh es
s cks
pants
$ _
```

Here we have mapped all "o"'s to spaces. Quoting the space is clearly needed; remember also to quote ; & ( ) | ^ < > newline, and tab. You can express both printable and nonprintable characters in either string using the familiar escape sequences with the octal ASCII value of the character. With printable characters, though, it is usually less confusing to use the characters themselves. The octal values of the most common control characters are listed below:

Character	Escape Sequence
Bell	´\07´
Backspace	´\010´
CR	´\015´
Escape	´\033´
Formfeed	´\014´
LF, Newline	´\012´
Tab	´\011´

The leading zeros are optional but recommended in view of the C language rules for octal numbers that are also mandated in many Unix commands. For example, the expression [x*n] is used in tr to represent a string with *n* repetitions of x. If *n* is written as 10 you'll get ten x's, but if you write 010, only eight are formed!

For those characters that may confuse the shell, you must either quote or escape them with \: ´&´ ´(´ ´)´ ´|´ ´^´ ´<´ ´>´ ´[´ ´]´ and ´\´, or \& \(\) \| \^ \< \> \[\] and \\.

The *in_string* and *out_string* arguments can use ranges as follows:

```
$ tr ´[a-z]´ ´[A-Z]´ <items
SHOES
SOCKS
PANTS
$ tr ´[a-m]´ ´[A-M]´ <items
shoEs
soCKs
pAnts
$ _
```

In the first example, all lowercase letters are converted to uppercase. Next, only the letters in the range "a"–"m" (inclusive) are replaced by their uppercase equivalents. A variant on this, already mentioned *en passant*, is the expression [x*n]. This stands for *n* repetitions of the character x. *n* is taken as octal if written with a leading 0, otherwise decimal. If you omit the *n*, the character x is "repeated" as many times as needed. This trick is vital when mapping an unknown number of *in_string* matches into a single *out_string* character.

tr does not allow the full power of the regular expression, but Unix has the venerable sed that fills this gap. You'll see sed in action in the next chapter.

The tr -d option lets you delete any character matched in the *in_string*. No *out_string* is allowed with the -d option.

```
$ tr -d ´[a-m]´ <items
shos
sos
pnts
$ tr -d so <items
he
ck
pant
$ _
```

In the first example, all lowercase letters in the range "a"–"m" (inclusive) have been removed from the output. In the second case, just the two letters "s" and "o" have been suppressed.

The -c option complements (or inverts) the set of characters in the *in_string* with respect to the whole ASCII character set (\001 to \377). In other words tr -c so says match every character *except* "s" and "o":

```
$ tr -cd so <items
sossoss
$ _
```

Note that -cd combines the options -c and -d. Every character in items except "s" and "o" matches and is therefore deleted. This includes newlines!

Finally, the -s (for squeeze or squash) option works as follows. After the normal translation has been performed, tr looks for any set of repeated characters in the output that matches a character in the *out_string*. If there be any such, all but one occurrence will be squeezed out. A common application is removing unwanted spaces or tabs. For instance,

```
tr -s '\011' ' ' <in_file >out_file
```

will convert each tab in *in_file* to a space, then squeeze multiple space sequences down to just one space. The result appears in *out_file*.

The translate and dd Commands

Two commands related to tr are translate and dd (both in man section C). They perform more specialized conversions such as loading data from magnetic tape files that use non-Unix formats. For example, to translate to and from EBCDIC (a code still used with some IBM mainframes) and ASCII files, you can write

```
translate -ea ebcdic_file ascii_file
translate -ae ascii_file ebcdic_file
```

translate will also convert binary files to a special ASCII format called *uuencode* so that you can transmit such files by email. Sending raw binary files via modems is usually hazardous since some bit patterns may be misinterpreted as transmission controls. The -bm option is used before transmission (binary to mailable); at the other end, the -mb option converts back from mailable to binary.

The dd command is used for both copying and conversion between different files and media. The syntax is as follows:

dd [*option1=value1*] [*option2 =value2*] ...

For example,

dd if=*in_file* of=*out_file* conv=lcase

will convert all alphabetic characters in *in_file* to lowercase equivalents and copy the result to *out_file*. Table 14.3 lists many of the options available to you.

TABLE 14.3: Common dd Options

dd Option	Value
if= (input file)	Input file name (default is standard input).
of= (output file)	Output file name (default is standard output).
ibs= (i/p block size)	Number of bytes in input block: *n*k means $n \times 1024$ bytes. *n*b means $n \times 512$ bytes. *n*w means $n \times 2$ bytes.
obs= (o/p block size)	Number of bytes in output block.
bs= (i/p and o/p block size)	Number of bytes in input and output blocks.
skip=	Number of i/p records to be skipped before conversion or copying starts.
conv=	ascii converts EBCDIC to ASCII. ebcdic converts ASCII to EBCDIC. lcase converts to lowercase. ucase converts to uppercase. swab swaps pairs of bytes. Several conv values can be supplied separated by commas, e.g., conv=ascii,ucase.

Putting It All Together

Perhaps we should pause here and take stock. I've thrown a whole slew of commands at you with short, illustrative examples. It might be helpful to see how these commands can be combined to perform more useful work. Unix, as you've seen, encourages the symbiosis of simple commands by means of the filter and pipe

mechanism: the output of one command can be piped into another, and so on through a long chain of filters until the desired result emerges on the standard output or redirected to a file. Knowing which filters and options to use requires practice. Let's "walk through" a real problem to indicate the mindset you need to develop.

A classic exercise is to determine the most frequently used words in a text file. The first task is to separate the words. We would like to translate the file so that each word sits on its own line. What is a word? Consider the following text:

```
"What is Life?<tab>Perhaps,we will never know what life is!"
```

Certainly, spaces delimit words, but we do not want "Life?", "Perhaps,we", and "is!" to count as words. We'll need to convert any sequence of nonletters, such as spaces, tabs, and punctuation marks, into a single newline. This should remind you of the tr filter. In particular, the -s option is indicated to squeeze out duplicates. The -c (complement) option, too, will be useful since we are looking for *non*alphabetic characters. Consider

```
tr -sc '[A-Z][a-z]' '[\012*]' <inf >outf1
```

The *in_string* gives all alpha characters, so the -c reverses the match to give all nonalpha characters. The *out_string* is the newline, '\012', repeated as many times as necessary to match each character in the *in_string*. So, each nonalpha character in inf will be changed to a newline. The -s option ensures that multiple newlines are squeezed down to a single newline. Applying our tr filter will give us an outf1 file like this:

```
What
is
Life
Perhaps
we
will
never
know
what
life
is
```

Are we going to treat "What" and "what", and "Life" and "life" as different words? If not, we'll need another tr pass to remove any case sensitivity:

```
tr '[A-Z]' '[a-z]' <outf1 >outf2
```

Now we have

```
what
is
life
perhaps
we
will
never
know
what
life
is
```

Later, of course, we aim to pipe these elements to avoid the intermediate files. The next step must be to sort outf2 to bring together occurrences of the same word:

```
sort <outf2 >outf3
```

outf3 now gives us:

```
is
is
know
life
life
never
perhaps
we
what
what
will
```

We next bring in uniq -c to filter out multiple occurrences and give us a count of each word:

```
uniq -c <outf3 >outf4
```

outf4 now contains

```
2 is
1 know
2 life
1 never
1 perhaps
1 we
```

```
2 what
1 will
```

We can now sort again, reverse numerically on the first field, alphabetically (ascending) on the second field to give us a list by decreasing frequency:

```
sort +0 -1nr +1 -2 outf4 >outf5
```

We now have the required output in outf5:

```
2 is
2 life
2 what
1 know
1 never
1 perhaps
1 we
1 will
```

To limit the output to the n most frequently used words, we can tag on a final head filter:

```
head -n outf5 >outf6
```

Omitting the n option gives a default of the ten most frequent words. Putting all this together, and setting n to 20, we have the sequence,

```
tr -sc '[A-Z][a-z]' '[\012*]' <inf >outf1
tr '[A-Z]' '[a-z]' <outf1 >outf2
sort <outf2 >outf3
uniq -c <outf3 >outf4
sort +0 -1nr +1 -2 outf4 >outf5
head -20 outf5 >outf6
```

Piping the commands avoids the need for all the intermediate named files:

```
tr -sc '[A-Z][a-z]' '[\012*]' <inf |
tr '[A-Z]' '[a-z]'   |
sort |
uniq -c |
sort +0 -1nr +1 -2 |
head -20 >outf
```

You can enter each line as shown. The final | on each line will invoke the secondary prompt >, at which point you enter the next command line. Alternatively, you can submit one long line via the keyboard. Long lines like this, exceeding the normal 80-character screen width, are rather awkward, so it's useful to break up the line

with the continuation escape character \ followed by newline (Enter). The \ hides the newline from the shell, so you won't get a secondary prompt:

```
tr -sc '[A-Z][a-z]' '[\012*]' <inf | \
tr '[A-Z]' '[a-z]'  | sort | uniq -c | \
sort +0 -1nr +1 -2 | head -20 >outf
```

Better still, you can save the whole sequence in a shell script. Let's call the script lwf (list word frequency) in keeping with the Unix penchant for obscure acronymy. lwf would be quite restrictive in the above listed format: it would work only on the files inf and outf for a fixed value of *n*! You can easily make lwf more popular by replacing inf with $1, *−n* by $2, and outf by $3:

```
$ cat lwf
:
# @(#)lwf -- list word frequency -- skb 3/16/95
#
# usage lwf in_file [-number] [out_file]
#
tr -sc '[A-Z][a-z]' '[\012*]' <$1 | \
tr '[A-Z]' '[a-z]'  | sort | uniq -c | \
sort +0 -1nr +1 -2 | head $2 >$3
$ _
```

If you want to use this script, remember to set execution permission with chmod u+x lwf. You will recall that the positional parameters, $1, $2,..., are set by the arguments supplied to the script command. So,

```
$ lwf stan.poem -30 stan.lwf
```

would find the thirty most frequent words in stan.poem and record the list in stan.lwf.

Summary

You added the following utility commands to your toolchest:

```
sort
uniq
head
tail
split
cut
```

```
paste
find
tr
translate
dd
```

and saw a typical shell script that exploited some of these comands. In the next chapter you'll meet sed, grep, and awk, three popular and well-established Unix commands with many shell-script applications.

CHAPTER

FIFTEEN

grepping, sedding, and a Little awking

- The grep family

- The fgrep command

- The egrep command

- The grep family summary

- The sed stream editor

- sed syntax

- Using awk

Preamble

Unix file and command names provide a colorful lexicon. The nice ones are pronounceable, like cat, yacc, grep, awk, and finger; the nasty ones require some thought: how do you say setuid, uucp, lpsched, and vi? They can also be divided by their comprehensibility factor: can you glean the functionality from the name? For example, find and kill, more or less, betray their intent, although find does a lot more than locate, and you will recall that kill simply sends signals that *usually* kill a process. Others, like sed (stream editor) and lp (line printer), are clear once you have the acronymic breakdown. But the purposes of many commands, such as cat, awk, and nice, are not immediately obvious and call for some historical amplification. awk, for example, honors the surnames of the three programming wizards who devised it: (Alfred) Aho, (Peter) Weinberg, and (Brian) Kernighan. What awk does, though, is not immediately clear from this fact.

Exactly which parts of speech (noun, verb, adjective, and so on) the Unix tokens represent is also a constant worry, especially to prescriptive grammarians. The latter believe that fixed, golden-age rules descended, way back when, from some Mount Sinai specifying linguistic usage, and that breaking these rules will destroy our civilization. A noun is a noun is a noun, and must know its place in the parse tree. Descriptive grammarians, on the other hand, simply observe the creative evolution of language, as writ and spoke by the folk, and report what they see and hear. They find that one of the glories of natural language, and English in particular, is that if a word can usefully serve as both noun and verb, that's what will emerge as common usage in spite of the defenders of the faith. The token cd (change directory), for instance, can stand for the name of the command (noun) but is also appropriate when discussing the action itself. It is certainly unambiguous and economical to say "You now cd back HOME," rather than "You now invoke the cd command with your HOME directory as argument." And when a usage is unambiguous and economical, it catches on and joins the canon.

All of which serves to explain the title of this chapter. You are about to learn the arts of sedding, grepping, and awking! The French also have ways of adapting words to different parts of speech: Apprenons l'awkage, la greperie et la sedition!

The three commands to be discussed in this chapter have a certain common theme: they all scan text files in various ways. They differ greatly in complexity. grep, the pattern searcher, is the simplest. Next comes sed, a stream editor that can search for patterns and edit files. Finally, awk is a fully loaded pattern processing language

with flow control and arithmetical operators. In fact you can use sed to perform nearly every grep operation, and you can use awk to do almost everything that grep and sed can do. The reason that grep survives and flourishes is that file searches for a given string or pattern are commonly needed, and grep offers a simple syntax dedicated to such tasks. Similarly, sed is more convenient in the many situations where awk would be overkill.

The grep Family

grep (in man section C), originally devised by Doug McIlroy, stands for "global regular expression print." There are two variants, egrep and fgrep, hence my reference to the grep *family*. We'll describe the standard grep first, then list the family variations.

grep is the cure for those frustrating moments when you cannot recall which files contain what. You wrote several memos last month about office equipment maintenance. Which of them covered the copier contracts? All you need is the command

```
grep -l copier memo.*
```

and the names of all memo files in your current directory that contain the word "copier" will be displayed. Without the -l option, you also get the lines displayed that contain the target string.

grep searches the standard input (or a list of one or more files) and displays (prints) on the standard output certain information when matches are found with a given pattern. The search patterns can use the regular expressions that you met in the ed chapter. Options are available to control the amount of data that displays when a match is found. The basic syntax is

```
grep [options] [-e] ´pattern´ [filenames] [>out_file]
```

The optional *filenames* argument is a list of files (separated by spaces) that grep will search for the given *pattern* argument. The *pattern* argument is usually quoted as shown—I'll explain when and why in a moment. If *filenames* is missing, grep will scan your standard input. Of course, it is rarely useful to grep your own keyboard input! What is common, though, is to pipe the output of other commands into grep. You can even grep the output from another grep.

The output from grep can be redirected, as indicated, or piped to other commands in the usual way. Remember that the shell will expand any wildcard characters (* and ?) in the *filenames* argument and apply grep to the resulting list of files.

Normally, if you are searching a single file, grep will output each line that contains a match with the given pattern:

```
$ cat hamlet
To be or not to be,
That is the question.
Or maybe not
$ grep 'or' hamlet
To be or not to be,
$ grep 'T' hamlet
To be or not to be,
That is the question.
$ grep Guildenstern hamlet
$ _
```

If you are grepping several files, the file name will be displayed before each match. You can suppress this file name display by using the −h option.

The search patterns 'or' and 'T' precede the file name hamlet. Note that a matching line appears once even if the pattern occurs more than once in that line. If there's no match, as in the search for "Guildenstern", grep remains silent, although the exit status value returned by grep reflects the failure. A value of 0 means that matches were found; a value of 1 indicates no match. (Be sure to remember this apparent anomaly: zero means success, nonzero means failure.) Shell scripts can make use of this fact to control conditional searches or to check if a file name exists that matches a certain pattern.

Quoting the Search Pattern

The single (forward) quotes round the search pattern are not essential in the previous example, but it's a good habit to acquire since your patterns may contain symbols that would otherwise be interpreted by the shell. As you saw in Chapter 13, the metacharacters $, *, [, ^, (,), `xxx` (backquoted strings), and \ have special meanings to the shell and must be *quoted* to suppress these meanings. Recall that double quotes are often adequate, but they do not "hide" all the metacharacters: $, `xxx`, and \ retain their special meanings within double quotes. Single characters in a search pattern can

also be hidden from the shell using the escape character, \. To search for a literal *, for example, your pattern could be ´*´, "*", or *.

If your search pattern contains spaces or tabs, you must definitely quote the pattern:

```
$ grep or not hamlet
grep: cannot open not
$ grep 'or not' hamlet
To be or not to be,
$ _
```

In the first attempt, grep takes not as a file name. As luck would have it, no such file was found!

Word Searches and the -w Option

Matches are made without regard to word boundaries, so that ´or´ would match "for" and "oregano". To get a "word-only" search, you can try ´or´ with surrounding spaces, but this would miss the word "or" in some contexts. Some grep implementations provide the −w (word) option to overcome these problems. This is a good moment to warn you that implementations vary somewhat in the options provided with grep, so take care!

Case-Sensitive Searches

Note that the match is usually case-sensitive, so that ´or´ did not match the "Or" in line 3 of hamlet. Similarly, ´T´ did not match the "t" in the final "not". You can make the search case-insensitive with the −y or −i options. The −i (ignore case) option is the better one to use if you have it. The −y option on some older systems must be used with care. It takes lowercase letters in the pattern and matches them with lower- or uppercase versions of those letters. However, in some early versions of grep, uppercase letters in the pattern match only uppercase letters in the file even if you use −y. (There may also be problems using −y with range patterns such as [a-z].) The good news is that most current versions of grep have a −y option that works sensibly with uppercase characters in the pattern. More recent versions of grep offer the −i option which gives completely case-insensitive matching: both

'Y' and 'y' will match both "Y" and "y". Experiment to see how your grep behaves. Here are some examples:

```
$ grep -y 'or' hamlet
To be or not to be,
Or maybe not
$ grep -i 'T' hamlet
To be or not to be,
That is the question.
Or maybe not
$ _
```

You can also use regular expressions to achieve case-insensitivity:

```
$ grep '[Oo]r' hamlet
To be or not to be,
Or maybe not
$ grep '[Tt]' hamlet
To be or not to be,
That is the question.
Or maybe not
$ _
```

The expression [Oo] matches either of the characters inside the brackets.

The -n Option

With the -n option, you also get the line number of the matching line:

```
$ grep -n 'or' hamlet
1:To be or not to be,
$ grep -in 'T' hamlet
1:To be or not to be,
2:That is the question.
3:Or maybe not
$ _
```

Note that options can be written separately: -i -n or together, in any order: -ni.

The -h Option

You can grep several files with a single command,

```
$ grep 'or' hamlet lear
hamlet:To be or not to be,
lear:'Faith, once or twice she heaved
```

by simply listing the file names after the pattern. Note that grep now helpfully reports the name of the file where the match was found. If you don't want the file names displayed, the −h option will suppress them:

```
$ grep -h 'or' hamlet lear
To be or not to be,
'Faith, once or twice she heaved
```

If you call for line numbers, they appear after the file name:

```
$ grep -n 'or' hamlet lear
hamlet:1:To be or not to be,
lear:43:'Faith, once or twice she heaved
```

You can combine −h and −n if you wish:

```
$ grep -hn 'or' hamlet lear
1:To be or not to be,
43:'Faith, once or twice she heaved
```

The -c Option

If you just want to count the number of matching lines without seeing them, use the −c option:

```
$ grep -ic 'T' hamlet
3
$ _
```

The -v Option

The −v option reverses the sense of the search: it will display the lines that do *not* match the search pattern. If the file payables, for example, has line entries with customer, amount, due date, and a string that either says Paid or " " (blank) depending on the status, you could run the following command:

```
$ grep -vi 'Paid' payables
Smith $450.12 09/12/95
Jones $ 78.89 08/12/95
```

to give you a list of unpaid accounts. The following example

```
$ grep 'To' $MAIL | grep -v '[Ss]tan'
```

would list messages not addressed to Stan.

The -b Option

The grep -b option has no immediate equivalent in sed or awk. It displays the disk block number of each matching line:

```
$ grep -b 'or' lear
3:'Faith, once or twice she heaved
```

This is often useful for service and diagnostic work.

The -l Option

The -l option displays only the names of the files where matching lines are found; the lines themselves are suppressed:

```
$ grep -l 'or' hamlet lear
hamlet
lear
```

You saw the -l earlier when we needed just the memo file names that discussed copiers.

The -e Option

The -e is useful when the search pattern begins with a hyphen. You can imagine the confusion if you want to search for the string "-n", say. Writing grep -n *file* is not going to do the job. And neither will grep '-n' *file* or grep "-n" *file* since '-n' and "-n" still look like an option to grep. The solution is grep -e -n *file*. The -e warns grep that the next string is to be taken as the pattern even though it looks like an option. The -e must come immediately before the pattern and after any other options. grep -e -ni -n *file* is an error (grep will look for a file named -n!). The correct form is grep -ni -e -n *file* (search for "-N" and "-n" and show line numbers).

The -s Option

The -s option suppresses the error messages that grep will normally display if the file arguments are faulty. For example, a file might not be found, or if found, you might not have read permission. In shell scripts, these messages are often a nuisance that the -s option can circumvent.

Regular Expressions

grep uses the regular expression developed for ed, so I'll just recap the highlights here. (Refer to Chapter 8 for more details.)

The dot

Outside a [*xxx*] pattern, the dot (period) matches any single character, so that .ust matches "dust", "must" and so on. Inside a [*xxx*] pattern, the dot loses its metacharacteristic and matches a literal ".".

^ and $

The metacharacters ^ and $ usually limit the matches to the beginning and end of a line. As with the dot, exceptions occur when ^ and $ appear inside [*xxx*] patterns; I'll cover these later.

```
$ grep -i '^or' hamlet
Or maybe not
$ grep 'not$' hamlet
Or maybe not
$ _
```

Here, '^or' matches only the leading "Or", and 'not$' matches only the final "not". Recall, too, the useful pattern '^xxx$' which will match a line containing the single string "xxx". The '^$' pattern matches only blank lines, characterized by successive newlines. As with ed, however, there is no regular expression that directly matches the newline character (so you cannot use grep '\n' *file*, for example).

The *

The pattern 'r*' matches zero or more occurrences of any regular expression r. The pattern '.*' therefore matches any sequence of characters, including the empty sequence. The pattern '..*' matches any nonempty string. These turn out to be more promising than might appear at first sight! Consider the following:

```
$ ls -l | grep '^d..*stan. '
drwxrwxrwx   3  stan1   group   272 Nov 15 1995 stan1
drwxrwxrwx   3  stan2   accnt   678 Nov 25 1995 stan2
$ _
```

The output from ls -l (namely the fully listed contents of the current directory—excluding dot files) is piped into grep. The ^d restricts the search to the subdirectories

(all lines starting with "d"). grep then matches lines that contain "stan" followed by a single character followed by a space. The . . * matches all the rubbish between "d" and "stan". (This is a rather artificial example, since you could use the −ld option to list just the subdirectories.)

You could achieve a similar goal with two greps:

```
$ ls −l | grep ´^d´ | grep ´stan. ´
drwxrwxrwx    3    stan1   group    272 Nov 15 1995 stan1
drwxrwxrwx    3    stan2   accnt    678 Nov 25 1995 stan2
$ _
```

Grepping the piped output from commands such as ls and who is quite common. The line

```
ls −l | grep ´^-..*\.mail$´
```

will match all file names (excluding dot files and directories) ending with .mail. The initial "-" in the permissions field matches ^-, indicating a file. Note the essential \ used to escape the final period. We want to match a *real* dot! Without the \, grep would treat the period as a metacharacter matching any single character. The final $ returns matches at the end of the line. To check if Mary is logged in, you can grep the output of who:

```
$ who | grep ´mary´
mary    tty2      Oct 15 12:32
$ _
```

The absence of a response would indicate that Mary is not logged in.

Regular expressions with [ ]

The expression ´[abc]´ matches any one of "a", "b", or "c". Ranges are allowed: ´[0-5]´ matches any single digit between "0" and "5". You can combine regular expressions: ´[A-E]8[0-2]Z´ will match "B81Z", "D80Z", and so on.

Inside the brackets [] some metacharacters may have different meanings, and some resume their literal meanings! The dot and $ are taken literally inside []: ´[.*]´ matches "." and "*".

A [inside [] is also taken literally: ´[a[]´ will match "a" and "[". To match a "]", however, you must escape it: ´[a\]]´ will match "a" and "]".

A leading ^ inside [ ] means reverse the sense of the match. Thus ´[a-m]´ matches any single character in the alphabetic range from "a" to "m", while ´[^a-m]´ matches any single character *not* in the range "a" to "m". The latter includes "n" to "z", of course, but also includes "A" to "Z" and many other characters! In other positions within [ ], the ^ is taken literally: ´[a^]´ will match "a" and "^".

Tagged Regular Expressions

Tagged regular expressions let you search for quite complex patterns that depend on parts of the text that have already been matched. You tag a regular expression by surrounding it with the symbols \(and \). Each such expression encountered in a pattern, from left to right, is assigned an internal register number, starting at 1 and increasing up to a maximum of 9. The characters matched with the nth tagged expression is stored in the nth register. Its contents can be referred to anywhere in the pattern using the sequence \n.

Consider the pattern ´\([a-c]\)x\1´, which has just one tagged expression, namely [a-c]. The sequence \1 will be replaced by whatever matches [a-c], so the whole pattern will match "axa", "bxb", and "cxc". The pattern

```
´\([a-c]\)\([d-f]\)x\2\1´
```

has two tagged expressions. \1 represents the [a-c] match, as before, and \2 represents the [d-f] match. This pattern therefore matches "adxda", "aexea", "afxfa", "bdxdb", "bexeb", and so on (a total of nine such strings). Replacing x with . and extending the ranges lets you search for five-letter palindromes (words like "radar" that are spelled the same in either direction):

```
grep -iw ´\([a-z]\)\([a-z]\).\2\1´ dictionary
```

A six-character palindrome would be detected by the following:

```
grep -iw ´\(.\)\(.\)\(.\)\3\2\1´ dictionary
```

Here we would match sequences such as "*&!!&*" as well as the more familiar palindromes.

A more practical example would be searching for any repeated adjacent strings to trap common typing errors such as "the the". Consider:

```
grep -i ´\(..*\) \1´ essay
```

The tagged expression `..*` matches any string with at least one character. The whole pattern therefore matches "xxxx xxxx" and so on. Note that the expression `\n` can be used anywhere in the pattern, even before the *n*th tagged expression occurs. For example,

```
´\2\1\(.)\)\)\(.\)´
```

is legal. This will match: "xyyx", "abba", and so on. The reason is that `grep` scans the whole pattern and knows in advance where all the tagged expressions are.

The fgrep Command

`fgrep` is a simplified version of `grep` that searches for fixed strings only. `fgrep` does not allow regular expressions but makes up for that deficiency in two ways: first, it is much faster than `grep`, especially with large files; second, you can have any number of search strings in the one `fgrep` command. These strings can either be entered on the command line (separated by newlines) or they can be stored in an expression file (whence the name `fgrep`: file **grep**, though some say, *fast* grep). You give the name of the expression file as an argument, and `fgrep` extracts pattern strings from it line by line. `fgrep` does a parallel search, so that each line is scanned in turn for matches with each of the given strings. Let's look at the syntax:

```
fgrep [options] ´strings´ [-f expfile] [filenames] [>out_file]
```

The `fgrep` options are slightly different from those of `grep`. The options −h, −b, −c, −i, −y, −l, −n, and −v all work the same as for `grep`. The −s option (suppress error messages) is *not* available with `fgrep`, but `fgrep` has a −x option not found with `grep`. The −x option restricts matches to exact, whole-line matches.

The −f option tells `fgrep` to open the named *expfile* (if possible) and take each line of this file as a search string. A good application is the simple, personalized spell checker. We all have "problem" words that we regularly misspell. You can make a file of such words, one per line, using the *bad* variations you usually employ. Then you let `fgrep` check your essays:

```
$ cat mywatch.words
supercede
abreviate
alimoney
allimony
```

```
allimoney
comittee
embarassment
logomarchy
overide
$ fgrep -in -f mywatch.words essay
12: which has been superceded by C++. This means
36: the Fortran/Algol logomarchy is over.
$ _
```

You can also enter multiple search strings directly in the command line:

```
$ fgrep -c 'Unix
> XENIX
> AIX' chap1
34
$ _
```

Notice that you must start with a quote (single or double would be fine here), enter a newline after each search string entry, and finally close the quote before typing the target file name.

Remember that fgrep does not allow fancy searches with regular expressions. Its main application is rapidly searching files for a number of key words. With a large expression file, there is an initial, noticeable pause while fgrep digests its contents, but the subsequent searching time is independent of the number of strings being hunted.

The egrep Command

The final member of the grep family is egrep (*e* for exponential). egrep allows the -f *expfile* option of fgrep. Unlike fgrep, though, egrep can use regular expressions. It would be nice to report that egrep and grep support the *same* range of regular expressions, but alas, no. egrep has some additional search tricks, but does not support the tagged expressions of grep and ed.

Table 15.1 lists the additional regular expressions not found in grep or ed. The symbols *r*, *r1*, and so on, stand for any egrep regular expression.

TABLE 15.1: Regular Expressions for `egrep`

Regular Expression	Matches
r+	One or more occurrences of *r*
r?	Zero or one occurrences of *r*
r1 | *r2*	Either *r1* or *r2*
(*r1* | *r2*) *r3*	Either *r1r3* or *r2r3*
(*r1* | *r2*) *	Zero or more occurrences of *r1* | *r2* (e.g., *r1*, *r1r1*, *r2r1*, *r1r1r2r1*,...)

The | metacharacter means logical OR and is often pronounced as "or." This character has no special meaning to grep and fgrep, but if you were searching for a literal "|" with egrep, you would have to escape it with \|.

Who Takes Precedence?

With these new egrep tricks, you have to be aware of operator *precedence*. When you have a complex sequence of regular expressions joined end to end (*concatenated*, as we say in these parts), you need to know which metacharacters apply to which pieces of the pattern. To avoid ambiguities, there are rules governing the order in which the various regular expression operations are carried out. This is a standard problem in many areas of computing. Computer language designers must assign operator priorities so that the user (and the machine) know exactly how a complex expression will be handled. The rule is that higher precedence operations are carried out before the lower precedence operations (hence the term "precedence"). You may have met a similar problem in arithmetic and algebra: in the expression A + B × C, it matters greatly whether you add A + B first, then multiply by C, or whether you multiply B × C, then add A. In some languages, precedence simply goes left to right (or right to left) regardless of the operators involved. In others, multiplication has a higher precedence than addition, regardless of position. In some cases, different operators may have the same precedence, meaning that you can perform the operations in any sequence. For example, with A × B / C you can (in theory) do the multiplication or the division first and get the same answer. (In practice, the results may differ because of precision limitations.)

The point is that there are no absolute, God-given precedence rules. You simply learn the man-made rules for a particular system, and break them at your own peril. Fortunately, most systems allow you to "override" the normal precedence rules by using parentheses. For example, if multiplication has a higher precedence than addition, you could write (A + B) × C to ensure that C multiplies the sum A + B. Without the parentheses, you would be adding A to the product B × C. The following egrep examples include the use of parentheses.

```
$ egrep -n 'or|the' hamlet
1:To be or not to be,
2:That is the question.
$ cat qfile
question
maybe
$ egrep -f qfile hamlet
That is the question.
Or maybe not
$ cat ur.1
XENIX is a version of the
UNIX operating system
for the IBM PC range.
Usually, you will find that
$ egrep '(U|XE)NIX' ur.1
XENIX is a version of the
UNIX operating system
$ egrep 'U|XENIX' ur.1
XENIX is a version of the
UNIX operating system
Usually, you will find that
$ _
```

Notice how the parentheses are used to change the normal precedence of the metacharacters and other regular expression operations. 'U|XENIX' matches both "U" and "XENIX" because | has a *lower* precedence than concatenation. So, XENIX is "formed" before the OR operation with U. '(U|XE)NIX', on the other hand, forms NIX, does an OR with the result of (U|XE), and therefore matches "UNIX" and "XENIX" but not the "U" in "Usually".

With *r**, *r+* and *r?*, the precedence works the other way round: these three metacharacters have a *higher* precedence than concatenation. So, for example,

'stan*'   Matches "sta", "stan", "stann", "stannn", …

`'(stan)*'`	Matches "", "stan", "stanstan", …
`'stan+'`	Matches "stan", "stann", "stannn", …
`'(stan)+'`	Matches "stan", "stanstan", "stanstanstan", …
`'stan?'`	Matches "sta" and "stan" only
`'(stan)?'`	Matches "" and "stan"

The matches shown as " " mean *zero* occurrences of the pattern. These must be used with care! The following example will serve as a warning:

```
$ egrep '(stan)*' ur.1
XENIX is a version of the
UNIX operating system
for the IBM PC range.
Usually, you will find that
$ _
```

Zero or more occurrences of "stan" occur in every line of ur.1!

Taking grep and egrep operations together, Table 15.2 shows them in decreasing order of precedence.

TABLE 15.2: Regular Expressions in Descending Precedence for grep and egrep

Regular Expression	Meaning
c	Normal (nonmeta) character
\m	Escape a character
^	Start of line
$	End of line
.	Any single character (excluding newline)
[xyz...]	Any one of x, y, z, …
[a–z]	Range
[^...]	Any single character not listed
\n	The nth tagged expression (grep only)
r*	Zero or more r's
r+	One or more r's (egrep only)
r?	Zero or one r's (egrep only)

TABLE 15.2: Regular Expressions in Descending Precedence for `grep` and `egrep` (continued)

Regular Expression	Meaning
r1r2	Concatenation: r1 followed by r2
r1| r2	r1 or r2 (egrep only)
\(r \)	Tagged regular expression r (grep only)
(r)	Regular expression r: lowest precedence

The grep Family Summary

Table 15.3 summarizes the `grep` family options. All Unix systems provide at least the following options: −b, −l, −c, −n, −s, and −v. The others may not be present on older versions.

TABLE 15.3: grep Family Options

Option	Action
	fgrep only:
−x	Matches whole line exactly
	grep, fgrep and egrep:
−h	Suppresses file name display
−b	Displays disk block number of matching line
−l	Displays only file names where matches found
−c	Counts and displays number of matching lines
−n	Numbers each matching line
−v	Displays lines that do not match
−i	Ignores case when matching
−y	Older version of −i
−e	Matches following expression, usually one that starts with "-". Avoids clash with an option

TABLE 15.3: grep Family Options (continued)

Option	Action
grep only:	
-s	Suppresses error messages
-w	Matches whole words only
egrep and fgrep:	
-f *expfile*	Matches strings stored in *expfile*

The regular expressions supported by each of the grep family are summed up in Table 15.4 (see the earlier sections of this chapter and also Chapter 8 for more details).

TABLE 15.4: grep Family Expressions

Regular Expression	Matches
grep, fgrep and egrep:	
x	Ordinary characters match themselves (newlines and metacharacters are excluded)
xyz	Ordinary strings match themselves
grep and egrep:	
\m	Matches literal metacharacter m
^	Start of line
$	End of line
.	Any single character
[xy^$z]	Any one of x, y, ^, $ or z
[^xy^$z]	Any one other than x, y, ^, $ or z
[a-z]	Any single character in given range
[^a-z]	Any single character not in given range
*r**	Zero or more occurrences of *r*
r1r2	Matches *r1* followed by *r2* (concatenation)

TABLE 15.4: grep Family Expressions (continued)

Regular Expression	Matches
	grep only:
\(*r*\)	Tagged regular expression: matches *r*
n	Set to what matched the *n*th tagged expression (*n* = 1 to 9)
	egrep only:
r+	One or more occurrences of *r*
r?	Zero or one occurrences of *r*
r1 | *r2*	Either *r1* or *r2*
(*r1* | *r2*)*r3*	Either *r1r3* or *r2r3*
(*r1* | *r2*)*	Zero or more occurrences of *r1* | *r2* (e.g., *r1*, *r1r1*, *r2r1*, *r1r1r2r1*,...)

The sed Stream Editor

sed (meaning stream editor, and described in man section C) was mentioned in the chapter on the ed editor. sed, originally designed by Lee McMahon, offers most of the ed editing features with identical commands. The difference is that sed is a complex filter known as a *stream* editor, whereas ed is an interactive editor. This makes sed more useful in a shell script, where you usually know in advance what editing steps are needed to convert one or more input files (representing the input streams of characters, by default, your standard input) to an output file or stream (by default, your standard output). You can picture sed supplying a script of editing commands, not unlike the sequences you would enter manually during an ed session, in order to transform the input stream into the output stream.

What's a Stream?

The picturesque word *stream* is widely used in computer science to represent a dynamic sequence of elements with certain properties. Each element in a stream is of the same *data type* (for example, bits in a bit stream, characters in a text stream, and

so on). The number of elements is called the *length* of the stream. You can read just one element at a time from the stream's *current position* (after such a read, the current position usually advances to the next element), and you can write to the stream but only by appending an element at the end of the stream. Streams that allow only reading are called input streams; those that allow only writing are called output streams; those that allow both reading and writing are called input/output streams (I/O streams for short).

In discussing sed, we will be concerned with text streams, namely sequences of ASCII characters. Input (read-only) streams are associated with stdin (the standard input, usually the keyboard); output (write-only) streams are associated with stdout (the standard output) and stderr (the standard error output). The I/O streams are usually represented by Unix text files (assuming that they have the appropriate read and write permissions). In other contexts, streams may be associated with special files representing various I/O devices such as modems or magnetic tape drives.

sed Syntax

Large tracts have been written covering all the tricks of sed. Here, I'll concentrate on the most common applications. From the following examples, you'll see that your knowledge of ed can be readily exploited.

There are two basic ways of using sed:

```
sed [-n] [-e] 'edit_command'  in_file
```

and

```
sed [-n] -fedit_script in_file
```

They *can* be combined, but let's take one gulp at a time.

The *in_file* represents the input stream that is to be edited. If you omit the *in_file* argument, sed will operate on your standard input. sed will output all the lines of *in_file*, whether changed by sed or not, excluding, of course, any lines deleted by your edit. This output is usually displayed (printed) on your standard output, as you might expect from a well-behaved filter. You do have the option, however, to suppress some or all of the output. The −n option (think of it as no output) suppresses all output except for specific lines designated in the edit command.

The trick with −n is to append the p (print) command to those edit commands for which the output is needed. You'll see how presently. *in_file* itself, of course, is not modified by sed. Whatever emerges from your sed operation can be written or appended to a file with the usual *>out_file* and *>>out_file* redirections, or piped to another command.

> **WARNING** It is entirely irresponsible to redirect the output of sed to the selfsame file that you are sedding!

The *edit_command* inside single quotes is an ed-like command, such as s/sun/moon/g (change "sun" to "moon") or 1,5p (with the −n option, this would print only lines 1 to 5). The surrounding single quotes are not always essential but are so highly recommended that beginners should treat them as mandatory. Two keystrokes can save you considerable angst. So many of the sed command characters have special meanings to the shell that it is easier to quote the whole edit command. You'll recall the similar caveats in force for the grep family.

You can have more than one *edit_command* in a single sed command. Simply enter −e before each *edit_command* and they will be processed in turn by sed.

The −f (file) option of sed is rather like the −f option in egrep and fgrep. The *edit_script*, following the −f, is the name of a file containing a set of ed-like commands (rather like a shell script). This allows some fancy operations. For example, suppose you need to keep several different versions of a large file, the results of various editing sessions. It is possible to save disk space by keeping just one version of the file, together with edit scripts that will generate the other versions. The edit scripts simply record the differences and are usually much shorter than the text files. In fact, Unix provides a command called diff that will generate an edit script. You give diff the two file names, say A and B, as arguments. The output is the sequence of ed commands that will produce B when applied to A.

The −e and −f options can be combined. The −e option is the default. If you have only one −e and no −f commands, you can omit the −e. In all other cases the −e is needed. The −f is never assumed, so

```
sed scriptfile in_file
```

would default to

```
sed -e scriptfile in_file
```

which is almost certainly an error, rather than the intended

```
sed -f scriptfile in_file
```

Likewise, it is wrong to write

```
sed ´command´ -f scriptfile in_file
```

rather than

```
sed -e ´command´ -f filename in_file
```

If an -f option is present, the -e is not assumed by default.

The edit_command

The *edit_command* works in the same way as ed with line numbers, line number expressions, addresses, and regular expressions. You will usually be using sed with the pattern matching addresses rather than with line numbers. Here are some examples:

```
sed ´s/sun/moon/´ myfile
```

Recalling your ed schooling, you will deduce that the above will replace the *first* occurrence of "sun" in each line of myfile with "moon". Without redirection, the output will appear on your screen. All lines will appear, whether changed or not.

```
sed ´s/sun/moon/g´ myfile
```

goes a bit further: the g (global) option will change *every* occurrence of "sun" in myfile to "moon".

```
sed -e ´s/sun/moon/g´ -e ´s/day/night/g´ myfile
```

Here you see two successive commands, requiring the -e option. sed operates by copying a line of myfile into a *pattern space*. It then applies each edit command in turn to the pattern space before outputting the result to the standard output. Of course, only those commands that "match" will affect the pattern space. There is one exception to this sequence: the q (quit) function will exit sed by branching to the end of the script:

```
sed ´/sun/q´ myfile
```

will output until a line containing "sun" is encountered. That line (if one exists) will be displayed; then sed terminates. As with ed, the full syntax for a command is

```
[address1 [,address2]] function [args]
```

Watch! If you are sedding more than one file, the line numbers accumulate across these files. If your first file has 200 lines, the first line of the second file will be address 201.

The *function* argument is also referred to as a command or command letter. The addresses specify the range of lines to be edited. If both addresses are missing, sed assumes that every line is targeted. In other words, the default address arguments are 1,$ (from line 1 to the last line). If one address is given, the other defaults to the first or last line of the file. In the above s commands, for example, we gave no address arguments, so each line was a potential candidate for subsitution. Addresses can be supplied to narrow the editing, using either line numbers (or line symbols such as $ for last), or *context* addresses. The latter are our old friends, the regular expressions. Consider the following:

```
sed '1,4s/sun/moon/g' myfile
```

Here, the substitution will be limited to the first four lines of myfile. The rather daunting

```
sed '/^Example/,/QED$/s/sun/moon/g' myfile
```

will only substitute "moon" for "sun" in those lines in the inclusive range selected by the two context addresses. The first says: select the first line that begins with "Example"; the second says: select the first line that ends with "QED". If these selections happen to be the same line, just that line is selected. If the line with "QED" precedes the line with "Example", only the "Example" line is selected. Normally, though, the command would select a set of lines, and in each of these the substitution would be applied. This process is repeated throughout the file, so it might edit several sets of lines starting with "Example" up to and including lines ending with "QED".

Each function, designated by a single letter, expects a certain number of addresses (zero, one, or two), and a certain set of arguments (including none). The q function,

for instance, takes a single address and no arguments. It simply stops sed when that address is matched. We'll now run through the more popular sed commands.

Substitution

The s (substitute) function has the following syntax:

```
[address1 [,address2 ]] s/regexp/replacement/flags
```

As you've seen, the regular expression matches are replaced by the replacement string within the given address ranges. The most common flag argument is g as shown earlier. The full set of flags is as follows:

n	A number 1-512 specifies that only the *n*th occurrence of *regexp* will be replaced.
g	Global substitution rather than just substituting the first occurrence on each line.
p	Displays (prints) the line if a replacement was made.
w *wfile*	Writes the line to the *wfile* if a replacement was made.

The w flag lets you write just the changes to a specified file while writing the whole, edited file elsewhere:

```
sed '/sun/moon/gw changes' myfile >tmp
```

The replacement string can be a new line, allowing you to insert extra line spacing:

```
sed 's/$/\
> /' myfile
```

This gives you double-line spacing since each end-of-line, indicated by $, is replaced by a newline. To get a newline in the replacement string, you have to enter \ followed by the Enter (↵) key. After the secondary prompt, you complete the entry with /'; then type the file name.

Reversals with a Bang!

A useful dodge to remember is that you can reverse the matching by placing ! (pronounced "bang" or "not") before the function. Thus:

```
sed '1,4!s/sun/moon/g' myfile
```

says, do the substitution on all but the first four lines of `myfile`. Similarly,

```
sed '/^Example/,/QED$/!s/sun/moon/g' myfile
```

performs the substitution on each line outside the ranges discussed earlier.

A more practical application of ! is where you want to edit only nonempty lines. An empty line, remember, matches the regular expression '^$', so

```
sed '/^$/!s/^/    /' myfile
```

says *"Don't* substitute on empty lines." Hence this command will insert a tab at the beginning of each nonempty line. This is a useful operation known as *indenting*. The replacement string is a real tab that is hard to see on the printed page.

Deletion

The d (delete) function takes two addresses, and deletes the range of lines selected:

```
sed '4,5d' myfile
```

deletes lines 4 and 5, while

```
sed '/sun/d' myfile
```

will delete *every* line containing "sun". Note that the "missing" second address defaults to $, the last line. You can delete every line *except* the ones containing "sun":

```
sed '/sun/!d' myfile
```

I must stress again that `myfile` is not affected by this operation! The deletion affects only the output of sed. To effect a lasting edit, you must redirect and then copy:

```
$ sed '/sun/d' myfile >tmp
$ mv tmp myfile
$ _
```

Take the following variant:

```
sed '/sun/,/moon/d' myfile
```

What is deleted? Well, the range selected is, inclusively, from the first line holding a "sun" to the first line holding a "moon". If there are such lines, they will not appear on your standard output.

Appending and Inserting Text

As with ed, you can append and insert text using the a and i functions. The difference is that the added text must be part of the edit command (or script file), and care is needed if the text straddles more than one line. What you need is the escape character, \, to hide all but the final newline from the shell:

```
sed '3a\
Now is the hour'
myfile
```

This will add "Now is the hour" after line 3 of myfile. The i function inserts before the given address.

The y Function

The y function is simple but effective: it replaces characters on a 1-to-1 basis:

```
sed 'y/abc/ABC/' myfile
```

Here, each "a" is replaced by "A", each "b" by "B", and so on. You can set up any mapping of characters by listing the "from" and "to" strings as shown. The two strings must be of the same length to avoid error messages and embarrassment.

The p Function

This is the familiar print (display) command from ed, but there are few new wrinkles. Since sed already sends its output to the screen by default, p is less useful than with ed. In fact, if you try the following command:

```
sed '/sun/p' myfile
```

you'll find that matching lines are displayed twice! Where p does earn its lunch is when used with the −n option. The −n option normally suppresses the standard output, but you can override this with a judicious p! (You can look on this as inhibiting the inhibition.) If you want to see only the matching lines, you can do the following:

```
sed −n '/sun/p' myfile
```

This is remarkably similar to grep 'sun' myfile. And you can display all lines except those with a "sun" by using

```
sed −n '/sun/!p' myfile
```

which is the same as grep -v ´sun´ myfile. As I said earlier, sed will do almost everything that grep will do (however, the results of the grep -b option cannot be achieved by sed).

Come All Ye
Tramps and 'awkers

awk, named for the triumvirate Aho, Weinberger, and Kernighan who designed it, is a complete language with its own band of dedicated enthusiasts. Some have described awk as a cult within a cult, and indeed awk does have its own bible: *The AWK Programming Language,* Alfred Aho, Brian Kernighan, Peter Weinberger (Addison-Wesley, 1988). Officially defined as a "pattern scanning and processing language," awk can be, and regularly is, coaxed into solving all manner of problems not immediately connected with patterns. awk uses a syntax that incorporates many features of the C language, so a knowledge of C is a great help if you wish to master awk (and conversely, of course). A useful rule-of-thumb is that if a job is too difficult for "normal" shell tools and scripts, try awk. If awk can't solve the problem, use C. Failing that, move up to C++ (Bjarne Stroustrup's object-oriented extension of C which is rapidly gaining popularity).

In this section, I'll concentrate on some of the simpler features of awk that you can exploit without becoming a full-time hacker. The basic idea of awk is not unlike that of grep and sed: you scan one or more files, record by record (usually line by line), looking for pattern matches, and you perform some action whenever a match is found. The power of awk arises from the fact that the pattern-checking tools are more elaborate, and the actions you can trigger are more extensive than those of sed. In fact, you can initiate complete programs with conditional loops and arithmetical operations whenever a match is found. The general syntax is

```
awk [-F re] [parameter...] [´prog´] [-f progfile] [in_file...]
```

in_file... specifies the list of files to be processed. As with sed and grep, awk does not modify the input files. If no files are given, awk processes the standard input. The results of awk appear on your standard output, so all the familiar Unix filter operations are available: redirection with <, >, and >>, and piping with |. The *prog* argument is a string, single-quoted, as you would expect, to hide stuff from the shell.

(Quoting is explained in the grep section.) The *parameter* options let you assign values to various variables. A typical *prog* argument looks like this:

```
'pattern { action }'
```

The *pattern* argument can be any of the egrep regular expressions, using the syntax /re/, plus a few more pattern-matching tricks as you'll see later. The *action* argument, always surrounded by braces, is a sequence of statements (separated by semicolons) that awk will interpret and execute for each *record* of the input file(s) that gives a pattern match. I'll explain records later. The default record for awk is the familiar line, so for the moment you can think of awk as processing the input files one line at a time. The *action* section can be quite long and complex, straddling many lines, or many pages even. As with shell scripts, you can insert comments using the # character:

```
'{ myaction }' # all mine!
```

Everything following # to the end of the line is ignored, so try to avoid '{ myaction # all mine! }'. This would generate a syntax error, since awk would not "see" the final brace. As I pointed out in Chapter 13, liberal use of comments is encouraged, especially where the program uses the kind of arcane tricks that Shakespeare warned us about:

"Bloody instructions, that return to plague the inventor…" (Macbeth)

You can omit either the *pattern* or the *action* arguments (but not both). No *pattern* means match *all* records; the default *action* is to display on the standard output. A simple *action* is the print command:

```
awk '/sun/ { print }' myfile
```

This will display all lines of myfile that contain the string "sun". (In this example, you could actually omit the { print } argument, since this is the default action.) Of course,

```
grep 'sun' myfile
```

will do exactly the same job, so we have proved our earlier claim that awk can grep! Omitting the *pattern* argument means that all lines will match, so

```
awk '{ print }' myfile
```

displays each line of myfile. This example turns out to be less efficient than the equivalent cat myfile.

The following is legal but ineffective:

```
awk '{}' myfile # where's the beef?
```

The above empty action does nothing on every line of input!

As with sed, you can select a range of lines by using two patterns separated by a comma:

```
awk '/[Ss]un/,/[Mm]oon/ { print }' myfile
```

This would display the lines from the first one matching "sun" or "Sun" to the next one matching "moon" or "Moon". The selected output from print can be redirected or piped by using >, >>, or | within the action:

```
awk '/sun/,/moon/ { print >my.extract }' myfile
```

Before looking at more complex examples, note that the -f option works just like -f in sed and egrep. You can put all your awk commands and actions in a separate program file, and pass its name in the -f *progfile* argument.

awk Fields

One of the tricks of awk that gives it great power is the ability to isolate and process separate *fields* of the lines being scanned. You've met fields before in several contexts. For example, the sort command uses fields to achieve sorts over different parts of a line. Both grep and sed are pure "line-based" utilities and it is not so easy to manipulate subsections of a line. The fields in a line can be accessed by awk using the notation $1, $2, and so on, rather like, but not to be confused with, the positional variables in a shell script. Suppose you had a file called books:

```
$ cat books
Author      Title       Prices
Smith       Ants        $39.95
Jones       Cats        $29.95
Brown       Dogs        $19.95
$ _
```

The author field can be referenced as $1, the title as $2, and the price as $3. The symbol-pair $n is called a field variable, where n is the field number. The special symbol-pair $0 represents the whole line, that is every field exactly as entered in the file. A built-in variable, NF, holds the number of fields, so $NF means the last field. NF and several other built-in variables can be accessed in your awk programs, rather like

the predefined shell variables you first met in Chapter 6. (You'll encounter some important differences, though, so take care.)

By default, fields are defined as any contiguous set of nonwhite-space characters separated by white space (spaces or tabs, or newlines for the last field). Under the normal white space separator regimen, any number of spaces/tabs serve to separate the fields and the fields themselves never contain white space. In the books file, $2 represents the title string with no leading or trailing spaces/tabs, no matter how much white space separates the columns.

The −F option lets you change the built-in variable FS (field separator) from spaces/tabs to any single nonspace character (including a single tab). Once you change the default separator, though, your fields *will* include any leading spaces. I'll return to the −F option soon.

awk Records

awk actually processes one *record* at a time. Records are determined by the character stored in the built-in variable, RS (record separator). The default RS is newline, so the standard awk record is one line of text, just like sed. awk, however, lets you change the RS, so your records can be parts of lines or multiple lines. This adds considerable flexibility in creating database applications. Before exploring these options, let's look at the default separators: white space for fields, newlines for records. The following examples show the field variables in action:

```
$ awk '{ print $0 }' books
Author     Title      Prices
Smith      Ants       $39.95
Jones      Cats       $29.95
Brown      Dogs       $19.95
$ awk '{ print $2 }' books
Title
Ants
Cats
Dogs
$ awk '{ print $3, $1, "Qty..." }' books
Prices Author Qty...
$39.95 Smith Qty...
$29.95 Jones Qty...
$19.95 Brown Qty...
$ _
```

The first example is a long-winded version of awk { print } books, since print defaults to print $0. As you can see, the print command can take one or more field arguments in any order. You can even repeat a field if you want to:

```
$ awk '{ print $3, $1, $3 }' books
Prices Author Prices
$39.95 Smith $39.95
$29.95 Jones $39.95
$19.95 Brown $39.95
$ _
```

print allows fixed-string arguments such as "Qty...". You usually need a comma between each argument, as shown. If the comma is omitted, the two fields will print coalesced as one. Note the spacing in the last example. Input field separators do not pass through to the output. Each comma in the print argument list simply generates a single OFS character (output field separator). By default, this is a space, but (as you've guessed), awk lets you change the OFS variable to any other character (tab being a common choice for pretty alignments). You can also tidy up the appearance using the tab character, \t, directly in the print arguments:

```
$ awk '{ print $3, $1, "\tQty..." }' books
Prices Author    Qty...
$39.95 Smith     Qty...
$29.95 Jones     Qty...
$19.95 Brown     Qty...
$ _
```

An interesting and useful aspect of awk's field variables is that they are *true* variables. Although $n starts life holding the nth field, you are free to assign new values to it during execution. For example:

```
$ awk '{ $1 = "O/S"; $3 = "N/A"; print $0 }' books
O/S        Title     N/A
O/S        Ants      N/A
O/S        Cats      N/A
O/S        Dogs      N/A
$ _
```

Remember that the input file is not changed, so you haven't lost the authors and prices from the books file.

You can use all the familiar `egrep` regular expressions to select lines from a file:

```
$ awk '/[Dd]|Smith/' books
Smith     Ants      $39.95
Brown     Dogs      $19.95
```

Here we match any line that has either "D", "d", or "Smith".

printf

For more complicated output formats, you can use the `printf` command (standing for print formatted). I won't go into all the `printf` tricks, but here's a typical example, showing how you can number each line of output. The built-in variable `NR` provides the line number. Unlike the shell variables you met in Chapter 6, the built-in awk variables like `NR` do not require a leading `$` to reveal their values. (`$NR` would mean the `NR`th field, which is something else!)

```
$ awk '{ printf "%03d %s\n", NR, $1 }' books
001 Author
002 Smith
003 Jones
004 Brown
```

`printf` crawls out, almost intact, from the C language with a plethora of options for formatting numbers and strings in any conceivable layout. `printf` takes a format string, followed by the arguments to be printed. The format string, within double quotes, contains a set of formatting specifications, each starting with a `%`, one for each argument to be printed. In the above example, `%03d` formats the `NR`, and `%s` formats the field `$1`. `d` means format a decimal number; `03` means pad with leading zeros to a width of 3. `s` means format a string. The final `\n` should be familiar: this provides a newline. Unlike `print`, `printf` does not automatically generate a newline at the end of each display, so you have to provide one as shown (or suffer a messy layout). You can also insert `\t` in your format strings to generate a tab:

```
$ awk '{ printf "\t%03d \t%s\n", NR, $1 }' books
001     Author
002     Smith
003     Jones
004     Brown
```

A predefined variable, `OFMT`, determines the output format for numbers in the absence of an explicit `%` specifier. The default format is `%.6g` which handles a decimal

floating-point with a precision of 6 digits. (awk handles all numbers internally in floating-point format.)

The -F Option

The −F option lets you change the field separator character. You simply follow the −F with a single character (or regular expression). A typical application is −F: to set the separator to a colon. The /etc/passwd file, for example, uses colons to delimit fields:

```
$ cat /etc/passwd
root:gf54JQxxZ32Fd:0:1::/:/bin/sh
...
stan:oIg65rfRdffn8:24:12:Stan Kelly-Bootle:/usr/stan/:/bin/sh
fred:qEsgs3324Fcc2:25:12:Frederick Lemaitre:/usr/fred/:/bin/csh
joe::27:14:Joseph Lussac:/usr/joe:
...
$ _
```

NOTE

For security reasons, many recent Unix implementaions no longer hold the encrypted password in \etc\passwd. A ":*:" appears if the user has a password; otherwise an empty field, "::", indicates no password has been assigned. Some systems will always show ":*:" whether the user has a password or not.

awk can be used to investigate important properties of your system's password file. Consider the following:

```
$ awk −F: '$2 == ""' /etc/passwd # note: print is implied
joe::27:14:Joseph Lussac:/usr/joe:
$ _
```

This example may offer a quick method of uncovering those users who are not password protected! To see how it works, note first that −F: tells awk that fields will be defined in terms of : as separators. $2 now refers to the second field in /etc/passwd, namely the encrypted password field. The pattern-matching expression $2 == "" tests whether this field is null (empty) or not, that is, whether there is *anything* between the second and third colon. Remember that once FS is defined

as :, any white space between the colons would "belong" to that field. I stress this because beginners often confuse spaces, nulls, and field separators. The == operator (also imported from C) is known as a *relational* operator since it tests for a relation between two expressions; in our case, it tests for equality between $2 and the empty string " ".

WARNING	Distinguish carefully between == (equality testing) and = (assignment). Confusing them is yet another common source for programming errors in awk and C.

The == operator gives you a neat way of selecting a range of line numbers:

```
$ awk 'NR == 5, NR == 20' myfile
```

will print from line 5 to line 20, inclusive. Recall that two patterns separated by a comma establish a range. You could list all lines except line 33:

```
$ awk 'NR != 33' myfile
```

The "not-equals" operator is !=. As in C, ! carries the hint of negation in several contexts. Let's look at awk's other relational operators.

awk Relational Operators

awk allows the tests shown in Table 15.5. These operators can be used in both the *pattern* and *action* sections. In the *pattern* section, the conditional test is implied: all you need write is, say, $2 == " ", and awk will seek a match. In the *action* section, however, you need explicit conditional and flow control operators such as if, else, and while that I'll explain later.

The exact meaning of a relational operator depends on the data type of the two variables or expressions being compared. With numbers and strings, equality and inequality tests obey the obvious rules. You can test x == 3 as well as str == "stan". With numbers, the comparisons >, >=, and so on, follow the usual arithmetic rules: 2 > 1, -1 > -2, etc. With strings, comparisons are made lexicographically (dictionary order), so that "b" > "a", "aa" > "a", and so on.

TABLE 15.5: Tests Allowed by awk

Relational Operator	Meaning
x == y	x equals y?
x != y	x not equal to y?
x > y	x greater than y?
x >= y	x greater than or equal to y?
x < y	x less than y?
x <= y	x less than or equal to y?
x ~ re	x matches the regular expression re?
x !~ re	x does not match the regular expression re?

The test $2 == " " used in the previous example can also be expressed as follows:

```
$2 ~ /^$/
```

The ~ (tilde) is often pronounced "contains." The pattern test asks whether $2 contains (or matches) the regular expression /^$/, which matches only an empty field. Note a subtle difference here between awk and sed: with awk, ^ and $ can designate the start and end of fields or lines. In sed, /^$/ matches only an empty line. You can also write

```
$2 !~ /./
```

with the same result: /./ matches any character, so we seek a $2 field that does not contain any character. Only a null (empty) field can make this statement! Yet another version of this test uses length, one of many built-in awk functions that add to the fun:

```
length($2) == 0
```

The expression length(str) is set to the length (number of bytes) in the string str. A zero length means an empty string. A more common use of the length function is tracking overlong lines, which can be useful before printing a file:

```
$ awk 'length($0) > 80 { print NR }' myfile
367
569
$ _
```

This example displays the line numbers of all lines exceeding eighty characters.

Multiple Tests

awk's pattern checking powers are considerably enhanced by the provision of three logical operators: ! (NOT), || (OR), and && (AND). (Note especially the double symbols needed for OR and AND.) These operators let you test for complex combinations of matches:

```
'( length($1) >= 4 ) && ( NR % 2 != 0 )'
```

Here we are seeking lines that satisfy two conditions: the first field must contain at least four characters AND the line number must be odd. You never know, that could be useful one day. The test for oddness deserves study: NR % 2 gives the remainder after dividing the line number by 2. A nonzero remainder indicates an odd numbered line.

The expression p||q is true if either p is true or q is true or *both* are true (we call this the inclusive OR). awk uses a shortcut when testing multiple conditions such as p||q: if p is found to be true, no time is wasted evaluating q! awk already knows that p||q is satisfied. Likewise when testing p&&q, if p is found to be false, the truth or falsehood of q is not explored. Here is || in action. The pattern

```
( ($1*$2) > 0) || ($6 == "Late")'
```

will match any line where either Qty × Price (fields 1 and 2) is positive or Status (field 6) is "Late" (or both).

Notice the parentheses used to group each pattern. I recommend them for added legibility even if they are not essential for controlling precedence. You met the "precedence" problem in the egrep section, but in awk with its richer supply of operators, precedence is much more difficult. I'll list the precedence order in Table 15.6, but it is much safer to use parentheses. If you are seriously contemplating a career in programming, of course, you will need to master the AND (logical conjuction), the OR (logical inclusive disjunction), and the NOT (logical negation).

You've already met the NOT (or reverse) operator under several guises. In sed, the same symbol ! is used to reverse the sense of a match, but it is placed between the pattern and the action. In awk, the ! always goes before the expression to be negated: !x is pronounced "NOT-x." Any pattern, however complex, can be negated by a preceding bang (!).

TABLE 15.6: Increasing Precedence of Operators for awk

Group	Operators
1	= += −= *= /= %=
2	||
3	&&
4	> >= < <= == != ~ !~
5	String concatenation: "x" "y" becomes "xy"
6	+ −
7	* / %
8	++ −−

Begin and End

Two special expressions, BEGIN and END, can be used in the *pattern* argument. Any action listed (within braces) after BEGIN will be performed before awk starts scanning the input, and any action listed after END will be performed after all the input has been scanned. BEGIN is used to display headings and to preset (initialize) variables. END is used to display any final results, such as field totals. Consider:

```
$ awk ´
> BEGIN { FS = ":"; print "Security Check" }
> $2 == "" { count++ ; print }
> END { print count, "User(s) not passworded." }´ /etc/passwd
Security Check
joe::27:14:Joseph Lussac:/usr/joe:
1 User(s) not passworded.
$ _
```

Let's examine some of the new awk constructs introduced here. First, I've given you a fresh way of setting the field separator. Rather than use -F:, you can assign ":" directly to the FS variable. Note the single = means "assign from the right to the left." We do this within a BEGIN section so the assignment occurs only once before the real work starts. We've also sneaked in a print statement to display the heading "Security Check" (again, we need only one of these). When you the type the closing brace,}, you signal the end of the BEGIN section. The thrill of awk is that you can list

as many action statements as you wish between the braces, as long as you remember the separating semicolons. Statements can also be separated by newlines. (C programmers will recognize the { } and ; as block and statement delimiters.)

The secondary prompt tells you that awk is waiting for more input. In fact, you could enter the whole command on one line, but for legibility I've divided it into three convenient sections. Long commands like these, of course, are eminently suitable for embedding in shell scripts (as discussed in Chapter 13), or in program files using the *-f progfile* option.

Next we have two action statements that will be triggered when the pattern $2 == " " tests true. The first action is count++ which increments (increases by 1) the variable count. count is your first encounter with *user-defined* variables. You can give your own variables any convenient, mnemonic names provided you avoid clashing with awk's predefined (built-in) variables such as NF, FS, OFS, and NR (the full list appears below in Table 15.7).

awk variables differ from those used in C in several important respects. First, awk offers only strings, one numerical data type, and arrays of these, a much simpler choice than in C. Second, with C you have to *declare* variables, giving their names and data types (int, char, and so on), before they can be used (well, *nearly* always).

TABLE 15.7: Predefined Variables for awk

Variable Name	Meaning
ARGC	Number of command-line arguments
ARGV	Array of command-line arguments
FILENAME	String = name of current input file
FNR	Current record number in the current file (starts at 1 for each input file)
FS	Input field separator character (default = space)
NF	Number of fields in current record
NR	Current record number (over all input files)
OFMT	Output format for numbers (default = %.6g)
OFS	Output field separator (default = space)
ORS	Output record separator (default = newline)
RS	Input record separator (default = newline)

In most cases, too, you also have to initialize C variables explicitly before they can be safely used. There are no explicit declarations with awk: it is sufficient to *use* a variable name. Upon its first appearance in an awk statement, a variable is data-typed as a string, number, or array according to its context. If you are adding numbers to a variable, for instance, awk will rightly conclude that the variable has numeric pretensions. Similarly, if you assign a string to a variable, or do some other string-like maneuver, awk data-types it as a string. (I'll cover arrays later.) When in doubt, awk assumes a string data type. awk then initializes the new variable: numbers to 0, and strings to " " (the null or empty string). awk is quite tolerant compared with strongly typed languages such as C and Modula-2. Strings and numbers are freely converted one to the other as demanded by the context. You can write X = "1" + 3, for example, without protest and X will be set to 4!

With this essential detour completed, let's return to the analysis of the last example. In the case of count++, the ++ (or postincrement) operator tells awk that count is to be treated as a number. count will therefore start off with the value 0, but each matching line triggers the statement count++, which adds 1 to count. count++ is a convenient shorthand for

```
count = count + 1
```

and is typical of C's economical syntax (a big reason for its popularity with programmers who hate typing). The postdecrement operator -- works in the same way: count-- decrements count by 1, as if you had written count = count -1. (C programmers should note that awk has no equivalent to C's preincrement or predecrement operators.)

When we reach the END section, count will hold the total number of matched lines. Our example prints this total with an explanatory legend. The print statement in the line

```
$2 == "" { count++ ; print }
```

displays the matching lines. Try omitting the print statement: you'll just get the final total and legend. You'll find this situation in many awk jobs: long files are scanned to give summaries, totals, averages, and the like, but the mass of detail is not usually displayed.

awk and Math

awk supports the usual arithmetical operations, a few fancy variants borrowed from C, and several useful mathematical functions. They are all listed below in Table 15.8.

TABLE 15.8: Mathematical Operations and Functions for awk

Operation	Function
x + y	Adds x to y
x - y	Subtracts y from x
x * y	Multiplies x and y
x / y	Divides x by y
x % y	Gives the remainder when x is divided by y
x = y	Assigns value of y to x
x++	Increments x by 1
x--	Decrements x by 1
x += y	Same as x = x + y
x -= y	Same as x = x - y
x *= y	Same as x = x*y
x /= y	Same as x = x/y
x %= y	Same as x = x % y
int(x)	Truncates x to whole number
rand	Gives a random number between 0 and 1
srand(x)	Sets x as new seed for rand
cos(x)	Gives the cosine of x
sin(x)	Gives the sine of x
atan2(x,y)	Gives the arc tangent of y/x
exp(x)	Gives e^x (e raised to the power x)
log(x)	Gives the logarithm of x (to base e)
sqrt(x)	Gives the nonnegative square root of x

Of special interest are the compound operators, +=, -=, and so on, which save a great deal of typing. Going back to the books file and modifying it slightly to help the arithmetic, let's calculate the average price of our meagre catalog:

```
$ cat sbooks
Author     Title      Prices
Smith      Ants       39.95
Jones      Cats       29.95
Brown      Dogs       19.95
$ awk 'BEGIN { print "Summer Price List" }
> NR > 1 { sum += $3; print $2, "$" $3 }
  END { print "Average price = $", sum/(NR-1) }' sbooks
Summer Price List
Ants $39.95
Cats $29.95
Dogs $19.95
Average price = $ 29.950
```

The NR > 1 pattern says, "Ignore the first line." NR gives the current line number, and we wish to avoid doing sums on the header line given by NR equal to 1. On all subsequent lines, we accumulate the price in field $3 into the user-defined variable sum, since sum += $3 means sum = sum + $3. At the end NR will be equal to the total number of lines, which is one more than the number of prices. Hence the average price is sum/(NR-1). One little trick to note: awk automatically concatenates adjacent strings, so "$" $3 gives "$" followed by the price. If the variable X contains the string "this", then

```
'{ print "all" X "week" }'
```

would display "all this week". Even with numeric expressions, concatenation occurs: if X holds 1 and Y holds 2,

```
{ print X Y }'
```

will display "12". (print XY, of course, will display the contents of the variable XY, whatever *they* may be.)

Let's smarten up the previous example by displaying the current date on the price list. This will introduce a few more tools available in the awk toolbox.

```
$ awk 'BEGIN { print "Summer Price List";
> print "'"`date`"'" }
> NR > 1 { sum += $3; print $2, "$" $3 }
  END { print "Average price = $", sum/(NR-1) }' sbooks
Summer Price List
```

```
Sun Jun 11 04:56:48 GMT 1995
Ants $39.95
Cats $29.95
Dogs $19.95
Average price = $ 29.950
```

The exuberance of quotes around `date` may have caught your attention! The inner expression `` `date` `` is our old friend the backquoted command, which the shell replaces with the output of `date`. Before awk can print it, though, this output has to be "stringized," and this is achieved by surrounding `` `date` `` with quotes. We can't get by with a simple `` '`date`' ``, however, because we already have single (forward) quotes surrounding the awk program. So, we end up by double-quoting each single (forward) quote. The rest is history, as they say. You are not alone, by the way, if you find this expression weird and wondrous in equal parts. Even Brian Kernighan and Rob Pike who devised it describe it as "remarkable." (*The Unix Programming Environment*, Prentice-Hall, 1984)

But there is more to follow. Suppose you feel that the full date as issued by `date` is not appropriate to a commercial document. Perhaps you want just the day, month, and year as nature intended. In the following variant, we use one of awk's many string functions to create an *array* of strings from which we can select parts of the date. The function `split` works as follows:

```
split( string, array, fs )
```

takes a string and breaks it into fields according to the given field separator, *fs*. If you omit the *fs* argument, `split` takes the current value of FS as the separator. In our case, we'll just accept space as the current FS and omit the *fs* argument. If *string* is "Sun Jun 11 04:56:48 GMT 1995", `split` will form six fields and load them into *array*. Thereafter, you can access the fields by indexing as follows:

```
array[1] is "Sun"
array[2] is "Jun"
array[3] is "11"
array[4] is "04:56:48"
array[5] is "GMT"
array[6] is "1995"
```

The syntax should be clear: the numerical index is enclosed in brackets after the name of the array. Here's our latest price list example:

```
$ awk 'BEGIN { print "Summer Price List";
> split( "'"`date`"'", today);
> print today[3], today[2], today[6] }
```

```
> NR > 1 { sum += $3; print $2, "$" $3 }
 END { print "Average price = $", sum/(NR-1) }´ sbooks
Summer Price List
11 Jun 1995
Ants $39.95
Cats $29.95
Dogs $19.95
Average price = $ 29.950
```

awk Flow Control

No self-respecting language is complete without some form of execution flow control. The basic idea behind flow control is that a program can be written in a general way to cover a multitude of foreseen circumstances. Depending on values encountered in certain variables, the program will select a set of statements and bypass others. Flow control also lets you iterate a set of commands until a certain condition prevails. As a simple illustration, let's modify our books file to include stock levels:

```
$ cat books
Author    Title     Price     Stock
Smith     Ants      $39.95    3
Jones     Cats      $29.95 .  0
Brown     Dogs      $19.95    81
$ _
```

We can write a simple awk program that selects books with dangerously low stock levels:

```
$ awk ´BEGIN { lowlevel = 5 }    # establish warning level
> NR > 1 { if ($4 <= lowlevel)
>          { print $0; count++ }
>        }
> END { if (count == 0 ) print "No low stock"
>       else if (count == 1) print "1 book low"
>           else { print count, "books low" }
>    }´ books
Smith     Ants    $39.95     3
Jones     Cats    $29.95     0
2 books low
$ _
```

I repeat an earlier caveat that once an awk program of more than one or two lines is debugged and proves useful, you would enter it into a file and use the -f *prog-file* option, or develop a suitable shell script.

The `if` and `else` statements work in an obvious way:

```
if (expression)
    action1
else
    action2
```

If the *expression* tests true, *action1* is executed and *action2* is ignored; otherwise, if *expression* tests false, *action1* is ignored and *action2* is executed. The tested expression is known as a *Boolean* expression: it's either true or false (no fuzzy in-betweens). Thus, `count == 0` is only true if awk found no books below the low stock level. Notice how I set this level in a variable and tested `$3 <= lowlevel`. I could have simply tested for `$3 <= 5`, but the given approach adds legibility and makes any future changes in the low level value much easier.

If *action1* involves several statements, they must be enclosed in braces to form a "single" action (known as a *block*). Even single actions, especially complex ones, are sometimes enclosed in braces to aid legibility. You can nest the `if`'s and `else`'s (with care) to set up sequences of actions to any degree of complexity.

There's nothing sacred about the layout of the given example. You can slap the code down on a single line without upsetting awk. All you need to remember is that an awk statement ends with either `;`, newline, or `}`. The parentheses around the expression to be tested *are* essential, but where you position the actions is a matter of taste. Certain rules have emerged over the years that give program texts a *structured* appearance. This is a great aid to the human reader in grasping the flow and logic of a program, but awk don't pay no mind.

There are two other control flow statements that I'll mention briefly: `while` and `for`. `while` lets you repeat an action until some condition tests false:

```
'BEGIN { i = 1 }
{
   while ( i <= NF ) {
   sum += $i
   i++
   }
}'
```

will add each field to `sum`. `i` starts at 1 and is incremented until it exceeds the number of fields, `NF`. Once it reaches `NF+1`, the `while` condition becomes false and the loop ends. If you are new to programming, you will almost certainly encounter the dreaded endless loop in your early coding attempts. Suppose, for example, that you

omitted the i++ statement in the last snippet. The while loop would keep adding $1 to sum with no end in sight! Perhaps an overflow error condition might intervene, but the condition tested by while, namely i <= NF, is permanently true. Always make sure that some action inside the loop is going to (eventually) make the while condition false. Forewarned is forearmed.

The for loop equivalent to the while example looks like this:

```
´{
    for ( i = 1; i <= NF; i++ )
        sum += $i
}´
```

After for you supply three statements (some or all may be empty) inside parentheses:

1. The loop initializer

2. The loop condition

3. The loop modifier

If the loop condition is true, the loop action, sum += $i in our case, is executed followed by the loop modifier. The loop condition is then tested again, and so on. For any while loop there is an equivalent for loop, and vice versa, so the choice is up to you. Both loops allow you to exit "prematurely" by using the break statement:

```
´{
    for ( i = 1; i <= NF; i++ )
        if ($i == "STOP LOOP") break
        sum += $i
}´
```

A more spectacular exit right down to the END pattern is available with the appropriately named exit statement.

```
´{
    for ( i = 1; i <= NF; i++ )
        if ($i == "END PROG") exit
        sum += $i
}´
```

awk Round Up

With a complex utility like awk, you can expect to make many false starts and iterations before your program works correctly. awk is relatively helpful in reporting any programming errors: it will indicate which line or expression has a syntax violation. You will often encounter the colorful error message: awk bailing out at line so-and-so. In awk circles, there are many black parachute jokes. I hope this brief introduction to awk has whetted your appetite. There are many features such as associative arrays that I have not mentioned. Appendix C lists several resources for continued study. You'll also see more awk applications in the next chapter where I delve more deeply into shell scripts.

Summary

In this chapter you met three widely used Unix tools in order of increasing complexity:

grep (global regular expression print)	A simple tool for locating string patterns in text files. The fgrep and egrep commands are close relatives.
sed (stream editor)	A non-interactive, "on the fly" version of the ed line editor. sed is used mainly in shell scripts to manipulate character streams (also known as text files).
awk (Aho, Weinberger, Kerninghan)	A sophisticated pattern processing language with flow control and arithmetical operators.

This trio provides a host of text manipulation features, ranging from simple pattern matching to complex edits and translations.

En route, you encountered

- Regular expressions for defining search patterns. You saw that, alas, the definition of "regular expression" is far from regular. The base set of regular expressions is common to ed, grep, egrep, sed, and awk, but there are additions and quirks as you move around these commands.

- The importance of quoting (escaping) certain metacharacters to hide them from the shell.
- The idea of operator *precedence* when combining certain operations. When in doubt, parenthesize, parenthesize…

CHAPTER

SIXTEEN

Advanced Shell Scripts

- The while loop

- The test command

- The read command

- if only

- Error handling

- The best case scenario

- Positional parameters

In this chapter, I'll build on the basic shell features introduced in Chapter 13 and the utilities covered in Chapters 14 and 15. The goal is the practical exploitation of the programming tools provided by the Bourne shell. I'll make the example scripts as useful as possible without too much heavy syntactical spade work. I'll analyze the scripts, show how they work, and offer suggestions on adapting them for your own applications. I'll also take the opportunity to revisit some of the trickier aspects of the shell: variables, assignments, and quoting.

The Menu, Please

Let's start by creating a simple menu from which you can select commands with a single keystroke. You've heard of painting-by-numbers: I now present Unix-by-numbers. Although naive, our first menu introduces several fundamental shell techniques and some new commands. Also, it provides a template for almost any kind of menu you may wish to create. If you find that you are regularly invoking commands with complex arguments, you can consider embedding them in a menu where they can be executed painlessly. Using ed or vi, create a file called mymenu.

```
$ cat mymenu
:
# @(#)simple 3-choice menu -- skb 1995
#
quit=n
clear
while test "$quit" = "n"
do
   echo "          Menu"
   echo "---------------------"
   echo
   echo "1.    List Users"
   echo "2.    Show Date"
   echo "3.    Quit"
   echo
   echo -n "Enter choice: .\b"
   read choice
   case $choice in
      1) who;;
      2) date;;
      3) quit=y;;
      *) echo "Invalid choice!\07\07"
```

```
        sleep 5;;
    esac
done
$ chmod +x mymenu
$ what menu.1
mymenu:
        simple 3-choice menu -- skb 1995
$ _
```

As the chapter proceeds, I'll explain how this script works. There will be several detours, so be patient. The layout of the script follows the guidelines for structured code that I discussed in the awk discourse (Chapter 15). Apart from the spacing between words (which the shell uses to parse commands), the shell ignores white space, so you are free to indent and align your code in any way you like. The aim is legibility, so you can see at a glance the overall flow structure of your script.

> **NOTE**   The term *blanks* refers to the characters designated in the string $IFS (internal field separators). These are space, tab, and newline by default. The term *white space* (also written *whitespace*) refers to any combination of space, tab, and newline characters. Unless you alter the value of IFS, therefore, the terms blank(s) and white space are essentially synonymous.

If you run mymenu, the screen clears, and the menu will be followed by the "Enter choice" prompt. The cursor awaits your input. You'll be able to execute who by selecting menu item 1, date from item 2, and exit back to the shell prompt with item 3. Any other selection will display Invalid choice, ring the bell, pause for five seconds, then redisplay the menu. We'll examine the code in detail with diverse digressions to clarify the new commands.

Helpful Comments

Two general points that apply to all the scripts in this chapter: First, I will assume that you are working in your own directories, that your PATH is set to include your working directory, and that you have the appropriate default read/write permissions. Second, if you want to run your scripts in the usual way (simply typing the

script name), you must remember to use chmod as shown to provide execution permission for your script files.

> Scripts can always be executed using sh *script_name*, but providing execution permission is usually more convenient. Executable scripts can be invoked directly by name just like any other Unix program. Also, you have *better* control over who gets to use your scripts.

If any of these conditions is overlooked, expect to get a "file not found" or similar message when you try to run a script.

The first three lines in mymenu establish good scripting habits. The leading : (null command) does nothing, but it does indicate to other programs that this is a Bourne shell script. For example, C shell users will be able to run mymenu without taking any special action. /bin/csh tests the first character of a shell program. If this is a # character, the program is assumed to be a C shell script and it will be executed by a spawned /bin/csh. On the other hand, when csh sees an initial non-# character (such as :), it invokes /bin/sh, the Bourne shell, to process the script. Bourne and C shell procedures have different syntaxes, of course, so /bin/csh will not always make much sense of a Bourne script, and vice versa.

The second line is a comment signaled by the leading # symbol. Any word *beginning* with # will be ignored, together with the rest of that line. You can write while #comment or while # comment, but # in the middle of a word will be taken literally: while#comment does not make a comment! The line continues with a special pattern, @(#), that is used by the what command.

```
$ what mymenu
# @(#)simple 3-choice menu -- skb 1995
$ _
```

what *filename* looks for lines in filename containing the pattern @(#) and displays what follows until it meets a tilde (~), greater-than sign (>), newline, backslash (\), or null. You should use this feature to give each script a title/author/date legend, and, with more complex scripts, a syntax/usage message. You can have as many such @(#) lines as you wish. By following this entirely optional convention, you make it easier

for you and your colleagues to check what a script is supposed to do. File names seldom reveal their full import.

The third line is also a comment, providing a blank line to improve legibility.

The while Loop

The script consists of a `while` loop that will execute relentlessly as long as the `quit` variable contains the value "n". The `while` construct is one of several *conditional* or *flow control* mechanisms that play a key role in all programming languages. Without them, a program would just roll on performing commands in the same fixed sequence. Allowing the execution to branch to alternative sequences, depending on user input or intermediate results, is the very heart of programming. The `while` shell command is conceptually the same as the `while` you met in awk (Chapter 15). The syntax, however, is rather different. The shell `while` follows the following format:

```
while w_list
do
       d_list
done
    ...
```

`w_list` is called the *while list*, and consists of one or more commands, separated by semicolons or newlines. These commands (which can contain arguments, redirections, pipes, other scripts, and all the other command mechanisms) are executed in the usual way. What happens next depends on the exit status returned by the last command executed in the `w_list`.

You will recall from Chapter 13 that each command returns an exit status (often known simply as the *return value*) to the current shell, which is a number used to indicate how the command performed. You can access this number via the special parameter $?. Although commands can be programmed to return completely arbitrary exit status values, there are certain ground rules that only cads and scoundrels dare to break. A zero exit status means *true* (the command was successful); a nonzero exit status means *false* (the commands failed for some reason). This is contrary to the convention used in C (zero=false, nonzero=true), but has the merit that programmers can use different nonzero exit status numbers to indicate the *reason* for failure. Truth shines out alone, but falsehood wears many faces. For example, `grep` returns zero if a match was found (success), 1 if no match was found (failure), and 2 if there was an error in the arguments (another kind of failure).

So far, we have noted this exit status phenomenon without making much use of it. But now it looms large: the while command takes note of the exit status of the final command in *w_list*: if *true*, the *d_list* of commands between do and done (known as the *do list*) is performed, and control then returns to the while command. The *w_list* is executed again, and so on. If the final exit status from *w_list* is *false*, the *d_list* commands are skipped and execution resumes with the command following done. Less verbosely, the while loop repeatedly executes the *d_list* while the *w_list* returns *true*. Now you know why it's called a while loop. The words do and done serve as block markers (the equivalent of braces in C and awk) for the do list. You should indent the commands in the do list so they stand out as one "unit" or block of code.

To be absolutely, technically exact, we should say that while examines the exit status of the last *simple* command executed in the w_list. As you've seen, commands can be complex affairs invoking showers of other commands. Indeed, there may be nested while and other conditional commands lurking in the w_list, and so on to unfathomable depths. Amidst all this generated activity, there will be a final, simple command with an exit status of interest to the outermost while command. It is this that determines whether the while loop will terminate (exit status *false*) or loop again (exit status *true*).

NOTE If the do list ends with done &, the whole loop will be executed as a background process.

break and continue

There are two commands you can place in the do loop itself that alter the above scenario. The aptly named break command causes an exit from the while loop, sending control directly to the command following done. If you have nested while loops, you can use break *n*, where *n* is a number defaulting to 1, to "break" out of *n* loops. A continue command in the do loop stops execution of the do loop and returns control to the enclosing while loop. Again, if you have nested while loops, the continue *n* sends control to the *n*th enclosing while command. After a break, the while loop is over; after a continue, the while loop continues.

break is useful when a condition arises in the loop that prevents further action. continue is used when a particular item in the loop cannot be processed, but you

want the loop to carry on processing further items. A typical example in *pseudocode* might be

```
while grab_next_item; any-left?
do
    if quota_full then break
    if item_empty then continue
done
```

We call this pseudocode because it does not have to follow the precise syntax of any computer (or natural) language. Rather, it can informally represent the logic and flow of an algorithm, and provide you with a useful guide for converting the algorithm into working code.

Endless Loops and the trap Command

Whenever you use the flow control commands such as while, you must always guard against endless loops. Some action in the loop should eventually lead to a *false* exit status when the while list is executed, or some condition in the do loop should invoke a break; otherwise the do loop will repeat blindly forever. There are occasions when an intentionally endless loop is useful. But such programs should warn the user and indicate the appropriate action for terminating the loop and (eventually) returning to the shell prompt. This is usually achieved with the key or Ctrl combination assigned to interrupt the program. The interrupt key is usually Rubout, Break, or Del but the default can be changed with the stty command:

```
stty intr ^a      # change interrupt key to Ctrl-a
```

Such changes are usually temporary and are intended to prevent "accidental" interruption during critical parts of a script. Your script can also trap (intercept) a user interrupt (and other unexpected signals) with the trap command and perform any set of actions before an eventual exit to the shell. trap is an internal shell command. The syntax is

```
trap ['commands'] [signo ...]
```

The optional *signo* arguments are the signal numbers you met with the kill command in Chapter 9. Each signal number (0-22, but the range varies with different systems) represents a type of signal that one process can send to another (using kill) or respond to when received from another process (using trap). Signal number 9 is the unique "killer" signal that cannot be trapped or ignored. Zero represents

the signal generated upon exit to the shell, 15 is the signal number for software termination (the default with the kill command), and 2 represents an interrupt signal generated by the currently assigned interrupt key. Another useful signal number to know is 1 for *hangup*. This is generated if the line is disconnected for any reason while a process is running. (The name comes from those occasions when someone hangs up the phone and cuts your link to the computer.) These signals represent a variety of "unexpected" calamities, and trap gives you a tool for ignoring them or handling them gracefully (except for the untrappable 9). When the specified signal numbers are trapped, the commands in the *commands* argument are executed. If *commands* is empty (" " or ' '), the signals are ignored by the shell.

Suppose your script generates a temporary file junk$$ in your home directory. $$ is the special shell parameter holding the process number for the current shell process. This is a useful trick for generating uniquely named files. Good housekeeping mandates that you erase this file before the program exits. A user interrupt or hangup could well frustrate this endeavor. The following line

```
trap "rm $HOME/junk$$; exit" 1 2
```

placed immediately after the file creation will trap signal types 1 and 2. Instead of an immediate exit, trap will run the command rm $HOME/junk$$ followed by an exit command. The latter, naturally, exits the current shell process. With no argument, exit will return an exit status equal to that of the last command executed. If the rm command failed (file not found), a nonzero exit code would be returned. By writing exit *n*, where *n* is a positive integer, you can set the exit status to *n*. You may recall my earlier statement that the exit status value is entirely a programming convention: successful operation should return zero, failure should return nonzero. You can now see how easy it is to break this convention. Unix relies on intelligent cooperation without heavy policing.

NOTE   **If you enter exit at the prompt, you'll terminate your login shell process, which means you'll be logged off the system.**

If the trap argument *commands* has more than one command, the whole argument must be quoted, since trap expects just one command argument (possibly empty). The double quotes are needed in the above example to allow $ substitution to occur.

In the absence of any arguments, `trap` displays a list of the commands associated with each signal number.

The `trap` *commands* `0` command lets you invoke *commands* when the shell is exited. If you set this trap in your login shell, any desired set of actions can be triggered when you log off.

The until Loop

This is a good moment to mention a simple variant of the `while` loop called the `until` loop. As the name might suggest, the `until` command will loop *until* a certain condition prevails rather than *while* a certain condition prevails. So, `until` simply reverses the sense of the `while` loop condition. Informally, you could say that

```
while X
do
   d_list
done
```

is equivalent to

```
until NOT-X
do
   d_list
done
```

Choosing between `while` and `until` really depends on the type of condition you are testing for. Sometimes the "positive" `while` condition is the natural (and easiest) one to test for; on other occasions, the "negative" `until` condition is more natural. Compare the following snippets:

```
while sleep 60
do
    who | grep stan
done
...
until who | grep stan
do
    sleep 60
done
...
```

Both versions will poll the list of users every 60 seconds to see if `stan` has logged in. The `until` version has the merit of exiting immediately if `stan` is already logged in; the `while` version sleeps for a minute before checking, and even after `stan` has

logged in, it will continue to report the fact every minute until either stan logs off or you interrupt the process.

The do List

The do list in mymenu displays the menu with a series of echo calls. You could display the fixed text of the menu with one big echo argument containing embedded newlines. I think that a separate echo for each line improves legibility and makes it easier to add or change lines.

Before we explore the do list, let's study the anatomy of the while command in more detail.

With awk, while is followed by a single Boolean expression. With the shell, however, while can be followed by any number of commands, of which the last one provides a "Boolean" value as a side effect. I mention this because you may find awk commands embedded in a shell script and you must avoid confusion between the two sets of grammars. In practice, the shell while is usually followed by a single command intended to control the loop. The most common of these single commands is called test.

The test Command

The test command is not an internal shell command like while, although it is rarely used outside shell programs. (More recent Unix versions have made test a built-in command, but this does not affect the usage outlined here.) test exists solely to return an exit status depending on its options and arguments. It is used after the conditional commands, while, until, and if, to provide a Boolean value for flow control.

> **NOTE** You should check whether you have an external /bin/test command. If so, resist the temptation to call any of your own programs test. If such programs are in directories in your PATH ahead of /bin, your scripts may misbehave.

In `mymenu`, the `while` loop is controlled by the following test:

```
while test "$quit" = "n"
```

Here, `test` compares the two strings `$quit` and `"n"` and returns *true* (zero) if the strings are equal. If the two strings are unequal, `test` returns *false* (nonzero). The `while` loop will therefore iterate as long as `$quit` evaluates to `"n"`. Remember that `quit` is a user-supplied variable, so `$quit` represents its current value.

> **NOTE** Note carefully the *essential* double quotes around each string and the *essential* spaces either side of the = sign.

The `test` command is so widely used that typing four characters proved irksome in the terse Unix environment. The following shorthand was therefore introduced:

```
while [ "$quit" = "n" ]
```

The character [must be treated like a command name (because it is!), so space is essential after the [. Further, since [invokes the `test` command in a certain way, it expects space before the closing]. This format for `test` is a more legible one in many contexts. Which version you use is a matter of personal taste, but you should be familiar with both in order to read and understand other programmers' code.

Variables, Values, and Quotes Revisited

The whole business of variables, values, and quotes, together with the syntax for assignment, substitution, and string comparison is a constant headache for beginners, so I'll digress a moment to clarify the situation.

When you assign a value to a variable, as in

```
quit=n
```

no white space (spaces, tabs, or newlines) is allowed on either side of the = sign. The right-hand side is interpreted by the shell as the string value, "n", to be stored in `quit`. You could write `quit="n"` or `quit='n'` with exactly the same effect. You need quote the right-hand side expression only if (1) it contains white space that is truly

part of the value to be assigned, or (2) it contains metacharacters that have special meanings to the shell.

There is no magical difference between assigning strings and numbers to a variable. `quit=n` and `quit=45` are equally valid. In `quit=45`, `quit` simply receives two characters that happen to be digits. You'll see soon that there are arithmetical (integers only) operations on `$quit` that could exploit this numerical value, but `quit` itself is not data-typed in the way that C variables are. (In the `awk` section of Chapter 15, I explained the concept of data typing.) Shell variables are actually string variables. If the string represents a whole number (positive or negative), you can extract its value, perform sums, and store the result as a string.

After `quit=n`, we have the single character "n" sitting inside the variable called `quit`. But if you `echo quit`, you'll simply display the string "quit":

```
$ quit=n
$ echo quit
quit
$ _
```

The shell must be "teased" into revealing the value of the variable called `quit`, and this is done by prefixing `quit` with the substitution metacharacter $:

```
$ quit=n
$ echo $quit
n
$ _
```

The shell "gets to" `$quit` first, "sees" the $, unlocks the value of `quit`, and passes this value as the argument to `echo`. Single (forward) quotes hide the $ from the shell:

```
$ quit=n
$ echo '$quit'
$quit
$ _
```

so no substitution takes place. Double quotes do not hide the $:

```
$ quit=n
$ echo "$quit"
n
$ _
```

Here the shell performs the substitution and passes the value "n" to echo. Since $quit and "$quit" echo in the same way, you may wonder whether the double quotes are useful. The reason is that quit may be assigned a value such as

"Now is   the hour" (note the extra spaces):

```
$ quit="Now is     the hour"
$ echo $quit
Now is the hour
$ echo "$quit"
Now is     the hour
$ _
```

In the first example, the shell passes four arguments to echo, namely the strings "Now", "is", "the", and "hour". The extra spaces between "is" and "the" are swallowed by the shell. echo displays the four arguments separated by single spaces.

In the second case, the double quotes around $quit preserve the embedded white space, and only *one* argument is passed to echo, namely the exact string stored in quit.

More test Options

With this in mind, let's return to the while loop test:

```
while test "$quit" = "n"
```

test has many applications, but here it is used to compare two strings. The test command syntax for string comparison calls for *three* distinct arguments: *string1*, =, and *string2*. This immediately alerts you that the spaces around the = *must* be present. "$quit=n", "$quit"="n", "$quit" ="n" or "$quit"= "n" are all wrong. The need for three arguments also implies that any white space in the strings being compared *must* be hidden from the shell. In the case of the fixed, literal right-hand string, either 'n' or "n" would be fine. On the left-hand side, only double quotes will work. As you saw earlier, "$quit" allows the $ to substitute and, equally importantly, passes the result as *one* argument to test.

But what if you need to compare strings containing a real, literal $? You would usually escape the $ with \ (backslash) since this hides the $ even within double quotes:

```
test "\$30" = "$val"
```

This would compare the string "$30" with the string stored in val. '$30' would also work. Table 16.1 summarizes how the different quoting methods work with each metacharacter.

> **NOTE** The syntax for string comparison with `test` uses a *single* = character (unlike the == equality test in awk and C).

TABLE 16.1: Quoting Methods

Quote	Metacharacter					
	\	$	*	'	"	'
'	n	n	n	n	n	t
'	y	n	n	t	n	n
"	y	y	n	y	t	n

n = not interpreted (hidden from shell)
y = interpreted by shell
t = terminates the quote

Testing Empty Variables

In addition to testing variables and strings for equality and inequality, `test` can tell you if a variable is empty (null) or not. You've met the notations " " and ' ' for the empty string. There are several ways a defined variable (also known as a *set* variable) such as `quit` can become empty:

- Unless `quit` is assigned a value, it *is* empty
- The assignment `quit=` (no right-hand value)
- The assignments `quit=""` or `quit=' '`

> **NOTE** The terms *empty string*, *null string*, and *string of length zero* all mean the same in this book.

If quit is empty, echo $quit simply displays a blank line:

```
$ quit=
$ echo $quit
$ _
```

What happens here is that the substitution operation $ applied to a null variable returns no value whatsoever, so echo does not receive an argument. If you try

```
$ echo

$ _
```

you'll get the same result. (Kernighan & Pike quotes Doug McIlroy's famous parable concerning the fair maid Unix and her dubiously crystal clear *echo*.)

NOTE   Variables are defined (or set) within a shell simply by being named without a preceding $. The occurrence of $quit, for example, does not define quit. If quit has not been defined, or has been defined without a value being assigned, $quit returns the empty string. Recall, also, that variables defined in a shell are not automatically defined in any of its subshells. You need an explicit export *var_name* statement in the parent shell in order that *var_name* will be known to its subshells.

The related operation unset quit actually removes quit from the shell's list of variables. quit is now undefined (unset), so asking if it is empty or not is a metaphysical question. echo will do its best:

```
$ unset quit
$ echo $quit

$ _
```

By the way, you can unset several variables in one fell swoop:

```
unset x y z
```

but, for obvious reasons, you cannot unset any of the predefined shell variables.

echo reacts to an empty, defined variable in the same way it reacts to an undefined variable. So, echo is not the ideal test for emptiness *or* existence! But worse follows:

```
$ quit=" "
$ echo $quit

$ echo "$quit"

$ _
```

quit now contains a space, so it's not empty in spite of appearances. In the second line, $quit produces a space which is immediately swallowed by the shell; echo gets an empty argument, hence the blank line. In line 4, a real space is passed to echo and is displayed, but you'll have to take my word for it.

Happily, test provides a more positive way of checking if a variable is empty or not. There are several options. Before I show them, recall that $? is the special shell variable that holds the exit status value of the last executed command. I'll use this to show the exit status of test with different options and arguments. First, we have the simplest test for null strings:

```
test var
```

or, to remind you of the synonym:

```
[ var ]
```

This returns true if *var* is not null, and false if *var* is null. For example,

```
$ quit=
$ test $quit
$ echo $?
1
$ test "$quit"
$ echo $?
1
$ quit=" "
$ test $quit
$ echo $?
1
$ test "$quit"
$ echo $?
0
$ _
```

When quit is empty, test returns 1 meaning *false*. When quit is nonempty, test returns 0 meaning *true*. So, test here is testing for "nonempty=true, empty=false." These negative queries are somewhat confusing, rather like the lawyer browbeating the witness: "Is it not the case that you have not denied that you refused to stop beating your spouse?"

The first two tests need careful attention. When you test the unquoted $quit, test receives no argument at all, yet it correctly reports an empty string. When you test the quoted $quit, test does receive an argument, namely " ". Again, the result is correct: $quit is empty. test *var* (like echo) treats no argument the same as a null-string argument. Many Unix commands, including some test variants, are less tolerant: if they expect an argument, they insist on one. The point is that in many contexts the empty string " " actually counts as a valid argument, as opposed to no argument at all!

The next examples use the −n and −z options for test. First the syntax:

```
test -n var
test -z var
```

The semantics here are less confusing. −n asks "Is the string length nonzero (string nonempty)?" and −z asks "Is the string length zero (string empty)?" Think of −n as "nonzero?", and −z as "zero?" Now the examples, and a little surprise:

```
$ quit=
$ test -z $quit
test: argument expected
$ echo $?
1
$ test -z "$quit"
$ echo $?
0
$ _
```

The lesson here is that text −z insists on precisely one argument. The unquoted $quit does not provide one, so you get an error message and a nonzero exit status (failure). When you quote $quit, test −z gets its argument, the null string, and returns *true*: quit is indeed empty. Similarly, test −n insists on an argument, but reverses the sense of the test:

```
$ test -n $quit
test: argument expected
$ echo $?
```

```
1
$ test -n "$quit"
$ echo $?
1
```

This time the test is for nonempty, so the answer is *false:* quit is not nonempty. See if you can follow the next examples where quit contains a space:

```
$ quit=" "
$ test -z $quit
test: argument expected
$ echo $?
1
$ test -z "$quit"
$ echo $?
1
$ test -n $quit
test: argument expected
$ echo $?
1
$ test -n "$quit"
$ echo $?
0
$ _
```

I make no apologies for grinding on about test, empty variables, null strings, and their quirky symbiosis. It's one of those subjects that pervade Unix: you start with a bewildering set of apparently unconnected facts, then suddenly the light dawns, and everything becomes obvious and intuitive. In spite of the mystical overtones, an awareness of the differences between an empty argument and no argument turns out to be useful when writing robust programs. A robust program is one that survives rough treatment, such as unexpected input. Your scripts should always anticipate peculiar input (including no input) from the user, issue a polite, helpful warning, then reprompt for correct input. The unfriendly script is the one that exits with an untrapped error from the shell itself.

Testing Numbers

test also lets you compare two integers, although the syntax is rather ungainly:

```
test "$X" -eq "$Y"
```

returns *true* (zero) if *X* equals *Y* numerically. Note that you are no longer testing for string equality. Ponder the following:

```
$ X=9; Y="00009"
$ [ "$X" = 9 ]
$ echo $?
0                       <true>
$ [ "$X" -eq 9 ]
$ echo $?
0                       <true>
$ [ "$Y" = 9 ]
$ echo $?
1                       <false>
$ [ "$Y" -eq 9 ]
$ echo $?
0                       <true>
$ [ "$X" = "$Y" ]
$ echo $?
1                       <false>
$ [ "$X" -eq "$Y" ]
$ echo $?
0                       <true>
$ _
```

The string tests reveal "9" and "00009" as unequal, but the numerical tests treat them as equal. You should repeat these tests with strings such as " 9 " and "09 ".

In addition to testing for numerical equality, `test` allows the following comparisons:

`"$X" -ne "$Y"`	Tests true if X not equal to Y
`"$X" -gt "$Y"`	Tests true if X greater than Y
`"$X" -ge "$Y"`	Tests true if X greater than or equal to Y
`"$X" -lt "$Y"`	Tests true if X less than Y
`"$X" -le "$Y"`	Tests true if X less than or equal to Y

Testing Files

The `test` command can also be used to check the existence of files and directories and what permissions have been set for them. The syntax is

```
test option file
```

The option is a single letter with some mnemonic significance, as shown below:

Option	test *option file* returns *true* if *file* exists and
-r	is readable (file or directory)
-w	is writeable (file or directory)
-x	is executable (file or directory)
-f	is a regular file (not a directory)
-d	is a directory
-c	is a character special file
-b	is a block special file
-u	its set-user-ID bit is set
-g	its set-group-ID bit is set
-k	its sticky bit is set
-s	has size greater than zero
-t[*fds*]	the open file with file descriptor *fds* is associated with a terminal device. (Default *fds* is 1.)

These provide considerable scope for checking on files before dangerous or illegal operations are attempted by your script. Recall my advice about averting abrupt program termination. A good example might be a script called `safecopy`. The user supplies two file-name arguments, *source* and *dest*. The script can access these as $1 and $2. The number of arguments is stored in $#. We could test the following:

- `test "$#" -eq 2` to ensure we have two arguments.
- `test "$1" = "$2"` to prevent spurious copying. (A more refined test would look at implicit and explicit paths, since two distinct strings can represent the same file.)
- `test -r "$1"` to see if *source* exists and is readable.
- `test -f "$1"` to see if *source* is a file (not a directory).
- `test -w "$2"` and warn if *dest* exists and is in danger of being overwritten.
- `test -d "$2"` to see if *dest* is a directory.

Multiple Tests

As the previous example indicates, you often need to test for a set of conditions, and test allows you to do this. You can combine Boolean expressions with the logical operators NOT, AND, and OR as you saw in the awk syntax in Chapter 15. The way you do it with test is less elegant than awk but quite manageable, as shown in Table 16.2.

TABLE 16.2: Mathematical Operations and Functions for test

Operator	Example	Meaning
!	[! expr]	NOT expr: *true* if expr tests *false*. *False* if expr tests *true*.
-a	[expr1 -a expr2]	expr1 AND expr2: *true* if both expressions *true*. *False* if either or both *false*.
-o	[expr1 -o expr2]	expr1 OR expr2: *true* if either or both expressions *true*. *False* if both *false*.

The [ ] notation here is much neater. The test versions would be test ! expr, test expr1 -a expr2, and test expr1 -o expr2. Here's a typical example:

```
filename=/usr/stan/richard.iii
if [ -r "$filename" -a -f "$filename" -a -s "filename" ]
then
    echo "$filename is a readable, regular, nonempty file"
    more -d "$filename"
else
    echo "Cannot display $filename"
fi
```

The if/else tests are quite obvious, but I'll cover them in detail later. We start by testing that filename meets three conditions before applying more to display its contents. It must be readable, a regular file (not a directory), and finally, it must have more than zero bytes. When combining logical operators, you need to watch the order in which they are applied. The test operators have built-in precedence rules that you can override by using parentheses. Before we examine these possibilities, let's review the basics. Just as

```
(x + y) x z
```

is not the same arithmetical expression as

```
x + (y x z)
```

the expression

```
(A OR B) AND C
```

is different from

```
A OR (B AND C)
```

In fact, George Boole's claim to fame was demonstrating the close affinity between arithmetical operators and the *Boolean* operators named for him.

The traditional way of evaluating complex Booleans is the *truth table*. The following truth table compares (A OR B) AND C and A OR (A AND C). We consider all the possibilities allowing A, B, and C to be true (T) or false (F). Let X = A OR (B AND C), Y = (A OR B) AND C.

A	B	C	X	Y
T	T	T	T	T
T	T	F	T	F
T	F	T	T	T
T	F	F	T	F
F	T	T	T	T
F	T	F	F	F
F	F	T	F	F
F	F	F	F	F

The differences in the X and Y columns establish that the two expressions are indeed distinct. Now consider the two expressions ! (A OR B) and (! A) AND (! B).

A	B	! A	! B	A OR B	! (A OR B)	(! A) AND (! B)
T	T	F	F	T	F	F
T	F	F	T	T	F	F
F	T	T	F	T	F	F
F	F	F	F	F	T	T

The last two columns are identical, so we have proved a useful identity:

```
! ( A OR B ) = ( ! A ) AND ( ! B )
```

It can be shown in the same way that

```
! ( A AND B ) = ( ! A ) OR ( ! B )
```

The built-in rules for `test` gives highest precedence to the string, file, and arithmetical operators (=, -eq, etc.), then comes –a (AND), and finally –o (OR). Higher precedence operations are evaluated before the lower precedence operations. This means that if you write

```
[ "$x" = "$y" -a "$n" -lt 0 -o "$m" -gt 30 ]
```

it will be interpreted, using conventional algebraic notation, as

```
if ( x=y AND n<0 ) OR ( m>30 )
```

If you wish to alter this interpretation, `test` lets you use parentheses (but they must be quoted):

```
[ "$x" = "$y" -a \( "$n" -lt 0 -o "$m" -gt 30 \) ]
```

You now have the distinct Boolean test:

```
if x=y AND ( n<0 OR m>30 )
```

Two vital facts about the parentheses: they must be quoted (the backslash offering the most convenient method) and they must have surrounding white space. The reason for quoting is that parentheses already have a meaning to the shell. You may recall that

```
( comm1; comm2 ) &
```

means run the two commands *together* as a background subshell process. The reason for the white space around \ (and \ ) is that, like the operators, the parentheses represent real, separate arguments to `test`.

Back to the Menu

In `mymenu`, the `quit` variable is set to the literal string value "n" before the `while` loop, and retains this value until you select item 3 to quit the menu. Once `quit` is set to "y", the `while` loop terminates. To be exact, the `while` loop would terminate if `quit` received any value other than "n". So you could concoct any number of equivalents to the given test:

```
while [ "$quit" != "y" ]
```

This loops while `quit` does *not* equal "y". You could also use:

```
until test "$quit" = "y"
```

or even,

```
until [ "$quit" != "n" ]
```

Note that the ! is the logical NOT operator, reversing the sense of the test. It can go in front of the = or in front of the whole expression. For instance, the last test could also be written as

```
until [ ! "$quit" = "n" ]
```

Of these five variants (and many more are available), the one used in mymenu seems the most "natural."

The read Command

The next element of our menu is the mechanism for inviting and receiving user input using the read command. The line

```
echo -n "Enter choice: .\b"
```

displays the argument string without a final newline because of the -n option. (The same effect can be obtained by adding \c at the end of the string.) The \b pair backspaces the cursor over the "." character. This is an optional trick; the idea is to display a dot for each input character expected. Typically, if a name of ten letters maximum was sought, the prompt would show

```
Enter Name: .........
```

and ten backspaces would bring the cursor to the entry point. The next line is

```
read choice
```

This reads one line from the standard input and places it in the user-defined variable, choice. In other words, the read command waits for the user to type something and when a newline is detected, read transfers the input to the argument variable. In fact, read can do more than that. If you supply more than one argument to read, the first word of standard input goes into the first argument, the second word goes into the second argument, and so on. Any excess words end up in the last argument. For example, if you had

```
read x y z
```

and the user typed "To be or not to be", x would pick up "To", y would pick up "be" and z would pick up "or not to be".

The read command has a useful property. Its exit status will be *true* (zero) until an end-of-file condition occurs during input. Once the end-of-file is sensed, read returns *false*. If read is getting its input from the keyboard, it will return *true* until Ctrl-D is typed. If input is being redirected from a file, read returns *true* until the end of the file is reached. This can be exploited in while loops. If myscript contains the following:

```
while read line
do
    process_line
done
```

you can use myscript <data_file to read lines and process data from data_file until it runs out of lines to process. Without redirection, myscript would accept and process manually typed lines until Ctrl-D is keyed.

NOTE From System V Release 2 onward, you can also redirect from a file to the read command: read line <data_file.

Sometimes read is used as a pause rather than as a way to invite useful data. The following snippet illustrates the familiar "Hit Enter to continue…" situation:

```
echo "Hit Enter to continue...\c"
read junk
```

It is worthwhile making this into a shell script, called pause. We can use it later to tidy up the menu.

if Only

In mymenu, choice will contain the item number selected by the user. Of course, there is no way of telling what the user may be inclined to type. Users are like that! The program must never assume that the value in choice contains only sensible responses to the prompt. Our script must now branch to the appropriate command depending on the value in choice, or warn if the value is unacceptable. We could proceed by testing the value of choice with a series of if/then/else statements.

As with `awk`, the shell's `if` conditional statement is quite straightforward (but watch out for the inevitable syntax variations):

```
if command-list
then
    action1
[else
    action2]
fi
next-command
```

The *command-list* follows all the rules given for the while list. If the last simple command executed returns *true*, *action1* (any list of commands) will be executed followed by *next-command*. Otherwise, if *command-list* returns *false*, the `else` branch (if present) is taken and the *action2* commands are executed followed by *next-command*. Analogous to the `do`/`done` block markers, we have the `if`/`fi` pair.

> **NOTE** It's critical to match each `if` with an `fi`—otherwise, the shell will not know which sections of code to execute. Furthermore, you'll get a syntax error!

The `else` section is not essential: it all depends on the logic of your program:

```
if [ "$#" -ne 2 ]
then
    echo "This command needs 2 arguments"; exit
fi
...
```

Once the number-of-arguments test is passed, the rest of the script can roll on without a specific `else` clause.

The contrary situation can occur. Sometimes you may want to skip the `if`/`then` action and simply perform the `else` section (for example, it may be easier to test for the "negative" condition). The trick is to use the null command, : (colon), the subject of the next section.

Busy Doing Nothing

Whenever the Unix syntax demands a command argument but you don't have a command to perform, you can use `:`. The null command satisfies the syntactical demand for a command but does nothing. You've seen it in a rather passive role as the first character in a Bourne shell script. A more active application is the "while forever" loop:

```
while :
do
  process
  if [ "$x" -eq 0 ]
  then
      break
  fi
done
...
```

The command list after `while` must contain at least one command. In a "while forever" loop, the while condition is deliberately made permanently true, and you rely on a `break` command in the do list to end the loop. The null command returns a zero exit status (true), so it offers one solution as shown above. A more legible solution is the `true` command. This also does nothing except guarantee a zero exit status. So you'll often see `while true`, as well as `while :`. There is a corresponding `false` command, guaranteed to return a nonzero exit status without doing anything else of note. You can create an "until-hell-freezes" loop with `until false`. Again, you must create a break with the `break` command if you want your loop to end (other than by a user interrupt). Another common use for `:` is to provide an empty statement after `then`:

```
echo "Enter author's name : \c"
read author
if grep "^$author " /usr/stan/books >/dev/null
then
    :
else
    echo "$author not found" >&2    # redirect to standard error
    exit 1
fi
...
```

If grep finds the target author (exit status 0, meaning *true*), we want to do nothing immediately. We are more interested in grep's failure. But if/then expects a command, so a blank line after then will invoke a syntax error. The : averts this tragedy.

Note the useful >/dev/null trick. You often meet the situation where a command in a shell script sends unwanted output to the screen. Here, we are using grep simply to see if a given pattern is matched, namely ^$author (the given author at the beginning of a line). Unless we take avoiding action, we risk the unnecessary distraction of matching lines on the standard output. The answer is to redirect unwanted output to /dev/null, a special "trash can" system file that takes everybody's rubbish without complaint. By the way, you cannot recover discarded data from /dev/null. If you read from /dev/null, you get an immediate end-of-file. In fact, that's a useful property of /dev/null: sometimes you need an immediate end-of-file!

Error Handling

The error message in the previous example introduces two important aspects of Unix commands:

```
echo "$author not found" >&2
exit 1
```

We exit with a nonzero status code so that if your script is incorporated in another script (by you or somebody else), other commands can check for failure and take appropriate action. The general idea is that if prog1 calls prog2 and prog2 exits with exit *n*, then prog1 can access *n* as $? to determine the cause of the exit. Since prog2 may have called prog3, and so on, this sequence exit checks can be nested indefinitely.

Without an argument, exit returns the status of the last command executed, and oftimes this will provide a suitable status value to the calling program. In the previous example, however, the last command performed before the error exit is a *successful* grep command! We must therefore use exit 1 (or any agreeable positive integer) to signal failure to any surrounding command.

The message from echo is redirected from the standard output to the standard error using the symbol & followed by 2, the file descriptor allocated to standard error (see below). You can write either >&2 or >& 2, but no spaces are allowed between > and &.

ADVANCED USERS ONLY

Three standard files are opened automatically and have preassigned file descriptors as follows:

0	Standard input
1	Standard output
2	Standard error

Unix assigns a unique numerical fd (file descriptor) to each file that is opened for processing. C and other languages allow programmers to access files via their fd's (until the file is closed). At the shell script level, you will usually only be concerned with the three standard fd's listed above.

The syntax for accessing a file with fd (file descriptor) n is

command >& n	redirect output from command to file with fd n
command <& n	redirect input from file (with fd n) to command
command 2> file	redirect standard error output from command to file
<&–	close the standard input
>&–	close the standard output
n>&–	close the file with fd n
1>&2	send standard output to standard error
2>&1	send standard error to standard output

Most of the standard Unix commands use >&2 (or equivalent) to send error messages to standard error rather than to standard output. Your own scripts should follow the same strategy. Although standard output and standard error are both, by default, assigned to your screen, they are separate "files." If your error messages are sent to the standard output, there can be a problem. If you redirect the standard output to a real file, your error messages will also be redirected, usually with depressing consequences. If you send errors to standard error, of course, they will appear on the screen, by default, even if standard output has been redirected. You can redirect from standard error to a file, though, just as easily as you redirect standard output to a file. The syntax is either

```
command 2>file     # NO spaces allowed between 2 and >
```

or

```
command 2> file    # space OK here
```

The following examples may clarify the situation.

```
$ ls amelia
amelia not found
$ ls amelia >junk
amelia not found
$ _
```

The error message appears on the screen (standard error) in spite of the standard output being redirected.

```
$  ls amelia 2> errfile
$ _
```

Standard error is now redirected to errfile, so no error message appears. Look at the contents of errfile:

```
$ cat errfile
amelia not found
$ _
```

The elif Command

Nesting a sequence of if / then / else / fi conditions can become quite complicated:

```
if test "$choice" = 1
then
      who
else if test "$choice" = 2
      then
           date
      else if test "$choice" = 3
           then
                quit=y
           else echo "Invalid choice!\07\07"
                sleep 5
           fi
      fi
fi
...
```

To simplify such chains, the `elif` can be used in place of `else if...fi`:

```
if test "$choice" = 1
then
      who
elif test "$choice" = 2
then
      date
elif test "$choice" = 3
then
      quit=y
else echo "Invalid choice!\07\07"
      sleep 5
fi
...
```

This is still rather awkward. The `case` statement offers a simpler (and faster) solution.

The Best case Scenario

Most languages have a `case` multibranch flow control mechanism. (BASIC has ON X GOTO..., C and Pascal have `case`) In theory, `case` is not needed since there is always an equivalent sequence of `if`'s and `else`'s. In practice, the `case` mechanism offers safer, faster, and more legible coding. The `case` syntax is easier to use than to define exhaustively. Here is the overall scheme:

```
case word in
pattern1)   command-list1 ;;
pattern2)   command-list2 ;;
pattern3)   command-list3 ;;
...
esac
next-command
```

The complete `case` statement starts with `case` and ends with `esac` (`case` spelled backwards). The *word* argument is an expression whose value will determine which branch to take. Each branch is "labeled" by a pattern, and whichever pattern first matches *word* will invoke its associated command list. After which, control moves to beyond `esac` to what I've called the *next-command*. The last command in each *command-list* must end with *two* semicolons.

NOTE The pair of semicolons is in fact optional after the final command list, but it's safer to use them after every command list. If you ever need to add an extra pattern at the end of a `case` statement, the penultimate command list will not need changing!

Before I clarify the syntax, let's look at the menu example:

```
...
   case $choice in
       1) who;;
       2) date;;
       3) quit=y;;
       *) echo "Invalid choice!\07\07"
          sleep 5;;
   esac
done
...
```

If `choice` receives 1 from the `read` command, a match is made with the first pattern: `1)`, so the `who` command is invoked. All the other patterns are then skipped, and control moves out of the `case` statement. Similarly choices 2 and 3 invoke just the commands associated with the `2)` and `3)` patterns. What if `choice` contains a 9? The first three patterns do not match, but the fourth pattern is `*` that matches zero or more occurrences of *anything*. In fact any `choice` other than 1, 2, or 3 gets "trapped" by the final `*` pattern (including null). For this reason, you'll find that most `case` statements end with this catch-all pattern. The patterns available in `case` are a special set of regular expressions, as tabulated below:

Pattern	Matches
`*`	Anything (including nothing)
`?`	Any single character
`[abc]`	Any one of "a", "b", "c"
`[a-m]`	Any one character in the range
`pat1|pat2`	Either `pat1` or `pat2`

These patterns borrow both from `ed` and the file substitution patterns used by the shell, with some private quirks thrown in to add to the fun. `ed` uses "." (period)

rather than "?" to match any single character. ed also uses "*" differently. With ed, r* matches zero or more occurrences of r. With case, r* matches r and r followed by any character. In addition, you can quote metacharacters with double or single quotes, or with \, to match their literal values. The menu uses single character patterns, but it's common to find more complex patterns:

```
case $day in
[Mm]onday|[Ll]undi)        monday_wash;;
[Tt]uesday|[Mm]ardi)       tuesday_dry;;
...
[Ss]unday|[Dd]imanche)     sunday_school;;
*)                         echo "Not a day...";;
esac
```

It is quite legal for a pattern to have an empty command list, meaning ignore the matching cases. For example,

```
case $choice in
    0) ;;
    1) who;;
    2) date;;
    3) quit=y;;
    *) echo "Invalid choice!\07\07"
       sleep 5;;
esac
```

would take no action if 0 was entered as the choice.

Branching with && and ||

There's a neat alternative to the if/then branch. Rather than write

```
if command1
then
    command2
fi
```

you can achieve the same ends with

```
command1 && command2
```

In other words, if *command1* returns 0 (success), *command2* will be executed; if *command1* returns nonzero (failure), *command2* will be ignored. You can slot in *command1* && *command2* at any point in a script where a command is legal. Once you get used

to this construct, it can save you the time spent laying out the if / then statements. For example,

```
grep "^$author " $fil >/dev/null && cat $fil >> biblio
```

will append the file $fil to biblio if the given author is found in $fil. If grep fails for any reason, the cat command is skipped.

The construct

```
command1  ||  command2
```

works the other way round: if *command1* fails, *command2* is executed; if *command1* succeeds, *command2* is ignored.

```
grep "^$author " $fil >dev/null || echo "$author not found"
```

You met the symbols && and || in a similar context in the awk section (Chapter 15). In awk they stand for the logical AND and OR operators used with Boolean expressions. In the shell, && and || have a slight affinity to AND and OR, but only in the context of two commands.

More Menu

To make use of some of the commands discussed so far, let's add a few choices to the menu:

```
$ cat newmenu
:
# @(#) simple 6-choice menu -- skb 1995
#
quit=n
prevdir=`pwd`
dir=prevdir
clear
while test "$quit" = "n"
do
   echo "          Menu"
   echo "---------------------"
   echo
   echo "Your current directory is `pwd`"
   echo
   echo "1.    List Users"
   echo "2.    Show Date"
   echo "3.    Display a file"
```

```
      echo "4.     Change working directory"
      echo "5.     Return to original directory"
      echo "Q.     Quit"
      echo
      echo -n "Enter choice: .\b"
      read choice
      case $choice in
      1) who | more
         pause;;
      2) date
         pause;;
      3) echo "Enter file name: \c"
         read fil
         if [ -r "$fil" -a -f "$fil ]
         then
            clear
            more -d $fil
         else
            echo "Cannot display $fil"
         fi
         pause;;
      4) echo "Enter target directory: \c"
         read dir
         if test -d "${dir:=`pwd`}"
         then
            cd $dir
         else
            echo "$dir: no such directory"
         fi
            pause;;
         5) if test "$dir" != "$prevdir"
            then
               cd $prevdir
            fi
            pause;;
         Q|q) quit=y;;
          *) echo "Invalid choice!\07\07"
             sleep 5;;
      esac
   done
 $ _
```

In addition to the new items, we've made a few minor improvements. who | more will give page pauses if your system is busy (moral: always assume the worse case!). The original choice of 3 for the quit option left much to be desired. By making

it "Q" or "q" we have less renumbering to do as we add new items, and, some would claim, it's a more natural choice. Note how we store the original directory:

```
prevdir=`pwd`
```

The backquoted pwd runs the pwd command *in situ* (right then and there) and returns the current working directory, which is then assigned to the variable prevdir. A quick test on your quota of "quote" understanding: do we need any additional quotes around the expression `pwd`? Single forward quotes would definitely be wrong. '`pwd`' would pass the literal five-character string `pwd` to prevdir since single forward quotes hide the command substitution meaning of the backquotes. Double quotes would work fine but they are not needed here. The pwd command returns a single, well-behaved value with no white space or metacharacters. We also store the initial working directory in dir. This value may change later if item 4 is selected.

The pause command is the small script I mentioned earlier, made executable with chmod.

```
$ cat pause
:
# #(@) pause til Enter key pressed...      skb 1995
#
echo "Hit Enter to continue...\c"
read junk
$ chmod +x pause
$ _
```

Menu items 3 and 4 illustrate the file test commands used to avoid abrupt exits if illegal names are entered by the user. If we simply invited user input for dir and invoked cd $dir without testing, the shell might well intervene. Remember that read puts you at the mercy of Homo sapiens, a species capable of typing anything or nothing. So, we have to decide how to handle nondirectory input (test −d being the obvious ploy); we also need to cope with a null input. If the user presses Enter (or spaces followed by Enter) rather than typing a decent directory, dir will be empty or white space. cd $dir will give us cd with a null argument which is quite valid: it returns the user to his or her HOME directory. If this is what we want, we could write

```
if test ! "$dir"  -o  test -d "$dir"
then
    cd $dir
```

This says, if dir is null or a valid directory, invoke cd.

The new menu, though, takes a different tack. If the dir entered is null, we set it to the current directory. This means that a null entry leads to no change in the current directory. The code to achieve this uses one of the clever conditional parameter substitutions that I mentioned way back in Chapter 13:

```
if test -d "${dir:=`pwd`}"
```

The ${dir:=`pwd`} expression says: if dir is set and not null, replace the whole expression with $dir; otherwise, assign to dir the value given by `pwd`, and then replace the whole expression with the new $dir. We then test $dir to see if we have a valid directory. If so, we cd to $dir. To help you keep track of which directory you are in, we display `pwd` each time the menu is displayed.

Do I need to remind you that directory changes made within this script are *not* remembered when you exit back to the shell? What you can do with this menu is cd to the appropriate directory before selecting item 3 to display a file.

Positional Parameters

As a naive example of the use of positional parameters n, suppose we allow the menu to take an item number argument. I'll call the new menu qmenu (q for quick). qmenu 1, for instance, would immediately invoke menu item 1. To reduce repetition, I'll limit qmenu to two choices. The example will illustrate some of the multiple tests I've been discussing. Testing that the right number of arguments has been supplied, as well as checking that the arguments are valid, is an essential part of safe scripting.

```
$ cat qmenu
:
# @(#) quick 2-choice menu -- skb 1995
#
if [ "$#" -gt 1 ]
then
     echo "Usage: qmenu [1|2]"; exit
fi
if [ "$#" -eq 1 -a \( "$1" -le 0 -o "$1" -gt 2 \) ]
then
     echo "Invalid argument: must be 1 or 2"; exit
fi
if [ "$#" -eq 0 ]
then
```

```
      quick=n
  else
      quick=y
  fi

  quit=n
  clear
  while test "$quit" = "n"
  do
    echo "          Menu"
    echo "----------------------"
    echo
    echo "Your current directory is `pwd`"
    echo
    echo "1.    List Users"
    echo "2.    Show Date"
    echo "Q.    Quit"
    echo

    if [ "$quick" = "n" ]
    then
        echo -n "Enter choice: .\b"
        read choice
    else
        choice=$1
        quick=n        # back to normal menu in next loop
    fi
    case $choice in
        1) who | more
           pause;;
        2) date
           pause;;
      Q|q) quit=y;;
        *) echo "Invalid choice!\07\07"
           sleep 5;;
    esac
  done
  $ _
```

The test shown below

```
  if [ "$#" -eq 1 -a \( "$1" -le 0 -o "$1" -gt 2 \) ]
  then
      echo "Invalid argument: must be 1 or 2"; exit
  fi
```

illustrates the use of quoted parentheses to override the precedence of the Boolean operators. We are testing that

> Number of arguments equals 1
>
> AND
>
> (argument is less than 0 OR greater than 2)

Since -a has a higher precedence than -o, the parentheses are needed. Without them, you would be testing

> (Number of arguments equals 1 AND argument is less than 0)
>
> OR
>
> argument is greater than 2

Note the use of the variable quick. It is often helpful, both for execution speed and legibility, to use a variable to store the result of some complex test. Later on, you simply test the variable rather than repeat the original test (indeed, in many situations the original test may become impossible because other conditions and states have changed). There are no dogmatic rules in such cases: only constant practice and experiment will hone your skills.

The for Loop

The for loop has a do list between do/done keywords, just like while. The difference lies in how the do list is executed. With while, the do list can iterate any number of times (or none at all), depending entirely on the return value of the command list. The for loop iterates a specified number of times, although, as with while, you can use the break command to exit the loop at any time. The key difference is that with a for loop, a given variable is successively assigned different, specified values each time round. Here's a simple example before we tackle the formal syntax:

```
for x in a b c
do
    echo $x
done
```

The do list is the single command echo $x, which will be executed just three times. In the first loop, x is set to "a"; for the second loop, x is set to "b"; in the third and final loop, x is set to "c". The output from this snippet will be:

```
a
b
c
```

The number of iterations is determined by the number of words occurring after in. Changing the for line to

```
for x in a b c d
```

for example, would produce one more loop with x set to "d". The output would be:

```
a
b
c
d
```

Now consider:

```
for x in "a b" c d
do
    echo $x
done
```

Yes, as you probably guessed, we only loop three times, since "a b" represents one word. The output will be

```
a b
c
d
```

The words after the in statement can be any expressions that can provide values (including null) to be assigned to the "roving" x variable. The shell will perform file-name substitutions in such expressions before the for loop starts, so:

```
for filename in *
do
        process $filename
done
```

is a neat way of applying the command process to each file (excluding dot files) in the current directory. * will generate a list of all such files, and then assign each one in turn to the variable filename. Similarly,

```
for filename in poem.[1-3]
do
      process $filename
done
```

will process the three files poem.1, poem.2, and poem.3 if they exist.

The most common application for the for loop is scanning the command line and processing each command argument. Since $* represents all the arguments entered with a command, you can write

```
for arg in $*
do
    process arg
done
```

Here arg will assume, in turn, the value of each word produced by the sequence $1, $2, up to the final argument. Recall that $# represents the total number of arguments. There's a subtle *gotcha* here. If $1 is an argument containing white space, such as "a b", the for loop will see it as *two* words, and will loop twice, with arg set to "a" and then with arg set to "b". Even if you write

```
for arg in "$*"
```

the for loop will still see $1 as two words. The solution is to use

```
for arg in "$@"
```

I mentioned $@ briefly in Chapter 13. When $@ is unquoted, it behaves exactly like $*. You can picture $@, $*, and "$*" all producing the same sequence of positional parameters: $1 $2...$n, so that any spaces lurking within them provide unwanted words to the for loop. Once you double-quote $@, however, the shell provides the sequence "$1" "$2"..."$n". Each parameter is now double-quoted and each therefore presents a single word to the for loop, regardless of any internal white space. Unless you are *absolutely* certain of the contents of each $n, the safest way to scan an argument list is with "$@".

Here's a simple testbed for you to play with this mechanism.

```
$ cat teststar
:
# @(#) test 'for' loops with $*
#
echo "We have $# arguments"
for arg in $*
do
    echo $arg
done
$ cat testat
:
# @(#) test 'for' loops with "$@"
#
echo "We have $# arguments"
for arg in "$@"
do
    echo $arg
done
$ chmod +x teststar
$ chmod +x testat
$ teststar jim mary stan
We have 3 arguments
jim
mary
stan
$ testat jim mary stan
We have 3 arguments
jim
mary
stan
$ teststar "jim mary" stan
We have 2 arguments
jim
mary
stan
$ testat "jim mary" stan
We have 2 arguments
jim mary
stan
$ _
```

The crunch is that "jim mary" stan looks like two arguments to both test scripts, but teststar nevertheless passes three word arguments to for. testat behaves

more reasonably: two arguments beget two words for the loop. Having belabored the importance of `"$@"`, I can now announce that `"$@"` is the *default* if you have no in arguments at all! `testat` could be written as

```
:
# @(#) test 'for' loops with "$@"
#
echo "We have $# arguments"
for arg
do
    echo $arg
done
```

The `for` provides a powerful tool for creating a host of useful scripts. The "roving" variable can assume values from a wide variety of sources, not just the positional parameters inherited from the command line. Consider a command such as `date` that produces six words. The following session shows how you can pass these six words to a for loop:

```
$ for x in `date`
> do
> echo $x
> done
Wed
Jul
5
09:15:32
GMT
1995
$ _
```

Yes, you can type this sequence directly. The secondary prompt will prompt you until `done` is entered. It's quite useful for experimenting with small loops prior to making scripts. Note the difference when you quote `date`:

```
$ for x in "`date`"
> do
> echo $x
> done
Wed Jul 5 09:15:32 GMT 1995
$ _
```

The set Command

There is a more powerful way of accessing the components of date's output, similar to the one you saw with awk. The set command, which is built into the shell, lets you assign your own values to $1, $2,... by breaking down the words in any expression. Remember that the positional parameters are not true variables, so you cannot directly reassign their values with $*n=X*. They start life with values dictated by the command's arguments, and only shift and set can alter them. set offers a simple way of assigning values to the positional parameters:

```
$ set `date`
$ echo $1
Wed
$ echo $5
GMT
$ echo $#
6
$ for x
> do
> echo $x
> done
Wed
Jul
5
09:15:32
GMT
1995
$ set
...
PATH=/bin:/usr/bin::/usr/stan/bin
PS1=$
PS2=>
SHELL=/bin/sh
TERM=ansi
x=1995
$ _
```

What magic is this? set has taken the words generated by date and passed their values, one by one, to the variables $1,...$6. The for loop with the default in "$@" argument proves that all six parameters have been set. It also sets $# to the number of parameters set.

set is often used to count the number of "words" in an expression, a "word" being any sequence of nonwhite-space characters surrounded by white space.

set is a rather overburdened command. As you can see from the previous session, if you enter set with no arguments, it displays the names and values of all variables defined in your environment, whether local or exported. set can also take options with or without an expression argument.

set takes many options from -- to -x, and thereby lurks a little snag. If you try to set an expression that begins with -, set will interpret it as an option with weird results. So set -- *expr* must be used to turn off the normal - action.

The two most useful options for budding script writers were mentioned in Chapter 13: -v and -x. These are used when debugging a shell script. With all but the most trivial scripts, it can be most frustrating when your program does not behave as intended. And programming being what it is, you must expect bugs. One debugging trick is to embed lots of temporary echo $x and echo "while loop reached" commands in your script in order to see whether values are being assigned as intended, and whether loops are looping correctly. set offers more help.

The -v (for verbose) option causes all shell input lines to display as they are read by the shell. The set -x (for execute) option puts the shell into *trace* mode until a set +x turns the trace mode off. You can enter set -x and set +x at the prompt while testing a script. While trace mode is on, you can see the executed commands displayed with a preceding + sign. Trace also shows you the variable assignments as they take place. The nice thing is that all the standard substitutions are made first (file-name wildcards, variables, and backquoted commands). Tracing does not automatically extend to any subshell activity, but you can insert set -x and set +x directly in any script. You can combine the two options with set -vx.

Doing Sums

My final section will cover briefly the arithmetical tools available in the shell. First, the bad news. The shell offers only integer arithmetic. If you want floating point decimals, you must use awk, dc (a stack-based arithmetic package), or bc (an interactive calculator with a C-like syntax). See man section C for details.

The less-bad news is that shell sums are quite easy. I touched on the fact earlier that shell variables simply hold strings of characters. To convert a string such as "23" into a number, you use the command expr in man section C. expr is rather like the

VAL function in BASIC. expr takes any sequence of "number strings" together with the five familiar arithmetical operators:

+   Plus

−   Minus

*   Multiply (must be backslash quoted!)

/   Divide

%   Modulus (also known as remainder)

The operators *, /, and % have higher precedence than + and −. expr evaluates its arguments and displays the result on the standard output. For example,

```
$ expr 2 + 3
5
$ expr 2 \* 3
6
$ a=4
$ a=`expr $a + 3`
$ echo $a
7
$ expr $a + 6
13
$ _
```

There are three quirks to remember. First, you must space between the numbers and operators (but you've met similar problems with other commands where the syntax demands distinct arguments):

```
$ expr 3+2
3+2
$ _
```

Second, you must backslash the * (multiply), else the shell substitutes file names! Lastly, when assigning the results of an expr operation, the command must be backquoted as shown.

Script Review

Our simple examples have introduced many of the constructions needed to craft more complex shell scripts. A common theme in all programming endeavors is putting together small "self-contained" chunks of code (called modules) to achieve a

complex goal. In mymenu, we have a `case` statement embedded in a `while` loop. In the extended version, some of the `case` branches involve further input and tests.

Summary

Here are the topics and commands introduced or amplified in this chapter:

The comment character #.

The special pattern @(#), used by the `what` command.

Control constructs:

```
while X do Y done
until X do Y done
break and continue
if W then X else Y ... [elif Z...] fi
case X in label) Y;; ... esac
for X in Y1 Y2 ... do Z done
```

The positional parameters $n. $0 is the name of the program, $1 to $9 hold the first nine arguments. Use `shift` to access any arguments beyond the ninth.

Using braces to avoid ambiguity in parameter substitutions: ${name}x appends x to $name, which is not usually the same as $namex!

Conditional expressions of the form ${Var: opValue}, where op can +, −, = or ?.

The `test` command: `test` X or synonym [X] can test strings, files, and numbers.

The `set` command sets shell options and reassigns positional parameters. `unset` "undefines" shell variables.

Shell sums with `expr` and +, −, *, /, and %.

CHAPTER

SEVENTEEN

Reaching Out to Remote Computers

- UUCP

- Unix and networking; reaching the promised LAN

- Introducing TCP/IP and Ethernet

- Distributing files over the network

- Client-server computing

- Accessing the Internet

- `finger`, `ftp`, and `telnet`

- Mailing other networks

In Chapter 5 you saw the `mail` program in action, sending and receiving email to and from users on the same Unix system. In this chapter you'll see how easy it is to converse with other Unix (and non-Unix) sites. As well as mail text, you can send (upload) files of any type to other systems or receive (download) files from other systems. The other systems must cooperate, of course, and we will explain how their help is solicited.

We'll also explore some of the widely used commercial and noncommercial Unix networks and the services they offer. Telecommunications is one of the most useful and rapidly growing areas of computing. Vast amounts of digital data pass each day through copper wire and optical fibers, not to mention the luminiferous ether, to and from computers and terminals in all five continents. Analog voice data now takes second place compared to the volume of digital data. The applications are legion. Transactions on the Tokyo stock exchange are available within seconds on the Wall Street analyst's disk drive. Clusters of corporate PCs interact with mainframes, LANs (Local Area Networks), and WANs (Wide Area Networks). Weather and military satellites gather and transmit billions of bits each day to dedicated supercomputers. Over 76,000 different sites carry USENET to over 2.5 million users, all wired to exchange information via Unix systems large and small. Are you getting your share?

Transmission speeds are also increasing from year to year. 14,400 baud modems are now available at prices that would have bought a now-laughable 2,400 baud device five years ago. The software to support these advances has also escalated in size and sophistication. New protocols emerge regularly to improve accuracy, handle the connectivity jungle better, and simplify the user interface.

In the modern context, telecommunications and networking includes not only exchanging mail and files, but being able to access resources at a remote computer, for example, executing commands on a far distant Unix system.

I'll start this chapter by exploring the UUCP network and the collection of programs that underpin many of the Unix telecommunications tools, then introduce several important networking concepts, and then close the chapter with a look at the programs you can use to explore the wonderful world of the Internet.

UUCP

There is a specific command available on almost every Unix system called uucp (Unix-Unix copy in man section C) that you can use directly to send and receive files. It is just one element in the UUCP network software, a varied collection of programs and files that knits together Unix systems worldwide and beyond. Note the uppercase UUCP to distinguish the network and the complete family of commands from uucp, one particular program in that family. Most of the commands in UUCP start with the (lower-case) letters uu (thus, uuname, uulog, and so on), which makes them easy to spot in a crowd. There are many situations where UUCP commands will be invoked behind the scenes without your direct involvement. For example, when commands such as mail and mailx (described in Chapter 5) are used to send mail to remote UUCP sites, it is actually the UUCP family of programs that do the work.

UUCP has undergone much change and improvement since the first version released in 1976. The most prevalent version now is the one released in 1983, known unofficially as the HoneyDanBer UUCP (named for the three principal authors: Peter Honeyman, David A. Nowitz, and Brian E. Redman); the official title is rather more prosaic: BNU for short, or Basic Networking Utilities in full. The older Version 2 UUCP and a BSD variant are still around, so you should check which version is available on your machine. If you have the older versions, expect a few minor differences in some of the features, file names, and command options.

TIP

A quick check on UUCP versions: Look in the /usr/lib/uucp directory. Version 2 UUCP has a file called L.sys. BNU UUCP replaces this with a file called Systems. If you have a Sun running SunOS 4.0 or later, you will not see either file. You will find your L.sys file, (as well as some others normally found in /usr/lib/uucp) in /etc/uucp instead.

UUCP is designed for use with standard serial cables, modems, and telephone service. If you have an Ethernet LAN, with or without a connection to the Internet, you do not have to use UUCP; you will usually need ftp instead. Most of the time, you won't have to make this choice, since a specific remote computer will only be

accessible by one type of connection. More on ftp—and the Internet—later in this chapter.

Making Contact

There are some essential requirements before you can use UUCP. First, there must be a physical link between the two UUCP computers. In addition to the sites "directly" reachable from your system, there may be many more that can be accessed indirectly via other networks such as USENET or the Internet. Links with non-Unix commercial networks such as CompuServe and MCIMail are also available. The basic connectivity principle is simple: if site A has a link with site B, and B has a link with site C, B may be able to act as a bridge handling mail and file transfers between A and C. If A and C are nodes of distinct networks, and B is able and willing to act as a bridge, B is called a *gateway*. Your link with yet another site, say D, may call for a chain of connections, A to B, B to C, and C to D, involving a varied mix of machines and protocols. With the many thousands of UUCP and networked systems currently running, it is almost certain that a path exists between any two given sites. In fact, it is often the case that you have a choice of paths. Certain sites, known as *backbones*, are especially "well-connected," so once you find a path to a backbone, you can usually reach out and touch anybody!

Second, UUCP must be installed on *both* the local and remote sites. Installing UUCP is a fairly complex operation best left to your vendor or a knowledgeable system administrator, although menu-based tools, such as the SCO UNIX sysadmsh, are now available to simplify matters. This initial setup establishes various configuration files that determine how and when communications links are to be made: port numbers, dialup and security procedures, and so on. The system administrator also establishes a unique UUCP name, often called the *node name*, for the site and sets up a list with the name of each remote UUCP system that can be reached directly. You need to know your own node name as well as the names of any remote system you wish to contact via UUCP.

NOTE   It is also possible to set up one side of a UUCP link as a passive system—a system that can be called by other systems, but that will never originate calls of its own.

An important point that affects UUCP (and many other transmission protocols) operation is that UUCP is a "store-and- forward" system. Your commands are spooled (or queued or batched) by UUCP, just as you saw with the print services in Chapter 10. For example, mail to remote sites is stored locally and sent at convenient intervals. The timing of the transmissions is dictated by parameters set in various files by the system administrator. UUCP is very flexible. Sometimes, transmission will occur as soon as a link is established between the two sites. Often, the remote site is dialed during off-peak hours to reduce the telephone bill.

UUCP Applications

UUCP provides several important services:

- Determining your local node name
- Exchanging mail between Unix sites using `mail` or `mailx`
- Executing commands on a remote Unix system using the `uux` command and the non-uucp `cu` and `tip` commands
- Transferring files between Unix sites using the `uuto`, `uupick`, and `uucp` commands
- Checking the status and progress of your UUCP jobs with the `uustat`, `uulog`, and similar commands

In the following sections, we will describe how you can use all of these commands.

The uuname Command

The uuname command is used to determine your local node name as well as the names of all UUCP systems that are immediately known to your system:

```
% uuname
basis2
ola
isis
mtxinu
beast
...
% _
```

uuname without an option lists the names of all the UUCP systems known to your site. uuname with the −1 (local) option tells you your local system name. uuname with the −c option lists all the systems known to the cu command. This list is often the same as that given by uuname, but cu (call up) is not strictly speaking a UUCP command. I'll explain the differences in a moment.

Who You Gonna Call?

Suppose you know that Anne, with login name anne, is a valid user on the system called isis. uuname tells you that isis is "reachable" directly from your system, known as basis. Sending mail to Anne is as simple as mailing someone on your own system:

```
% mail isis\!anne
From:    basis!stan (Stan Kelly-Bootle)
To:      isis!anne (Anne B. Margaret)
Subject: This is a test!

Dear Anne: let me know if you don't receive this memo.
Stan
.
% _
```

Note that the recipient's login name is prefixed by the target system name and a bang (!). The general syntax for UUCP addresses is

```
system_name!user_name
```

With the C shell you must escape the bang with a backslash. This is because the C shell interprets ! as the history substitution prefix (see Appendix A). With the Bourne shell you could simply mail isis!anne, since ! is not a Bourne shell metacharacter. I tend to use \! always, out of habit, regardless of which shell I am running. The bangs in the text of your mail shot, of course, are not "seen" by the shell and need not be escaped. You signal the end of your mail text in the usual way with either a period in the left-hand margin or with a Ctrl-D (end-of-file). (Try which of these works on your system.) If the mail has been wrongly addressed, you will get an error message, but not necessarily right away. Anne will eventually get a You have mail notice, and she can use mail on her machine to read something like this:

```
You have mail

$ mail
```

```
From uucp Sun Jul 9 10:31 PST 1995
>From stan Sat Jul 8 9:24 PST 1995 remote from basis
Status: R
From:     basis!stan (Stan Kelly-Bootle)
To:       isis!anne (Anne B. Margaret)
Subject: This is a test!

Dear Anne: let me know if you don't receive this memo.
Stan
? _
```

The header indicates the sender, the sender's system name, the time of the original composition, and the time of receipt. (Your header format may differ.)

If and when Anne responds, she would mail me at basis\!stan. All of your usual mail facilities are available, including the simple transmission of small (less than 64K bytes) files using redirection.

With mail you can only *send* files, and these files cannot exceed 64K bytes. For larger files, you must use uuto (send only) or uucp (send or receive), covered later in this chapter. Another disadvantage to using mail to send files is that the header mail attaches to the file can be a nuisance: your recipient may have to delete it before making use of the received file.

Mailing Binary Files

The only files you can physically transmit are pure ASCII text files. The reason is that many of the nontext control codes have special meanings to the telecommunications hardware and software. (Indeed, the control codes are so-named because they are used to control devices such as modems!) In order to transmit binary coded files, they must first be translated to text format, then translated back again to binary by the receiver. UUCP offers the uuencode and uudecode commands (both in man section C) to achieve this. To send a binary file called prog by mail, you could use the following command line:

```
% uuencode prog /usr/anne/prog | mail isis\!anne
% _
```

The first argument is the name of the file to be encoded. The second argument is the ultimate path name to be assigned when the file is decoded at the remote site. The output of uuencode is then piped through the usual mail *addressee* command. Anne at isis will receive a strange-looking encoded ASCII message in her mail. She then saves this message into a file called, say, prog.encoded. This file will

be about 35% longer than the original binary prog file. prog.encode contains a header encoding the permissions field and the destination name, /usr/anne/prog. She can recover the binary data by entering

```
$ uudecode prog.encoded
```

uuencode creates a file called prog in the usr/anne directory. This will be a copy of the original prog with the same permissions. For those sites regularly exchanging binary files, the whole encoding and decoding process can be automated by creating a special "decode" user account to receive encoded files. You then set the send-mail environment variable in .mailrc (the local mail resource file) to a suitable shell command. The default sendmail is /bin/rmail, the standard tool for delivering mail. The replacement for rmail can invoke uudecode automatically on all messages arriving at the "decode" user.

Forward, Please!

Now suppose that Joe is on a system called scouse, a node name not known to my basis system. To reach Joe I need to find a willing backbone: an intercessory site that (1) is known to basis and (2) knows scouse. If, say, mtxinu fits the bill, I could mail Joe as follows:

```
% mail mtxinu\!scouse\!joe
Joe: whadya know?
sTaN (tm) (basis!stan)
% _
```

I can reach mtxinu, and mtxinu can reach scouse. Then Joe can reply to me using mtxinu\!basis\!stan. Or perhaps he knows a different path between us.

Chains between cooperating sites can be of any length. The general syntax is

```
system_name1!system_name2!system_name3..!user_name
```

where each system knows the following one, and the final system has your target *user_name* as a registered user. This mechanism is known as *forwarding*: each system forwards your mail to the next one named in the address chain (also known as the network path name).

The backbone sites are "better-connected" than others and equipped to forward mail. You can soon build up a list of these to help establish network addresses. Business cards often show net addresses: research!skb, mtxinu!bison!dick, and so on. The first node listed is usually a backbone site.

Several utilities exist to help you determine possible routes through the network. If you have uuhosts available, entering uuhosts *target_name* will list possible paths from your site to *target_name*. A path database managed by pathalias and a mailing program called uumail are available on some systems. These let you uumail scouse!joe without worrying about the routing. You can also use a command called uupath to query the path database.

The .mailrc File

As your address list grows in size and complexity, it is worth exploring the features available in the extended versions of mail. You can preset many parameters in a file called $HOME/.mailrc. This is your personal mail resource file, as opposed to the system-wide (or global) mail resource file called /usr/lib/mail/mailrc. At startup time mail will execute the global resource file (if present), then your personal resource file (if present). The idea is very similar to the profile files you saw in Chapter 6. You should first see if you have a .mailrc in your home directory. If not, create one with ed or vi. If you already have a personal mail resource file, list the contents to see what defaults are being set for you. The two commands that are relevant here are alias and set. alias lets you assign shorthand strings for lengthy addresses. set lets you assign values to the special mail environment variables. You can add lines to your .mailrc file such as the following:

```
$ cd
$ cat .mailrc
alias dave beast\!uunet\!david
alias mark mtxinu\!scouse\!isis\!mkh
alias edd mary joan stan alf
set Sign="Your old pal, Stan Kelly-Bootle"
set sign="Contributing Editor, UNIX Review"
...
$ _
```

You can now use dave and mark in lieu of the longer addresses. You can mail edd rather than mail mary joan stan alf. The Sign variable is used as follows: whenever you enter ~A (tilde A) during mail input, the string value set in Sign will appear in your mail text. Similarly, ~a (tilde a) will cause the string assigned to sign to appear. The tilde must be entered at the beginning of a line. There are nearly thirty of these special tilde escape commands (see your mail or mailx manual).

Executing Commands on a Remote System

Running commands on a distant system takes several different forms. The cu command (and a Berkeley variant called tip) is not part of the UUCP family but is mentioned in this chapter since it offers related services. cu stands for *call up*; it lets you call a remote site (including non-Unix systems), log in (assuming you have a valid account and password), and perform interactive work. This may sound like normal remote operation from a dialup terminal, but with cu you are connected to both your local Unix system and the remote site. cu lets you "toggle" between the two systems, running commands locally and remotely as the mood takes.

The UUCP remote execution command, uux, is less flexible than cu. With uux, you set up commands that are batched and executed remotely at some future time. The scheduling, as with file transfer, is determined by configuration files established by the system administrator. Remote execution can also be delayed (or rejected) by the receiving system for obvious reasons: you may be trying to access protected directories, or the remote device requested may be offline. You are usually informed via mail if your requested command has been executed successfully. So uux only provides "interactive" computing if you are of a patient disposition! Commands sent by uux are usually background jobs that run non-interactively by specific permission of the remote site.

The most common use of uux is resource sharing. If another site has a fancy laser printer, for example, you may be allowed to print your local files on the remote laser. In return, you could perhaps share your expensive plotting device with the other site. uux can invoke the appropriate lp command on the remote system and also enlist the help of uucp to download the files (which may even be stored at a third site!) to be printed. Several batching operations are now involved. First, the local UUCP would queue the lp command and transmit it at some convenient time. Accessing the files might also invoke a batch process. Finally, the remote site would spool your print requests. If all goes well, your files will be printed and mail will advise you accordingly. With UUCP, however, you can track the progress of these operations without waiting for the mail to arrive. You'll meet the uustat and uulog tracking commands later on.

UUCP Security

From the previous overview, it should be clear that security is a critical aspect of UUCP. Since each site has its own security awareness and protection schemes, it is hard (and possibly dangerous) to give you a definitive picture. You must find out what rules are imposed on your particular system and on the systems you wish to "talk" to. Most systems keep an extremely tight control over who can read and write files or execute commands from remote systems. Clearly, you must prevent intruders reading sensitive files. You must also stop strangers overwriting your files or depositing *Trojan Horses*. Trojan Horses are program files (often deviant versions of familiar commands) that can lurk unnoticed for long periods before wreaking havoc on your system. *Worms* and *viruses* are other threats that have been widely publicized. A common solution to such invasions is for each site to have a public directory called PUBDIR which holds subdirectories for incoming and outgoing files. This is often the *only* area that can be accessed from outside. Attempts to read or write files from/to directories outside this public area can be disallowed even if the target directories and files have the appropriate local permissions. PUBDIR insulates file transfers from the main file hierarchy and reduces the chances of accidental or deliberate corruption of your system.

PUBDIR usually represents the path name /usr/spool/uucppublic. This directory may have a general subdirectory called receive for holding incoming files. There may also be special subdirectories set up to handle file transfers for specific users or to/from specific sites.

It is important to realize that with UUCP there are two levels of access permissions at work. In addition to the usual file read/write/execute and directory read/write/search permissions that control access within your own system, UUCP allows the system administrator to place overriding restrictions for UUCP access to specific nonpublic directories.

Any directory to which UUCP sends files must have the read/write/search permissions set for "others." Further, files being transferred must be readable by "others" and must reside in directories that are readable/searchable by "others." For example, if you examine PUBDIR and its subdirectories with ls -ld you'll see that they all have rwx set for "others." The reason for this apparent contradiction is that UUCP as a *user* (called uucp and belonging to the group other or bin) needs to access directories and files that it does not *own* in order to transmit them! The pseudo user name uucp should not be confused with the uucp command, of course. If the

file to be sent is owned by you and has, say, rw-rw---- permissions, a UUCP process running under the user uucp cannot read it. End of transmission! Even if you are root, UUCP must have "others" read permission. The file must have at least r-- in the "others" permission field. Similarly, the directory holding the file to be transmitted must have "others" search permission (at least --x in the "others" field).

The converse problem can arise. Once a file or directory is copied by UUCP, the permissions of the originals are retained, *but* the copy is now owned by the user uucp! As the receiving user, you may well inherit files that you cannot delete because you lack write permission on the received directory. Another point that may confuse you: when I talk about UUCP *copying* a directory, this does not imply copying its files and subdirectories. UUCP simply *creates* the named directory on the target system: you need to specify (using wildcards, perhaps) the actual files to be copied into that directory. Later on, I'll show you methods that overcome this limitation. There are ways of creating special files that contain an entire directory together with its files, subdirectories, their files, and so on down the hierarchy.

A common solution to the permissions hazards is to set up your own public directory, such as /usr/stan/public, with full permissions (use chmod 0777). This can hold files (each set with chmod 0666) for UUCP operations without you having to relax the permissions on your normal working directories and files. To avoid tedious repetition, I'll often use the word *file* in the wider Unix sense to include both directories and files. I'll also assume that the directories and files involved in all the following UUCP examples have the appropriate permissions set. Failing these, expect messages such as "remote access to path/file denied." And note that such rejections may take some time reaching you!

In the next section, I'll show you the simplest way of exchanging files, using the uuto and uupick commands.

Using the uuto and uupick Commands

The uuto command is actually a Bourne shell script offering a simplified file-copying service based on uucp. (You can list uuto if you wish, and see how it works. Consult your colleagues, however, before making changes!) If you don't have uuto on your system, you'll have to learn the more complex syntax of uucp to be described later. uuto copies files to a public directory on a remote system and automatically advises the recipient by mail when they arrive. You need to know the remote system path name

as explained in the `mail` section above. For example, to send the file `memo` to `anne` on the `isis` system, enter

```
$ uuto memo isis\!anne
$ _
```

If your recipient is not directly reachable, you need to go via a cooperating gateway:

```
$ uuto memo mtxinu\!scouse\!joe
$ _
```

You can send several files with `uuto` simply by listing them with white-space separators:

```
$ uuto memo poem ode isis\!anne
$ _
```

Where will the `memo` file to `isis\!anne` be written? For security reasons, `uuto` sends files to a subdirectory (typically called `receive`) of the public directory, `PUBDIR`. By default, the variable `PUBDIR` is set to `/usr/spool/uucppublic`. The full path name of the `memo` file as received at `isis` will be

```
/usr/spool/uucppublic/receive/anne/basis/memo
```

For this reason, `uuto` is known as the public Unix-to-Unix file copy utility. When the file arrives at `isis`, Anne will receive a mail message something like

```
From uucp Sat Aug 12 10:45 PST 1995
 /usr/spool/uucppublic/receive/anne/basis/memo
from basis!stan arrived
```

This path name is quite an eyeful, but it turns out to be a rational and useful scheme. Breaking down the path, you can see that the general format is

```
$PUBDIR/receive/rec_user_id/send_system/filename
```

So the path name tells you the sender system, the target user, and the file name. On a busy system with hundreds of users receiving many files from different systems, you might find thousands of entries in the `$PUBDIR/receive` directory. Each recipient has his or her eponymous subdirectory, and each sending system has its own subsubdirectory. When you think about it, any remote file transfer scheme has to guard against the inadvertent overwriting of files. If both `basis!stan` and `mtxinu!stan` (different Stans!) send different files called `memo` to `isis!anne`, chaos

can ensue if they hit the same directory on isis. Under the uuto protocol, Anne would receive two files:

```
$PUBDIR/receive/anne/basis/memo
```

and

```
$PUBDIR/receive/anne/mtxinu/memo
```

When Anne gets her UUCP mail, she knows which files have arrived and where they are. Although she can use mv to move the files into her own directory (the public area is accessible to all, remember), the uupick command is specially designed to simplify this operation. There are excellent reasons to move received files from the public area as quickly as possible. First, of course, is the obvious point that the files are vulnerable in PUBDIR. Second, the public directories are considered as temporary abodes and are regularly purged by the system administrator.

Here is a simple example of uupick in action:

```
$ cd /usr/ann/public
$ uupick
remote from system basis: file memo
?
m
10 blocks
remote from system scouse: file junk
?
d
?
q
$ _
```

First, Anne moves to her public directory. This has rwx permissions for everyone and provides a convenient place to collect incoming directories and files. Like other UUCP programs, uupick will usually move files only into directories that have read/write/search permissions for "others." uupick works rather like mail in receive mode, prompting with ? for your action. You then respond with either m for move, d for delete, Enter to skip, q for quit, and so on.

When Anne enters uupick with no options, each subdirectory of $PUBDIR/receive/anne is scanned, looking for files received from all sender sites. You can limit this search to a specific sender site by using the −s sender_name option. For example,

```
$ uupick −sbasis
```

would scan only the $PUBDIR/receive/anne/basis directory and report just the files sent by basis. If you already know the file name, you can add this as an argument:

```
$ uupick -sbasis poem
remote from system basis: file poem
?
...
```

For each file found, uupick displays the sending system name and file name followed by the ? prompt. If a directory has been received, uupick tells you:

```
$ uupick
remote from system basis: directory accounts
?
...
```

Your response after the ? prompt determines what happens next. You can move the file to your current directory with m or delete it with d. If you just press Enter at the prompt, nothing happens to the current file, and uupick passes on to display the next file (if any). uupick exits when it runs out of files, or you can quit at any time with a q. Table 17.1 lists all the interactive commands available with uupick.

TABLE 17.1: Interactive Commands Available with uupick

uupick Option	Action
Enter	Moves to next entry, if there is one; current file remains in public directory
*	Help: lists available commands
d	Deletes current file from public directory (no copy made); directories are deleted recursively using rm -rf
m[*dir*]	Moves current file to *dir* (default is the current directory)
a[*dir*]	Moves all files received from current site to *dir* (default is the current directory)
p	Displays contents of current file
q or Ctrl-D	Quits uupick
!*command*	Escapes to shell and executes *command*

Returning to uuto, there are two useful options, –m and –p, you should know about:

```
$ uuto -m memo isis\!anne
$ uuto -p poem mtxinu\!joe
$ uuto -mp accounts scouse\!mary
```

The –m option tells UUCP to mail the *sender* when the file has been successfully transferred. Recall that the *recipient* is always mailed when the file arrives.

The –p (copy) option works as follows. The poem file you are sending will be copied into your local spool directory before uploading. It is this copy that will be transferred regardless of any changes you might make to the original poem. Without the –p option, UUCP will transfer the file from its particular directory. Since you never know exactly when the transfer will be scheduled, you may not be sure which version of a rapidly changing file is sent. (You may recall the same problem when passing files to the printer services.) A worse scenario is where you delete poem thinking that it has been safely uploaded! The –p option would have saved your bacon. Another point about –p concerns permissions. If poem is owner-only readable, –p will make an unprotected copy suitable for later UUCP transfer. (Some versions of UUCP will actually default to –C if the file to be sent lacks the proper permisssions; see Table 17.2 later in the chapter.)

uuto copies *to* public directories on remote systems. For more general file transfers, to and from public and nonpublic directories, you need the more powerful uucp command, the subject of my next section.

The uucp Command

The uucp command differs from uuto in several respects:

- uuto copies files only *to* a remote system. uucp copies *to* and *from* any two systems (local to/from remote or remote to/from remote).

- uuto copies files to the PUBDIR public directories. uucp can copy files to and from any directories that have appropriate permissions, including PUBDIR. Because of this difference, uucp requires that you supply full path names for the remote files.

- uuto lets you use uupick to automate the handling of received files. With uucp you must handle the files with mv, cp, and similar commands.

Here are some examples:

```
$ uucp memo isis\!/usr/spool/uucppublic/memo.anne
$ uucpisis\!/usr/spool/uucppublic/poem /usr/spool/uucppublic/stan/
$ uucp chap.* isis\!/usr/mary/
$ uucp isis\!/usr/mary/prog.\* /usr/stan/
```

The first line copies the file `memo` in my current directory to the file `memo.anne` in the public directory at the `isis` system. The second line copies the file `poem` from a public directory on `isis` to the `stan` subdirectory of `PUBDIR` on my system. Here, we are copying files *from* a remote site, a feat that neither `uuto` nor `mail` can perform.

The third example sends all files matching `chap.*` in my current directory to Mary's home directory on `isis`. If all goes well, Mary will find the files `chap.1`, `chap.2`, and so on in `/usr/mary/`. The final `/` is vital! Without it, `uucp` would copy into a file called `usr/mary`. The wildcard `*` is *not* escaped since I want *my* shell to expand it.

The fourth and final example demands careful study. Here we are downloading files from the remote to the local site, a trick that `uuto` cannot do. The last line copies all `prog.*` files in Mary's home directory to my home directory. In this case, the wildcard `*` *must* be escaped. Can you see why? The reason is that this `*` has to be expanded by Mary's shell rather than by my shell. `uucp` must pass the `*` to the other site. Without the backslash, my shell would get to it first with chaotic results.

Of these four examples, only the first could be achieved with `uuto`. With the `uuto` command, the second transfer would only be possible if a user at `isis` undertook to send the file to me. Note that with `uuto` the `PUBDIR` paths are implied; with `uucp`, they must be explicitly stated. But before you go crazy typing these long path names, make note of a handy short cut: `~/` (tilde slash) can be used in place of `/usr/spool/uucppublic/`:

```
$ uucp memo isis\!~/memo.anne
$ uucp isis\!~/poem ~/stan/
$ _
```

TIP Care is needed when using the tilde with the C shell. A leading tilde is expanded by the C shell to the path name of the user's home directory. Tildes embedded inside paths are ignored by the C shell and will therefore be expanded by UUCP to give PUBDIR. You can escape the tilde with a backslash to protect it from the C shell. On recent Unix versions, you can use uucp as the shorthand for the PUBDIR directory when using the uucp command regardless of which shell you are using.

In theory, you can use uucp to transfer files directly between ordinary user directories, as shown above. But recall my earlier warnings that such transfers will only work if the source and destination directories are readable, writable, and searchable by "others," and if the files are readable by "others." Further, the source and destination must be allowed by the appropriate read and write permissions in the Permissions files at each site. In most cases, unless you make special arrangements with both the local and remote sites' system administrators, you will be forced to use PUBDIR directories.

The basic uucp syntax is quite simple:

```
uucp [flags] from to
```

This syntax is very much like the cp (copy) command. You specify the source file(s) in the *from* argument, possibly with wildcards and paths, followed by the destination in the *to* argument. With uucp, the *from* and *to* arguments can also specify the system names of the sites involved, as explained in the mail and uuto commands. The defaults are quite natural. If you omit the system name, uucp assumes your local system name. (It's quite legal, but rarely useful, to send yourself files with uucp: *from* and *to* can both be the same system.) Directory defaults need some care. In the following example,

```
$ uucp chap.* isis\!/usr/mary/
```

the *from* path defaults to my current directory. Since I specify a directory in the *to* argument, the files copied will be in that directory with the file names unchanged. If I specify a directory that does not exist in the target, uucp will create one (permissions allowing). Suppose I send

```
$ uucp chap.* isis\!/usr/mary/tmp/
```

If Mary had no tmp subdirectory, uucp would create one and then copy the chap.* files there. This can sometimes be a nuisance to Mary, so uucp has a useful –f option that says don't create the destination directory if it's not there:

```
$ uucp -f chap.* isis\!/usr/mary/tmp
```

As with uuto and its –p option, uucp has the –C option that lets you control whether a copy of the file being sent is spooled immediately, or whether uucp takes the current file when it is ready to transmit. The option letter is different, but the effect is the same. The –m option is the same for both uuto and uucp: the *sender* is notified by mail when the file transfer has succeeded. uucp also has the –n*user* (notify) option to mail the named user when the file arrives. Table 17.2 summarizes the main uucp options.

TABLE 17.2: Common Options for uucp

uucp Option	Action
–f	Prevents creation of destination directories
–C	Copies source file to spool directory before transmission
–j	Displays UUCP job id
–m	mail sender when transfer succeeds
–n*user*	mail *user* on remote system when transfer succeeds

Keeping Track with uustat and uulog

Since UUCP simply takes your requests and spools them, you need a method of checking the status of your commands. If your command is complete nonsense, of course, UUCP is able to reject it immediately:

```
$ uucp poem
usage uucp from ... to
uucp failed completely
$ _
```

The lack of instant error messages, however, does not imply success! Your command is floating around in the bowels of Unix, and various daemon processes will be prodding it from time to time beyond your immediate ken.

> **NOTE**
>
> Daemons (pronounced "daymons"), you will recall, are background processes that perform regular tasks for the Unix kernel. For example, `cron` is the clock daemon that can execute arbitrary commands at dates and times specifies by the `at`, `batch`, and `crontab` commands. Other more specialized daemons, such as the printer daemon, are set to scan the status of queues and invoke the appropriate action.

Beginners have been known to panic at the apparent lack of response and repeat their UUCP command; this simply risks the future duplication of the job (not always a sound idea). The next section offers a solution to this problem.

Tracking UUCP Jobs

Each time you invoke a UUCP command, either directly with `uuto` and `uucp`, or indirectly with `mail`, the appropriate requests are queued and assigned a unique UUCP job id. The word *job* resists a precise definition: take it as identifying a group of tasks for achieving a certain UUCP command. The requests are stored in various files in subdirectories of the `/usr/spool/uucp` directory that make up the UUCP database. As jobs are processed, this database is updated, so tracking their progress is really a matter of interrogating the UUCP database. To protect you from long-winded files such as `/usr/spool/uucp/.Log/uucico`, UUCP supplies the `uustat` and `uulog` commands that pull out and list the relevant status information.

`uustat` (man section C) lists the status of all (or selected) recent UUCP jobs. The word *recent* is relevant since UUCP's housekeeping process, known as the *cleanup daemon*, regularly (you can set the intervals) deletes old jobs (you can set the age) from the queue. Even incomplete jobs that for some reason have been lurking around too long will be expunged (although you can *rejuvenate* such jobs with the `-r` option). With no options, `uustat` lists the following data about each of your own UUCP pending jobs:

Job id	A unique id for this job
Submit time	The date and time your job entered the queue
Mode	S = send request; R = receive request
System	Name of target site

User id	Login name of user invoking the job
Job	For uux: name of program to be executed remotely
	For uucp: size and name of file being transferred

Table 17.3 summarizes the options that modify the action of uustat.

TABLE 17.3: Options Modifying Actions of uustat

uustat Option	Action
-a	Lists all jobs for all users in queue
-u*user*	Lists jobs queued by given *user*
-s*system*	Lists jobs queued for the remote site given by *system*
-m	Lists status of all connected sites (lists queue-count, last-action-date, and status)
-q	Lists jobs queued for each site (lists queue-count, last-action-date, and status)
-k*jobid*	Kills the UUCP request given by *jobid* (must be issued by owner of this job or by the superuser)
-r*jobid*	Rejuvenates the job given by *jobid* (sets the date-last-modified to the current date on all files associated with *jobid*)

Only uncompleted jobs can be killed with uustat -k*jobid*, and naturally you need to know their job ids. You should run uustat without options first to obtain the job id of the job you wish to cancel. Furthermore, you can kill only your own jobs unless you are the superuser (root). The superuser can kill any UUCP request. Of the uustat options, only the -u and -s options can be combined in the one uustat command. Together, they will select those jobs for a given user and a given remote site. For example:

```
$ uustat -sscouse -ustan
```

will list Stan's UUCP requests aimed at the remote system scouse.

uulog provides a more detailed account of what UUCP is doing by listing the various status messages saved (logged) by UUCP processes in various log files in subdirectories of the /usr/spool/uucp/.Log directory. As with uustat, you can use the -s and -u options to limit the listings to a given remote system or a given user id.

So far in this chapter we have looked at a simple UUCP connection between two Unix computers. In the next few sections, we'll describe the position Unix occupies in the larger world of networking, and conclude the chapter with a discussion of the world's largest computer network, the Internet.

Unix and Networking; Reaching the Promised LAN

The largest growth area in computing today is the connection of PCs and workstations into local area networks (LANs). Networks allow users to share resources, such as file servers, printers, and communications hardware, as well as data. Networks are providing the basis for important business applications, often based on the client-server model, and in many corporate environments the network is seen as a cost-effective replacement for the large mainframe computer of days gone by.

In this section, we'll look at each of the major components of networking and examine the ways the Unix community has solved some of the complex problems associated with networking.

Introducing TCP/IP and Ethernet

One of the most common kinds of Unix system in use today is a group of workstations and servers connected together using an Ethernet cabling system and the TCP/IP suite of protocols. TCP/IP is a whole set of communications protocols that define how computers of the same or different type communicate with each other. Two of these protocols, Transmission Control Protocol and Internet Protocol, give TCP/IP its name, but they perform very different functions:

- IP moves information between computers in the form of a datagram, a message unit that contains source and destination information as well as the data itself.

- TCP ensures that the datagrams that comprise a transmission are reassembled in the correct order at their final destination, and requests that any missing datagrams be resent until they are all received correctly.

NOTE   See Appendix C, "Unix Resources," for sources of more information on TCP/IP.

Other protocols provided as part of TCP/IP include the following:

- Address Resolution Protocol (ARP) translates between Internet and Ethernet addresses.

- Internet Control Message Protocol (ICMP) is an error message and control protocol.

- Reverse Address Resolution Protocol (RARP) translates between Ethernet and Internet addresses; RARP is the reverse of ARP.

- Simple Mail Transport Protocol (SMTP) manages mail via TCP/IP.

- Simple Network Management Protocol (SNMP) performs distributed network management functions.

- User Datagram Protocol (UDP) provides an alternative delivery system, but without the guaranteed delivery features of TCP.

Users rarely have to deal directly with TCP/IP, but a system administrator may have to configure or even troubleshoot TCP/IP. In SCO UNIX, the `netconfig` program is used to install the device drivers, configure the kernel, and modify the startup files, and `ifconfig` is used to configure the network interface card.

NOTE   TCP/IP packages are also available for the Macintosh, DOS, Microsoft Windows, and OS/2 systems.

Computers on the network can be connected in a variety of ways, including thick or thin Ethernet coaxial cable, twisted-pair wiring, or fiber-optic cable. The original Ethernet standard specifies baseband transmission at 10 megabits (10 million bits) per second, but recent developments known by various names including fast Ethernet are pushing this transmission speed to 100 megabits per second.

Distributing Files over the Network

Several elegant systems exist in Unix that allow for *transparent* file sharing across the network. Transparent in this context means that you don't know or care where the files are physically located, because they always act as though they are on the local computer. The only time you might need to know where they are actually located is for reasons of efficiency, security, or disaster recovery. Sooner or later in your travels in the Unix world, you will encounter the Network File System (NFS) and the Network Information Service (NIS). Let's look at both of these facilities.

NFS

The Network File System was originally developed by Sun Microsystems almost a decade ago, and now it is hard to imagine a Unix system without it. NFS allows a computer on the network to use the files and peripheral devices of another computer as if they were local.

NOTE A similar file-sharing scheme, Remote File Sharing (RFS), is from AT&T and is part of SVR4.

NFS uses a client-server model (more on this model in the next section), in which a server exports directories available for sharing, and a client mounts the directories in order to access the files contained in them. In this way, NFS avoids keeping copies of the same file on many computers, and lets users access a single copy of a file on the server. This also means that you use traditional Unix commands to access remote data. Any Unix system on the network can be an NFS server, an NFS client, or both at the same time. You can mount a remote file system by hand, which can reduce overhead by only having file systems mounted when they are needed, but the process is best accomplished by commands contained in the startup files.

NFS is platform-independent, and is available on mainframes, minicomputers, RISC-based workstations, and some personal computers. This means that NFS can be used to share files among computers running different operating systems. NFS has been licensed to and implemented by more than 300 vendors.

NIS

Network Information Service was formerly known as the Sun Yellow Pages (YP), and is used to make configuration information consistent on all machines across the network. It does this by specifying that one computer holds the master database of all the system administration information on the network, and then making this database available to all the other computers on the network. This arrangement makes it easier to maintain the database than it would be if there were several copies of the database kept in several locations, because it neatly avoids the problems of inconsistent updating.

NFS and NIS both use a session protocol known as RPC (Remote Procedure Call) which unfortunately is beyond the scope of this book. Suffice it to say that RPC allows a computer to make a procedure call that appears to be local, but which is actually executed remotely, on a different machine on the network.

Client-Server Computing

In the past, traditional computing has used a hierarchical architecture based on nonprogrammable "dumb" terminals connected to a mainframe or minicomputer. In this scheme, the database was on the same computer that was running the application.

A client-server architecture replaces this structure by dividing the application into two (or more) separate parts or processes; a front-end client and a back-end server. The client component provides the user with the power to run the data-entry part of the application, and this part of the client is usually optimized for user interaction with the system. The server component, which can be either local or remote, provides the data management, administration, and system security features and manages information sharing with the rest of the world.

How does a client-server application differ from a network, and what benefits does it bring? Networks usually focus on sharing resources system-wide. In a client-server system, the emphasis is on processor sharing and application cooperation. This allows a mix-and-match approach to selecting the right level of computing power: workstation, minicomputer, or mainframe.

NOTE   X Window systems reverse the sense of the terms client and server; for more on this, see Chapter 19.

Typically, a client-server approach reduces network traffic, because relatively small amounts of data are moved over the network. This is in sharp contrast to the typical network, where entire files are constantly being transmitted between the workstation and the network file server.

Database applications were some of the first to embrace this concept, particularly with Structured Query Language (SQL, usually pronounced "sequel"). SQL has grown into an industry standard database language. It is relatively easy to implement, robust, powerful, and easy for users to learn.

UnixWare from Novell

Novell Inc. is a leading network operating system developer, and independent surveys show that Novell can claim up to 60 percent of the PC-based network operating system market with products such as Novell NetWare 3.x, 4.x, and Personal NetWare.

In mid-1993 Novell completed the purchase of USL from AT&T (for more on this aspect of Unix history, see Chapter 20), and in late 1993 released UnixWare 1.1, based on SVR4.2.

UnixWare's list of features is indeed impressive:

- The ability to run programs written for SVR4, SCO UNIX, SCO XENIX, DOS, and Microsoft Windows

- The ability to communicate with traditional Unix systems using TCP/IP and NFS, and Novell systems using IPX/SPX

- The ability to load systems from UnixWare or NetWare servers across the network

- Interchangeable Open Look or Motif window managers (for more on Open Look and Motif, see Chapter 19)

- Support for the Veritas fault-resilient, journaling file system (VxFS) as the default file system for hard disks. Compared with the standard System V file

system, VxFS suffers less if the operating system halts abnormally and requires less repair, making recovery after the crash much faster

- The ability to use NetWare server services
- Support for advanced PC hardware

UnixWare offers both a single-user version in the Personal Edition (originally shipped without TCP/IP), and a complete, multiuser system called the Application Server. Following SunSoft's lead, neither system includes a C compiler. Only time will tell how Novell will proceed with NetWare and UnixWare development, whether Novell will port UnixWare to other processors, and how certain Unix features that we consider to be standard will fare.

Accessing the Internet

In this section I will attempt the impossible: I will try to explain the Internet and show you how to access this vast wealth of information using just a few simple commands. No one person can understand all of the Internet; the resources available are just so vast that they are beyond comprehension. Something I *can* do within the confines of this chapter is tell you how to find out more about the Internet by actually using the Internet as a tool for information access, rather than concentrating on the mechanical components of the network.

I will explain how to transfer files from one system to another, and show you how to log on to a remote computer using common Unix commands. I will also quickly cover some of the other Internet utilities that are generally available, but which are not part of Unix.

What Is the Internet, Anyway?

You may hear the Internet described as a "network of networks," or as "the world's largest network," and while both statements are true, they do not give any real indication of how large the Internet really is. The Internet was originally established over 25 years ago to meet the research needs of the U. S. defense industry, but it has grown into a huge global network serving academic research in all fields. Astonishing as it sounds, no one person runs the Internet, and no one organization pays the costs.

> **NOTE** While many Internet boosters are fond of quoting statistics, the most important thing to remember is that the Internet is a means to an end, a mechanism for accessing an incredible wealth of information.

Much of the work is done by volunteers, with some of these volunteers serving on the Internet's guiding committees. Almost two million computers and 15 million users are connected into the Internet, and the rate of growth is still increasing rapidly with no end in sight. With all these computers and users connected to the Internet, there must be a way to identify each site in a unique way. To do this the Internet uses domain addressing.

UUCP Addressing versus Domain Addressing

So far in this chapter, we have used UUCP addressing for mail and mail routing, but there is another addressing scheme known as *domain* or *Internet* addressing. Domain addressing follows the pattern

   user_name@*system_name.domain*

Note that, unlike UUCP addressing, the user name comes before the system name, and that @ symbol (pronounced "at") is used rather than the bang. The domain, following a period, may consist of several subdomains also separated by periods. Table 17.4 lists the Internet top-level domains.

TABLE 17.4: Organizational Top-Level Domains

Domain	Category
com	Commercial organization
edu	Educational establishment
gov	U.S. government organization
int	International organization
mil	Branch of U.S. military
net	Networking organization
org	Nonprofit organization

In addition to these top-level domains, geographical domains are used to indicate the country in which a network is located. Usually, these geographical domains are the standard two-letter international abbreviation, such as ch for Switzerland or dk for Denmark. The exception to this rule is Great Britain. Its international abbreviation is GB, but its domain name is uk, for United Kingdom.

Underneath these domains and subdomains, and usually hidden from sight, the IP (Internet Protocol) address specifies the exact routing to the Internet host with a set of four numbers separated by periods, such as 116.37.10.30. These numbers work much like a telephone number, and you can use an IP address anywhere you would use a regular address. The part of the system that keeps track of addresses is called the *Domain Name System* or *DNS*. DNS is a TCP/IP service that translates domain addresses to and from IP addresses; this is all done out of sight, and there is little reason to delve further into the details.

You can find out about Internet domains with the whois and nslookup commands:

whois   Provides information about a domain such as its full name and location

nslookup   Provides the IP address of any domain, as well as information of interest to system administrators

Other programs that perform the same function that may be available on your system include dig and host.

If your system has the appropriate mail-forwarding software, the Internet format has the advantage that your mail can be routed to the remote site without the need to specify the intermediate gateways. Check with your vendor or local guru as to which addressing formats are viable for your system. In general, UUCP-style addresses are used within the UUCP network, while domain-style addresses are used for the Internet. For information on how to send mail to systems outside the Internet, such as CompuServe or MCIMail, see the section "Mailing Other Networks" near the end of this chapter.

Fingering a Remote Computer

Of all the commands that access the Internet, the finger command is the easiest to use. The command displays information about users by listing the .plan or .project

files in each user's home directory. When used with a domain address, `finger` will tell you about a remote user; however, there are many people who exploit `finger` information in a rather novel way.

The University of Wisconsin has a computerized Coke-vending machine. To buy a drink, you log in to a terminal next to the machine and use the appropriate commands. You must have paid in advance to have credit in your account. The command

```
finger coke@cs.wisc.edu
```

displays the instructions for this system. The information on your screen is being sent from the remote computer. Congratulations, you are using the Internet.

There are many other nontraditional uses of `finger` information, including the baseball scores displayed by the command

```
finger jtchern@sandstorm.berkeley.edu
```

or the recent earthquake activity displayed by

```
finger quake@geophys.washington.edu
```

If `finger` can't find the address you typed, you will see the message

```
finger stan@sybex.com
unknown host: sybex.com
```

But if you see the response

```
finger: command not found
```

the `finger` command is not available to you; check with your system administrator.

The `ping` command will also tell you whether a remote host can be reached, but because of the load it can impose on the network, `ping` should not be used during normal operations or from automated scripts. The best use of `ping` is as a trouble-shooting aid for system administrators.

Transferring Files with ftp

The `ftp` program allows you to transfer files to and from a remote computer, and work with files and directories on that remote computer. From a historical standpoint, `ftp` is part of the Berkeley heritage (while `uucp` originally comes from AT&T).

When you use ftp, you start a client program on your computer that connects to a server program running on the remote computer. You issue commands using ftp that are translated into instructions that the server program executes for you.

You start ftp as follows:

```
ftp [options][hostname]
```

Most of the *options* are used for debugging ftp and are not used very often; *hostname* can either be a domain address or an IP address. Once the connection is complete, ftp enters command mode and is ready to receive your commands. If *hostname* is not specified, ftp enters the command mode immediately.

You can use ftp to connect to any computer on which you have an account and password, but most Internet users do not have accounts on all the machines from which they may want to copy files; the administration would just be a nightmare. To solve this problem, a particularly important application of ftp, known as *anonymous* ftp, is used instead; indeed, many people do not use ftp in any other way. You simply log in to the remote computer with the user name anonymous and your user id as a password. You cannot use anonymous ftp with every computer on the Internet; only those that have been set up to offer the service. The system administrator decides which files and directories will be open to public access, and the rest of the directories on the system are off limits, and cannot be accessed by anonymous ftp users. As an extra level of security, most anonymous ftp sites will only allow you to download files from them; you are not allowed to upload files to them. Having said all that, the world open to anonymous ftp is simply enormous; there are literally thousands of anonymous ftp computers on the Internet, and countless files you can download.

Once you have started ftp and established a connection to the remote computer, you will see the prompt

```
ftp>
```

meaning that ftp is ready for a command. Depending on the version of the ftp program you have, the number of commands may vary. Type ? or help at the prompt to see the commands available on your system. You will notice that many of the ftp commands are very similar to Unix commands we covered in earlier chapters, such as ls to list files, pwd to display the name of the current directory, or cd to change to another directory. The most useful ftp commands are listed in Table 17.5.

TABLE 17.5: The Most Useful ftp Commands

Command	Action
Basic Commands	
quit	Closes the connection to the remote computer and terminates ftp
?	Displays a list of the ftp commands
? *command*	Displays a short summary of the specified command
help	Displays a list of the ftp commands
help *command*	Displays a short summary of the specified command
!	Pauses ftp and starts a shell on the local computer
! *command*	Executes the specified shell command on the local computer
Connecting Commands	
open [*hostname*]	Establishes a connection to the specified remote computer
close [*hostname*]	Establishes a connection to the specified remote computer and continues to execute ftp
user [*name*[*password*]]	Identifies the user to the remote computer
Directory Commands	
cd [*directory_name*]	Changes the working directory on the remote computer to that specified by *directory_name*
cdup	Changes the working directory on the remote computer to its parent directory
dir [*directory_name*]	Displays a listing of *directory_name* on the remote computer
lcd [*directory_name*]	Changes the working directory on the local computer
pwd	Displays the name of the current working directory on the remote computer

TABLE 17.5: The Most Useful ftp Commands (continued)

Command	Action
File Transfer Commands	
get [*remote_filename* [*local_filename*]]	Downloads the file from the remote computer specified by *remote_filename*, and renames the file *local_filename* on the local computer
mget [*remote_filenames*]	Downloads the specified files from the remote computer
mput [*local_filenames*]	Uploads the specified files to the remote computer
put [*local_filename* [*remote_filename*]]	Uploads the file specified by *local_filename* to the remote computer and renames the file *remote_filename*
Option Setting Commands	
ascii	Sets the file transfer type to ASCII
binary	Sets the file transfer type to binary
hash	Toggles the hash sign (#) printing for each block of data transferred
prompt	Toggles interactive prompting
status	Shows the current status of ftp

Once you have made a connection using ftp, and found your way to the right directory on the remote system, you only need a few commands to move files across the Internet to your local computer. You can become an ftp expert with just five commands: ascii, binary, get, put, and quit.

> **NOTE**
>
> Several file designations are common on the Internet: *filename*.tar indicates an archive created by tar; *filename*.Z indicates a file created by the Unix compress program and you must use the Unix uncompress program to restore the file to its original size before you can use it; *filename*.tar.Z indicates a compressed archive; *filename*.zip is a compressed file created by the PKZIP program; *filename*.tar.gz is a compressed file created by the GNU zip programs gunzip and gzip; *filename*.txt is a text file; *filename*.1 is an nroff source file; and *filename*.ps is a PostScript file ready for printing on a PostScript printer.

The default file transfer type is ascii, but it makes good sense to set the mode before a transfer. Use the ascii command before transferring a purely text file, and use the binary command to create an exact byte-for-byte copy of a file.

The get command downloads a file from the remote computer to your local computer, and the put command uploads a file from your local computer to the remote computer (these commands are sometimes called recv and send instead of get and put). The get command must always include the name of the file you want to download, and it can also include the name you want to use for this file after it is on your system (you don't have to use the original name).

For example, to download a text file called faq (an Internet name for a file containing a set of frequently asked questions and their answers) located in the directory /pub on the remote computer, and name the file faq.txt on your local system, the sequence might look like the following:

```
ftp> cd pub
250 CWD command successful.
fpt> ascii
ftp> get faq faq.txt
200 PORT command successful.
150 Opening ASCII mode data connection for faq (50007 bytes).
226 Transfer complete.
```

After a get command, ftp reports the number of bytes transferred and the elapsed time that the transfer took to complete. If you have no more files to transfer, all that

remains is to use the `quit` command to close the connection to the remote computer and terminate `ftp`.

Connecting to a Remote Computer with telnet

`telnet` is a remote access program that you can use to manually log into a remote computer on the Internet. Unlike `ftp` (which makes a connection for the sole purpose of transferring files), a `telnet` connection is a general-purpose connection useful in three main ways:

- When you have a login on a remote computer and you want to do some work on that computer.

- When you want to use an Internet client-server program, but you do not have a client program installed on your usual machine.

- When you want to access an application that is only available on the remote machine.

The usual form of `telnet` is

```
telnet [host[port]]
```

where *host* may be a domain address or an IP address, and *port* specifies the port number on the remote computer you want to log into. Once a connection is established, anything you type on your keyboard is passed to the remote computer, and anything displayed by the remote computer appears on your screen. To pass a command to the `telnet` program itself (rather than to the remote computer), you can toggle into command mode by typing the `telnet` escape character, usually `Ctrl-]`, and you will see the prompt

```
telnet>
```

on your screen. Table 17.6 lists the most common `telnet` commands; type `man` `telnet` to see the on-line documentation available on your system.

You can use `telnet` to perform any operation that you would normally do using a terminal connected directly to the remote computer; for example, you can even open a `telnet` connection to a third computer somewhere else on the network.

TABLE 17.6: The Most Common `telnet` Commands

Command	Action
?	Displays a list of the `telnet` commands
? [*command*]	Displays a short summary of the specified command
open *hostname*	Establishes a connection to the specified remote computer
close	Breaks the current connection and returns to the `telnet` command mode
quit	Breaks the current connection and terminates `telnet`
set *escape value*	Specifies the character to switch into `telnet` command mode
status	Displays the current status of `telnet`, including the name of the remote computer you are connected to

`telnet` does not have a file-transfer option; if you are using `telnet` and you want to transfer a file, you must exit `telnet` and use `ftp` to perform the transfer.

Other Internet Animals

So far in this section we have looked at two Unix commands, `ftp` and `telnet`, commonly used in computer-to-computer communications. Due to the vast amount of information available on the Internet, several special-purpose tools have evolved to help manage access to this information. These are not Unix commands, but you may well find them available, and we will describe each of them briefly in the following sections. As always, more information is available on the Internet.

Educating archie

`archie` is a program that helps you locate files on the Internet accessible with anonymous `ftp`. At periodic intervals a special program accesses all known anonymous `ftp` sites and collects a list of all the public files available on each system. This information, including domain name, directory path information, and file names, is collated into what is known as the Internet Archives Database, and when you use `archie` to find a file, all it has to do is check in this database. The database currently

contains information on over 2.5 million files from more than 1,500 anonymous `ftp` sites all over the world, and is available on the following servers:

Country	Server Name
Australia	`archie.au`
Austria	`archie.edvz.uni-linz.ac.at`
Austria	`archie.univie.ac.at`
Canada	`archie.uqam.ca`
Finland	`archie.funet.fi`
Germany	`archie.th-darmstadt.de`
Great Britain	`archie.doc.ic.ac.uk`
Israel	`archie.ac.il`
Italy	`archie.unipi.it`
Japan	`archie.kuis.kyoto-u.ac.jp`
Korea	`archie.sogang.ac.kr`
New Zealand	`archie.nz`
Spain	`archie.rediris.es`
Sweden	`archie.luth.se`
Switzerland	`archie.switch.ch`
Taiwan	`archie.ncu.edu.tw`
USA Maryland	`archie.sura.net`
USA Nebraska	`archie.unl.edu`
USA New Jersey	`archie.internic.net`
USA New Jersey	`archie.rutgers.edu`
USA New York	`archie.ans.net`

You can access archie in three ways:

- By using an archie client program on your local computer. Type archie, and you should see the prompt change to archie>. This is the most convenient way to use archie, and is the one we will describe in the next section. If you get an error message instead, archie is probably not available.

- By querying a server by email. Address your email to user archie at the server nearest to you (for example, archie@archie.au), and make sure the body of your message contains the word help. You will get back a short guide on how to use the archie email interface.

- By connecting to a server with telnet. This is the least popular and least convenient method.

Start archie by typing

`archie [options] string`

These are the most commonly used options:

Option	Action
-c	Makes the search case sensitive
-s	Makes the search case insensitive
-o *filename*	Stores the results of the search in *filename*
-m#	Limits the search to # results (95 is the default)
-h *server*	Queries the archie database specified by *server*
-r	Searches using a regular expression

string is the search string or text pattern you are looking for. Choose your search string carefully so that you are not overwhelmed with information.

The result of an archie search is a list of ftp site addresses with files or directories that match the string you specified, along with the file size, date of last modification, and directory name. The list is sorted by site domain address.

gopher

gopher is a powerful, menu-driven system you can use to access information on the Internet without worrying about domain addresses or directory names; indeed, you don't even have to know where the file you want is located. gopher is so good at hiding all the mechanical parts of the Internet that the term "gopherspace" was invented to represent the mass of information resources managed by gopher.

To use gopher, just select an item from the menu. Each time you make a selection, gopher does whatever is needed to perform that action, all behind the scenes. Some menu items lead to more menus; others will get files for you and display their contents.

gopher works in cbreak mode, which means that you don't have to press the Return key after a single-key command. Use the arrow keys to navigate the menus, press ? for help information, and press q to quit.

One of the best features of gopher is that you can use a bookmark to save a menu item in a bookmark list. This means that you can jump straight back to this location in a future gopher session without having to navigate (or remember how to navigate) all the intermediate steps. To add a menu item to your bookmark list, move to it and press a (for add); to add a complete menu to your list, type A instead. To view your list, press v (for view), and to return to the previous menu, press u (for up).

veronica

veronica is a gopher-based tool used to search gopherspace for menu items that contain specific words, much the same way that archie searches for ftp information. You can use veronica to find gopher-based information without performing a manual menu-by-menu search. veronica is usually available as a gopher menu selection, and is a good candidate for a bookmark; then use the v command to view your bookmark list and select veronica.

When you start a veronica search, you are asked to enter the search string you want to look for, and veronica returns a gopher menu containing items that match your search string; this can save you a lot of time.

Wais

Wais (pronounced ways) is an abbreviation for Wide Area Information Service, a service that can search through hundreds of collections of data, each called a source. You tell Wais which sources to use, and what you would like to find, by specifying

a set of keywords. Wais then searches through each of these sources to find those that meet your criteria and outputs a list of articles. You then go through the list and select those you want to look at. Wais will retrieve the text and display it on your screen.

Several Wais clients are available via anonymous `ftp`, including `swais` (simple Wais) and `waissearch` for Unix systems, and `xwais` for those systems using X Window (see Chapter 19 for more on X Window).

World-Wide Web

The World-Wide Web, also known as WWW, W3, or just the Web, is an information browser based on the concept of hypertext. Hypertext is a method presenting information so it can be viewed by the user in a nonsequential way, regardless of how the original information was organized. Hypertext lets you browse through information, choosing to follow a new path (or link) each time the information is accessed.

NOTE   **A program written by Matthew Gray at MIT that meanders from one Web server to another, collecting statistics as it goes, found that there were almost 1 000 Web servers containing almost 250,000 hypertext documents.**

What makes the Web such a powerful tool is that a link may point to any type of Internet resource; a session, a text file, a `gopher`, a USENET newsgroup, and so on, and the Web accesses each resource using the appropriate method. Unfortunately, there is no application that does for the Web what `archie` does for `ftp` and `veronica` does for `gopher`—at least, not yet.

There are many browsers available, both line and full-screen, for Unix, X Window, Microsoft Windows and other systems, via anonymous `ftp` from `info.cern.ch`. For information, look in the directory `/pub/www` for a file called `README.txt`.

If you have an X Window system, try the Mosaic browser. Mosaic was written at the National Center for Supercomputer Applications (NCSA) at the University of Illinois in Urbana, and is available via anonymous `ftp` from `ftp.ncsa.uiuc.edu`. The program is called `xmosaic`; look in the `Web/xmosaic-binaries` directory for the version for your system. Mosaic is also available for Microsoft Windows and on the Macintosh.

Talk, Talk, Talk

The Internet Relay Chat (IRC) is a 24-hours-a-day conversation where people from all over the world talk about anything and everything. IRC is difficult to explain in a short paragraph, so to learn more, look for a file called `IRCprimer` in any of the following places: the `pub/unix/irc/docs` directory on `nic.funet.fi`, the `irc/support` directory on `cs.bu.edu`, or the `pub/irc/doc` directory on `coombs.anu.edu.au`. You may find several versions of the file: the extension `.txt` indicates a text file, `.ps` indicates a PostScript file, and `.Z` indicates a compressed file. Get the file using anonymous `ftp`. Be careful—IRC is great fun and is known to be addictive.

Introducing USENET

USENET is an international, noncommercial, news-sharing network linking many thousands of Unix sites. USENET represents the best of the original Unix philosophy. It's a free-rolling, unmercenary, informal (almost anarchic) affair developed by and for Unix users. USENET is more a way of life than a traditional bulletin board. And USENET is easier to use than to define. There are no enrollment or usage fees, apart from your CPU and connect time. The latter is usually minimal since you'll probably connect with a "local" call and exchange information during off-peak hours. If you have one of the many versions of the Net News software (all available at no charge) and a link, via UUCP or similar, to a USENET feeder, you can join in the fun. The feeder sites are backbones or gateways, collecting and relaying all or selected news to other USENET sites. You can post news items and queries and browse through similar items posted by others. The items are filed by category into many hundreds of newsgroups, ranging from abstruse Unix technicalities to lonely hearts! Consult the list of contacts in Appendix C, "Unix Resources," if you are ready to risk USENET addiction.

Using News Readers

A *news reader* is a program that manages the newsgroups that you subscribe to and lets you read the USENET articles themselves. `vnews`, `rn`, and `nn` are all screen-oriented news readers commonly available at many sites. The `tin` and `trn` news readers are also screen-oriented, but they can also organize news articles into threads, where a thread is an original article followed by all the responses to that article. This makes it much easier to follow a conversation and avoid redundant responses.

Many news readers are available via anonymous `ftp`, and you can get more information from the USENET group `news.software.readers`.

Mailing Other Networks

To end this chapter, we will describe a few of the most commonly used mail gateways, and show you how to use an Internet-style address to send mail to users of these networks.

CompuServe

A CompuServe user id consists of two numbers separated by a comma. To send mail to a CompuServe account from the Internet, just replace the comma with a period, and add the domain address `compuserve.com`. So if the original user id was

```
12345,678
```

the complete address now becomes

```
12345.678@compuserve.com
```

To send mail from CompuServe to an Internet user, use the following form:

```
INTERNET:user@host.domain
```

In other words, add the prefix `INTERNET:` to the domain address.

MCI Mail

MCI Mail customers may have a user name or an identification number. To send mail from the Internet to MCI Mail, use either the name or the number and the domain `mci_mail.com`, as in

```
accountname@mci_mail.com
```

To send mail from MCI Mail to an Internet user, use the following form:

```
create <cr>
TO:   username
EMS:  Internet
MBX:  user@host.domain
```

Summary

In this chapter we have covered the major methods of communication between Unix computers:

- The uucp family of commands
- Mail to remote sites
- Networking concepts including NFS, NIS, and client-server computing
- The Internet, and an introduction to the most popular Internet navigation tools, including finger, anonymous ftp, gopher, veronica, Wais, and the World-Wide Web
- USENET, USENET news groups, and news readers
- Mailing other networks

CHAPTER

EIGHTEEN

Basic System Administration

- What's involved

- Superuser rules

- Putting the boot in

- The halting problem

- File systems and filesystems

- Backing up

- New accounts

Every computer system, large and small, needs "administration." Even the single-user PC running DOS, when you think about it, requires a host of miscellaneous activities to maintain smooth operation. These include mundane tasks such as the procurement, formatting, and filing of diskettes; regular and unplanned maintenance of the hardware; monitoring disk integrity with CHKDSK; checking disk usage and purging old files; periodic backing up of programs and data; installing new hardware and applications software; upgrading from DOS n to DOS $n+1$; maintaining documentation, and so on. Less mundanely, one hopes, users may have to recover from disasters such as disk crashes. For PC users, these are do-it-yourself jobs that merge into the general pattern of computer operation and are seldom seen as formalized "administration."

With larger, multiuser systems, these and other tasks must be planned and scheduled with greater care and delegated to specialists. Individual users are discouraged or prevented from performing the global operations associated with administration. Many maintenance and administration chores require the use of the whole system, so ordinary users must be warned that normal service is being interrupted. And, clearly, one needs a central authority for bug-fixing, for assigning user id's and priorities, allocating and policing disk and time quotas, and for smoothing out the inevitable resource conflicts between users.

Unix System Administration

In the Unix culture, system administration has always played an ambivalent role compared with the site-management strategies adopted for the proprietary operating systems of large commercial companies such as IBM or DEC. Unix, as you have seen, was developed by programmers for programmers, so for some time there was a certain laissez-faire indifference towards such apparently trivial and wimpish administrative tasks as backing up and assigning user id's. The early Unix manuals offered no specific guidance for administrators: there were lots of tools, and programmers were expected to use them or invent their own tools to fine-tune performance or perform backups. In the early days, if a programmer found bugs in the utilities, or even in the kernel itself, they would often be fixed on the spot without too much formality.

As Unix grew and entered the prim world of commerce, more attention was paid to having some central site authority, and the Unix system administrator was born (he or she requires such an unlikely mix of technical and political skills that they say a good one is in fact born not made). Compare the paucity of early SA documentation with the 300+ page *System Administrator's Reference Guide* and the equally voluminous *Operating System System Administrator's Guide* issued with SCO UNIX. Of great significance is SCO's `sysadmsh`, a system administration shell that presents clear menu selections for the most frequently used SA jobs. Similar shells are emerging from other Unix vendors which present an equally friendly interface for the smaller sites that cannot justify full-time, guruesque supervision. You have to be logged in as `root` (or superuser) to use these admin shells, of course, but once you acquire a basic understanding of the terminology and the rationale for the SA functions, the syntactical complexities of the SA commands are replaced by navigating plain English (or the language of your choice) menus. In this chapter, therefore, I will not describe any of these admin shells in detail, but will concentrate on the underpinning logic of the commands that the menus offer. After all, it is rather condescending, not to say boring, to tell you that to back up you need to select "Backup" from a menu, then select the media type and device from a submenu, and so on.

There are hundreds of commands dedicated to SA duties, now in their own ADM section of the man pages. I will concentrate on those that are needed to keep a Unix system running smoothly. The other duties that seem to go with the territory, such as being priest-confessor, patient font of wisdom, soother of frayed spirits, and shoulder-to-cry-on, must either come naturally, or be left to develop with time and experience.

Some of the essential jobs for a system administrator are the same whether the site supports 4 or 400 terminals, and whether it runs 2 or 24 hours a day. The large Unix mainframe systems, of course, will have highly trained, full-time SA's, often several on duty at all times, sharing the load. But I also have in mind the growing number of PC- and workstation-based Unix systems with a handful of users, one of whom is the designated part-time SA. Or possibly, the SA chores rotate, so everyone needs to know the standard procedures.

What's Involved

At the top of the list is the obvious task of ensuring satisfactory service to the users. This requires knowing how to perform the following tasks:

- Start up and shut down the system.
- Set up new accounts and remove old ones.
- Establish defaults for various user processes.
- Organize groups and assign group id's.
- Provide global defaults for various commands and files.
- Set up uucp and links to other sites.
- Maintain a central printer service.
- Establish crontab for regularly scheduled jobs.
- Cope with lost passwords.
- Handle security.
- Maintain a written log of system changes and other pertinent events.
- Maintain log files.
- Check the file system integrity.
- Back up data and systems files.
- Update the online and offline documentation.
- Disseminate the ground rules and read the Riot Act.
- Recover from miscellaneous disasters.
- Cope with hardware and software changes.
- Monitor performance, disk usage, and resource allocation.
- Provide help and guidance in person and via email.

I will not deal with the initial setup procedures when the units are unboxed and assembled. Most vendors will provide help for this, and in any case, it's hardly possible to give useful advice apart from RTFM (Unix slang for "Read the Manual!").

Superuser Rules OK?

The first point to note, before I discuss these jobs in more detail, is that most system administration duties require the highest of privileges, namely *superuser* access to the system. The home directory of the superuser is /, the root directory, and the login name is therefore traditionally set as root (strictly speaking, the first user in /etc/passwd given user id 0 is the superuser. Many commands, though, rely on the fact that "root" is the superuser name, so it is unwise to change this). The token "root" has various meanings and parts of speech in Unix. When used as an adjective (root directory, root filesystem, root mode) or as a synonym for /, I'll use normal font. As a login name, you'll see root, as in root's password.

NOTE The /etc directory usually has read/write permissions for root only. Run an ls to confirm this fact. As a reminder, I will usually give the full /etc/*xxxx* path name for commands and files in /etc.

At most sites root's password is known only to the system administrator who changes it regularly. A common practice here to cope with sickness and death is to keep the current password for root in a secure place accessible only by a trusted nominee. As you saw in Chapter 7, root has the power not only to bypass the file and directory permissions set by any user, but can also change these permissions. root alone can add and remove users, and at any time (recall that /etc/passwd is writeable only by root). root alone can safely shut down the system or change its run level. For example, root can reduce the whole system to single-user mode (run level 1) for various maintenance chores. root alone can log in to any account without knowing its password. root alone can create special files with /etc/mknod, special filesystems with /etc/mkfs, and make filesystems available and unavailable with /etc/mount and /etc/umount.

NOTE In Unix terminology, the file system consists of one or more filesystems! See "File Systems and Filesystems" later in this chapter.

Even simple jobs such as changing the system date with the `date` command can only be performed by `root`. `root` alone can `kill` any processes. And `root` alone can grant permission to employ certain commands such as `crontab` (see Chapter 9). I stress the omnipotence of `root` because even a brief, temporary access to `root` by the wrong person is highly dangerous, allowing deeper penetration. This *trapdoor* syndrome has been the source of many security breaches. A phoney superuser, of course, could shut down the system or change passwords (including `root`'s password!) but is unlikely to attract attention so obviously. If the intention is unobtrusive long-term file peeking or snatching, the intruder may try to create an innocent-looking account. An important SA activity is maintaining security at the appropriate level and educating users about the possible loopholes. One aspect of this is maintaining both written *logs* and automated log files. For example, all attempts to log in as `root` via the `su` command (see later) can be automatically recorded in a designated `SULOG` file (usually `/usr/adm/sulog`) or displayed immediately on a designated terminal.

The whole concept of a single-passworded, all-powerful superuser is considered by some experts to be a major blemish in Unix security. Most of the large operating systems such as IBM's VM and DEC VMS employ multilevel privileges to control access. This approach is gaining ground with some high-security versions of Unix. The DOD (Department of Defense) has a National Computer Security Center that issues the *Orange Book* guidelines for grading a system's security level. Unix systems can be submitted for testing. Achieving the proper grade is clearly a marketing advantage in many applications. There are also commercial packages that plug or warn against security breaches.

Many sites have "special users" such as `admin` or `backup` who can log in with less powerful privileges than `root` to perform certain administration duties. The general rule, to reduce the chances of catastrophic error, is to log in at the lowest possible privilege level for the task at hand.

Assuming Power

Having seen the power of a superuser, you will be anxious to know how to become one. There are several ways but they all require knowledge of `root`'s password (sorry about that). First, note that even SA's do not spend all their time in root mode: they often have normal accounts named `sys`, `sysop`, or `mary` even, with normal file permissions for their nonprivileged duties, such as sending and receiving mail. At the login prompt, you can type `root`, followed by `root`'s password, and everything

works just like a normal login. If you are running as a normal user, you can log out then log in again as root. There's a shortcut, though: the su command.

If you are running as a nonroot user, know root's password, and have *su permission*, you can use the su (switch user or superuser) command (in man section C) to become root. If you are already running as root, su can be used to log in as any other user without knowing the user's password: powerful stuff! su has the following syntax:

```
su [-] [ name [ arg1 [ arg2, ...]]]...
```

The default *name* is root, so after entering su with no arguments, you will asked for a password. Type the password for root and you become superuser with the # prompt. To return to your previous drab existence, simply press Ctrl-D, and the $ or % prompt returns. If you are already root, you can enter su mary, say. You'll then be logged in with Mary's user id but no password is requested. There are a few subtle differences between su'ing to an account and logging into that account in the normal way. The differences concern the shell and its environment, and su has options to control these.

Whatever user you su to (root or mary), a new shell is spawned based on that user's /etc/password shell field (/bin/sh by default). However, you usually retain any previously exported environment variables from your earlier shell. You can alter this state of affairs with the – option. Provided that the new user's shell is /bin/sh (or similar), the – option sets up a new environment as though you had logged into the new account in the normal way. This is achieved by executing the appropriate profile files for the new user. The optional arg1,arg2,... arguments let you pass on commands to be executed by the new shell (see the su man pages for the grisly details). A Ctrl-D exits you back to your previous login state. System daemons regularly use su to "assume" other user identities.

Summing up, a superuser can su to root or any other account without logging out and in again.

Putting the Boot In

Starting, or booting up, a Unix system is usually the easiest part of the whole exercise. Often it is sufficient to switch on the power and let the machine's ROM trigger the booting sequence. The bootstrap idea is still quite magical to me after 40++ years of close observation! The initial code has to coax the system to read in (bootstrap) more

code, and so on until the boot program is read from disk, either floppy or hard disk depending on your circumstances.

> **NOTE** Some of the newer, sleeker, real-time Unix *executives* are completely ROM'd, so they boot up without disk help.

On some systems you are prompted first to name the boot device or program. This allows you to boot with different versions of the kernel, especially useful during experimental work. For example, before you can test new peripherals, their drivers have to be linked to the kernel, so there are occasions when you have several different kernels to choose from.

In my own installation, I have both Unix and DOS 6 on separate hard disk partitions on my 486-based PC. If I place a DOS 6 system diskette in drive A:, I boot up and am saddled with DOS 6 ("Serves you right," I hear you cry). In the absence of a diskette in drive A:, Unix is booted from the hard disk. In the event of hard disk problems, I can boot Unix from a specially prepared floppy. This points to an early SA caveat: Be Prepared! Test your emergency booting procedures from time to time, and have sufficient software on your external booting medium to allow proper diagnostics. (Your documentation will tell you how to prepare a boot diskette.)

Cleanup Time

The boot program loads the Unix kernel (and maybe other things) into RAM. What happens next depends on the particular system. SCO UNIX, for instance, performs an integrity check on the *root filesystem* using the fsck command (filesystem check in man section ADM). I'll explain these terms soon when I discuss proper shutdown procedures. If the filesystem is "clean," normal startup proceeds; otherwise, you are prompted through an fsck cleanup session. If your system does not perform such a check automatically, fsck can be run manually (in single-user mode) as an insurance against corrupted files (rather like CHKDSK in DOS, only more so). Note that data can be lost when cleaning a corrupted filesystem. Furthermore, fsck is one of Unix's most complex commands (it keeps asking you questions). So, corrupted filesystems should be shunned if at all possible. The most common cause for filesystem corruption is the failure to follow the correct close down procedures, but

a power surge or failure is also a possible candidate. Morals: (1) Read the next sections on how to turn off a Unix system correctly; (2) Invest in a UPS (uninterruptible power supply) or, at least, surge protector.

Next, again depending on your version, Unix may come up in multiuser (or *normal*) mode ready for action. Alternatively, you may be prompted to select a *run level*, usually a choice between multiuser mode and single-user mode (also known as *maintenance* mode). In the single-user case, you'll be prompted to enter root's password that I've been making such a fuss about.

Single-User Mode

Single-user mode gives you a bare-bones system and is usually reserved for emergencies or major scheduled maintenance operations. Emergencies would include restoring, rebuilding, and cleaning up the filesystem after some calamity. Typical cases of maintenance would include major hardware or software upgrades, normally performed at off-peak times to avoid inconvenience to users. Only root can run single-user mode, and, as the name implies, only one terminal is active (usually the system console): the rest of the system is dead to other users. Logging out of single-user mode (with Ctrl-D or logout) brings up multiuser mode.

Multiuser Mode

When you are in multiuser mode, any users who know root's password can play at superuser while the rest of the system supports ordinary users. Hopefully, only the privileged and responsible few will have that power.

Exactly how the system comes up depends on the contents of the /etc/inittab and /etc/rc2 (rc meaning "resource") files, both of which need root permission to edit. etc/rc2 is a longish sequence of scripts with names beginning with S*nn*, where *nn* runs from 00 to whatever. The number determines the order in which the scripts are obeyed. Thus, S00SYSINIT starts the ball rolling by initiating the kernel message logger; later comes S75cron to start the cron daemon, S80lp to start the printer scheduler, and so on. Note that single-user mode does not invoke /etc/rc2, so the features initiated therefrom are not immediately available.

The Halting Problem

DOS and other simple systems can be safely shut down by switching off the power, although you may need to park the disk heads first for complete peace of mind, and switching off while a spreadsheet is recalculating is not recommended. Multiuser systems such as Unix call for a more thoughtful halting stategy. Active users are rightfully miffed if their terminals die without warning. Even if the users have all logged out and gone home, there may be background jobs and daemons ticking away. Daemons get mad if their processes are suddenly curtailed.

A less obvious danger lies in the way the Unix file system works. For improved performance, Unix systems use a *buffered* file approach. When a file is "changed" the disk version of that file is not always updated immediately. Usually, portions of the file-to-be-changed are read into file buffers (dedicated areas of system memory, sometimes called *caches*), not just the blocks to be changed but adjacent blocks too. The changes may reside in memory for a while before being written to disk. Flags are set by the kernel to indicate if the "file-in-memory" needs to be written out. The kernel *flushes* these buffers periodically, maintaining *synchronization* between the buffer and the file itself. The time savings are considerable, since the need for relatively slow file and directory accesses is reduced to a minimum. The price, of course, is that a premature cessation of kernel activity may destroy the synchronization (the nasty word *unsychronization* is perhaps excusable for such a nasty phenomenon). As you saw in the "Cleanup Time" section above, the `fsck` command tests for a corrupted (unsynchronized) file system, and helps you to repair the damage. But in mending (cleaning) the file structure, some data may be lost. For all these reasons, Unix provides several commands for a graceful shutdown. For obvious reasons, they are accessible only to a superuser.

If you are in single-user mode (and therefore already a superuser), there is no need to warn other users to terminate their jobs, but you still have to flush any pending file I/O to ensure synchronization. On SCO UNIX, the `/etc/haltsys` command (in `man` section ADM) achieves this. The syntax is simple:

```
/etc/haltsys [-d]
```

Typing `/etc/haltsys` will flush the file buffers, mark the file system as *clean*, then halt all kernel activity without any grace period or warning. Any background processes will die, of course, so it is your responsibility to kill them safely before using

/etc/haltsys. A message then tells you that it is safe to power down or "Press any key to reboot." /etc/haltsys has only one option: −d withdraws the option to reboot, so all you can do is power down (you can read the d as *dead*). There is a variant of /etc/haltsys called /etc/reboot that does a haltsys followed by a reboot with no option to power down.

A much safer command is /etc/shutdown, available only to superusers (of course!). /etc/shutdown is especially useful in multiuser mode, but can be used in place of /etc/haltsys in single-user mode. shutdown actually calls haltsys but not until all active users have been warned and all pending processes have been gracefully killed. shutdown also has options to switch the system to other init levels.

TIP   /etc/haltsys should only be used directly in multiuser mode if some weird system error prevents shutdown from working.

The shutdown command syntax is quite daunting, but you'll rarely need all the options—and if you do, a shell script should be created since typing errors in the shutdown command can be quite disconcerting.

```
shutdown [-y] [-g[hh:]mm] [-i[0156sS]] [-f"messg"] [-Ffile] [su]
```

The −y option is *silent*: without it, shutdown asks you to confirm that you want to shut down the system. With the −y option, shutdown proceeds apace, no questions asked.

The −g option indicates the grace period in hours and minutes, or just minutes if you omit the *hh*: argument. The maximum grace period is 72 hours, and the default is one minute. Grace is the length of time before the shutdown begins. Users receive periodic messages that the system is going offline. The warnings are transmitted every hour if the grace period exceeds one hour; every 15 minutes if the grace period exceeds 15 minutes; otherwise every minute. Active users must save their files and finish up their work as best they can.

The −f option lets you vary the default warning message. Note that double quotes are needed around the *messg* string. −F is similar, except that you send the contents of the given *file*. The wall command can also be used for informing all users whenever you want to vary the periodic messages generated by the −g option.

The −i option specifies the *init level* (also known as the run level) to which the system will be brought. The default is 0 (safe-to-power-down state). Using either −i1, −is, or −iS will bring the system down to single-user state. shutdown actually calls init to change the run level. init (in man section M) is a general process spawner that takes an init level as argument. It plays a vital role in starting up a Unix system by creating the initial daemons and other processes under the guidance of the etc/inittab file.

/etc/shutdown also calls /etc/sync, a system primitive that updates the *super-block* to ensure synchronization. The super-block is the vital block 1 of every filesystem, holding the name and other essential information about the filesystem.

Yet another way to get from multi- to single-user mode is to use the su option (type both letters with no hyphens). The su synonym exists to maintain compatibility with XENIX. The following command,

```
/etc/shutdown −g10 −f"URGENT! Wind up and logout NOW!" su
```

starts sending the given warning ten minutes before switching to single-user mode. The message will be repeated every minute to all logged-in users. A common reason for a single-user shutdown is to back up files. It can clearly be counterproductive to start backing up files that users may be changing! Before I discuss the backup situation, though, a brief detour on filesystems is called for.

File Systems and Filesystems

The Unix file system consists of one or more filesystems! The essential *root filesystem* is the familiar hierarchy of directories and files starting at /, the root. The root filesystem is *mounted* automatically when you boot, and must be present (it contains all the basics to run Unix). For smaller installations, root may be the only filesystem you need for both system and user files. To improve performance on larger systems, you can store user files in separate filesystems, the most common of which is known as the /u or *user filesystem*. When a Unix hard disk system is initially formatted and partitioned, decisions have to be made regarding the number and type of filesystems needed, since later changes require reinstallation of the whole system.

Similarly, the SA will usually have to create partitions and new filesystems when new disk drives are added. This is, of course, a *big* subject that I can only touch on

briefly. As Unix systems grow, a whole panoply of skills and tools are enlisted to optimize performance for different work loads and application mixes. Fifty biologists modeling DNA molecules present a different challenge from fifty technical writers running vi and nroff. The filesystem organization is a vital factor here, as is the allocation of *swapping* areas. Swap spaces are disk partitions used to store processes that are temporarily swapped from RAM to disk (as you saw in Chapter 9). Clearly, the size of available RAM is a major part of the equation.

Filesystem names are stored in /dev along with other special files (device drivers and so on). The /etc/mkfs command (in man section ADM) is used (by root only!) to name and create a filesystem. You can specify the type of files to be stored (ACER, UNIX, XENIX, even DOS!), number of blocks, and various technical details. Before the system can access a filesystem, it must be "attached" to the root filesystem using the /etc/mount command that is also privileged. Thus,

```
# pwd
/
# /etc/mount /dev/u /u
# _
```

will mount the user filesystem /dev/u on the "directory" /u. The mounted filesystem looks rather like an ordinary directory under root, but the kernel knows better! Because of the low-level stuff associated with /etc/mount and /dev/u, commands accessing files in the /u filesystem will be correctly routed to the proper logical disk partition. Mounting nonroot filesystems is usually performed automatically by scripts in the /etc/rc2 file, but during maintenance and backups the SA often has to mount filesystems "manually." The reason is that when you boot up in single-user mode, only the root filesystem is mounted and accessible (/etc/rc2 is not invoked, you'll recall). In passing, note that fsck can be used to check any filesystem's integrity and clean up if necessary. Indeed, mounting a corrupt filesystem usually triggers a request to perform fsck.

Access to a filesystem can be removed, by root only, with the /etc/umount command (in man section ADM) meaning *unmount* (some talk of *demounting* or *dismounting* a filesystem):

```
# pwd
/
# /etc/umount /dev/u
# _
```

> **TIP**
>
> Unix spelling reminder: There is one "e" in `creat` and one "n" in `umount`!

Notice that `etc/umount` takes the *device* name as argument, not the filesystem directory. If you have a removable mass-storage device, it should be unmounted *before* it is physically removed. Otherwise, much puzzlement can be occasioned. The "directory" under `root` that represents the placeholder for the filesystem would still be visible. There are several "gotchas" with `/etc/umount`. A common error is to attempt an unmount when you are logged into the target filesystem: you'll get a "device busy" message until you log into `root`.

The reason for the filesystem digression should now be clear: the SA is intimately involved with filesystems even though the average user can function without any inkling that they exist. Both root and nonroot filesystems need to be backed up, of course, which leads me back to the mainstream of my dissertation.

Backing Up

Even with proper shutdowns and regular `fsck` checks, the data and programs stored in your file system are subject to diverse catastrophes and *forces majeures*. Backing up means copying some or all of your fixed, hard-disk files to an external medium (magnetic tape reels, cartridges, or cassettes; floppy disks; or removable hard disks) in such as way that the data can be copied back (restored) at some future date. The restoration, note, may have to be made on another machine of the same type, or possibly on an entirely different Unix system. The latter situation requires special attention, being associated with a form of madness known as upgrading.

The need for regular backups will be so self-evident to those readers who have ever lost a vital file that they may skip the following homily. To those with an "It can never happen to me" mentality, I urge them to reconsider. In your bowels, you know that I am right! By a quirk of fate, disaster always strikes the day after you have decided to forego a backup "just this once." Apart from power fluctuations and outages, disk and other hardware failures, files can be deleted accidentally or as a result (rare, one hopes) of software bugs. As Maxwell Smart

used to say, "We've established the *why*, so let's consider the *when, what, who,* and *how.*" As you'll see, these four turn out to be cunningly interrelated.

When?

The optimal frequency of backing up is best decided by posing the following question: If the disks all crash *now*, how much work would be involved in restoring the system using the data from my previous backup? Only you can answer this risk-analytic conundrum. You need to balance the effort and cost of each backup against the effort and cost of redoing lost work. This clearly depends on the rate of change of your data and the degree to which you can automate the backup procedures. Not to be considered, nowadays, is the cost of the backup medium and the cost of storage. The obvious point of *where* it's stored is quickly answered: Any 100% safe place! And as far away from the point of origin as is compatible with easy accessibility! It is quite alarming how often fires, floods, and earthquakes destroy both the disk drives and their backups.

What?

The frequency of backup also depends on what you back up. We can distinguish several basic backup strategies:

- Low-level backups mean copying a complete filesystem to your external medium. Restoration is simple: just copy the backup to the filesystems.

- High-level or incremental backups mean copying only the files in that filesystem that have changed since the previous low-level backup. Restoration requires careful application of each incremental backup to the last total backup in the correct sequence.

A typical schedule might be a weekly total backup and a daily incremental backup. Clearly, different filesystems can require different schemes. At a small-to-medium business site, the systems and applications programs in the root filesystem can be quite static after the initial tribulations have subsided, justifying monthly total and weekly incremental backups. The database on filesystem /u, say, representing life-sustaining invoice, inventory, payroll, payables, and receivables (especially receivables) information, is throbbing with activity. The concept of incremental backup is

hardly meaningful here, but it is often practical to maintain a smaller transac-tions filesystem for frequent backups throughout the day together with an over-night total backup. The backup tools are extremely flexible, allowing you to copy individual files, whole directories, or whole filesystems, or just those parts which have changed.

A related consideration is how long you should keep a particular backup copy. Total backups, since the effort is great and the medium cost trivial, should be kept for at least twelve cycles. If you do a monthly total backup, you would rotate twelve car-tridges (or whatever) labeled Jan through Dec. You could keep four weekly and seven daily incremental backups. The main challenge is to log, label, and store the backups sensibly and consistently, shunning complacency during those inevitably uneventful periods when the whole exercise seems pointless. A further point is to have a verification strategy. This involves both checking that the backup is indeed a faithful copy, and occasionally rehearsing the restoration procedure.

The choice of backup medium involves the following considerations:

- Floppies are cheap but require human intervention (consider the number of 1.44Mb diskettes when backing up a modest 100Mb filesystem). On the plus side, for smaller systems which rely on floppies for system installation and emergency booting, no additional hardware is required.

- Some form of tape drive or removable cartridge disk (reel-to-reel, streamer cartridge, or cassette) is essential for medium-to-large filesystem backup. The higher capacity allows fully automated operation.

Who?

At those sites where users have PCs or workstations with local storage media, some or all of the backup responsibilities can be likewise distributed. More often, though, the bulk of the mass storage (sic) is centralized, and the backup lot must itself fall on the center, namely the SA. As you've seen, backing up a filesystem ideally re-quires single-user mode to ensure that the files are unchanged. This in turn requires superuser privilege. Having said that, regularly scheduled backups can be scripted and automated to the point that they run unattended (with tape backups) or safely delegated to trusted nonsuperusers (with floppies). This is an area where admin shells such as SCO's sysadmsh earn their gravy. Both scheduled and unscheduled

backups, as well as restorations, can be invoked with a few keystrokes. SCO's edit-able `schedule` file lists the various backup levels and even displays a color code for labeling the medium.

How?

I've saved the worst question for the last. Over the years, because of the importance rightfully accorded to backing up, a myriad of commands have evolved to do the dirty work. I will restrict myself to the three most common approaches: the `dump`, `cpio`, and `tar` commands. It is worth noting that many of the backup commands also serve a wider market: the distribution of software and databases to the wide world of Unix users, where the emphasis is on standard formats and portability. Here are some of the key points to be considered in choosing a backup utility:

- Does the backup allow easy restoration of individual files, or must you scan the entire backup?

- Does it allow *incremental* backups as an option? That is, is it smart enough to save only files that have changed since the previous backup?

- Can backed-up files be "split" across backup volumes?

- Are the backups portable to other systems in the event of prolonged down-time or the urge to upgrade?

The `/etc/dump` command and its sibling `/etc/restor` have been around a long time. `/etc/dump` copies a whole filesystem with a simple command syntax. For example,

```
# /etc/dump 0uf /dev/bak /dev/u
# _
```

copies everything in `/dev/u`, the user filesystem—files, directories, i-nodes, the lot—to the device called `bak` (which can be a floppy or tape drive of any sort). The `0uf` set of options translates as follows:

0   Dumps at level 0 (the whole filesystem).

u   Updates a file called `/etc/ddate` (used in subsequent incremental backups).

f   Takes the following argument, `/dev/bak`, as the destination device to receive the backup.

Before restoring a complete dump'd backup, you must prepare a nice, clean filesystem. /etc/restor simply dumps all the saved stuff back to the new filesystem. /etc/dump and /etc/restor are not overly bright (some device errors during copying are simply ignored) and you should run fsck after each dump. Nor are they overly portable, since the i-node information is filesystem-dependent. However, the simple syntax is an advantage where portability is not a factor.

The cpio Command

You briefly met the cpio (copy file archives in and out) command during the discussion on find in Chapter 14. cpio (in man section C) is not a privileged command, so it is widely used (in conjunction with find) by nonroot users to selectively back up personal files. root, of course, can also use it, and it forms the backbone (sic) of many admin shell backup procedures. cpio is extremely flexible and the syntax is correspondingly horrendous. cpio can split big files across multiple volumes and can cope with special files (device files and pipes) and empty directories (a good backup should record such things, when you think about it). Another signal advantage is that cpio backups have a standard format which leads to high portability. By changing the order of the arguments, cpio also performs the restore operation. On the downside, restoring an individual file from a cpio backup can be painful: you need to read through all the previously saved volumes until you hit the target. If any corrupted files are encountered *en route*, later files are inaccessible.

The tar Command

The versatile and popular tar (tape archive) command (in man section C), like cpio, produces archived backups on floppies or tapes, restores such backups, and can be used by nonroot users (read and write permissions allowing). Whole directories (and their subdirectories) or individual files can be backed up, and large files can split across volumes of the backup medium. This splitting can save much time and frustration when backing to floppies. tar also packs each floppy to the max, reducing the number of floppies needed (not to mention all that inserting and removing nonsense). The tar syntax is a tad simpler than cpio's, but it does not copy special files or empty directories. However, restoring individual files is much easier than with cpio: you can start restoring from the volume that contains your wanted file.

Before you back up to floppies, make sure you have enough formatted and labeled floppies (each one representing a separate *volume*) on hand. tar will prompt you as each floppy becomes full.

You can set up the name and characteristics of your default backup device in a file called /etc/default/tar. This file can hold several such devices, which you can select via the command line. Or, with the f option, you can supply a specific device name with the command, as in the following example:

```
$ assign /dev/floppy
$ tar cvfk /dev/floppy 720 chap*
$ _
```

Here, a nonroot user assigns the floppy drive for his or her exclusive use (see assign in man section C), then archives all files in the current directory that match chap*. The argument 720 specifies the capacity of the diskette in kilobytes. The cvfk options have the following meaning:

c   Creates a new archive file and starts writing at the beginning (see later for the r option, which appends to an existing nontape archive).

f   Takes the /dev/floppy argument as the target archive name. Without this option, tar takes the default from a device name stored in /etc/default/tar. This file also stores defaults such as blocking factor and volume size. tar can also read and write from standard input and output, which is useful for piping.

v   The verbose option causes tar to display file names as they are archived.

k   Tells tar to take the 720 argument as the device volume size in kilobytes.

The options for tar work differently from most Unix commands. The first *function* letter must be either r, x, t, u, or c with no hyphens. This first letter can be followed by one or more function modifiers (no intervening spaces or hyphens). Those function modifiers that take further arguments need their arguments listed after the group of option letters in the correct sequence. Thus in the above example, we have

the function letter c followed by two modifiers f and k. f takes the argument /dev/floppy, and k takes the argument 720.

You cannot run ls, say, on a tar archive to see the files that you've saved, but tar itself has a display option:

```
$ tar tvf /dev/floppy
blocksize = 10
chap1
chap2
...
```

The t option says list the file names. The v and f options are as described earlier. The following command restores the tar backup:

```
$ tar xvf /dev/floppy
$ _
```

The option x says *extract* (also known as *unarchive* or *de-archive*) *all* the files saved on the given floppy. To extract particular files, you can add file name arguments (including wildcards used with care) after the device. Where will the extracted files go to? Great question. The equally great answer is: It all depends! In the above example, I saved chap* without specifying an absolute path name, so when I restore, the chap* files will be written to my current directory (assuming I have proper write permissions). Internally, tar attached ./ to each chap* file. If I had written /usr/stan/chap* when backing up, using an absolute path name, tar would try to restore the files to the /usr/stan directory regardless of my current directory. And thereby hangs *two* dangers: I must have write permission, of course, but the more vexing problem is whether the target directory still exists! A tar'd backup might lie around for months, possibly years, so the original directories embedded in the archive might well have disappeared. To avoid this aggravation, it's wiser to use only relative path names. And, naturally, restore only into directories where you have write permission.

tar can also be used with both directory and file name arguments. Using wildcards when extracting can cause hardships. If I tried tar xvf /dev/floppy chap*, for instance, it is the *shell*, not tar, that expands the *, so only files in the current directory matching chap* will be extracted! It is therefore safer to spell out the files, or simply restore everything in a given directory.

Some other useful tar options follow:

r   Appends files (writes at end of an existing archive). NOT valid with mag tape archives.

u   Update option: archives only those files which are not already archived, or those files which have been modified since they were last backed up. NOT valid with mag tape archives.

w   Wait option: displays each file name and invites y/n response before the current action is performed (allows selective backup and selective restore).

b   Changes the default blocking factor to the following numerical argument (used with raw mag tape archives only).

m   Mod-time option: normally the modification time stamp on a file is set to the time when the file is extracted. m says do *not* change the modification time when extracting.

e   Prevents the split of a file across volumes: if the file about to be saved will not fit on the current volume, the e option prompts with an "Insert new floppy" (or similar). Without the e option, tar will save until the volume is full before prompting: a file might therefore be split across several volumes.

n   Tells tar that archive is *not* a mag tape. This can speed up certain operations.

p   Used with the x option: extracts the files and directories using their original permissions.

A   Suppresses absolute file names by stripping any initial / characters.

New Accounts

The SA has the important task of greeting new users and getting them online smoothly. Assuming that terminal or dial-in facilities are in place, the key steps are:

- Assign a user name and id. The traditional, friendly method of using first names is fine until the second Henry arrives! Several strategies are possible to avoid duplications: you can have smitha, smithjc, and so on, using surname and initials, or follow the Bard with henry1 through henry8.

- Change /etc/passwd to include the newcomer. You may need to assign an initial password. You will certainly advise the user as to your password philosophy.

- The /etc/passwd file also names a home directory (/usr/henry) with the correct ownership (use mkdir and chown) and permissions (use chmod), and default shell (which might be a restricted shell initially, such as /bin/rsh).

- If necessary, assign the user to a login group by editing /etc/group and using chgrp.

- Establish the appropriate .profile or .login files for the user (and explain how it can be personalized).

- Assign the default CPU priority for use with the nice command.

- Set other parameters as required, such as number of login attempts, password change intervals, and auditing information.

Most of these jobs require superuser privileges. The admin shells such as SCO's sysadmsh, of course, also need you to be logged in as root to access the new user routines. Although the direct editing of /etc/passwd and /etc/group is still used at some sites by (one hopes) experienced SA's, the admin shells are far superior and much safer. sysadmsh lets you add and modify user accounts from easy-to-read screen forms.

Having settled in the new user, you will never hear from him or her again! If only. The truth is that you have simply added one more soul to wash, feed, and mother-hen. I wish you well.

Summary

I've given you an overview of the SA's duties. In one impossible slogan: Keep the users happy at all times. I touched on the security issue and the dangers of the all-powerful superuser concept. The following commands and topics were introduced:

- su for switching your user identity. A superuser can move around accounts (including root) without logging out first.
- Booting up and shutting down: the synchronization problem and how to avoid file corruption by using haltsys and shutdown.
- Checking and mending a corrupt filesystem with fsck.
- The run-level concept and init: the differences between single- and multi-user modes.
- The filesystem concept and the mkfs, mount, and umount commands.
- The importance of backups: why, when, what, who, how, and where.
- Three of the backup tools: dump, cpio, and tar: their pros and cons.
- Adding new users and groups.

CHAPTER

NINETEEN

X Window Exposed

- An introduction to X

- X Window managers: Open Look and Motif

- Using X

- X marks the spot: the future of X

Throughout this book, we have worked with a character-based shell, but in this penultimate chapter, we will take a look at Unix's graphical face, and describe the X Window System, usually known simply as X. X has become very popular in the modern Unix world, as it helps to overcome or avoid many of the limitations of the traditional Unix character-based interface.

In a graphical user interface (GUI), applications execute in windows using a consistent set of menus and dialog boxes, along with other graphical elements such as scroll bars and icons. Instead of typing commands at the prompt, you use a mouse or trackball (or other pointing device) to point to pictorial elements on the screen, and click (or double-click, or drag) one of the mouse buttons to make the desired action occur.

NOTE The X Window System is complex enough that a whole book could easily be devoted to it. You will find details of several periodicals and books on X in Appendix C, "Unix Resources." If you want to write X programs yourself, one publisher in particular, O'Reilly & Associates, has produced a library of almost twenty technical books in its X Window System Series.

The use of graphical elements in the user interface was pioneered at Xerox Corporation's Palo Alto Research Center (PARC) in the early 1970s. Unfortunately, the computational hardware required to support such an interface was very expensive. The early work at PARC greatly influenced Steve Jobs, cofounder of Apple Computer, and the design of the ill-fated Apple Lisa computer (and then later, the very successful Apple Macintosh), as well as workers in many other environments. Since then GUIs have emerged for most computing environments. Figure 19.1 shows a typical Sun workstation display.

The fundamental idea behind using a windowing system with a consistent look and feel is that you do not have to learn new commands when you move to a new application. Instead, you take advantage of habit to perform similar tasks. After a while, you know that you will always find the Open command in the File menu, and the Resize command in the Window menu. Many Unix commands, on the other hand, use the same letter as an argument to produce completely different results. For example, -l when used with ls does one thing, but when used with who

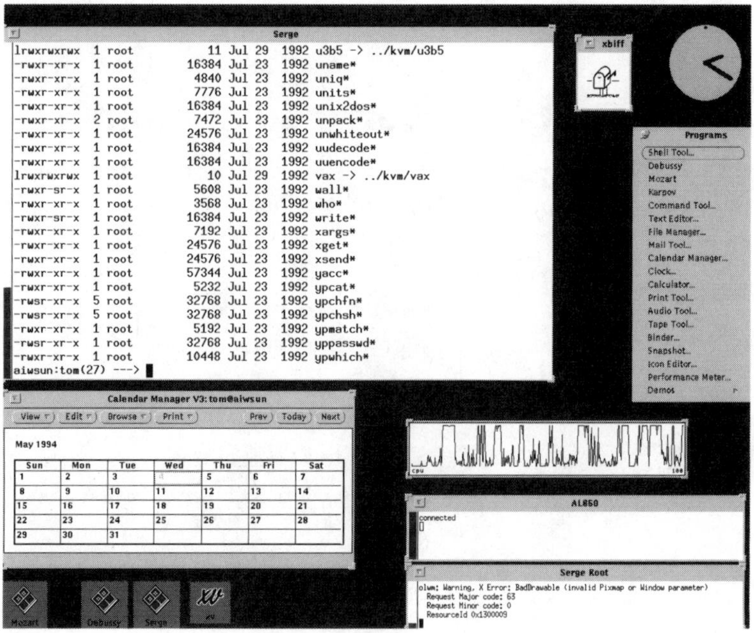

FIGURE 19.1:

A typical Sun workstation graphical user interface

does something completely different. With a well-designed windowing system these kinds of inconsistencies disappear.

An Introduction to X

X development began in 1984 at the Massachusetts Institute of Technology (MIT) as a joint project between the Laboratory for Computer Science and Project Athena. Much of this early work was sponsored by DEC and IBM. By 1986, X was becoming a significant factor in computing, and the version that is currently in use, X Version 11 (or X11), was released in 1987. In 1988, MIT, Apple, AT&T, DEC, HP, and Sun contributed $150,000 each to form the X Consortium. Since then, X has been enhanced, mostly under the guidance of the X Consortium, which continually monitors standards for the system and ensures compatibility with earlier releases.

X Version 11, Release 6 is the most current version, although most users will continue to use Release 5 for many years. But what is X, and how does it work?

Clients and Servers Revisited

X is a windowing system that provides for multiple resizable windows so that you can have many applications displaying on your screen at the same time. Unlike most windowing systems that have a specific built-in user interface, X is a foundation upon which almost any style of user interface can be constructed. The unique feature of X is that it is based upon a network protocol rather than on the more usual programming procedure calls.

NOTE   In the X Window System the terms client and server do not have the same meaning as in the "Client-Server Computing" section in Chapter 17.

The X System consists of three main parts:

- The server software, which controls your display, keyboard, and mouse
- The client software, or applications programs, which are completely separate from the server
- A communications link that connects the client and the server

Figure 19.2 shows these three elements, and in the next section we'll look at these system components in more detail.

The Server

The server controls the display hardware. It accepts requests sent across the communications link from client application programs to open a window on the screen, to change the size or position of a window, and to draw graphics and display text in these windows. The server sends back events to the clients, telling them about keyboard or mouse input.

FIGURE 19.2:

The client represents the application while the server controls the display.

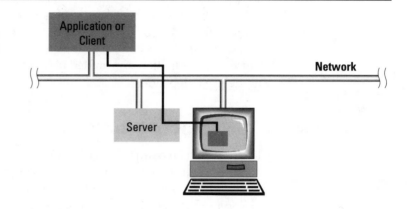

A server can manage simultaneous communications from many clients. This means you can run several applications at the same time, each with its own separate window on your screen.

The Client

The client is the application program that, in addition to providing the code needed to support X and the graphical user interface, performs a specific function for the user, such as managing a database or sending email. A client can work with any display, as long as there is a communications link to the server.

X is not limited to one server and one client, and in fact many combinations are possible. Several clients may interact with a single server when several different applications display on a single screen, or a single client can communicate with several servers and display the same information on several different screens.

The Communications Link

The third major element is the communications link. All communications between server and client must use this link, but it does not matter what form the link takes. There are two main implementations:

- Client and server execute on the same computer, for example, a workstation running X. In this situation, the link will be some form of interprocess communication (IPC) such as shared memory (named pipes or streams).

- Client and server run on different computers, for example, across a network. X is independent from the network, so almost any physical link can be used: Ethernet, token ring, X.25, and serial lines have all been used. The two computers do not even have to have the same processor or operating system, because the information transmitted between the server and the client is always device independent.

How the X Protocol Works

The X Protocol is the real definition of the X System, and it defines just four types of messages that can be transferred over the communications link. Requests are sent from the client to the server, and replies, events, and error messages are sent from the server to the client. This chapter is not the place to detail the decisions made and the tradeoffs evaluated in defining what should be a client function and what should be a server function. Several of the books listed in Appendix C, "Unix Resources," contain detailed information about the protocol.

X Compared with Other Windowing Systems

Many other systems offer a windowed environment, but none of them can offer the combination of features that makes X such a powerful force.

`telnet` (see Chapter 17) lets you log in to a remote computer and then run programs as though they were executing on your own local computer. However, `telnet` cannot manage graphics or multiple applications.

The Macintosh interface is a consistent GUI, and with System 7 allows multitasking, but the interface is fixed and cannot be changed. Also, the interface is an integral part of the operating system—you can't run a Macintosh without its GUI.

Microsoft Windows is also a consistent GUI that allows a form of multitasking, but again the GUI is fixed and cannot be changed. Also, it can only be used with applications written for the PC; it cannot run a program on a VAX containing a built-in GUI and run the display to a PC.

What the Users See in X

The GUI that you see as a user consists of two separate X components:

- The application interface, which cannot be changed without changing the original program. This controls the flow of the program and what appears in the menus and the dialog boxes.

- A separate client program, known as the window manager, which controls how you move, resize, arrange, and close the windows on your screen.

This relationship is shown in Figure 19.3.

Because the window manager is not part of the application, you can change to a different window manager if one is available. However, at any given moment, all the applications windows on your screen work in the same way because they are all under the control of one window manager. See the section "X Window Managers: Open Look and Motif" later in this chapter for more information.

FIGURE 19.3:
A separate client program known as the window manager controls the windows on your screen.

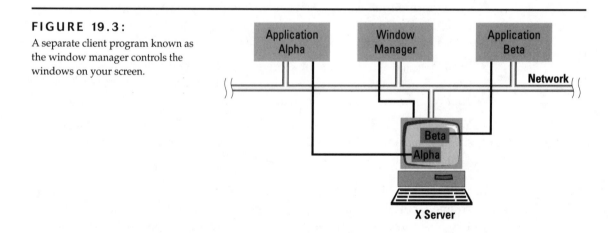

X-Terminals and PC X Servers

X-terminals are special terminals built to run X. An X-terminal consists of a simple and fast computer with a built-in X server, and includes a mouse, keyboard, graphics screen, and a network interface. The X server itself is usually stored in read-only memory (ROM) so that no disk storage is needed. In fact, a good way to think of an X server is to think of it in terms of a terminal.

Packages that allow an X server to run on a PC are also available, effectively transforming the PC into an X terminal. These packages are available for the Macintosh and for PCs running DOS, Microsoft Windows, OS/2, and Windows NT. Many of the packages also include the software necessary to add TCP/IP to the system.

X Benefits

Along with the well-known and well-understood benefits of using a well-designed and consistent GUI (ease of use, short learning times for new applications, direct manipulation of individual interface elements, and multiple applications in overlapping windows), the X System brings many other important benefits. These are some of the most important:

- Once a network has been set up to use X, a user can access any application on any computer on that network. This can be particularly useful if an application must be run on a specific machine due to memory, disk space, or computational speed requirements, or if the network consists of a number of computers with different operating systems. By using X, anyone can access the application on the large computer and display the output on their own workstations at their desks. This is by far the most important X benefit.

- X can disguise the structure or architecture of a network, and can simplify subsequent growth of the system. Indeed, you may not even know that your application is running on a network.

- You can also run non-windowed applications with X by using a special X client called a *terminal emulator* (more on this in the section "Using the xterm Terminal Emulator" later in this chapter).

The code that implements X is widely available, and over time has shown itself to be extremely portable. Implementations are available for computers ranging from PCs to massive supercomputers. X is so completely independent of both the underlying computer hardware and the operating system, that carefully written software will compile and run on any system anywhere.

In the next section, we'll look at two popular X implementations, and then examine how to use X in more detail.

X Window Managers: Open Look and Motif

The X Consortium controls the technical development of the X Window System, but not the implementation of the window manager. The window manager is just another X client (although it enjoys certain special privileges) that performs the following functions:

- Creates and removes windows.

- Resizes and moves windows.

- Converts windows into icons and icons into windows (you may be unlucky enough to hear this process referred to as "iconization"). An icon is a small image that represents an application that is not running or that is running in the background.

- Controls the management of overlapping windows, the top window always being completely visible, while only portions of other windows may be visible.

The X System does not require you to run a specific window manager. You can use any window manager that performs the basic functions. Many X clients can run under any window manager, but some clients do depend on the facilities provided by a specific window manager.

NOTE   If you check the FAQ (frequently asked questions) in the comp.windows.x USENET newsgroup, you will find descriptions of well over 30 different window managers.

twm (Tab Window Manager, or alternatively, Tom's Window Manager after its creator, Tom LaStrange) was one of the first non-MIT window managers, and offered the user lots of custom options. uwm (Universal Window Manager) is still popular for its speed, although it is considered by some to be outdated.

Window managers enforce the "look and feel" of the window system, usually as style guides. twm and uwm do not have strict style guides, but the two major commercially available X standards that have emerged, Open Look (olwm) and Motif (mwm), most certainly do.

A style guide usually specifies more than the simple objects that form the user interface; it also describes the ways in which these objects can be configured in an interface. For example, the Motif style guide specifies that a pull-down menu should be in a menu bar located at the top of the main window, while Open Look interfaces quite often have menus and command buttons distributed throughout. Open Look lets you pin up a menu on your screen, even if the menu's parent window is buried and out of sight. Motif counters this with the tear-off menu.

Open Look was developed by AT&T and Sun Microsystems, and is derived from user interface work performed at Xerox in the early 1980s. Sun was chiefly responsible for the design of the interface. Open Look was also included in AT&T's release of SVR4.2.

Motif was developed by the Open Software Foundation (OSF), a collaboration of hardware and software vendors including DEC, IBM, and Hewlett-Packard. The OSF released the first version of Motif in 1989, along with a style guide and a plan for application certification—two elements required for a consistent user interface. In appearance and function, Motif is similar to Microsoft Windows, and this may be important for users who want to integrate their X applications with existing Windows software.

The Common Open Software Environment (COSE) has now established OSF/Motif as the standard look and feel for Unix user interfaces, which leaves a large body of Open Look-based software that will probably be converted to Motif sometime in the future.

Using X

To use X you will need the following:

- An X server for your system, or, if you are not using a workstation, an X-terminal instead.

- Client application programs. X software can run directly; older, non-X applications can run under X by using a terminal emulator such as xterm. See the section headed "Using the xterm Terminal Emulator" later in this chapter for more information.

- A window manager to manage your application windows.

- Certain standard default files, usually supplied as part of the application, that define font usage, colors, and layout.

- If your system supports shared libraries and your application uses them, these libraries must be present on each computer that runs the applications.

If you work in a networked environment and run the applications on a remote computer, you will also need access to the appropriate network hardware and software.

Logging In

Many systems start X automatically, and you log in under X in the same way you normally would. The xdm (X Display Manager) program handles logins and manages X sessions, and is normally called as part of the system initialization. After you have logged in xdm runs xterm by default, or an application you specify. You can also run xdm remotely with X-terminals and PC X servers to provide a login window; one copy can manage multiple terminals or PCs.

If X was not started automatically, you can start it with the xinit program, usually located in the main X directory; /usr/bin/X11 on many systems. Either way, you can use an initialization file that contains commands executed when X starts; the location of the file and the file name depend on whether X was started manually or automatically:

- If X was started automatically, the initialization file is usually located in your home directory and called .xsession. The contents of .xsession are executed before the initialization files associated with your shell.

- If X was started manually, the initialization file is called .xinitrc (on SCO's Open Desktop, the .xinitrc file is usually called .startxrc). As a minimum, this file should contain commands to call xterm in the background and a window manager in the foreground. If .xinitrc does not exist, xinit starts the X session by running an xterm window.

If you do not use an initialization file, you will just be accepting system-specific default values for the more than 30 environmental variables.

X Resources

It is possible to specify X resources at the command line, but the commands are long and the options are many, and so are prone to error. However, these options are sometimes used in shell scripts, and you will find details in an X client's man pages. Many clients follow the naming conventions used with xterm options, and we will get to xterm in the next section. You can also use a resource database file, usually called .Xdefaults in your home directory if it is a local database. If it is a system-wide file, look in /usr/lib/Xlib. You will have to see your system administrator for information on configuring these files, because this is a subject well beyond the scope of this book.

NOTE   **Two terms you will hear sooner or later in connection with X are** *toolkit* **and** *widget.* **The X toolkit is a set of predefined functions that an applications programmer uses to create the user interface, and a widget is a user interface element created within X guidelines. Widgets actually provide the look and feel of an interface, in terms of the appearance of the menu, scroll bar, and pushbutton widgets.**

There are other ways you can adjust the look and feel of an application. SCO's Open Desktop provides the Controls window so you can select your own color scheme, configure the mouse, select fonts, or choose a background pattern or image. SunSoft's OpenWindows Workspace Properties window lets you alter window frames, change colors, configure your mouse, and even create your own icons. Many individual application programs will often give you a way to configure their own resources.

But what do you do when you want to use X with a program that is not an X program? The answer is straightforward enough: use X and the xterm terminal emulator.

Using the xterm Terminal Emulator

The xterm terminal emulator program provides an X window that behaves just like a terminal, sometimes known as a virtual terminal, under the control of the shell specified by the SHELL environment variable, with /bin/sh as the default. xterm emulates two ancient terminals, the DEC VT102 text terminal and the Tektronix 4015 graphics terminal. You are unlikely to have either, but that is not important. What is important is that you understand what this emulation gives you.

NOTE   The name of the X terminal emulator may vary depending on the Unix you use. In SCO Open Desktop, xterm is known as scoterm, and in Hewlett-Packard systems, as hpterm; in Sun systems you will find cmdterm, and shelltool in addition to xterm, and in UnixWare you will find a Terminal window.

Put simply, a terminal emulator program pretends to be a real terminal, and so gives you a window that acts just like a physical terminal running your shell. It can display any input you type at the keyboard, as well as run programs just like any normal shell. Therefore, you can still run all the old character-based programs and utilities described in the first part of this book such as ls, pwd, and even vi, all without leaving X. Figure 19.4 shows a typical xterm window.

Running your character-based applications in this way gives you several other advantages too:

- You can cut and paste between xterm and other X windows, giving a degree of communication between the older programs and your X clients.

- You can customize your keyboard and map function keys separately for each window.

- You can scroll text output or log your session to a file.

- You can connect each xterm window to a different host computer so you can perform work on several different computers, all from one physical terminal.

FIGURE 19.4:

An xterm window

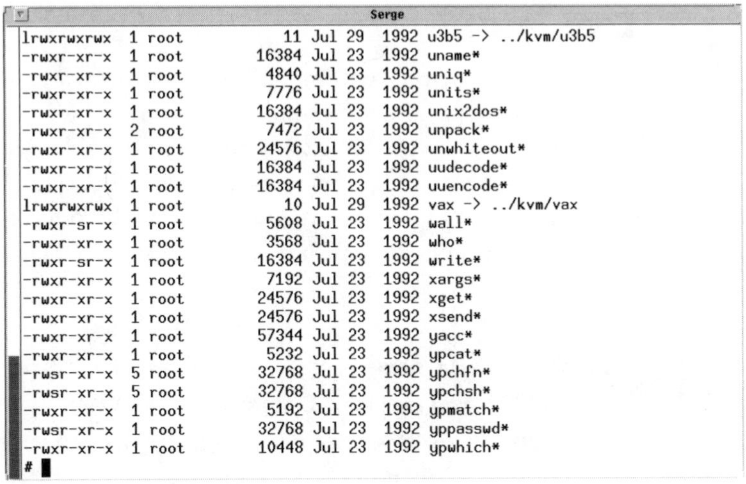

```
                                            Serge
lrwxrwxrwx  1 root           11 Jul 29  1992 u3b5 -> ../kvm/u3b5
-rwxr-xr-x  1 root        16384 Jul 23  1992 uname*
-rwxr-xr-x  1 root         4840 Jul 23  1992 uniq*
-rwxr-xr-x  1 root         7776 Jul 23  1992 units*
-rwxr-xr-x  1 root        16384 Jul 23  1992 unix2dos*
-rwxr-xr-x  2 root         7472 Jul 23  1992 unpack*
-rwxr-xr-x  1 root        24576 Jul 23  1992 unwhiteout*
-rwxr-xr-x  1 root        16384 Jul 23  1992 uudecode*
-rwxr-xr-x  1 root        16384 Jul 23  1992 uuencode*
lrwxrwxrwx  1 root           10 Jul 29  1992 vax -> ../kvm/vax
-rwxr-sr-x  1 root         5608 Jul 23  1992 wall*
-rwxr-xr-x  1 root         3568 Jul 23  1992 who*
-rwxr-sr-x  1 root        16384 Jul 23  1992 write*
-rwxr-xr-x  1 root         7192 Jul 23  1992 xargs*
-rwxr-xr-x  1 root        24576 Jul 23  1992 xget*
-rwxr-xr-x  1 root        24576 Jul 23  1992 xsend*
-rwxr-xr-x  1 root        57344 Jul 23  1992 yacc*
-rwxr-xr-x  1 root         5232 Jul 23  1992 ypcat*
-rwsr-xr-x  5 root        32768 Jul 23  1992 ypchfn*
-rwsr-xr-x  5 root        32768 Jul 23  1992 ypchsh*
-rwxr-xr-x  1 root         5192 Jul 23  1992 ypmatch*
-rwsr-xr-x  1 root        32768 Jul 23  1992 yppasswd*
-rwxr-xr-x  1 root        10448 Jul 23  1992 ypwhich*
#
```

- By using telnet from an xterm window, you can run applications on computers that do not have any X Window support of any kind.

- You can open multiple terminals at once in different windows, and you can run several copies of the same program if you wish.

The form of the xterm command line is

    xterm [*options*]

The command-line options can be long and complex. A – usually turns on an option, while a + usually turns it off—just the opposite of what you might expect. You can also abbreviate an option to its shortest unique form, so you can use –bg for –background, or –fn for –font. Table 19.1 lists the most frequently used xterm command-line options; remember that you can use many of these options with other X clients.

When using xterm or any other X client, it is always a good idea to spell the command out in full, as most of them use long English-language names. You should also remember to keep commands standard; you can always expect foreground, background, and so on.

TABLE 19.1: Common xterm Command Line Options

Option	Description
-bd *color*	Specifies *color* as the window border color
-bg *color*	Specifies *color* as the window background color
-bw *width*	Specifies a window border of *width* pixels
-e *program*	Executes *program* and uses *program* as the window title (unless you also use the -title option)
-fg *color*	Specifies *color* as the window foreground color
-fn *font*	Specifies the name of the fixed-width font to use
-help	Displays a list of command options
-j or +j	Turns on or off jump scrolling, also known as speed scrolling, which makes xterm much faster when you are scanning through long text files
-l	Sends xterm input and output to the default log file called XtermLog.*n*, where *n* is the five-digit decimal number that represents the process id number
-lf *filename*	Specifies *filename* as the log file
-ms *color*	Specifies *color* for the mouse pointer
-rv	Simulates reverse video by swapping the foreground and background colors. +rv prevents this swapping when reverse video is set as the default
-sb or +sb	Displays a scroll bar on the xterm window, and saves text that is scrolled out of the top of the window in a text buffer for later viewing
-sl *number*	Specifies the number of lines in the text buffer
-title *string*	Specifes *string* as the title of the window if the window manager requests a title

NOTE You will always see two separate independent cursors in an xterm window; the mouse cursor and the text cursor.

You can open an xterm window with scroll bars if you enter

```
xterm -sb &
```

Remember that the & starts the program running in the background. See Chapter 9 for more on background and foreground processes. To store commands and output from those commands into a log file called foocmds, use

```
xterm -l -lf foocmds &
```

When you start an xterm window in this way, it runs another instance of the shell specified by the SHELL environment variable. If you would rather create an xterm window that runs a program and then disappears when that program terminates, use

```
xterm -e program
```

If you are using several command-line options, be sure that the -e option is the last one you type. Everything after the -e is treated as a command. In this case, the xterm window title will also show the name of the command that followed the -e, unless you also used the -title option to specify that something else is to be used instead.

xterm has menus you can activate if you press the Ctrl key on the keyboard at the same time you press a mouse button:

- Ctrl and the left mouse button open the xterm menu. This contains selections you can use to start logging and to send signals of various kinds to the current foreground process.

- Ctrl and the middle mouse button open a menu containing options to set various terminal modes.

- Ctrl and the right mouse button may open a menu containing font selections. On some systems, however, Ctrl and the right mouse button do not open a menu.

There are also several more advanced systems available. While they are still basically terminal emulators, they also allow you to add an X front end to a character-based application without changing the original application. Such systems are occasionally termed *frontware*. The simplest systems add a set of pushbuttons to the side of the xterm window; these buttons are configured by a script file. More advanced

systems are completely programmable, and can provide much more complex front ends, to the point where the original character-based interface is no longer visible, and the user sees a fully functioning graphical user interface. The advantage of this approach is that the original application has not changed. You don't care what language it was originally written in because you don't even need the source code.

Using Other X Clients

Many other X clients are commonly available. Some you use as utility programs and others as configuration programs. There is, however, some variation between different X systems. These are some of the more useful clients:

Client	Description
bitmap	Lets you create and edit bitmap images
xbiff	Raises a flag on the mailbox icon to let you know that the mail has arrived
xcalc	Provides a scientific calculator
xcalendar	Displays a monthly calendar and lets you mark appointments
xclock	Provides a clock display with either analog or digital form
xcolors	Displays a color chart of available colors
xdpr	Runs xwd to make a screen capture and send the output to the printer
xfd	Displays font selections or the font specified by the −fn option
xfontsel	Displays fonts and lets you choose a new font
xkill	Kills an X client
xload	Displays a graphical image of system load
xlsfonts	Lists the fonts supported on your system

Client	Description
xman	Provides an X version of the regular man command
xrefresh	Refreshes the whole screen
xset	Allows you to specify screen and keyboard options
xsetroot	Sets the background of the root window to the color or bitmap you specify
xwd	Makes a partial or complete screen capture to a file
xwud	Displays images made using xwd

xclock and xbiff are often run in the background, so that their windows are always visible on the screen. The form of the xclock command is

```
xclock [options] &
```

The *options* include -analog for a conventional clock face, -digital for a 24-hour digital face, and -chime to chime once on the half hour and twice on the hour.

The form of the xbiff command is

```
xbiff [options] &
```

The flag on the xbiff mailbox is raised if you have mail and lowered when the mail has been retrieved. Both xclock and xbiff respond to X command-line options; see Table 19.1 for a list of the common options and your system manual for others specific to your X implementation.

Common public-domain tools include xloadimage, which displays various graphics files, and pbm, which converts graphics files from one file format to another.

Killing an X Client

One of the X clients listed in the previous section is worth a closer look. The xkill program forces the X server to close the connection to a client and is useful for removing unwanted windows, although in some cases the client may not always terminate cleanly. The command has the form

```
xkill [options]
```

The *options* depend on the particular implementation of X on your system.

X Marks the Spot: The Future of X

Some of the formal standard-producing organizations are developing X standards. For example, the ANSI task group X3H3 is working on the X Window data stream definition (in other words, the X protocol), including how it should operate over OSI networks, and the IEEE P1201.1 group is developing standards for the user interface. The European Commission has specified X and Motif as standards for its own use, and X has been specified as a standard for many U.S. government systems.

The religious wars between those who favor Motif over Open Look may also be drawing to a close. Sun has agreed to support Motif as part of the Common Open Software Environment (COSE) initiative, but it may be a long time before all the existing Sun and AT&T Open Look users switch over. Because there is often a fairly close mapping between Open Look and Motif interface objects, automatic conversion tools may make this transition less painful for those software developers concerned with porting X applications.

NOTE You can obtain the X System files over the Internet using anonymous `ftp` from `ftp.x.org.mit.edu`, from `gatekeeper.dec.com`, from `x11r5.b.uu.net`, or from several third-party vendors. You can get information about X from the USENET `comp.windows.x` newsgroup; to join, send an email message to `xpert-request@expo.lcs.mit.edu`. You can also access a set of programs and documentation by sending email with the single word `help` as the message to `xstuff@expo.lcs.mit.edu`. You might also consider joining the local chapter of the X User's Group by sending an email message to `xug@ics.come`.

The X version number (X11) refers to the protocol, and the version number is incremented when the protocol changes. The new version becomes incompatible with the old version and existing programs will no longer work. For this reason I don't think there will be a version 12, because that would require too much conversion of existing software. But that does not mean that X cannot change and add new functions.

Every so often MIT releases a collection of sample programs and programming libraries; these represent the release level. New releases might contain bug fixes, performance improvements, and improvements or enhancements to programming libraries.

The original designers of X went out of their way to ensure that X would never be limiting. An extension mechanism allows new features to be built into the server without producing a performance penalty. In fact, extensions are often used by system manufacturers to take advantage of hardware features. They are also used by the X Consortium itself to implement and agree on new features.

Even with the wide acceptance of X11, new developments continue. Works in progress include extensions to support various input devices, X for Japanese use, a multithreaded X server, and 3-D graphics.

Other interesting developments on the GUI front concern the evolution of the graphical desktop, a screen-based metaphor for a real desktop that contains icons representing applications and other accessories. The DeskSet bundled with Solaris, SCO's Open Desktop, and Hewlett-Packard's VUE (Visual User Environment) are all good examples. The only question is, can these desktop managers replace the shell command line, and will the evolution of the desktop give rise to the same kind of religious wars we have endured between the C shell and the Korn shell, and between Open Look and Motif?

Summary

This chapter described the X Window System, including the following discussions:

- The background to X System evolution
- The role of the client and the server, and the nature of the communications link
- The benefits of using X as a user interface
- A brief description of Open Look and Motif
- A description of how to use X
- A list of common X clients
- A brief look at the future of X

CHAPTER

TWENTY

Postscript

- History lesson

- Flavors of Unix

- Unix and the future

If you've stayed the course so far, I crave your indulgence for one more chapter. These few final words will cover two aspects of the future: what's next for you in your Unix studies? And what's next for Unix itself as a new millenium draws nigh?

Zu Neuen Taten (New Tasks Await You)

I borrow Brünnhilde's cry as she sends Siegfried off to new deeds of glory (Prelude to Wagner's *Götterdämmerung*). I'm less tempted to quote Siegfried's reply: "Forgive me if your lessons have left me still untaught!"

I hinted at the start of the journey that the climb would be a steep one with many craggy detours. And, of course, it is not easy to say when, if ever, the ascent is over. Unix is not a stationary target in spite of all the efforts at standardization. In fact, the current emerging standards require your close study: as different Unix versions converge, there will be new features and angles to learn. As with most aspects of the computer scene, just "keeping up" with Unix takes considerable effort. Luckily, there is no dearth of accessible resources to help you extend and hone your Unix skills. Among these resources are the following:

- System administrators and local gurus
- Books and magazines
- Seminars, conferences, and exhibitions
- Unix User clubs and associations
- USENET and other electronic networks

Indeed, the problem is choosing from the surfeit of resources. In Appendix C, I provide some pointers to obtaining helpful material and guidance.

Whither Unix?

To ruminate on the future of Unix requires some understanding of its turbulent past and bubbling present. Several basic, interrelated facts have influenced the Unix

story. First, Unix originated within a research environment (Bell Telephone Labs, owned by AT&T) free from the proprietary, commercial nexus of other contemporary operating systems. Second, the Unix kernel was small, clean, elegant, and understandable; its source code was in legible, portable C, freely available (or nearly so), and eminently modifiable. In the early 1970s, most commercial systems software was heavily guarded, highly priced, written in the lowest of low-level, hard-to-change languages, and firmly rooted to a single company's hardware (usually IBM's). Unix is structured so that the machine-dependent pieces are isolated and can be readily modified as you move from PC to Sun to VAX to Cray. The arrival of Unix was a sort of computing glasnost or DP perestroika, with the same melange of joy and pain.

Unix encouraged the programmers' penchant for experimental, born-free, undocumented hacking, building and breaking tools rather than meekly using hand-me-downs. In particular, other research establishments and universities quickly ported, extended and "improved" Unix in ways disallowed by the traditional, authoritarian commercial computer vendors. So, ironically, the fundamental strengths of Unix have led to various compatibility and control problems over the years as Unix emerged "from the Labs into the Real World." The elitist anarchy of Ur-Unix has had to survive the cold shower of plumpen commerce. The focus of the corporate world and its CPAs is the balancing of the bottom line of beans. How the job is done is unimportant as long as you are "timely and cost-effective." The surprise is that many of these apparently trivial office-management tasks turn on major computer-scientific problems (traveling salespersons, resource allocations, database integrity, accounts payable [the knapsack problem: which subset of amounts due can be settled with the check received], and so on). There are now over 300 Unix accounting packages available. The "maturation" of Unix needs to be explored.

History Lesson

Figure 20.1 shows a simplified version of the Unix family tree, and gives an overview of how Unix has evolved since its 1969 genesis. The leftmost column represents XENIX evolution. The next column represents AT&T's Unix System Development Lab (USDL), while the third column represents R&D within Bell Laboratories. The fourth column shows the evolution of Berkeley Unix, BSD. I will attempt to unravel this Gordian knot as we proceed through the next few sections.

FIGURE 20.1:

Unix evolution

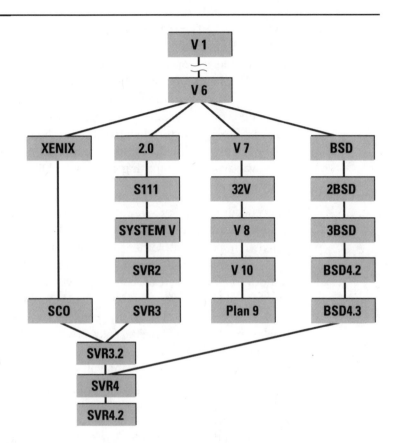

The UNIX Programmer's Manual, 2nd Edition, 1972, proudly announced that "The number of UNIX installations has grown to 10, with more expected." This was Version 1 written for the PDP-11/20. As you now know, these expectations were exceeded beyond belief in the following two decades. The touted numbers are hard to verify precisely, but by 1983 over 100,000 Unix sites were claimed. In 1985, one company alone (Tandy) shipped 14,000 XENIX-based systems. Some 450,000 Unix systems were shipped in 1990. The number of Unix users worldwide is now about five million and they use more machine time than the DOS-ridden community. (DOS still leads in unit sales, of course, but most Unix sites are multiuser.) Perhaps less predictable in 1972 was the eventual diversity of Unix versions.

The Big Three

Oversimplifying the early Unix genealogy, one can see that there were three major strands:

- Original AT&T from Versions 1–7 and Systems III–V
- Microsoft/SCO XENIX
- Berkeley (UCB) from 1BSD to BSD 4.4

This list does not tell the whole story, since a host of derivatives, clones, and extensions under fancy names (all ending with X, it seems) have been launched by other vendors, as we shall see. The key to all this is that System V Release 4.2 represents a reasonable convergence of all the three major families listed above.

AT&T

The first version of Unix, known as Unics, ran on a Dec PDP-7 computer, and in 1970 Ken Thompson and Dennis Ritchie moved it to the PDP-11/20. Ritchie also designed and created the first C language compiler so that he could write a portable version of the system. In 1973 Ritchie and Thompson rewrote the Unix kernel, the innermost part of the operating system, in the C language.

The so-called Fifth Edition (not to be confused with System V) was the first Unix licensed to universities for educational purposes; the Sixth Edition, also known as V6, was released in 1976 and distributed much more widely. The Seventh Edition, released in 1978, was the first Unix to have ease of portability as a major design goal; it was implemented on the Dec PDP-11, the Interdata 8/32, and the VAX. If one single Unix can be said to embody "classical" Unix, then the Seventh Edition is the one.

System V, released in 1983, was billed as the industry standard, so subsequent versions were called System V Release 2.0 (1984), System V Release 3.0 (1986), and System V Release 4.0 (1989). The latest release is System V Release 4.2, also known as Destiny. You'll find the System V versions abbreviated as SVR2, SVR3, and SVR4.

XENIX

Microsoft/SCO (Santa Cruz Operation) XENIX, a fully licensed version of Unix, was jointly developed from Version 7 circa 1979–81 for the Intel 8088/6 family and intended for commercial applications on the IBM PC. There were also versions for

the Motorola 68000 and Zilog Z8000, but these were overshadowed by the violent success of the PC which led to XENIX being, numerically, the most successful Unix of all time. (Some 200,000 XENIX licenses were reported by January, 1987.) XENIX added several important features to Unix, such as file-locking at the record level and semaphores for signal synchronization, vital elements for PC database and network applications. Whatever else they may say about Microsoft CEO Bill Gates, his parallel exploitation of MS-DOS, Windows, and XENIX revealed the ultimate Midas touch. Microsoft sold its interest in XENIX to SCO in 1987.

The People's Republic of Bezerkeley

The role of the Computer Science Department of UCB (University of California at Berkeley) in the Unix story has been enormous. The Berkeley Unix versions, distinguished by the designation BSD (Berkeley Software Distribution), started out as a series of enhancements to the Series 6 and 7 AT&T Unix, aimed at exploiting the VAX (a range of DEC mainframes widely used at UCB and other universities). Particular BSD features such as the C shell, `vi`, `termcap`, and support for TCP/IP communications protocols were included by most Unix vendors without becoming part of the official AT&T canon.

Because Berkeley was strictly a research establishment, BSD Unix was not supported in any modern sense; bug fixes were certainly not guaranteed. Eventually, a company called Mt. Xinu (Unix tm spelled backwards) was formed to support the Berkeley releases of Unix.

Why did the AT&T and BSD Unix versions evolve along different paths? Part of the reason was that, unlike AT&T, UCB was not a commercial enterprise selling and supporting hardware and software. It was an academic site producing bright, state-of-the-art, research-type software but with no support obligations. BSD Unix therefore appealed especially to the scientific and R&D user. However, it soon became unnecessary to advertise that your release of Unix included Berkeley enhancements; the enhancements were just taken for granted.

Finally, in June 1993, Berkeley released BSD 4.4, and disbanded the Computer Science Research Group (CSRG) at the same time, thus ending Berkeley's contribution to the development of Unix.

The Sun Also Rises

The spectacular growth of the RISC-based workstation market, SPARCed by Sun Microsystems, is another illustration of the Unix success story. Two factors led to Unix being the preferred operating system for Sun. First, Sun was started by Unix pioneers. Cofounder Bill Joy wrote the C shell and was a key figure in the BSD Unix enhancements. Not surprisingly, Sun/OS is very BSD influenced. (The recent Solaris 2.x operating system from Sun is based on SVR4.) Second, Unix was the only operating system that could be reasonably ported to the new breed of chips. The architectures and instruction sets of the RISC microprocessors represented a major break with tradition, forcing extensive modifications to compilers and other systems software. Operating systems such as DOS are CPU-dependent, being inextricably bound to the Intel 8088/80x86 architecture—and in any case it would hardly make sense to revamp a single-user, nonreentrant operating system such as DOS for the powerful RISC-based workstations. The other workstation manufacturers, including IBM and HP, who followed Sun have all adopted Unix (either willingly or reluctantly) as their prime operating system. With the advent of the Intel Pentium and the Motorola 68030/40 (CISC attempts to meet the RISC challenge), the distinction between PC and workstation is becoming difficult to define.

Unix on Intel

Several very high-quality Unix implementations are available for the Intel family of 386/486 and Pentium processors, including SCO UNIX, SunSoft's Solaris, Novell's UnixWare (more on this in a moment), and NeXT's NeXTStep. Unix is also available for the Intel architecture from several other vendors, as Table 20.1 shows. The bottom line of Unix on Intel processors is that the user has plenty of choices.

TABLE 20.1: Unix on Intel

Vendor	Operating System	Unix Heritage
Consensys	V 4.2	System V Release 4.2
Dell Unix	System V Release 4	System V Release 4
NeXT	NeXTStep 3.2 for Intel Processors	BSD 4.3 and Mach kernel
Novell	UnixWare 1.1	System V Release 4.2
SCO	SCO UNIX and Open Desktop 3.0	System V Release 3.2
SunSoft	Interactive Unix 4.0	System V Release 3.2
SunSoft	Solaris for x86 2.1	System V Release 4.0

NOTE Several low-cost Unix-like operating systems are also available for the Intel platform, including FREEBSD, NetBSD, and LINUX.

As these Intel-based systems are an emerging force in the Unix marketplace, let's take a short detour here and look at some of these systems a little more closely:

- SCO UNIX and Open Desktop is the current market leader in Intel-based Unix systems, and as such can boast of a large range of native applications, including CorelDRAW, dBASE IV, Lotus 1-2-3, Microsoft Word, the Norton Utilities, and SQL databases from Informix, Ingres, Interbase, Oracle, Progress, Sybase, and Unify. DOS and Windows applications run under emulation provided by Locus Advanced Merge. Connectivity options include TCP/IP, IPX/SPX from Novell, and NetBEUI/NetBIOS support for connections to Windows for Workgroups and Windows NT.

- NeXTStep for Intel Processors is known for the excellence of its GUI (based on Display PostScript rather than X Window) and the fact that it is a clear divergence from the more normal System V kernel, the foundation for most of the other Intel Unix systems. NeXTStep is based on BSD 4.2 and the Mach system kernel. Networking is strongly supported, and the software development environment is one of the most fully featured found anywhere. On the downside are the relatively small number of native applications and the stringent hardware requirements. DOS emulation is an add-on package from SoftPC.

- UnixWare 1.1 is the latest offering from Novell (see Chapter 17 for more on UnixWare), which, not surprisingly, supports both TCP/IP and Novell's networking protocol IPX/SPX for Ethernet and token ring networks. Most well-behaved SCO UNIX and SCO XENIX binaries will run well under UnixWare, as well as DOS and Windows applications running under emulation provided by Locus Advanced Merge.

- Solaris for x86 is an Intel version of SunSoft's Solaris for SPARC operating system. The graphical user interface is supported by Open Look, itself a victim of the COSE standard. SunSoft's Windows Application Binary Interface (Wabi), developed with Praxsis Technologies, allows users to run certain qualified Windows applications without Microsoft Windows. Wabi has been

licensed by IBM, HP, and Novell. DOS emulation is provided through a Sun-Soft add-on called Vix.

The NFS is available for all these systems, so networking and interoperability requirements are easily satisfied.

And Now Novell

In 1990, that part of AT&T Bell Laboratories maintaining System V was turned into a subsidiary called UNIX System Laboratories (USL), and Novell became a major shareholder of this new company. In 1991, USL and Novell formed a joint venture called Univel, and in the fall of 1992 released UnixWare 1.0 to run on 32-bit Intel-based hardware. UnixWare is based on System V Release 4.2. At about the same time, Novell agreed to purchase USL from AT&T, and the deal was completed in mid-1993. Now Novell owns USL, Univel, and also controls the future direction of the Unix System V operating system. At the end of 1993, Novell turned the Unix trademark and the certification process over to X/Open.

And the future? As Francis Bacon said, "Men must pursue things which are just in present, and leave the future to the divine Providence." In other words, time alone will tell. Novell has described and subsequently retracted many strategies for Unix-Ware recently. They seem unsure just how to promote UnixWare, whether as a compliment to or as a replacement for NetWare.

So Which Unix Is Unix?

We can now distinguish several broad categories of "Unix" in the marketplace:

- Pure Unix licensed directly from AT&T and now Novell

- Unix with enhancements from official VARs (Value Added Retailers), independent computer manufacturers, or independent software developers who have sublicensing agreements

- BSD Unix versions from UCB (a "noncommercial" product that some vendors have "commercialized")

- Unix clones and look-alikes

Table 20.2 lists some of the more common Unix systems and their developers. Table 20.3 lists the major manufacturers of Unix-based computers, including workstations, mid-range computers, and servers, by percentage of market share in 1993.

TABLE 20.2: Unix Versions Available

Vendor	Operating System
Alphamicro	Unimos
Amdahl	UTS
Apple Computer	A/UX
AT&T	System V
Ballistic Research Labs	BRL Unix
Carnegie-Mellon	Mach
Charles River	UNOS
Concept Omega	Thoroughbred
Cromenco	Cromix
DEC	Ultrix
FCC	MMOS
IBM	AIX
Interactive Systems	IN/ix
HP	HP/UX
Mark Williams	Coherent
Microport Systems	System V/AT
Mt Xinu	more/BSD
National Semiconductor	Genix
Opus Systems	Opus 5
Prentice-Hall	Minix
QNX Software Systems	QNX
Silicon Graphics	IRIX
Sun Microsystems	SunOS
VentureCom	Venix
Whitesmith	IDRIS

TABLE 20.3: Unix Computer Market Share, 1993

Vendor	Market Share Percent
Hewlett-Packard	19.5
Sun Microsystems	18.2
IBM	11.8
DEC	5.6
Silicon Graphics	5.5
Others	39.4

In this multibillion dollar (and growing) Unix market, inevitable tensions result. The key issues are (1) what exactly is Unix? and (2) who controls its destiny? There is a constant pressure to improve Unix as new algorithms are discovered and hardware price/performance improves. Faster, cheaper RAM, mass storage, and CPUs continually alter the equations that determine the optimum operating system strategies. Countering this urge to update Unix is the need to preserve compatibility with the huge investment of existing software. A divine tweak of the kernel could prove to be a major disaster if it entails recoding existing applications.

Many Unix vendors, including SCO, IBM, HP, SunSoft and others have agreed to support the Common Open Software Environment (COSE) to continue to unify Unix. The COSE environment standardizes Unix components from networking and the graphical user interface to multimedia and graphics. Whether this effort succeeds—and where it leaves non-COSE vendors such as NeXT—remains to be seen.

Unix and the Future

Unix now is a very different animal from the Unix of the 1970s. A typical system then consisted of a single processor serving a set of dumb terminals. Unix today is more likely to be a workstation running a windowing system, acting as a part of a large, complex network of computers. Unix in the early days was a small, not-very-commercial product aimed at a small, specific set of users, most of whom were professional programmers. Unix today is a large and complicated commercial offering, used in a wide range of applications, and often by people with little or no programming experience.

Over the last ten years or so, there has been considerable effort to achieve a single "definitive" Unix from the various major subspecies. Historically, nearly every computer standardization process has proved to be a slow and tedious affair. The exceptions have been where a dominant supplier has established what is known as an *ad hoc* standard. Dominance is usually associated with IBM or Microsoft, but Borland's Pascal is one of several exceptions. Whether or not an ad hoc standard is blessed by the multifarious national and international standards organizations, other vendors are generally forced to follow suit by the sheer weight of market forces. Changes in technology often topple or invalidate standards, but sometimes the major factors seem to be political and commercial. With software, the situation is even more complex, because the laws governing copyright and "look 'n' feel" are still being resolved in the courts. In the case of Unix, both technical and political considerations are apparent. As you've seen, Unix is such an extremely complex collection of interacting and extensible modules that it is not easy to see which parts can or should be "standard." The general idea is that you can meet or *exceed* a standard; that is, your enhancements must not remove or impair any existing features. Even as I write the broth is bubbling nicely, so I urge you to read UNIX Review for the latest installment of the intrigue.

What is beyond doubt is that Unix is here to stay. Unix is so deeply entrenched that it is hard to see a radically new operating system displacing it. It is certainly flexible enough to cope with demands far beyond its original design goals.

Already, real-time and high-volume transaction versions of Unix are available, and Carnegie-Mellon's Mach indicates how Unix can be pushed in new directions without losing object-code compatibility with other Unix versions.

Summary

In the longer term, one sees the whole concept of the operating system changing. Even today, one operating system can run "over" or "under" another, so the traditional arguments, based on the "either-or" principle, are losing validity. What is clear is that the "Open" concept pioneered by Unix will prevail. Software that locks you into a given hardware vendor will vanish—and good riddance.

APPENDIX

A

Shell Versions

- Invocation

- Termination

- C shell variables

- The Korn shell

This appendix briefly reviews the major differences between the Bourne and C shells. I also list some of the new features found in the Korn shell. Note that as a *rough* approximation, the Korn shell is a superset of the Bourne shell that also includes some C shell influences. For a more detailed account of the C and Korn shells, see the csh and ksh entries in man section C. Other sources are listed in Appendix C: Unix Resources.

The C shell was developed mainly by Bill Joy at UCB as part of the so-called BSD (Berkeley Software Distribution) enhancements to AT&T Unix Series 6 and 7 (see Chapter 20). The name derives from the fact that the C shell's syntax borrows widely from the language C. The recent Korn shell, devised by David Korn of AT&T, offers nearly all of the Bourne shell features plus several C shell additions such as history and alias as well as a few new tricks of its own.

In the early days, when the East Coast (AT&T) and West Coast (BSD) Unix versions started diverging, there was much theological *logomachy* (a war about languages) over which shell, Bourne or C, was the best. Although there are still vocal fans on each side, the violent arguments of yore have given way to the more mature view that each shell has its advantages and drawbacks depending on your application. The C and Korn shells are certainly more complex but this is the price you pay for the extra features and more powerful arithmetical operations. The Bourne shell is still the "standard" shell and has the merit of portability: its shell scripts will run under the C and Korn shells.

The C shell (unlike the Bourne shell) is not officially a part of Unix System V, but is now widely distributed with System V along with the Bourne shell. Many System V vendors have also started including the Korn shell in their package. To check which shells you have on your system, you can run ls /bin/*sh and consult the following table:

Filename	Shell
/bin/sh	Bourne
/bin/csh	C
/bin/ksh	Korn
/bin/rsh	Restricted Bourne

NOTE Some systems may keep `ksh` in `/usr/bin` or `usr/local`, so look around if it's not in `/bin`.

Invocation

Recall that shells are "simply" programs: they are not embedded deep into the operating system, so there is no magic about which shell you run. If you have `/bin/csh`, you can run the C shell, even if your default shell (set by the system administrator in your `/etc/passwd` entry) is the Bourne shell. And, of course, vice versa: If you have `/bin/sh`, you can run the Bourne shell even if your default shell is `/bin/csh` or whatever. (And similarly with `/bin/ksh`.)

The best way to switch from the Bourne to the C shell is as follows:

```
$ exec csh
% _
```

Going the other way is just as easy:

```
% exec sh
$ _
```

Note the switch of prompt between $ (Bourne shell) and % (C shell). I'm assuming that the usual default prompts are in force. (The Korn shell default prompt is also $, by the way.) Either or both may be different on your system. The primary Bourne shell prompt is determined by the value of the environment variable PS1, whereas the C shell prompt is set in the variable `prompt`. You'll see other environment variable differences shortly.

The `exec` (execute) command is unusual in that the argument command (`csh` or `sh` in the above examples) *replaces* the calling program (the current shell in the above examples). You'll recall that normally the current shell spawns a new process or subshell to run a command, after which control returns to the caller (usually the parent shell). With `exec` (a built-in command for both the Bourne and C shells), the specified command argument is executed but control does not return to the caller. In the previous examples, therefore, `exec` runs `/bin/sh` and `/bin/csh` like parent shells and control does not return to the original shell.

The C shell also has a related built-in command called source that works like the Bourne shell "dot" (.) command. Both "dot" and source commands execute their argument file without creating a new process, but (unlike the exec situation) control *does* return to the calling program.

Termination

When you log out of the C shell, a file called .logout is executed if found in your home directory. So if you want to perform specific housekeeping tasks, or simply display a "Farewell, come back soon!" message, you can place suitable commands in your .logout file:

```
% cat .logout
rm -i *.temp
echo Adios UNIX cara
% _
```

To prevent accidental logging off with Ctrl-D (EOF), you can set the special variable ignoreeof (ignore end-of-file) by including the command

```
set ignoreeof
```

in your .cshrc file (see "The C Shell Environment" below). Thereafter, Ctrl-D is disabled as the log off signal, and Ctrl-D will invoke the message Use "logout" to logout.

C Shell Variables

The C shell supports predefined and user-named variables rather like the Bourne shell, but...note the differences as shown in Table A.1. C shell variable names can contain any mix of letters and digits, but they must start with a letter. Names are generally case-sensitive but some environmental variables "co-exist" in two spellings (for example, setting SHELL may also set a related variable called shell).

TABLE A.1: Comparison of C and Bourne Shell Variables

Variable Type	Bourne Shell	C Shell
String	Yes	Yes
String arrays	No	Yes
Numeric	No*	Yes
Numeric arrays	No	Yes

Variable Assignment	Bourne Shell	C Shell
String	*NAME=string*	set *name* = *string*
String arrays	n/a	set array = (*str1 str2* ...)
Numeric	n/a	@ *var assop expr*
Numeric arrays	n/a	Declare: set *array* = (*n1 n2* ...)
		Assign: @ *array*[*m*] = *n*

* Bourne shell variables holding numeric strings can be manipulated arithmetically, but C shell numeric variables work like C language integers with the standard C language arithmetic and logical operators.

C Shell String Assignment

Note the different syntaxes for assignment in Table A.1. The Bourne shell uses a direct assignment: *NAME=string* with no spaces. With the C shell, you use the set command to assign string values to variables, and spaces are *optional* around the = sign. (Some environmental variables require the setenv command.) You can do multiple assignments on the same line. When assigning strings with embedded white space (or other funnies), you need double quotes:

```
% set myteam = Giants yourteam = Atlanta Braves
% echo myteam
myteam
% echo $myteam
Giants
% echo $yourteam
Atlanta
% set yourteam ="Atlanta Braves"
% echo $yourteam
Atlanta Braves
```

The $*var* trick works as for the Bourne shell.

C Shell String Arrays

You met arrays in Chapter 15. They allow you to associate a single name with an arbitrary sequence of items (of the same data type). The C shell offers both string and numeric arrays. You can extract particular members of the array by specifying an index or range of indices. You can also reset an element's value using its index. First, some self-explanatory examples of string array manipulation:

```
% set shells = (Bourne C Korn "Restricted Bourne" "")
% echo $shells
Bourne C Korn Restricted Bourne
% echo $shells[2]
C
% echo $shells[4]
Restricted Bourne
% echo $shells[2-3]
C Korn
% echo $shells[*]
Bourne C Korn Restricted Bourne
% set shells[5]=MyShell
% echo $shells
Bourne C Korn Restricted Bourne MyShell
% echo $#shells
5
% _
```

Arrays are initialized with set using a sequence of elements inside parentheses. The expression array[n] means the nth element of array (starting at 1!). Note that $#array echoes the number of elements, while $array[m-n] echoes a range of elements. The fifth element of shells starts life as " ", the empty or null string. Later on, I assign a value to it using set with shells[5]. The reason for this maneuver is that C the shell, like C the language, works with fixed dimensional arrays. The number of elements in the initial set assignment fixes the size of the array for eternity. A common trick, therefore, is assigning "spare" null elements to allow for future "expansion."

Some of the C shell's environment variables are string arrays, so you'll meet the above "set-array" syntax again when we discuss the C shell environment.

> **NOTE**
>
> If you are a C programmer, you'll notice a few differences in the C shell array syntax:
>
> - The first element is index 1 rather than index 0.
> - There is no explicit `char*` or `char X[]` data type declaration.
> - You initialize the array with (`string-list`) using parentheses rather than braces.
> - The items in *string-list* are separated by spaces rather than commas.
> - Double quotes are needed only to hide white space and metacharacters.
> - The index can be a range, [*m-n*], or the special character * (meaning *all*). In C, only a single index value is allowed.
> - C the language permits multidimensional arrays: char *X[3][4], but C shell arrays are single dimensional.

C Shell Numeric Variables

C shell arithmetic avoids the need for `expr` and backquoting as required by the Bourne shell. The C shell numeric variables are integers and use the following assignment syntax:

  `@ var assop [exp]`

where *var* is the variable's name, *assop* is one of the assignment operators listed below, and *exp* is any expression that evaluates to a valid number.

The assignment operators are

Assignment Operator	Meaning
=	@ x=y assigns y to x
++	@ x++ increments x by 1
--	@ x-- decrements x by 1
+=	@ x+=y assigns x+y to x

Assignment Operator	Meaning
-=	@ x-=y assigns x-y to x
*=	@ x*=y assigns x*y to x (product)
/=	@ x/=y assigns x/y to x (quotient)
%=	@ x%=y assigns x%y to x (modulus)

These are best understood through examples:

```
% @ chapters = 19
% @ chapters++
% echo $chapters
20
% @ chapters += 5
% echo $chapters
25
% @ pages = 304+15-5
% @ totalpages = $chapters * $pages
% echo $totalpages
7850
% _
```

The right-hand side can be as complex as you dare, using numbers and previously assigned numeric variables combined with the basic math operators +, -, *, / and %. The following C language operators are also available:

Operator	Meaning
		Bitwise inclusive OR
&	Bitwise AND
^	Bitwise XOR (exclusive OR)
!	Logical negation
~	One's complement
||	Logical OR
&&	Logical AND
==	Equality (test)

Operator	Meaning
! =	Inequality (test)
<	Less than
<=	Less than or equal
>	Greater than
>=	Greater than or equal
<<	Shift left
>>	Shift right

Any C textbook will explain these operators and their precedences. Use parentheses to override C's normal precedence, as explained in Chapter 15.

The backquoted command is quite popular for assigning values:

```
% @ words = `cat chap.1 | wc -w`
% _
```

The value returned by the backquoted command, namely the number of words in chap.1, will be assigned to words.

C Shell Numeric Arrays

Numeric arrays are declared and initialized with set just like string arrays, but individual elements are assigned with @ like simple numeric variables:

```
% set sales = (10 20 30 40 "")
% echo $sales
10 20 30 40
% echo $sales[3]
30
% @ sales[1] = 15
% @ sales[5] = 45
% echo $sales
% 15 20 30 40 45
```

The C Shell Environment

In Chapter 6 you saw that if your login shell is the Bourne shell, you can set up your environment via commands in the script .profile in your home directory. This file is executed automatically each time you log in, but not when you run a subshell (unless you invoke .profile yourself). If your login shell is the C shell, you have a little more flexibility. There are two scripts, .login and .cshrc (both in your home directory), in which you can set environment and other variables. .login is equivalent to .profile and is executed whenever you log in. .cshrc (C shell resource) is executed both when you log in *and* when you invoke a subshell. The latter situation usually occurs when you run a shell script from the command line. .cshrc is therefore used to set environment and user variables that are needed by other shells. It is also used to establish aliases as explained in Chapter 6 (and discussed further below).

NOTE Since .login and .cshrc are *dot* files, they do not show up in plain ls listings—you must use ls -a.

You use set and setenv to assign values to the various predefined and user-defined C shell variables. The predefined C shell environment variables are more numerous and complex than those of the Bourne shell. Some of the C shell environment variables exist to provide compatibility when running Bourne scripts. Several have the same names and functions in both shells (such as HOME, PATH, TERM, SHELL, LOGNAME, etc.), while others also occur in lowercase versions (such as mail), and yet others have entirely different names (prompt is used in place of PS1). There are several C shell variables not found in the Bourne shell that act as *toggles* to turn certain features on and off. The following is a short list comparing the most important environment variables in the two shells:

Bourne Shell	C Shell	Notes on C Shell Usage
HOME	HOME, home	Your home directory. HOME is set automatically. home is set to $HOME when you enter a shell.

Bourne Shell	C Shell	Notes on C Shell Usage
PATH	PATH, path	As for Bourne shell, PATH holds the sequence of directories that will be searched for a given command. A default value is assigned automatically. PATH can be reassigned with `setenv` in `.login`; path is always reset when PATH is changed (and vice versa). path can be set in `.cshrc` using `set` and the string array syntax `set path = (/bin /usr/bin $HOME/bin .)`
MAIL	MAIL, mail	See the section "C Shell Mail" below.
SHELL	SHELL, shell	Holds your default login shell. SHELL is set from the last field of `/etc/passwd`. Can be changed using, e.g., `setenv SHELL /bin/sh`. shell is set to `$SHELL` whenever you enter the C shell.
TERM	TERM	Identifies terminal type. Use `setenv TERM` *termtype* in `.login`. (Note: no = in `setenv`)
LOG-NAME	LOGNAME	Holds your login name. Set automatically.
PS1	prompt	Holds the primary prompt. Use `set` in `.cshrc` to change the default, `"% "`
CDPATH	cdpath	List of alternative directories to be searched when using the `cd` command. For example: `set cdpath = (/usr/stan/lib); cd obj` is the same as `cd /usr/stan/lib/obj`

Variables peculiar to the C shell include the following:

Variable Name	Meaning
argv	List of current command's arguments.
cwd	Full path name of current directory.

Variable Name	Meaning
echo	If set, the shell echoes each command or argument before execution.
history	Sets size of history list.
histchars	Two-character variable: holds the history character (default is !), followed by the history substitute character (default is ^). See "C Shell History Command" section below.
ignoreeof	If set, the shell ignores Ctrl-D (EOF) as logout from shell.
noclobber	If set, prevents accidental overwriting of files when using >.
noglob	If set, stops file-name expansion of wildcards.
status	The exit status of the last command (equivalent to the Bourne shell $? special variable).
time	If a command takes more than $time cpu seconds to execute, the command's timing will be displayed (user time, system time, real time, utilization percentage).
verbose	If set (e.g., via the −v command-line option), each command name will be displayed after history substitution.

C Shell Mail

The variable MAIL holds the path name of your system mailbox. MAIL applies only to the Bourne shell, but is often set by C shell users (using setenv in .login) to ensure that mail notifications arrive normally when they are using the Bourne shell. The C shell mail string array variable combines the functions of the Bourne variables MAIL, MAILPATH, and MAILCHECK and is usually set in .cshrc. The mail setting syntax is

```
set mail = ([checkfreq] mailfile1 [mailfile2 ...])
```

The *checkfreq* argument (in seconds) specifies how often the system should check for new mail (the default is 600 seconds, meaning check every ten minutes). The *mailfilen* arguments specify the mail files to be checked. *mailfile1* is usually /usr/spool/mail/$LOGNAME.

C Shell File-Name Metacharacters

In addition to the Bourne shell's *, ?, [abc], and [a-z], the C shell offers the following file-name metacharacters:

Metacharacter	Meaning
{*abc*, *def*, ...}	Match either *abc* or *def* or ...
~ (tilde)	Current user's home directory
~name	The home directory of user *name*

You'll soon see that ! and ^ also have special meanings in the history mechanism offered by the C shell. The point is that command lines or scripts that use these "C shell–only" metacharacters need special care when used in mixed Bourne and C shell contexts, for example when UUCP connects systems running different shells (see Chapter 17). Recall that backslash, \, escapes the following character in both shells.

C Shell History Command

The C shell provides a *history* mechanism whereby previously entered command lines are stored and can be retrieved (all or part) and modified to save tedious retyping. First, you need to set the variable history to establish the size of your history list; this mandates how many previous commands your shell will "remember." The default of 20 can be changed with

```
% set history = 45
% _
```

Usually, a command like this would be placed in your .cshrc script.

> **NOTE** There may be a practical limit to your maximum history list size depending on the amount of memory available to your shell. In any case, too large a history list can be self-defeating!

If you enter some commands and then type history with no arguments, you'll get a numbered display of up to $history (45 in my case) of the most recently entered commands (more accurately known as *events* since history records every *line* you submit, both the multicommand lines and the rubbish):

```
% history
1 cd /usr/stan/lib
2 ls -l
3 more container.c
4 pwd
5 history
% _
```

Note that the last entry is the selfsame history command that invokes the list! As the day wears on, earlier entries in the history list will be dropped if you exceed the history list limit (but the number assigned to each command is retained for each login session). You can recall a command from the history list by using the magic symbol ! (known as *bang* in the trade). At least that is the *default* history character: you can vary this by resetting the first character in the histchars variable. For example:

```
% !4
pwd
/usr/stan/lib
% !78
78: Event not found
% set histchars = "#^"
% #4
pwd
/usr/stan/lib
% set histchars = "!^"
% _
```

(I'll explain the second histchars symbol in a moment.) Notice how the retrieved command is displayed and then executed. The bang can be followed by the event

number of the command you wish to retrieve, or by a *negative* number indicating the relative position of the target command counting back from the current command:

```
% !-2
pwd
/usr/stan/lib
% _
```

You can recall the previous command with two bangs:

```
% pwd
/usr/stan/lib
% !!
pwd
/usr/stan/lib
```

The key concept here is that the shell performs *history substitution* on tokens such as !*n*, !-*n*, and !!. You've met command substitution with '*command*', and filename substitution with *, ? and [a-z]; now we see yet another imposition on the poor shell! The history substitution takes place in any part of the command line, and with practice can save you keystrokes:

```
% who
iwonka      tty01      Oct 9 09:32
stan        tty02      Oct 9 10:34
% !! >user_list
who >user_list
% _
```

Well, you've saved one keystroke, but who's counting?

The history mechanism also lets you search for the most recent event (command) that starts or contains a given pattern:

```
% history
1 cd /usr/stan/lib
2 ls -l
3 more container.c
4 pwd
5 history
% !l >libfiles
```

```
ls -l >libfiles
% !?wd
pwd
/usr/stan/lib
% !?stan?/docs
cd /usr/stan/lib/docs
% _
```

In other words, !*pattern* is replaced by the most recent history event that starts with *pattern*. !?*pattern* is replaced by the most recent event that contains *pattern* anywhere in the line. A second ? after the pattern means that any following text will be tagged on after the substitution has been made. Hence, in the final example above, /docs is appended to /cd/usr/stan/lib to provide the command shown.

You can also retrieve specified *arguments* (also known as *words* in this context, since the shell parses the command line into words) from earlier commands. The expression !*event_number*:*arg_number* is replaced by the shell to give the appropriate argument of the command found in event number *event_number*. The *arg_number* starts at one for the first argument (the command itself is number 0):

```
% history
1 cd /usr/stan/lib
2 ls -l
3 more container.c
4 pwd
5 history
% cp !3:1 container.backup
cp container.c container.backup
% _
```

The *arg_number* can be replaced by the special (greppish) symbols ^ (meaning the first argument) and $ (meaning the last argument), so the previous example could be written

```
% history
1 cd /usr/stan/lib
2 ls -l
3 more container.c
4 pwd
5 history
% cp !3:$ container.backup
cp container.c container.backup
% _
```

with the same effect. Later, you'll see that these examples are particular forms of a more general history syntax.

The history mechanism also lets you modify a retrieved command line, providing yet another time-saver if you have entered a long command with a single, arresting typo:

```
% cay /usr/stan/lib/experiment/nyquist.diag456
cay: Command not found
% ^cay^cat
cat /usr/stan/lib/experiment/nyquist.diag456
// skb - 091593
// nyquist.diag456
#typedef INT short
...
% _
```

The construct `^x^y` simply replaces the text *x* with the text *y*. The caret, `^`, is the default history-substitution character. This can be changed by resetting the second character in the variable histchars. Recall that the first character in histchars holds the history character (default is !).

There are more elaborate ways of selecting and editing an earlier command using a ex-type syntax:

```
![event-spec][:op1[:op2] ...]...
```

The *event-spec* picks a particular history entry, and the optional operators, separated by colons, perform a variety of operations on the selected event. If you omit the event specification, the default is always the previous event. You've already seen simple examples of this format. For example, in !3:1 the *event-spec* selects the event numbered 3, and the 1 operator extracts the first argument. Here's a complete list of event specifications that can follow the initial bang:

History Event Specification	Selects
n	The event numbered *n*
-n	Relative: the event *n* lines prior to current event

History Event Specification	Selects
!	Previous event
#	The line being entered (lets you select parts of the line to the left of your current cursor)
pattern	Most recent event starting with *pattern*
?*pattern*	Most recent event containing *pattern*
?*pattern*?*text*	Most recent event containing *pattern* (*text* is appended to selected event)

Having selected an event, you can use a sequence of colon arguments to extract or modify parts of the event. With no *opn* arguments, the whole event is selected. Some values of *opn*, as shown below, work with or without the colon. Conversely, if you specify some operations *without* selecting an event, the default is the previous event. Each colon *opn* operates on the output of the previous operation. Here are some of the most popular values for the operator arguments:

History Operation	Meaning
0	The command itself (excluding its arguments)
n	The *n*th argument of the selected event
^	Same as *n* = 1, the first argument (the : can be dropped)
$	The last argument (the : can be dropped)
%	The word matched by the immediately preceding ?*pattern*[?] search operation (the : can be dropped)
m–n	Range of arguments (from *m*th to *n*th)
–n	The range 0–*n* (the command and its first *n* arguments (the : can be dropped)
*	The range ^–$ (all the arguments). Null if selected command has no arguments
m∗	The range *m–$*
m–	As for *m*∗ but omitting the last ($) argument

The following operators modify the selected event or alter the normal history action:

History Operation	Meaning
h	Head: removes last element of a path name
t	Tail: removes all but the last element of a path name
r	Root: removes any extension (.*xxx*) from the file name, leaving the *root* name (not to be confused with the superuser root!)
p	Print: displays the selected event but does not execute it
q	Quote: quotes the selected part of the operation in order to prevent substitutions
x	As for q, but divides words at any white-space characters (spaces, tabs, or newlines)
s/*old*/*new*	Substitute: replaces first occurrence of *old* with *new*
&	Repeats the previous substitution

A modifier operation can be preceded by a g (global), extending the modification to all matches, not just the first. The special ^*old*^*new* construction you saw earlier (with ^ as the first nonblank character on a command line) is a shorthand for !!:s/*old*/*new*. The result is to substitute *new* for *old* in the previous command. (My SCO documentation gets this reversed, by the way.) A riveting fact is that you can use any character in place of the delimiter / in the s modifier syntax! So s@sun@moon works just like s/sun/moon or even szsunzmoon. However, be aware of the concomitant dangers: sssunsmoon using s as delimiter is definitely pushing your luck. If your delimiter occurs in either string, the result is chaos. ss\sunsmoon works because the s in sun will be taken as a "real," literal (quoted) s rather than as a delimiter. My advice is to use the delimiter /, as God intended, and in the rare event that you have a "real" / in your old or new strings, you can then use the quoting mechanism: s/\\user\/stan/\/user\/stan will replace \user/stan with /user/stan. Note that quoting is also needed for any other metacharacters and white space that appear in the two strings.

Here are some more examples of history in action (the event numbers in the left column are there as a guide—they will not appear on your screen):

```
(39) % echo w1 w2 w3 w4 w5
     w1 w2 w3 w4 w5
(40) % !!:s/w/W
     echo W1 w2 w3 w4 w5
     W1 w2 w3 w4 w5
(41) % !!:&
     echo W1 W2 w3 w4 w5
     W1 W2 w3 w4 w5
(42) % echo !!:5:s/w/W
     echo W5
     W5
(43) % !39:gs/w/W
     echo W1 W2 W3 W4 W5
     W1 W2 W3 W4 W5
(44) % echo /usr/stan/lib/container.c
     /usr/stan/lib/container.c
(45) % !!:h
     echo /user/stan/lib
     /usr/stan/lib
(46) % history
     39 echo w1 w2 w3 w4 w5
     40 echo W1 w2 w3 w4 w5
     41 echo W1 W2 w3 w4 w5
     42 echo W5
     43 echo W1 W2 W3 W4 W5
     44 echo /usr/stan/lib/container.c
     45 echo /usr/stan/lib
     46 history
(47) % !44:r
     echo /usr/stan/lib/container
     /usr/stan/lib/container
(48) % !44:t
     echo container.c
     container.c
     % !39:p
     echo w1 w2 w3 w4 w5
     % _
```

The C Shell Alias Command

I discussed the mechanics of aliasing in Chapter 10, so here I will just summarize the highlights. Yet another chore for the C shell as it parses each command line is to check the first word of each detected command against an internal list of current aliases. This list is created and modified using the built-in `alias` and `unalias` commands. The `alias` *name wordlist* command establishes *wordlist* as an alias for *name*. The `unalias` command (with wildcards allowed) simply removes one or more aliases. The shell replaces *name* with *wordlist* before performing history substitutions. There are many subtleties in the timing of, and interaction between, the history, alias, and other substitutions performed by the shell. For most practical purposes, it is sufficient to view the aliasing mechanism as a simple textual replacement aimed at reducing keystrokes since *name* is typically much shorter than *wordlist*!

Alias commands are placed in your `.cshrc` file:

```
%<34> cat .cshrc
#
# @(#) .cshrc 9/15/95 skb
#
# prompt with % followed by history event number
set prompt = "%<\!> "
set history = 45
alias myprint lp -onobanner -ocpi=elite
...
%<35> _
```

Note the new prompt, showing the history event number of the current command. This reflects the value `"<\!>"` set in the variable `prompt`.

To check on the current state of all your aliases, you use `alias` with no arguments:

```
%<35> alias
bye     clear;logout
c       clear
dir     ls -al
g       grep
gb      set gb=`/bin/pwd`; cd $gt; set gt=$gb
gt      set gt=`/bin/pwd`; cd !^
h       history
la      ls -F
ll      ls -l
m       more
motd    more /etc/motd
```

```
p          ps -ef
rm         rm -i
mycd       cd /usr/stan/\!\*
%<36> _
```

There are several points of interest in the above list. First note that you can alias an existing command such as rm. This needs care, of course, but here you are guarding against the rash deletion of files. rm *filename* will translate to rm -i*filename*, which seeks confirmation before deleting the file. The mycd alias works as follows:

```
%<45> pwd
/usr/stan/lib
%<46> mycd doc
%<47> pwd
/usr/stan/doc
```

In other words, mycd doc expands to cd /usr/stan/doc. The reason is that the argument to mycd (in fact whatever follows mycd on the command line) replaces the string \!* in the expanded alias. This is the familiar history operator !* (select all arguments), with suitable escapes to delay interpretation by the shell. If you've been paying attention, you may be worried by the fact that !* is supposed to apply to the previous command (45), not the current command (46). What actually happens is that when the mycd alias is matched during parsing, the expanded text, cd /usr/stan/\!*, is reread like a fresh input line and subjected to possible history substitution. To the history mechanism, mycd doc appears to be the previous command, so doc replaces !*.

Aliasing is recursive: each expanded text is searched for the presence of more aliases; if any are found, these are expanded and the process repeats. The shell can detect endless loops and will signal an Alias loop error:

```
%<56> alias x1 x2
%<57> alias x2 x3
%<58> alias x3 x1
%<59> x1
Alias loop
%<60> _
```

The gt (go to) and gb (go back) aliases let you jump to another directory, do some work, and then jump back to whence you came. These two aliases lean on each other without causing a loop:

```
gb         set gb=`/bin/pwd`; cd $gt; set gt=$gb
gt         set gt=`/bin/pwd`; cd !^
```

Note that an alias can invoke a sequence of commands. And observe the typical use of backquoted commands: for example, the variable gb is set to the current directory (as returned by /bin/pwd) when gb (the command) is invoked. There's no clash here between names of variables and names of commands: in the current jargon, they occupy different *name spaces*.

Let's see gt and gb in action:

```
%<60> pwd
/usr/stan
%<61> gt /usr/mary
%<62> pwd
/usr/mary
%<63> echo $gt
/usr/stan
%<64> gb
%<65> pwd
/usr/stan
%<66> echo $gb
/usr/mary
%<67> echo $gt
/usr/mary
%<68> _
```

C Shell Flow Control

The C shell has several different conditional and looping constructs compared with the Bourne shell. I will confine myself to a brief listing of the main differences. First, in place of the Bourne shell's test command, the C shell has a set of expression operators for testing the state of files and directories. As with test, these can be used with if, while, and other conditional statements:

Operator	Returns true if *filename* is:
-r *filename*	Readable
-w *filename*	Writeable
-x *filename*	Executable
-e *filename*	Found (exists)
-o *filename*	Owned by user

Operator	Returns true if `filename` is:
`-z filename`	Zero size
`-f filename`	An ordinary, nondirectory file
`-d filename`	A directory

The following list compares the two shells' control syntaxes:

Bourne Shell	**C Shell**
`if...then...else...` `elif...fi`	`if...then...else` `...else if...endif`
`for`	`foreach`
(not available)	`goto label`
`while (exp) do` `  command-list done`	`while (exp)` `  command-list end`
`until (exp) do` `  command-list done`	(not available)

`case (string) in`
`   label1) command-list1;;`
	`switch (string)`
	`  case pattern1:`
	`      command-list1`
	`  breaksw`

`   label2) command-list2;;`	`  case pattern2:`
	`      command-list2`
	`  breaksw`

`  *) command-list;;`	`  [default:`
	`  command-list`
	`  breaksw]`

`  esac`	`  endsw`

The Korn Shell

The Korn shell is a superset of the Bourne shell, so all Bourne shell scripts should run under ksh without problems. Here's a brief list of new (or somewhat different) things you'll find when using the Korn shell:

- The ENV variable stores the name of a file that will be run whenever you log in. So $ENV is rather like a supplement to .profile used to set up specific Korn shell environmental variables. Remember to set SHELL to /bin/ksh in .profile so that when you escape to the shell from vi, you'll escape to ksh.

- ksh lets you edit command lines using either vi or emacs type editor commands.

- ksh offers a history mechanism rather like the C shell's (the syntax is quite different though).

- ksh has a *job* control facility using a job *monitor.* Some versions allow you to move jobs between foreground and background operation.

- ksh has quite elaborate parameterized functions that you define with the function command.

- ksh supports C language integer arithmetic and arrays rather like the C shell's, but the ksh syntax is closer to the C language.

- The ksh pattern-matching features are more extensive than those of sh or csh.

- You can directly address more than ten positional parameters.

- ksh has a C shell-like alias command.

APPENDIX

B

ASCII Tables

- ASCII control characters

- ASCII character set

- IBM extended character set

Table B.1 shows the ASCII control characters, and Table B.2 shows the standard 7-bit ASCII character set (comprising characters 0–127), which is implemented on all computers that use ASCII. Table B.3 shows the 8-bit IBM extended ASCII character set.

TABLE B.1: ASCII Control Characters

Decimal	Control	Character	Decimal	Control	Character
0	None	NUL (Null)	16	Ctrl-P	DLE (Data link escape)
1	Ctrl-A	SOH (Start of heading)	17	Ctrl-Q	DC1 (Device control 1)
2	Ctrl-B	STX (Start of text)	18	Ctrl-R	DC2 (Device control 2)
3	Ctrl-C	ETX (End of text)	19	Ctrl-S	DC3 (Device control 3)
4	Ctrl-D	EOT (End of transmission)	20	Ctrl-T	DC4 (Device control 4)
5	Ctrl-E	ENQ (Enquire)	21	Ctrl-U	NAK (Negative acknowledgement)
6	Ctrl-F	ACK (Acknowledge)	22	Ctrl-V	SYN (Synchronous idle)
7	Ctrl-G	BEL (Bell)	23	Ctrl-W	ETB (End transmission block)
8	Ctrl-H	BS (Backspace)	24	Ctrl-X	CAN (Cancel)
9	Ctrl-I	HT (Horizontal tab)	25	Ctrl-Y	EM (End of medium)
10	Ctrl-J	LF (Line feed)	26	Ctrl-Z	SUB (Substitute)
11	Ctrl-K	VT (Vertical tab)	27	Ctrl-[	ESC (Escape)
12	Ctrl-L	FF (Form feed)	28	Ctrl-\	FS (File separator)
13	Ctrl-M	CR (Carriage return)	29	Ctrl-]	GS (Group separator)
14	Ctrl-N	SO (Shift out)	30	Ctrl-^	RS (Record separator)
15	Ctrl-O	SI (Shift in)	31	Ctrl-_	US (Unit separator)

TABLE B.2: ASCII Character Set

Decimal	Character	Decimal	Character	Decimal	Character
32	space	48	0	64	@
33	!	49	1	65	A
34	"	50	2	66	B
35	#	51	3	67	C
36	$	52	4	68	D
37	%	53	5	69	E
38	&	54	6	70	F
39	'	55	7	71	G
40	(	56	8	72	H
41	)	57	9	73	I
42	*	58	:	74	J
43	+	59	;	75	K
44	,	60	<	76	L
45	–	61	=	77	M
46	.	62	>	78	N
47	/	63	?	79	O

TABLE B.2: ASCII Character Set (continued)

Decimal	Character	Decimal	Character	Decimal	Character
80	P	96	"	112	p
81	Q	97	a	113	q
82	R	98	b	114	r
83	S	99	c	115	s
84	T	100	d	116	t
85	U	101	e	117	u
86	V	102	f	118	v
87	W	103	g	119	w
88	X	104	h	120	x
89	Y	105	i	121	y
90	Z	106	j	122	z
91	[	107	k	123	{
92	\	108	l	124	|
93	]	109	m	125	}
94	^	110	n	126	~
95	_	111	o	127	DEL

TABLE B.3: IBM Extended Character Set

Decimal	Character	Decimal	Character	Decimal	Character
128	Ç	152	ÿ	176	░
129	ü	153	Ö	177	▒
130	´	154	Ü	178	▓
131	â	155	¢	179	│
132	ä	156	£	180	┤
133	à	157	¥	181	╡
134	å	158	₧	182	╢
135	ç	159	*f*	183	╖
136	ê	160	á	184	╕
137	ë	161	í	185	╣
138	è	162	ó	186	║
139	ï	163	ú	187	╗
140	î	164	ñ	188	╝
141	ì	165	Ñ	189	╜
142	Ä	166	ª	190	╛
143	Å	167	º	191	┐
144	É	168	¿	192	└
145	æ	169	⌐	193	┴
146	Æ	170	¬	194	┬
147	ô	171	½	195	├
148	ö	172	¼	196	─
149	ò	173	¡	197	┼
150	û	174	«	198	╞
151	ù	175	»	199	╟

TABLE B.3: IBM Extended Character Set (continued)

Decimal	Character	Decimal	Character	Decimal	Character
200	⊫	224	∝	248	°
201	⊩	225	β	249	°
202	⊥	226	Γ	250	·
203	⊤	227	π	251	√
204	⊩	228	Σ	252	η
205	=	229	σ	253	^{2}
206	⊹	230	μ	254	■
207	⊥	231	τ	255	
208	⊥	232	Φ		
209	⊤	233	Θ		
210	⊤	234	Ω		
211	⊩	235	δ		
212	⊢	236	∞		
213	⊩	237	φ		
214	⊩	238	ε		
215	╬	239	∩		
216	╪	240	≡		
217	⌐	241	±		
218	⌐	242	≥		
219	▌	243	≤		
220	▬	244	⌠		
221	▎	245	⌡		
222	■	246	÷		
223	■	247	≈		

APPENDIX

C

Unix Resources

- Printed sources

- Unix networks and bulletin boards

- Unix seminars and exhibitions

The amount of information available about Unix—both in printed and digital form—is simply enormous. This appendix lists just a few resources that may be helpful in your ongoing Unix studies. Many of the books and files listed here are updated regularly, so make sure you get the latest version. Look in the online news and magazines for information on expositions and seminars in your local area. The Unix culture has always maintained a helpful attitude to information sharing, regardless of your current skill level.

Printed Sources

The following sections list written material, including books and magazines. Also, if you have access to the Internet, you might anonymous `ftp` to `rtfm.mit.edu` and get the file called `unix` from the directory `/pub/usenet/news.answers/books`, or anonymous `ftp` to `ucselx.sdsu.edu` and look for a file called `Unix-C-Booklist` in the `/pub/doc/general` directory.

General Unix Books

Bach, M. *The Design of the UNIX Operating System.* Englewood Cliffs, NJ: Prentice-Hall, 1986.

Bourne, S.R. *The UNIX System V Environment.* Menlo Park, CA: Addison-Wesley, 1987.

Christian, K. *The UNIX Operating System.* New York: Wiley-Interscience, 1988.

McGilton, H. and R. Morgan. *Introducing the UNIX System.* New York: McGraw-Hill, 1987.

Todino, G., J. Strang, and J. Peek. *Learning the UNIX Operating System.* 3d ed. Sebastopol, CA: O'Reilly & Associates, 1993.

Unix Versions

AT&T UNIX System V: System Manuals. Englewood Cliffs, NJ: Prentice-Hall, 1987.

Cutler, E. *SCO UNIX in a Nutshell.* Sebastopol, CA: O'Reilly & Associates, 1994.

Gilly, D., and O'Reilly Associates. *UNIX in a Nutshell*. 2d ed. Sebastopol, CA: O'Reilly & Associates, 1992.

Heslop, B. and D. Angell. *Mastering Solaris 2*. Alameda, CA: SYBEX, 1993.

Specific Unix Tools

Aho, A., B. Kernighan, and P. Weinberger. *The AWK Programming Language*. Menlo Park, CA: Addison-Wesley, 1988.

Dougherty, D. *sed & awk*. Sebastopol, CA: O'Reilly & Associates, 1990.

Hewlett-Packard. *The Ultimate Guide to the VI and EX Text Editors*. Redwood City, CA: Benjamin/Cummings, 1990.

Lamb, L. *Learning the vi Editor*. Sebastopol, CA: O'Reilly & Associates, 1990.

Peek, J. *MH & xmh: E-mail for Users and Programmers*. 2d ed. Sebastopol, CA: O'Reilly & Associates, 1992.

Sonnenschein, D. *Guide to vi—Visual Editing on the UNIX System*. Englewood Cliffs, NJ: Prentice-Hall, 1987.

Unix Shells and Shell Programming

Anderson, G. and P. Anderson. *The C Shell Field Guide*. Englewood Cliffs, NJ: Prentice-Hall, 1986.

Bolsky, M. and D. Korn. *The KornShell: Command and Programming Language*. Englewood Cliffs, NJ: Prentice-Hall, 1989.

Kernighan, B. and R. Pike. *The UNIX Programming Environment*. Englewood Cliffs, NJ: Prentice-Hall, 1984.

Kochan, S. and P. Wood. *UNIX Shell Programming*. Indianapolis: Hayden Book Co., 1990

Rosenblatt, B. *Learning the Korn Shell*. Sebastopol, CA: O'Reilly & Associates, 1993.

Waite Group. *Tricks of the UNIX Masters*. Indianapolis: SAMS/The Waite Group, 1986.

Unix System Administration

Hunter, B. and K. Hunter. *UNIX Systems: Advanced Administration and Management Handbook.* New York, NY: Macmillan, 1991.

Frisch, A. *Essential System Administration.* Sebastopol, CA: O'Reilly & Associates, 1991.

Garfinkel, S. and G. Spafford. *Practical UNIX Security.* Sebastopol, CA: O'Reilly & Associates, 1991.

Hunt, C. *TCP/IP Network Administration.* Sebastopol, CA: O'Reilly & Associates, 1992.

Loukides, M. *System Performance Tuning.* Sebastopol, CA: O'Reilly & Associates, 1990.

Nemeth, E., G. Snyder, and S. Seebass. *UNIX System Administration Handbook.* Englewood Cliffs, NJ: Prentice-Hall, 1989.

O'Reilly, T. and G. Todino. *Managing UUCP and Usenet.* 10th ed. Sebastopol, CA: O'Reilly & Associates, 1992.

Stern, H. *Managing NFS and NIS.* Sebastopol, CA: O'Reilly & Associates, 1991.

Unix Programming

Curry, D. *Using C on the UNIX System.* Sebastopol, CA: O'Reilly & Associates, 1989.

Kernighan, B. and D. Ritchie. *The C Programming Language, 2nd ed.,* Englewood Cliffs, NJ: Prentice-Hall, 1988.

Oualline, S. *Practical C Programming.* 2d ed. Sebastopol, CA: O'Reilly & Associates, 1993.

X Window

O'Reilly & Associates of Sebastopol, CA, publish a whole set of technical books on X; call (800) 998-9938 for a catalog, or use gopher with gopher.ora.com, then use the root menu to choose the Complete Listing of Titles option.

Johnson, E. and K. Reichard. *X Window Applications Programming.* Portland, OR: MIS Press, 1991.

Jones, O. *Introduction to the X Window System*. Englewood Cliffs, NJ: Prentice-Hall, 1989.

Communications and Networking

Anderson, B., B. Costales, and H. Henderson. *UNIX Communications*. Indianapolis: SAMS/the Waite Group, 1991.

Comer, D. *Internetworking with TCP/IP, volume 1*. Englewood Cliffs, NJ: Prentice-Hall, 1991.

Comer, D. and D. Stevens. *Internetworking with TCP/IP, volume 2*. Englewood Cliffs, NJ: Prentice-Hall, 1991.

Gaskin, J. *Novell's Guide to Integrating UNIX and NetWare Networks*. Alameda, CA: Novell Press, 1993.

Gofton, P. *Mastering UNIX Serial Communications*. Alameda, CA: SYBEX, 1991.

Negus, C. and L. Schumer. *Novell's Guide to UnixWare*. Alameda, CA: Novell Press, 1994.

Todino, G. and D. Dougherty. *Using UUCP and Usenet*. Sebastopol, CA: O'Reilly & Associates, 1986.

The Internet

Estrada, S. *Connecting to the Internet: An O'Reilly Buyer's Guide*. Sebastopol, CA: O'Reilly & Associates, 1993.

Falk, B. *The Internet Roadmap*. Alameda, CA: SYBEX, 1994.

Frey, D. and R. Adams. *!%@:: A Directory of Electronic Mail Addressing and Networks*. 4th ed. Sebastopol, CA: O'Reilly & Associates, 1994.

Hoffman, P. *Internet Instant Reference*. Alameda, CA: SYBEX, 1994.

Kehoe, B. *Zen & the Art of the Internet*. Englewood Cliffs, NJ: Prentice-Hall, 1993.

Krol, E. *The Whole Internet User's Guide and Catalog*. 2d ed. Sebastopol, CA: O'Reilly & Associates, 1994.

Unix History and Folklore

AT&T Bell Labs. *UNIX Programmer's Manual, volume 2, 7th ed.,* Bell Telephone Laboratories, Inc., Murray Hill, NJ: 1986.

Libes, D. and S. Ressler. *Life with UNIX: A Guide for Everyone.* Englewood Cliffs, NJ: Prentice-Hall, 1989.

Salus, P. *A Quarter Century of UNIX.* Menlo Park, CA: Addison-Wesley, 1994.

Stoll, C. *The Cuckoo's Egg.* New York, NY: Doubleday, 1989.

Unix Magazines

Advanced Systems
Integrated Media Inc.
501 Second Street
San Francisco, CA 94107
Telephone (800)685-3435
email editors@advanced.com

SCO World
Venture Publishing, Inc.
480 San Antonio Road
Mountain View, CA 94040
Telephone (415)941-1550
email letters@scoworld.com

UNIX Review
Miller Freeman, Inc.
600 Harrison Street
San Francisco, CA 94107
Telephone (800)829-5475
email editor@ureview.com

Unix World's open COMPUTING
McGraw-Hill
1900 O'Farrell Street
San Mateo, CA 94403
Telephone (800)257-9402
email `letters@uworld.com`

The X Journal
SIGS Publications
588 Broadway, Suite 604
New York, NY 10012
Telephone (212)274-0640
email `editor@unx.com`

The X Resource
O'Reilly & Associates
103 A Morris Street
Sebastopol, CA 95472
Telephone (800)998-9938
email `order@ora.com`

Unix Networks and Bulletin Boards

Most of the electronic conferencing and news networks have forums or conferences devoted to Unix. There are thousands of these networks ranging from small private bulletin boards (BBS) running on a single PC to the giant Internet. Indeed, many Unix vendors offer their own online information services giving up-to-date product information, patches, and even new device drivers.

Internet

The Internet is a huge resource, as we saw in Chapter 17, and there is much Unix and Unix-related material available, as you might imagine. Depending on the individual Internet site, you can transfer files using `ftp`, or you can log in at the site using `telnet`. You can also use `archie` or `gopher` at many sites.

Start your trip through the Internet by using `ftp` to get Scott Yanoff's Internet Services List from `csd4.csd.uwm.edu`; the file is called `inet.services.txt` from the `/pub` directory, and contains information on selected Internet sites, arranged by category. The file is updated on a regular basis, and is currently about 50K in size.

For information on `telnet` or `ftp`, anonymous `ftp` to `ftp.sura.net` and look for the files `how.to.telnet.guide` and `how.to.ftp.guide` in the `/pub/nic/net-work.service.guides` directory; for USENET information try anonymous `ftp` to `rtfm.mit.edu`, and get the file `part1` from the `/pub/usenet/news.answers/what-is-usenet` directory. Happy hunting.

USENET

The USENET, or User's Network, is a disparate collection of computers, most of which run Unix. Although there is a very close relationship between the Internet and USENET, they are not the same thing. Not every Internet computer is automatically part of USENET, and not all USENET computers can be accessed from the Inernet; you must connect to these computers with UUCP.

USENET has over 5,000 different discussion groups, varying in subject from the sacred to the profane, tens of thousands of USENET sites, and millions of users worldwide.

Of the 459 different discussion groups in the comp category, approximately 30 deal with Unix and Unix-related topics. The rest deal with hardware, software, and commercial applications, as well as the distribution of public domain and shareware programs. Alternative groups include `gnu`, devoted to the GNU Project of the Free Software Foundation, with about 30 separate discussion groups; `alt.bbs.unixbbs`, which lists Unix bulletin board systems; and `info.unix-sw`, which lists Unix software available by anonymous `ftp`.

Index

Note to the Reader: Throughout this index, **boldfaced** page numbers indicate primary discussions of a topic. *Italicized* page numbers indicate illustrations

Symbols

A

B

C

F

G

H

I

M

O

P

Q

R

T

U

V

W

GET A FREE CATALOG JUST FOR EXPRESSING YOUR OPINION.

Help us improve our books and get a **FREE** full-color catalog in the bargain. Please complete this form, pull out this page and send it in today. The address is on the reverse side.

Name _____

Company _____

Address _____

City _____ State ____ Zip _____

Phone (___) _____

1. How would you rate the overall quality of this book?

- ❏ Excellent
- ❏ Very Good
- ❏ Good
- ❏ Fair
- ❏ Below Average
- ❏ Poor

2. What were the things you liked most about the book? (Check all that apply)

- ❏ Pace
- ❏ Format
- ❏ Writing Style
- ❏ Examples
- ❏ Table of Contents
- ❏ Index
- ❏ Price
- ❏ Illustrations
- ❏ Type Style
- ❏ Cover
- ❏ Depth of Coverage
- ❏ Fast Track Notes

3. What were the things you liked *least* about the book? (Check all that apply)

- ❏ Pace
- ❏ Format
- ❏ Writing Style
- ❏ Examples
- ❏ Table of Contents
- ❏ Index
- ❏ Price
- ❏ Illustrations
- ❏ Type Style
- ❏ Cover
- ❏ Depth of Coverage
- ❏ Fast Track Notes

4. Where did you buy this book?

- ❏ Bookstore chain
- ❏ Small independent bookstore
- ❏ Computer store
- ❏ Wholesale club
- ❏ College bookstore
- ❏ Technical bookstore
- ❏ Other _____

5. How did you decide to buy this particular book?

- ❏ Recommended by friend
- ❏ Recommended by store personnel
- ❏ Author's reputation
- ❏ Sybex's reputation
- ❏ Read book review in _____
- ❏ Other _____

6. How did you pay for this book?

- ❏ Used own funds
- ❏ Reimbursed by company
- ❏ Received book as a gift

7. What is your level of experience with the subject covered in this book?

- ❏ Beginner
- ❏ Intermediate
- ❏ Advanced

8. How long have you been using a computer?

years _____

months _____

9. Where do you most often use your computer?

- ❏ Home
- ❏ Work

- ❏ Both
- ❏ Other _____

10. What kind of computer equipment do you have? (Check all that apply)

- ❏ PC Compatible Desktop Computer
- ❏ PC Compatible Laptop Computer
- ❏ Apple/Mac Computer
- ❏ Apple/Mac Laptop Computer
- ❏ CD ROM
- ❏ Fax Modem
- ❏ Data Modem
- ❏ Scanner
- ❏ Sound Card
- ❏ Other _____

11. What other kinds of software packages do you ordinarily use?

- ❏ Accounting
- ❏ Databases
- ❏ Networks
- ❏ Apple/Mac
- ❏ Desktop Publishing
- ❏ Spreadsheets
- ❏ CAD
- ❏ Games
- ❏ Word Processing
- ❏ Communications
- ❏ Money Management
- ❏ Other _____

12. What operating systems do you ordinarily use?

- ❏ DOS
- ❏ OS/2
- ❏ Windows
- ❏ Apple/Mac
- ❏ Windows NT
- ❏ Other _____

13. On what computer-related subject(s) would you like to see more books?

_____

_____

_____

_____

14. Do you have any other comments about this book? (Please feel free to use a separate piece of paper if you need more room)

_____

_____

_____

_____

PLEASE FOLD, SEAL, AND MAIL TO SYBEX

SYBEX INC.
Department M
2021 Challenger Drive
Alameda, CA
94501

Summary of Common Unix Commands

(continued from front inside cover)

COMMAND	ACTION
news	Display a news item
nice	Run a command at (usually) lower priority
nohup	Run a command after logout (inhibit hangups)
nroff	Format files for printing
nslookup	Display IP information about a domain
od	Display file in octal
passwd	Create or change login password
paste	Merge lines of files
pr	Format and print file
ps	Report status of active processes
pstat	Report system status
pwcheck	Check /etc/passwd (default) file
pwd	Display current working directory
rm	Remove (erase) files or directories
rmdir	Remove (erase) empty directories
rsh	Invoke the restricted Bourne shell
sed	The stream editor
set	Assign value to variable
setenv	Assign value to environmental variable (C Shell)
sh	Invoke the Bourne shell
sleep	Suspend execution for given period
sort	Sort and merge files
spell	Find spelling errors
split	Split a file into smaller files
stty	Set options for a terminal
su	Make a user a superuser (or a different user) without logging out first
sum	Compute checksums and number of blocks for files
tabs	Set tabs on a terminal
tail	Display last few lines of a file
tar	Copy (archive) and restore files to diskette or tape
tee	Create a tee in a pipe
telnet	Access remote systems

For every kind of computer user, there is a SYBEX book.

All computer users learn in their own way. Some need straightforward and methodical explanations. Others are just too busy for this approach. But no matter what camp you fall into, SYBEX has a book that can help you get the most out of your computer and computer software while learning at your own pace.

Beginners generally want to start at the beginning. The **ABC's** series, with its step-by-step lessons in plain language, helps you build basic skills quickly. For a more personal approach, there's the **Murphy's Laws** and **Guided Tour** series. Or you might try our **Quick & Easy** series, the friendly, full-color guide, with **Quick & Easy References**, the companion pocket references to the **Quick & Easy** series. If you learn best by doing rather than reading, find out about the **Hands-On Live!** series, our new interactive multimedia training software. For hardware novices, there's the **Your First** series.

The **Mastering and Understanding** series will tell you everything you need to know about a subject. They're perfect for intermediate and advanced computer users, yet they don't make the mistake of leaving beginners behind. Add one of our **Instant References** and you'll have more than enough help when you have a question about your computer software. You may even want to check into our **Secrets & Solutions** series.

SYBEX even offers special titles on subjects that don't neatly fit a category—like our **Pushbutton Guides**, our books about the Internet, our books about the latest computer games, and a wide range of books for Macintosh computers and software.

SYBEX books are written by authors who are expert in their subjects. In fact, many make their living as professionals, consultants or teachers in the field of computer software. And their manuscripts are thoroughly reviewed by our technical and editorial staff for accuracy and ease-of-use.

So when you want answers about computers or any popular software package, just help yourself to SYBEX.

For a complete catalog of our publications, please write:

SYBEX Inc.
2021 Challenger Drive
Alameda, CA 94501
Tel: (510) 523-8233/(800) 227-2346 Telex: 336311
Fax: (510) 523-2373

SYBEX is committed to using natural resources wisely to preserve and improve our environment. As a leader in the computer book publishing industry, we are aware that over 40% of America's solid waste is paper. This is why we have been printing the text of books like this one on recycled paper since 1982.

This year our use of recycled paper will result in the saving of more than 15,300 trees. We will lower air pollution effluents by 54,000 pounds, save 6,300,000 gallons of water, and reduce landfill by 2,700 cubic yards.

In choosing a SYBEX book you are not only making a choice for the best in skills and information, you are also choosing to enhance the quality of life for all of us.

Summary of Common
Unix Commands

(continued)

COMMAND	ACTION
false	Return a nonzero (*false*) exit status
fgrep	"Fast" version of grep
file	Report type of file
find	Find matching files and perform specified actions
finger	Report user information
format	Format disks and cartridge tapes
ftp	Transfer files to and from remote systems
grep	Search files for regular expression matches
haltsys	Gracefully shut down system (root)
head	Display first few lines of a file
join	Display the join (lines with common fields) of two files
kill	Send a signal to process (by default, terminate the process)
ksh	Invoke the Korn shell
lc	List directory contents in columns
line	Read a line (shell script usage)
ln	Create link to a file
logname	Get login name
lp, lpr	Send request to printer
lprint	Print on local printer
lpstat	Report printer status
ls	List contents of a directory
mail	Send and receive mail
man	Print reference pages from online manual
mesg	Grant or deny permission to receive write messages from other users
mkdir	Create a new directory
mknod	Build a special file
more	Display a file one page at a time
mount	Mount a special file, or report its status
mv	Move (rename) a file

(continues on back inside cover)